Advances in Unmanned Aerial Vehicles - Technology and Applications - Big Issues Solved with Drone Technology

Edited by Antoni Grau and Rodrigo Munguia

Published in London, United Kingdom

Advances in Unmanned Aerial Vehicles - Technology and Applications - Big Issues Solved with Drone Technology
http://dx.doi.org/10.5772/intechopen.1005919
Edited by Antoni Grau and Rodrigo Munguia

Contributors
Adhi Dharma Permana, Agus Dwiono, Agus Krisnowo, Ahmed Al-Maashri, Antoni Grau, Bagus Anang Nugroho, Beatriu Tort, Burhaneddin Bilgen, Desh Deepak Sharma, Dorottya Mészáros, Eduard Degollada, Fan Gao, Fauzie Dahmir, Guntur Haryanto, Hadj Bourdoucen, Hasan Bilgehan Makineci, Irfan Pratama Putra, Joaquin Vico Navarro, Joel George Manathara, Jonathan Prabowo, Juan A. Vila Carbó, Jumain Appe, Lorant Andras Szolga, Mochamad Taufik, Nabil Aouf, Navid Nasiri, Piyarat Vijuksungsith, Rattana Boonprasert, Rodrigo Munguia, Said Al-Abri, Sercan Bülbül, Siddhardha Kedarisetty

First published in London, United Kingdom, 2025 by IntechOpen
IntechOpen is the global imprint of INTECHOPEN LIMITED, registered in England and Wales, registration number: 11086078, 167-169 Great Portland Street, London, W1W 5PF, United Kingdom

For EU product safety concerns: IN TECH d.o.o., Prolaz Marije Krucifikse Kozulić 3, 51000 Rijeka, Croatia, info@intechopen.com or visit our website at intechopen.com.

British Library Cataloguing-in-Publication Data
A catalogue record for this book is available from the British Library

Advances in Unmanned Aerial Vehicles - Technology and Applications - Big Issues Solved with Drone Technology
Edited by Antoni Grau and Rodrigo Munguia
p. cm.
Print ISBN 978-1-83634-425-4
Online ISBN 978-1-83634-424-7
eBook (PDF) ISBN 978-1-83634-426-1

If disposing of this product, please recycle the paper responsibly.

Meet the editors

Antoni Grau received the M. S. and Ph.D. degrees in computer science from the Technical University of Catalonia (UPC), Barcelona, in 1990 and 1997, respectively. He is currently a Professor with the Department of Automatic Control at UPC, where he teaches lectures on computer vision, digital signal processing, and robotics at the School of Informatics in Barcelona and the Industrial Engineering School. His research interests include computer vision, pattern recognition, autonomous mobile robots, factory automation, and education on sustainable development. He chaired several international conferences. He is a Senior member of IEEE Industrial Electronics Society (IEEE-IES), co-chairing the Technical Subcommittee "FA11: Intelligent and Cooperative Robotics". He serves as the Associated Editor for the Transactions on Industrial Informatics.

Rodrigo Munguía received a Ph.D. degree in Automation and Robotics from the Technical University of Catalonia (UPC), Spain, in 2009. Previously, he obtained a M. S. degree in computer science in 2006 from the same institution, and a B. Eng. degree in electronic engineering from the University of Guadalajara (UdeG), Guadalajara, México, in 2002. He has worked as a software engineer in companies as IBM or Continental Automotive. Currently, he is a titular professor with the Department of Computer Science at the University of Guadalajara, México. His research interests include mobile robotics, unmanned aerial vehicles, navigation systems for autonomous vehicles, automatic control, optimal state estimation, sensor fusion, computer vision, and other related topics. He has authored more than fifty scientific and technical publications, including journal articles, book chapters, and conference proceedings. He is a member of the researcher's national system of México.

Contents

Preface

UAVs (unmanned aerial vehicles) are robots that have the particular ability to fly. This fact gives them characteristics that are significantly different from other types of robots as we know them—they cannot walk, roll, crawl, climb, or swim like robots specifically designed for those tasks. Another unique feature of flying robots is their ability to hover and mimic a helicopter, that is, to remain suspended in the air. This ability makes them especially useful and capable of monitoring, observing, analyzing, and recording scenes and images that can only be captured from the sky. Additionally, these robots are equipped with autonomous flight capabilities, while also allowing for remote control. These distinctive features, combined with the integration of various technologies, have allowed UAVs to fill a gap that had previously remained empty in the field of robotics.

This book aims to showcase some of the technologies embedded in UAVs that enable them to have these special characteristics, making them unique in the robotics world. One of the UAVs main sensors is its "eyes", and providing it with this sense gives it impressive capabilities in autonomous flying and environmental awareness. One chapter explores how this technology is integrated into UAVs and the performance it enables. Another key technology that makes UAVs exceptional is their ability to localize themselves, create maps, and navigate autonomously within them. Knowing the robot's exact position at every moment makes it smarter and more autonomous, enabling it to manage its actions effectively. Other chapters discuss the onboard technologies of flying robots, including the technological maturity of the systems. The level of readiness is a key factor in assessing how close we are to having a finished, market-ready product. Cybersecurity is also tightly linked to UAV technology; if external systems intercept a UAV's control signals, the consequences can be disastrous for both the operator and bystanders.

However, UAVs also play a crucial role on the planet, helping to maintain a healthy ecosystem and serving as valuable tools for its protection and conservation. In this regard, the book includes a section dedicated exclusively to this topic, where agriculture, living beings (both animals and plants), and the Earth's fossil materials are monitored, allowing experts to conduct research based on the data collected by UAVs. We hope this section serves as an example for other researchers, whether in UAV technology or other disciplines, to utilize UAVs for noble purposes.

Beyond these sustainability-related applications, UAVs have also historically been used for a wide range of commercial purposes. Some of these uses are presented in the section on general applications.

We believe this book will be of great interest to professionals who may incorporate UAVs into their work to expand their application portfolio, as well as to drone enthusiasts who want to continue learning and use them in their daily, professional, or recreational activities. If we achieve any of these goals, the work of the authors and editors will have been worthwhile.

Antoni Grau
Professor,
Polytechnic University of Catalonia,
Barcelona, Spain

Rodrigo Munguia
Professor,
University of Guadalajara,
Guadalajara, Mexico

Section 1

Technology Aboard

Chapter 1

Image Processing on Drone

Lorant Andras Szolga

Abstract

A new drone-based image processing technique for item and human detection is presented in this work. Unlike previous methods that relied on a steady network connection for optimal results, a Raspberry Pi 4 module was installed on the drone for local processing and detection. In the first investigation, a lightweight drone was constructed using some of the most advanced racing components, specifically chosen to meet particular needs. Convolutional neural networks and TensorFlow Lite were used in the second stage to develop a computationally efficient detection method on the Raspberry Pi. Multiple objects in a single image might be detected in a single algorithm iteration thanks to the chosen algorithm, Single Shot Detection (SSD). To securely mount the drone's battery, Raspberry Pi module, and additional battery, a container was created and 3D printed.

Keywords: image processing, drone, Raspberry Pi, TensorFlow, single shot detection (SSD)

1. Introduction

UAVs (Unmanned Aerial Vehicles), better known to the public as drones, are aerial vehicles that do not require a pilot on board. They are part of a system that also includes a ground controller, which can be either human or automated, and a communication medium that connects the two. The first use of a device officially called a "drone" was for ground-controlled aircraft used for target practice of shipboard guns in the 1920s and later for many other types of operations.

Although drones originated from their use in military operations too dangerous for a human crew, they quickly became very popular in a multitude of fields, from science (e.g., counting aquatic species populations), commerce (e.g., transporting online-ordered items), and agriculture (e.g., spreading insecticide) to recreation (e.g., toy drones for children). The trend of miniaturizing and simplifying drones has reduced their costs, making them increasingly accessible to the public. Many enthusiasts take aerial photographs with the help of drones or even participate in drone races built at home by each participant. As the community of drone enthusiasts continues to grow, it has given rise to numerous online communities dedicated to this hobby.

Beyond recreational use, mounting cameras on drones has opened new horizons regarding their utilization. Practically becoming an extension of the human eye, drones are frequently used today to monitor vast spaces, remote or dangerous areas for humans, or crowded crowds for cinematic purposes to create panoramic images. Since the drone with camera system allows for the visualization of many places that were previously inaccessible by other means, in recent years, the issue of establishing clear legislation on the legal domains of drone use has begun to be addressed [1] to respect private spaces and ensure people's safety. Thus, the advancement of technology has led to the need for new laws to keep pace with it. From using drone images in court to assigning IDs to each drone for easy identification, society has been forced to adapt to the emergence of new aerial vehicles. As presented in the paper [1], systems for identifying drones by ID and position have begun to emerge, thereby ensuring their continuous monitoring.

Since most drones today have an attached camera, another very important aspect is the ability to faithfully transmit the images obtained by these cameras. Surveillance using drones necessitates the rapid identification of specific objects, people, or events that represent the purpose of the surveillance. Thus, the need to process the images obtained from the drone naturally arises. This is only possible if the obtained images are clear, without excessive noise or image alterations due to transmission. In research [2], using a classic image transmission system to a ground station, the authors state that the noise associated with the transmission altered the images, which partially compromised the subsequent processing.

In research [3], the authors implemented a system of multiple Wi-Fi antennas across the vast domain of a farm. The drone, which aimed to detect cattle belonging to the farm, interacted with the antenna system by connecting to the nearest antenna. Thus, the system minimized noise and enabled a relatively clear transmission of images, thereby fulfilling its intended purpose. However, a major disadvantage of this type of system is its complexity and the need to install numerous antennas proportional to the area covered, which raises the system's cost and makes it unfeasible for an average person or a company with limited financial resources.

Thus, the solution adopted in the current project, which offers the best image quality-to-price ratio, is presented in the research [4]. The solution presented by the authors is installing a processor directly on the drone, thus enabling local image processing. Since the camera and processor are directly interconnected, the image quality is not affected by transmission, and the processing of the obtained images thus becomes much easier. Since processing is done at the drone level, only an alarm signal will be sent to the ground station if specific objects or people are detected, and this signal is much easier to transmit than a video stream. The disadvantage of this system is the increased energy consumption caused by the processor and the additional weight, which limits the time the drone can stay airborne. However, the current project also aims to provide solutions for these issues.

After the image transmission, a processing issue arises, which constitutes the software part of this work. Therefore, a presentation of the technologies used and their current status is necessary. The concept of Artificial Intelligence involves the imitation of human understanding and behavior by computers, which are naturally incapable of doing so. Because of this, machines can interpret their surrounding environment and make decisions that are appropriate to their situation.

Through Machine Learning, we understand the mimicking of the human cognitive learning process by a computer, where learning refers to the acquisition of the ability to adapt to new situations based on previous understanding of a multitude of similar situations. Based on well-defined algorithms tailored to the application it will perform, computer training begins by randomly guessing certain outcomes and showing the correct ones. The network adjusts each time based on how well or poorly it responds to the requirement. Thus, the network is expected to provide increasingly better responses after many such examples. This type of learning, known as supervised learning, is one of several types, including unsupervised learning and reinforcement learning, each with its own specific algorithm.

Closely related to machine learning is the concept of Computer Vision. It focuses on understanding the computer's environment based exclusively on image or video frame processing. Depending on the matrix of numerical values corresponding to each pixel or the succession of matrices in the case of videos, through image filtering techniques, it is possible to distinguish the presence or absence of certain characteristics in an image, other algorithms being used afterward to detect, for example, moving objects, to track a specific object, or to create a 3D map of an area. Examples of such algorithms are Frame Differentiation and Background Subtraction. However, one very important thing to mention is that training a machine cannot be done without a proper dataset. The more relevant training images a given dataset contains, the better the system will be trained, and the better the results will be produced. Nowadays, there is free online access to many such databases, which research groups or enthusiasts often offer.

Most Machine Learning and Computer Vision algorithms utilize objects called Neural Networks, named for their apparent similarity to the functionality of the nervous system and neurons. These are composed of nodes, called neurons, which are essentially variables that store a value between 0 and 1, and edges that connect the neurons. Each edge is associated with a certain weight and offset (bias). These weights and biases are the variables that change when the network is trained. The activation function is the last crucial element of a network, which assigns a value between 0 and 1 to each neuron. Depending on the application, it can be of the sigmoid type, ReLU (Rectified Linear Unit), or others. Such structures enable their training and use to make predictions or detect specific objects, as seen in the current project, where images from the camera mounted on the drone will be processed to identify moving objects.

Regarding the current state of convolutional neural networks as highly efficient object detectors, we have, for example, the SSD (Single Shot Detector) networks initially presented in research [5]. This type of network significantly streamlines the detection process by allowing an image to pass through the network only once, enabling the detection of multiple objects. SSD networks are based on dividing the image into grids and defining detection boxes of various sizes, thus searching for objects from different perspectives and sizes. Compared to other types of networks, such as YOLO (You Only Look Once) or R-CNN (Region-based Convolutional Neural Network), the SSD algorithm offers similar speed and accuracy while being much lighter in terms of computational resources, making it suitable for use in embedded systems. Based on the SSD algorithm, increasingly efficient and more accurate networks are being continuously developed, such as RefineDet, which was presented in the research study [6].

It will begin by selecting the drone components based on the current application and then explaining how they were built for optimal performance. In the second part, the design of a box placed on top of the drone will be shown, which will safely hold the batteries and the Raspberry Pi board. In the final part, the implementation of the object detection algorithm, implemented on the Pi 4 board, will be presented.

2. Drone design

This chapter describes the drone components based on the current application and explains how they were built for optimal performance.

Nowadays, there are many types of drones, each implementation having a specific application for which it was designed. Therefore, when selecting the components, the application's needs were considered, specifically capturing frames with a camera for subsequent detection. From this, the photographs must be as clear as possible, which translates into a flight as stable as possible for the drone to perform. The drone must remain airborne for as long as possible, necessitating a lower weight and a higher-capacity battery.

Considering these aspects, the selection of frame components was necessary. A larger frame results in a more stable flight, so I chose a 7-inch frame as the wheelbase, which still fits within the portable drone category but leans toward the larger spectrum. The options offered by retailers on the market were analyzed, and it was concluded that the HSKRC XL7 model (**Figure 1**) offers the best quality-price ratio, featuring a carbon frame.

The frame features a fairly simple design, with the main advantage being the multiple openings and holes on the upper side, which allow for the mounting of necessary components on the drone. With the frame chosen, it was time to select the other components. Because there are numerous options and directions we could take, a preliminary weight calculation was made for the drone using the average weight of components available on the market. This calculation is based on the fact that the drone's weight influences the choice of motors, which in turn affects the selection of other components (**Table 1**). After studying the most popular models on the market, the following average weights for the various components of the drone were established:

Additionally, the drone will feature a battery that powers the Raspberry Pi module, which weighs approximately 250 g, as well as the Pi module, weighing 45 g. From this, we can consider the average weight of the drone to be 900 g. Having this information, we can proceed to choose the motors. It is recommended that the force generated by a motor to counteract gravity (thrust) be equal to the drone's weight. Thus, for the motor, the Emax Eco II motor model was chosen, which has a volume specified by the index 2807 (28 mm—rotor diameter, 7 mm—stator height) and a rotation index of 1300 Kv (1300 RPM/1 V applied). The right choice can also be seen in **Table 2**, provided by the manufacturer, where the generated thrust can be observed:

For an average current (9.4A), the thrust produced is 900 g, approximately equal to the drone's weight. Following this, the propellers recommended by the

Figure 1.
HSKRC XL7 drone frame.

#	Component	Medium weight [g]
1	Frame	125
2	Flight controller + ESC	20 g
3	4 x Motors	180
4	4 x Propeller	10
5	Receiver	10
6	Battery	250
	Total	595

Table 1.
Medium weights of different components of a drone.

Motor type	The voltage (V)	Propeller	Current (A)	Thrust (G)	Power (W)	Efficiency (G/W)	Speed (RPM)
ECOII-2807-1300KV	25.2	HQ 7*4*3 3-blade propeller	2.2	300	55.44	5.41	6550
	25.2		4.2	500	105.84	4.72	9600
	25.2		6.5	700	163.80	4.27	11,100
	25.2		9.4	900	236.88	3.80	12,500
	25.2		13.4	1100	337.68	3.26	13,900
	25.2		51.2	2640	1290.24	2.05	Max

Table 2.
Emax Eco II motor datasheet specification [7].

manufacturer were selected, specifically the HQ 7*4*3, which is suitable for the chosen 7-inch frame. As the name suggests, these have a pitch of 4 inches, thus fitting within the average range of propellers, requiring little force to spin them.

The next components that must be chosen are the flight controller (FC) and the electronic speed controller (ESC) [8]. They are usually sold together under the name Stack. I chose an economical variant capable of providing the motors with sufficient current for any conditions without burning out, namely, the Mamba F405 MK2. This FC is based on an STM32F405 microcontroller. This is a 32-bit controller with a maximum operating frequency of 168 MHz and a supply voltage of 3.3 V. What makes it suitable for the chosen application is, in addition to the increased operating speed, the presence of an integrated Floating Point Unit (FPU) and a Digital Signal Processor (DSP), which facilitates easy data processing. There are twelve 12-bit Analog-to-Digital Converters and many serial communication interfaces for interfacing with various sensors, including I2C, SPI, UART, and CAN. UART is used for communication with the RF receiver, while I2C is used for connection with the gyroscope and OSD. An LQFP (Low-profile Quad Flat Package) type package is used for the controller to ensure the smallest possible size. As an auxiliary circuit on the flight controller, the MPU6000 is used. This is an integrated circuit for motion tracking, incorporating a 3-axis gyroscope and a 3-axis accelerometer to enable the controller to detect the movements made by the drone and make informed decisions. The circuit's range is programmable, with selectable ranges for the gyroscope of ±250°/sec, ±500°/sec, ±1000°/sec, and ± 2000°/sec. For the accelerometer, the available ranges are ±2 g, ±4 g, ±8 g, and ± 16 g. The information from the six channels is digitized by six 16-bit ADCs and sent to the controller *via* I2C at up to 400 kHz.

Since the various circuits on the PCB or connected to it require different supply voltages, the flight controller has three linear LDO voltage regulators: 3.3 V, 5 V, and 9 V, each with a maximum output current of 2A. The board also features a TVS (transient voltage suppressor) for protection against transient voltage spikes that could damage it.

The MOS transistors in the ESC's inverters can handle a current of IDmax = 50A, allowing each motor to draw up to 50A from the battery.

Next, it was necessary to choose the elements that would transmit commands from the pilot to the drone, namely, the transmitter and the receiver. After studying the reviews of experienced users, it was concluded that the best quality-price ratio is offered by the FlySky FS I6X controller, which will work together with the FlySky FS X6B receiver, both of which can be seen in **Figure 2**.

The transmitter can transmit information from 10 channels, including the four default ones (throttle, roll, pitch, and yaw) and six auxiliary channels. It will operate in the 2.4GHz band, utilizing Gaussian Frequency Shift Keying (GFSK) modulation and AFHDS (Automatic Frequency Hopping Digital System) technology to minimize interference from other transmitters. The receiver acts as a demodulator of the signals transmitted on the carrier, offering three options for communication with the FC: through PWM, PPM, or I2C. Ibus is FlySky's proprietary digital protocol. It works exactly like the SBus protocol regarding packet format and message size, only with the opposite polarity (Ibus—Inverted bus), thus having High in the idle/recessive state and Low being considered the dominant state, like the CAN protocol. This protocol was chosen because it is the most highly recommended by the manufacturer, taking into account noise tolerance and transmission speed considerations.

With all the components at hand, the drone could be constructed. It started with the construction of the carbon frame base. It comprises the central plate that connects the four arms where the motors will be mounted. The ESC will be mounted on the screws of the central plate, which must be positioned carefully, as the order of the motors in a counterclockwise direction in Betaflight [9] is 2, 1, 3, 4.

Each motor corresponds to three pins related to the three phases of the inverter branches. The order in which the three motor wires are soldered to the pins does not matter, as software can later modify the direction. In addition to the 12 pins corresponding to the motors, the ESC must have the power supply wires soldered. On

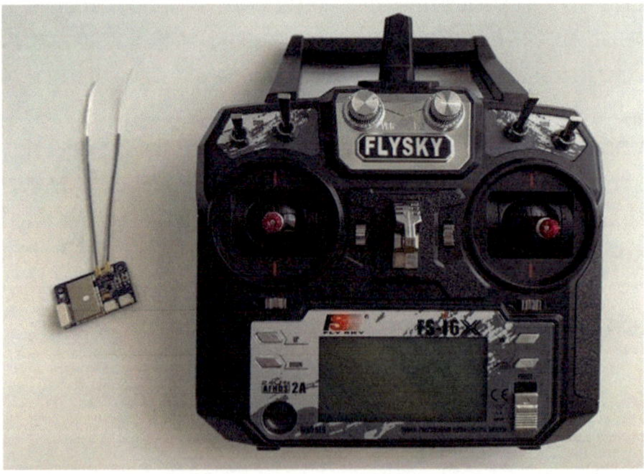

Figure 2.
FlySky FS X6B receiver and FlySky FS I6X controller.

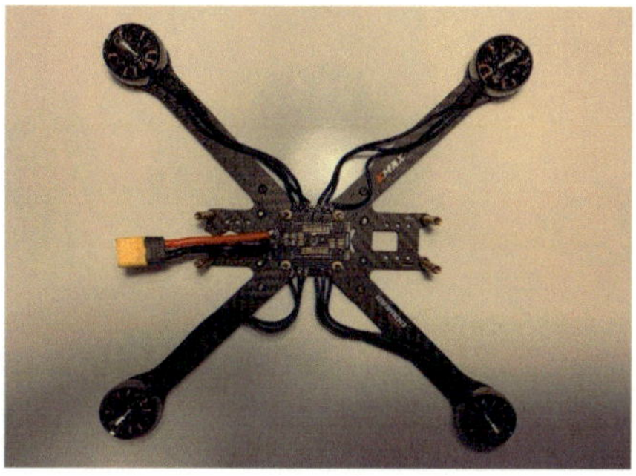

Figure 3.
ESC connections.

the Mamba ESC, the corresponding pins are U-shaped; next to them, small holes connect the filtering capacitor to the power terminals. I made these solder joints, as seen in **Figure 3**. The capacitor fits perfectly on the frame under the ESC, leaving enough space above it to place the FC. At the other end of the power wires, an XT-60 connector was installed, as Li-Po batteries typically come with this type of connector. Each wire was soldered to one of the two terminals of the connector, and a protective cover was placed over the solder joints to shield the connections from water or other impacts and shocks. Thus, the power connections for the entire system and the motors to the ESC were ensured. Thus, the power part has been completed, leaving only the signal part routed through the Flight Controller *via* the STM32 controller.

Since the VTX or OSD is not used in this application, the only soldering needed on the FC is for the receiver signals. It will transmit the command signals through an RX pin of a UART port. Thus, the receiver was assigned to the UART3 port, soldering the Ibus pin from the receiver to the RX3 of the controller. Additionally, the power supplies (VCC and GND) were soldered to the receiver. It needs 5 V to be powered through the linear voltage regulator on the flight controller. The connection between FC and ESC is made through a harness provided by the manufacturer. In addition to the battery's VBAT and GND power supplies, the harness contains four signal wires for the four motors. Thus, the FC and ESC are now ready to communicate, and the system is almost ready for flight operations.

After completing the soldering, a multimeter was used to test the various connections. The solder joints were made correctly, so no unwanted short circuits or solder bridges were formed by mistake. Thus, the propellers were mounted after the drone's cover was installed so that the front propellers spun outward from the drone's body and the rear propellers spun inward. Thus, the drone is fully assembled, and the complete system is shown in **Figure 4**.

After assembling the drone's hardware, it is necessary to program the firmware into the microcontroller's memory on the FC to ensure the correct transmission of information about motor speeds to the ESC controllers. The firmware most enthusiasts use is open-source, with numerous improvements from version to version, and is called Betaflight. To facilitate the easiest modification of parameters without the need to edit the code directly, the Betaflight team has released an application called Betaflight Configurator. This application uses the laptop's USB port to connect to the FC *via* a micro-USB port.

Thus, all the important flight parameters are configured from the application, namely, which UART port the Receiver is connected to, which protocol it will use,

Figure 4.
Equipped drone.

which protocol will be used to send information to the ESC, in which directions the motors will spin, what each channel of the transmitter will represent, what role the secondary channels will have, and so on. Everything in the app is quite intuitive, and you can also set the failsafe mode, which describes what the drone should do when it loses signal from the transmitter. The application uses a driver to program the controller from USB to UART. On the flight controller, control LEDs will signal when the controller has been flashed correctly. The application allows each motor to be tested individually to check its direction before flight. This is very important because incorrect rotation of the motors can lead to drone accidents. The four necessary channels for flight (throttle, roll, pitch, and yaw) and the auxiliary channels can also be tested.

3. 3D design for housing of the image processing unit

This chapter describes the step-by-step design of the housing mounted on top of the drone, which will hold together the image processing unit formed by the Raspberry Pi 4 board, the Pi Camera V2, and the external lithium-polymer battery.

For the 3D design, Autodesk's Fusion 360 facility was used.

First, the three big components were sized, which must be incorporated into the housing's interior design. Their dimensions are shown in **Table 3**.

The external battery is longer than the other two components. Considering the length of the drone's frame cover, 14.6 mm, a two-tier housing was created. On the first tier, close to the frame, the external battery will be positioned, and on the upper tier, the Li-Po battery and the Raspberry Pi will be located. The positioning principle is illustrated in the block diagram shown in **Figure 5**, where the housing is marked with red lines.

The housing design was divided into two major components: the body and the lid. It was decided that the Raspberry camera mount should be on the lid, which will capture frames later subjected to the detection algorithm. The camera must be positioned at an angle to look slightly downwards when the drone flies straight, as we will be interested in ground-level objects.

So, it started with the body's design. According to the idea above, it has two levels plus a few holes for the connection ports. After proper sizing and design, the results are shown in **Figure 6**.

Component	Length [mm]	Width [mm]	Height [mm]
External battery	145	70	15
Li-po battery	85	42	34
Raspberry Pi 4	90	56	17

Table 3.
Physical dimensions of the components.

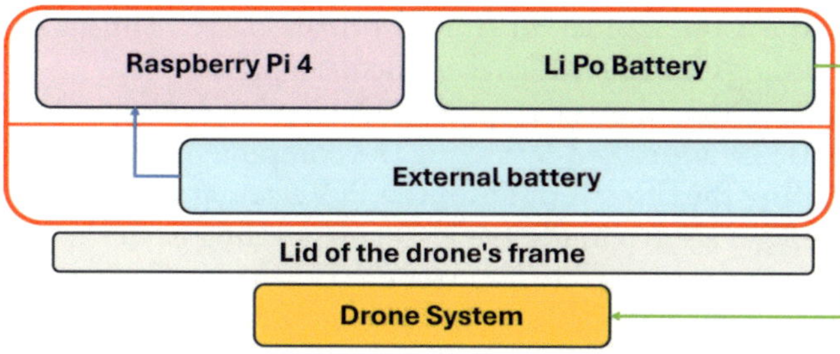

Figure 5.
Schematic of the housing mounted on top of the drone.

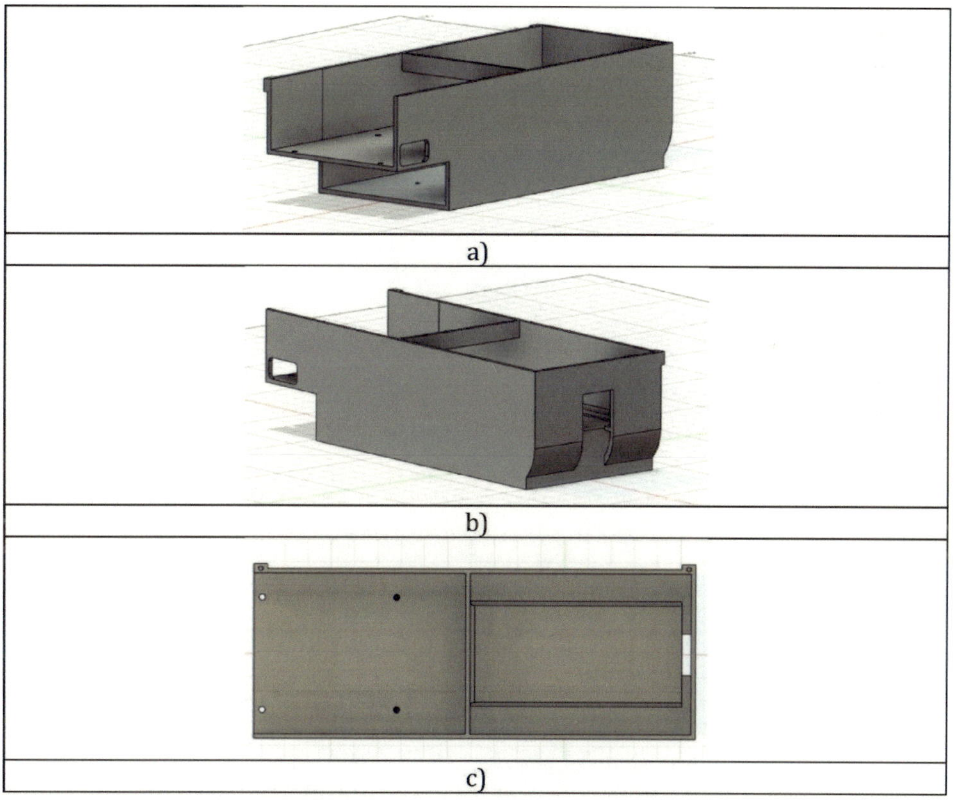

Figure 6.
3D design of the housing's body: (a) side view 1; (b) side view 2; (c) top view.

Corresponding to the external battery is the lower deck, which will slide over the mounting holes of the housing onto the drone's frame. For mounting, the lower tier is approximately the same size as the battery, so it will not have room to move when the drone is in the air and any vibrations due to turbulence occur. The connection between the battery and the Raspberry Pi board is made through the front part of the lower deck, specifically the visible opening on the left side of the upper deck, corresponding to the power port of the Pi 4 module. On the top deck, four holes were made to secure the Raspberry board, and the visible partition wall serves as a separator between the components on the top deck. A vibration-damping tray was created for the Li-Po battery and placed at the back of the upper deck. Behind the piece is a hole corresponding to the XT60 connector from the drone's ESC. Thus, all the ports have corresponding openings for the external connection part.

Next, the design of the lid was completed. During implementation, it was decided that the issue should be addressed by sliding the component laterally over the body, thereby encapsulating the tilted mount for the Pi V2 camera. The result of the design is evident in the images shown in **Figure 7**. Corresponding to the lower floor, at the front, an opening was created to connect the USB Type-C power cable for the Raspberry, which is smaller than the empty space in the body. For easy removal and attachment, the threading around the wall makes the transition smoother. With this design, there is a very small chance that the lid will detach from the body during flight, potentially causing damage to the components inside the housing.

The camera mount was designed to position the camera at a 22.5° angle and maintain a fixed position. Thus, the camera is slightly tilted, and its lens is directed toward the ground. As shown in **Figure 7b**, the bus cable connecting the camera to the CSI (Camera Serial Interface) port on the Raspberry Pi will exit the box through the opening on the top side of the lid. The camera will slide into the specially created slot for it. Unfortunately, the protocol used between the camera and the Raspberry Pi is closed source, being the MIPI interface. This interface is defined by the MIPI Alliance, which

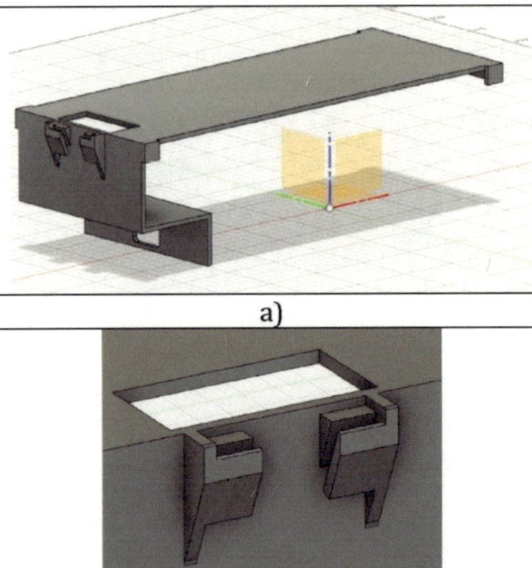

a)

b)

Figure 7.
3D design of the housing's lid: (a) side view; (b) camera mounting side view.

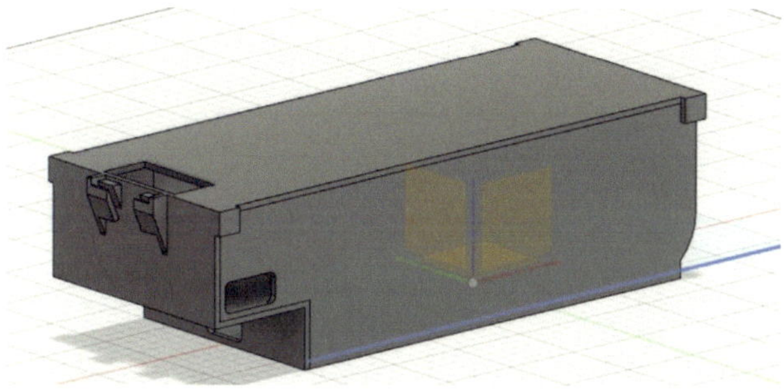

Figure 8.
3D view of the entire housing (body with lid).

includes major companies such as Apple, Samsung, and Huawei. These companies pay an annual fee to access the interface specifications, thereby enabling more efficient communication between cameras and their devices. On the Raspberry Pi board, the MIPI interface is transmitted through the CSI interface to the processor, which is used in this project for the camera. Thus, a complete integration of all the parts that will enter the interior and exterior of the housing is achieved. The connections between components will be made safely and stably, with special openings designed in the housing for this purpose. The complete 3D design assembly, with the lid attached to the body, is presented in **Figure 8**.

4. Object detection algorithm implementation

This chapter presents the implementation of the image processing software, specifically the detection algorithm for various object categories, using the camera mounted on the drone. It begins by explaining the reasoning behind the choice of algorithm, then presents the code written for its implementation and adaptation to the embedded platform on the Raspberry Pi 4 board.

To choose a suitable detection algorithm for our application, several aspects were considered: first, the limited computational capacity of the Raspberry Pi 4 board, so the chosen algorithm had to be as lightweight as possible from a computational standpoint, then the detection accuracy, as well as the maximum speed at which it could run. A few competitors stood out, namely, R-CNN (Region-based Convolutional Neural Networks), YOLO (You Only Look Once), and SSD (Single-Shot Detector). R-CNN-based algorithms were ruled out because they could not be implemented on embedded systems using TensorFlow Lite; therefore, the decision was between the last two. The research paper [5] highlights a comparison, as seen in **Table 4**, between the detection algorithms of interest.

As can be seen, the SSD models, numbered according to image size (300x300, 512x512), have better accuracy (mAP—mean average precision) than the YOLO models. However, the Fast YOLO model achieves a significantly higher frame rate. In the case of the present application, detection does not require extremely fast processing; the speed provided by the SSD algorithm is sufficient. That is why it was decided to go with the SSD—Single Shot Detector network for the implementation.

The SSD-type detector can detect objects in images from predefined object categories. The network's output consists of boxes that enclose the detected objects, along with the confidence percentages indicating the level of certainty in

Method	mAP	FPS
Faster R-CNN (VGG16)	73.2	7
Faster R-CNN (ZF)	62.1	17
YOLO	63.4	45
First YOLO	52.7	155
SSD300	74.3	46
SSD512	76.8	19

Table 4.
Detection algorithm comparison [5].

the detection (i.e., how sure we are that the detection was made correctly). This type of network utilizes 3x3 pixel convolutional predictors or filters. To ensure that the object's size does not influence the prediction in the image, feature maps of various sizes are employed, which combine different convolutional filters to obtain more complex features.

In **Figure 9** [10], the complete structure of the SSD network is shown. As observed, we will have a 300x300 pixel image as input to the algorithm used. This image will be used as input to a classic VGG16 [11] network, truncated to its last pooling layer, from which several feature maps will be extracted to assist in object localization. After the VGG16 truncated network, the image is passed through several additional convolutional layers of the detector, which introduces novelty to this implementation.

The basic idea is that we cannot know the area and orientation of the objects we will detect. That is why the idea behind SSD is to divide the image into multiple grids of various sizes, applying different predefined detection boxes of different sizes and aspect ratios within the grid cells. The determination of the types of boxes used for detecting certain types of objects is done during training, where the aspect ratio of the boxes is optimized. An example of such anchor boxes is presented in **Figure 10** [12].

Thus, the various types of anchor boxes will detect objects from the feature map at different sizes and orientations. As shown in the network structure presented above, 8732 presence/location predictions will be made for each object category in the image, after which the non-max suppression layer will be applied to eliminate redundant and overlapping predictions. This layer compares the

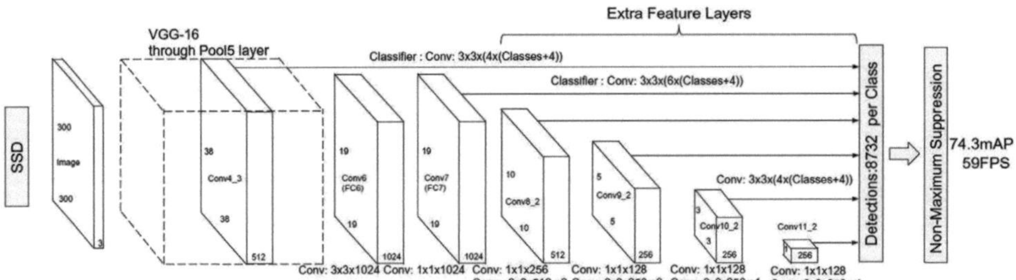

Figure 9.
The structure of the implemented SSD network [10].

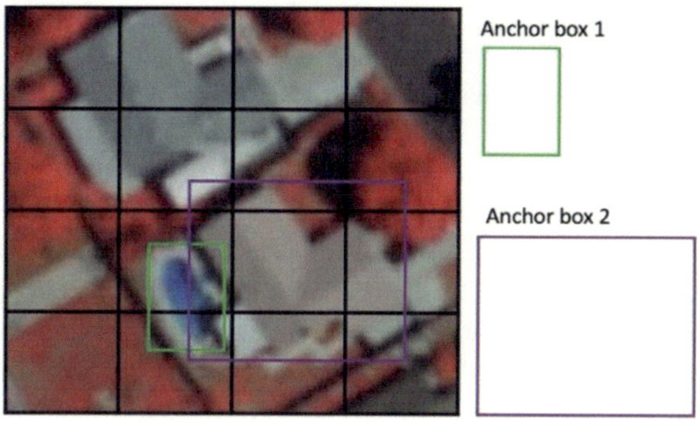

Figure 10.
Anchor boxes example [12].

prediction boxes that overlap significantly and retains the one with the highest prediction confidence. Thus, we will only keep the most reliable boxes in a region, which we will use as network outputs.

As a programming language for implementing a script that utilizes the SSD model for detection, Python was used, the most common language for image processing, due to its multitude of existing libraries and ease of use. In **Figure 11**, the block diagram of the implemented script is presented.

The program is simple and can run on the Raspberry Pi platform. The function libraries used in the program are *OS* for determining the locations of the files used; *OpenCV (CV2)* for processing the captured frames*; NumPy* for resizing arrays*; time* for calculating the frame rate; *threading* for generating a new Thread, as explained further below; and *TensorFlow Lite* [13] for model interpretation and inference.

The VideoStream class was designed with start, update, read, and stop methods for easy control of the video stream. In the start method, the initiation of a new Thread can be observed. This involves capturing frames from the camera in a separate location in the processor's user space, compared to the inference performed by the SSD detection model [14], which introduces execution parallelism to optimize the program's performance. After reading the file with the labels and creating a list with

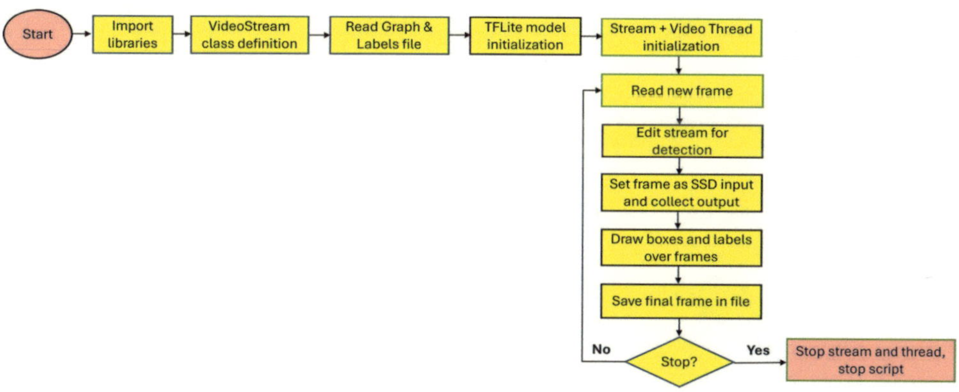

Figure 11.
Block diagram of the script.

them, the *tflite* file containing the model's graph will be interpreted. This was taken from the *TensorFlow GitHub* [15] to test the SSD model. The graph is quantized, meaning that all the values in it (weights, biases), as well as the activation levels resulting from the calculations, will be represented as uint8 (unsigned integers on 8 bits), which is specific to TensorFlow Lite. In comparison, TensorFlow models work with float values represented in 32 bits.

Next, the program will enter an infinite loop, where frames will be continuously read through the VideoStream class object. The SSD network's output for the respective frame will be obtained, anchor boxes will be drawn and labeled appropriately, and the resulting images will be written into *JPEG* files. Thus, the detection results can be accessed after the program is completed and the drone lands.

Next, the preparation of the Raspberry Pi 4 board for detection will be presented. After installing the latest version of the Raspbian operating system, Python IDLE was installed to facilitate the easy execution of Python scripts. Due to the nature of the application, the user will not have access to the mouse, keyboard, and screen when the Raspberry is mounted on the drone. That is why it is necessary to configure the system so that it automatically starts the Python script at system boot-up. This was a bit more complicated than it seemed at first glance because the script needs to be run after certain preparatory steps are completed; namely, the current directory is chosen as the folder containing the script and the models, in this case, *tflite1*, and a virtual environment is activated within the folder so that the library versions recommended by TensorFlow do not conflict with other versions present on the device. This was accomplished through the following steps:

1. A bash script was created to execute commands that would normally be written line by line in the command line:

2. A desktop file was created in the *autostart* sub-folder of the *.config* folder in the Raspbian system. This specifies which program to run when the system exits boot up. In this case, it was specified the bash script presented above, as seen in the image (**Figures 12** and **13**).

Thus, the script will run autonomously, no longer requiring manual initiation.

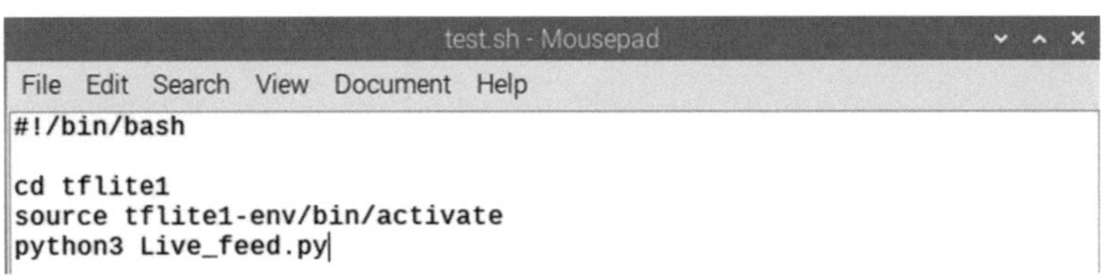

Figure 12.
The bash script created for the proper functioning of the application.

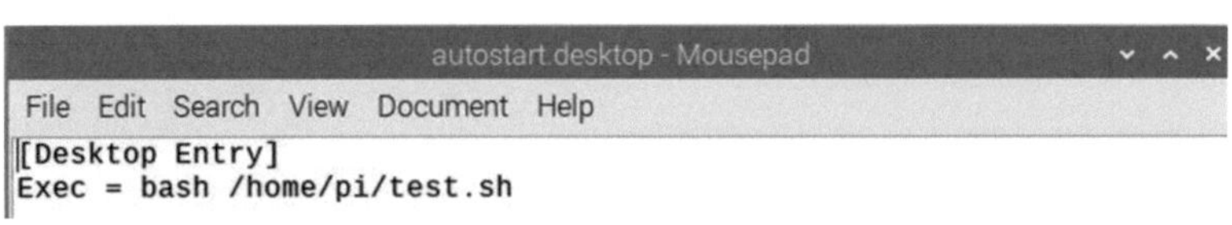

Figure 13.
The desktop file that specifies the execution of the bash script at startup.

5. Experimental results

In this chapter, the results obtained from the system testing are presented. These aspects include the lifespan of the batteries used, the drone's flight time, and the detection algorithm using the camera mounted on the drone, which is connected to the Raspberry Pi board. The main parameters that require increased attention are the proper functioning of the Raspberry Pi board and the camera, the correct operation of the script, the algorithm's detection accuracy, and the longest possible lifespan of the power supply components.

First, the 3D-printed result and the fully assembled drone are presented, including the printed housing, external battery, Li-Po battery, Raspberry Pi 4 module, and Pi V2 camera, as shown in **Figure 14**.

According to the design, the external battery is located on the lower level of the housing, as shown in **Figure 14**. In contrast, the upper level contains the Li-Po battery, the Raspberry Pi 4 module, and the Pi camera.

Thus, it continues with the tests regarding the operation of the various assembly components. The chosen external battery is manufactured by Tellur and can deliver a power of 18 W, which is sufficient for the Raspberry Pi 4 module, which requires a voltage of 5 V and a maximum current of 3A. The battery has a capacity of 10,000mAh, weighs 220 g, and connects to the Pi board *via* the USB Type-C port. The Pi board was initialized to run the script at boot-up, and all other peripherals, such as the mouse, keyboard, and monitor, were disconnected to simulate the drone's operation as accurately as possible. This test showed a discharge time of almost 3 hours from 100–50% of the battery capacity.

Figure 15 shows the 1100 mA Li-Po battery used for the drone. For this battery test, one of the major advantages of this type of battery was considered, namely, the linear discharge throughout the entire discharge range. The fully charged battery was 22.8 V (6 x 3.8 V). However, it started with a battery level of around 22 V due to the necessary battery configurations and preliminary tests. After approximately one minute of flight, the voltage was checked in the Betaflight app, and the voltmeter indicated a value of 21.5 V. Thus, considering that the drone alerts the pilot when the battery voltage drops below 10 V (the highest voltage regulator on the board is 9 V), we can calculate the possible flight time with this battery for a flight without tricks or sudden changes in altitude and direction as:

$$\Delta t_{flight} = \frac{\Delta V2}{\Delta V1} * \Delta t = \frac{12V}{0.5V} * 1\,min = 24\,min \tag{1}$$

If linear discharge is considered, using the battery from the tests with a capacity of 1100 mAh, a maximum of 24 minutes of flight time will be achieved before the battery needs to be recharged. This battery will limit the drone's flight time, leaving much room for future improvements. We could consider solutions such as mounting two batteries on the drone, along with a solar panel system, where one battery charges while the other discharges, allowing for seamless switching between them and thus increasing the drone's flight time. A disadvantage of such a system would be the increased weight of the drone and the need for a robust design to ensure the integrity of all components during flight.

Naturally, a battery with a higher capacity provides a longer flight time. However, this is not linear over the entire range of values because a battery with a very high capacity is also much heavier, which makes the drone heavier and drains the battery faster than the additional time introduced by the extra capacity.

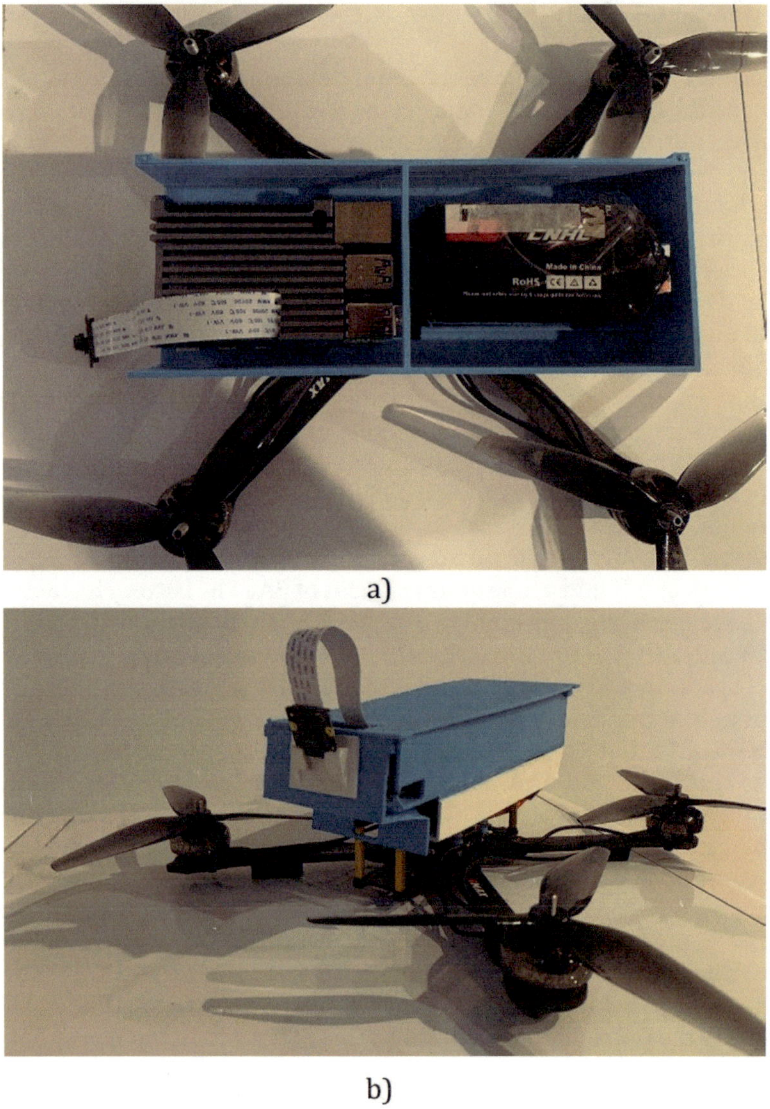

Figure 14.
The whole system: Drone + mounted housing with electronic components: (a) open lid view; (b) closed lid view.

Figure 15.
Li-Po battery used in tests.

Further, the software was tested, specifically the SSD detection algorithm. The first thing noticed at the beginning of the testing was the color spectrum in which the Raspberry Pi V2 camera captures scenes. Being the NoIR model (No Infrared Filter), it does not contain a filter for the infrared portion of the electromagnetic spectrum. For this reason, the colors of the captures are slightly distorted and shifted toward the red area. An example of this phenomenon is illustrated in **Figure 16**.

Although the colors in the images are shifted toward red due to the lack of a filter, the objects are still easily distinguishable, so this should not impede the detection algorithm. After verifying the camera's proper functioning, the detection algorithm was applied to the image above as a first test to assess its performance. The result is illustrated in **Figure 17**. It can be observed that the algorithm correctly detected both the water bottle and the keyboard. This demonstrates that the algorithm correctly receives the category labels from the *txt* file and accurately performs category detection.

Additionally, it can be observed that the boxes placing the detected object in the image are positioned correctly and drawn in green, as specified in the Python script. The confidence levels are also displayed correctly, above 50%, which is the minimum threshold for display. To display them, a small white rectangle is created and placed

Figure 16.
The color spectrum of the Pi V2 NoIR camera.

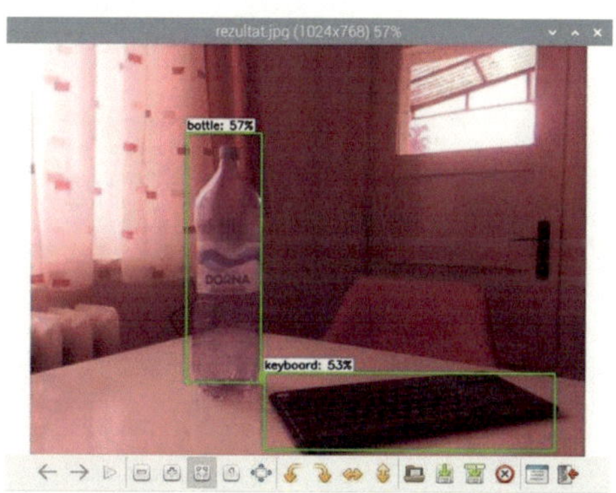

Figure 17.
The detection result for the test image.

above the detection box, where the category name is written in black, followed by the confidence level of the detection, expressed as a percentage. If we see that this works well, it is time to run the complete algorithm, which will read images one by one as frames of a video stream.

To test the complete detection algorithm, the auto-initialization sequence at boot-up was set, as presented in the previous chapter. Namely, the bash script was created that initializes the current directory and the virtual environment, after which the script runs. This script was written in the *autostart* subdirectory of *config*, meaning it will run when the external battery is connected. The initialization of the Pi board took approximately 20 seconds. Afterward, a walk around with the Raspberry Pi board in hand was taken, powered by the external battery that would also power the drone. The walk around the yard reveals various objects from predefined categories in the SSD algorithm. In **Figure 18**, the images saved by the script are displayed, along with the successful detections made by the algorithm.

It can be observed that the algorithm successfully identifies the categories of objects in various poses, directions, and perspectives. For the bicycle, two anchor boxes appeared, both correctly identifying the bicycle, which is an error on the part of the algorithm. The smallest anchor that best frames the bicycle also has the highest detection confidence. It can be observed that the algorithm achieves a detection frame rate of approximately 5.4 fps with this script and on the Pi platform, which is more than sufficient for this application.

The system does not function as intended at night or in low-light conditions. The system was tested in the same yard under nighttime conditions, with unsatisfactory results. The system fails to detect anything under these conditions, resulting in completely black images that cannot be used for detection. For nighttime detection, it will be necessary to use a camera with significantly better capabilities than the current one.

Next, the algorithm was tested in flight mode. **Figure 19** shows some of the results.

Despite the vibrations and unstable image, the algorithm detects the person in the frame without any issues, regardless of height or perspective changes, demonstrating the feasibility of using the algorithm on a device mounted on a drone. To ensure the accuracy of the result, the algorithm was tested using a second location at a different time of day under varying lighting conditions. The results are presented in **Figure 20**. In these lighting conditions, the brightness was significantly lower, and the camera was much more unstable, resulting in photos taken under much less favorable

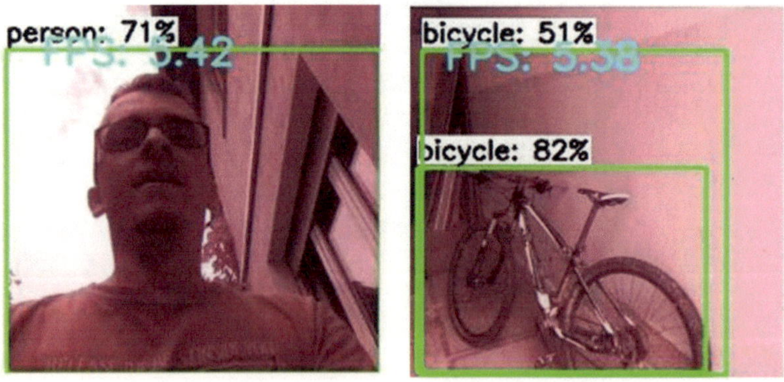

Figure 18.
Examples of successful detections made by the SSD algorithm.

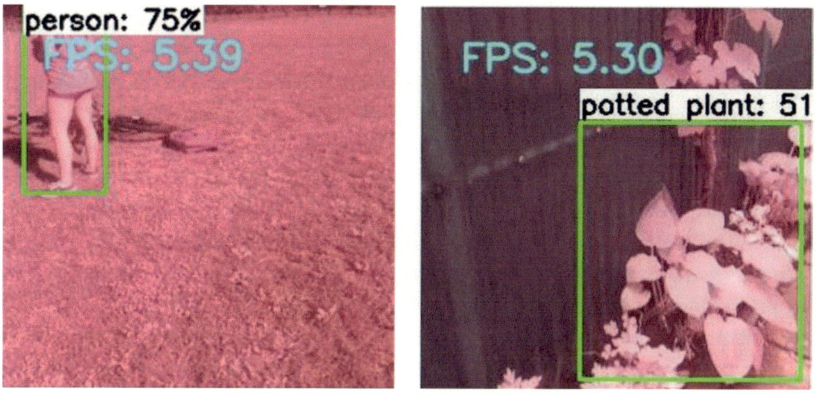

Figure 19.
Flight results in the first location.

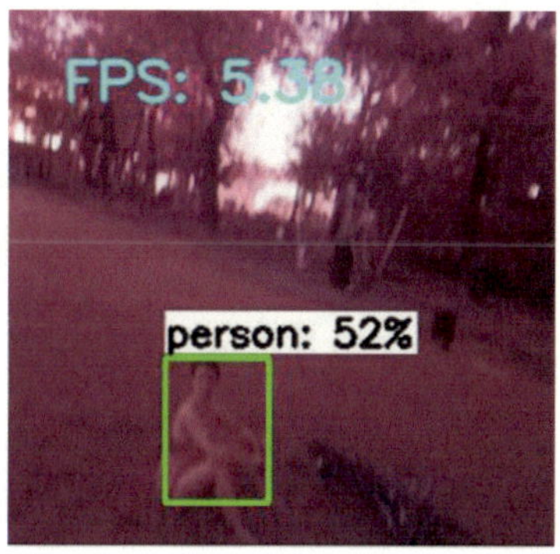

Figure 20.
Flight results in the second location.

conditions. However, when an object from the predefined categories of the algorithm, such as a person, appeared in the frame, it successfully detected them. For this reason, the algorithm's execution was a success.

6. Conclusions

This chapter will summarize the project's goal, outcomes, and areas for improvement.

The project's goal was to create a customized drone equipped with an artificial intelligence system that, when fitted, can recognize particular objects using a camera and a powerful CPU.

A drone was built on a 7-inch frame after first sizing it and selecting parts that would allow for the most stable flight. For optimal system synergy, the motors, propellers, flight controller, electronic speed controller, receiver, transmitter, and battery were selected based on the drone's total weight. The drone was prepared for flight after flashing the required flight firmware with the Betaflight Configurator. A two-tier housing was designed in Fusion 360 that will allow the Li-Po battery, the external battery that powers the Pi board, and the Pi board itself to be stored more efficiently. This housing is mounted on the top side of the drone's frame. Multiple objects can be detected in a single network pass thanks to the SSD algorithm, which was employed for detection. Because it was less computationally demanding and compatible with the Pi board, the Python script utilized a quantized model compatible with TensorFlow Lite.

The experimental part began by timing how long the two batteries took to drain. The system is unrestricted from this angle because the external battery can power the Pi board for a few hours. However, because the tested Li-Po battery had a flight time of less than 30 minutes, the system has a constraint that will need to be made up for by additional system enhancements.

The algorithm was executed successfully. Initially, it was tested without the drone. In most of the test scenarios, it was able to identify the relevant item categories. Finally, the complete assembly (drone with image capture and processing unit) was tested, and the outcomes were also favorable. The system effectively identified items from the given categories, even during abrupt altitude changes and shocks.

To improve the system for the future, several key points will be addressed. One is to activate the homing feature for the drone in the event of signal loss; the device could first be outfitted with a GPS module. Additionally, a technology installed on the drone that utilizes solar panels to charge when the weather is suitable could be used to extend the flight duration and the detection period. Thus, two batteries might be used, one charge and the other discharge at any given time, greatly extending the flight time. Regarding the detection algorithm, tests may be carried out using enhanced SSD algorithm variations that have recently emerged, improving accuracy and efficiency.

Author details

Lorant Andras Szolga
Technical University of Cluj-Napoca, Romania

*Address all correspondence to: lorant.szolga@bel.utcluj.ro

References

[1] Chamoso P, González-Briones A, Rivas A, Bueno FDM, Corchado J. The use of drones in Spain: Towards a platform for controlling UAVs in urban environments. Sensors. 2018;**18**:1416

[2] Yong SP, Chung ALW, Yeap WK, Sallis P. Motion Detection Using Drone's Vision. In: 2017 Asia Modelling Symposium (AMS). Malaysia: Kota Kinabalu; 2017. pp. 108-112. DOI: 10.1109/AMS.2017.25

[3] Rivas A, Chamoso P, Briones A, Corchado M. Detection of Cattle Using Drones and Convolutional Neural Networks Sensors. 2018;**18**(7):2048. DOI: 10.3390/s18072048

[4] Huang C, Chen P, Yang X, Cheng KTT. REDBEE: A visual-inertial drone system for real-time moving object detection. In: IEEE/RSJ International Conference on Intelligent Robots and Systems (IROS), Vancouver, BC, Canada. 2017. pp. 1725-1731. DOI: 10.1109/IROS.2017.8205985

[5] Liu W, Anguelov D, Erhan D, Szegedy C. SSD: Single shot MultiBox detector. In: Computer Vision—ECCV 2016 and Lecture Notes in Computer Science. Vol. 9905. Springer; 2016. pp. 21-37

[6] Zhang S, Wen L, Bian X, Lei Z, Li SZ. Single-shot refinement neural network for object detection. IEEE Transactions on Circuits and Systems for Video Technology. Feb 2020;**31**(2):674-687. DOI: 10.1109/TCSVT.2020.2986402

[7] Rotorama. Emax Eco II 2807 1300Kv [Internet]. 2024 [cited 2025 Apr 06]. Available from: https://www.rotorama.com/motory/emax-eco-ii-2807-1300kv

[8] IDrone Electronic Speed Controller (ESC) with XMC™, Gate Driver, OptiMOS™, Application Note; 2016, Copyright © Infineon Technologies AG 2016, https://www.infineon.com/dgdl/Infineon-Application-Motor_Control-Drone_Electronic_Speed_Controller_ESC-TR-v01_00-EN.pdf?fileId=5546d462580663ef015843a229fe54ea

[9] GitHub. Betaflight project repository [Internet]. 2024 [cited 2025 Apr 06]. Available from: https://github.com/betaflight

[10] Liu W et al. SSD: Single shot MultiBox detector. In: Leibe B, Matas J, Sebe N, Welling M, editors. Computer Vision—ECCV 2016. ECCV 2016. Lecture Notes in Computer Science. Vol. 9905. Cham: Springer; 2016. DOI: 10.1007/978-3-319-46448-0_2

[11] Neurohive. VGG16 – Convolutional Network for Classification and Detection [Internet]. 2018 Nov 20 [cited 2025 Apr 06]. Available from: https://neurohive.io/en/popular-networks/vgg16/

[12] Data Science Central. Drilling into the SSD Model for Object Detection [Internet]. Data Science Central; 2021 Oct 12 [cited 2025 Apr 06]. Available from: https://www.datasciencecentral.com/drilling-into-the-ssd-model-for-object-detection

[13] TensorFlow. TensorFlow [Internet]. 2024 [cited 2025 Apr 06]. Available from: https://www.tensorflow.org/

[14] Esri. How single-shot detector (SSD) works? [Internet]. ArcGIS API for Python; [cited 2025 Apr 06]. Available from: https://developers.arcgis.com/python/latest/guide/how-ssd-works/

[15] EdjeElectronics. TensorFlow Object Detection API Tutorial: Train Multiple Objects on Windows 10 [Internet]. GitHub; [cited 2025 Apr 06]. Available from: https://github.com/EdjeElectronics/TensorFlow-Object-Detection-API-Tutorial-Train-Multiple-Objects-Windows-10

Chapter 2

Enhancing Monocular-Based SLAM with Range-to-Base Measurements for MAV Navigation in GPS-Denied Environments

Rodrigo Munguia and Antoni Grau

Abstract

This paper presents a novel enhancement to monocular-based Simultaneous Localization and Mapping (SLAM) by integrating attitude, altitude, and range-to-base measurements aimed at mitigating drift and improving system observability. The proposed approach leverages range data relative to a known base position, enabling micro aerial vehicles (MAVs) to reduce error accumulation, maintain map consistency, and operate reliably in GPS-denied environments. This integration supports robust long-term autonomous navigation with minimal drift. The approach is theoretically underpinned by a nonlinear observability analysis, which establishes the benefits of incorporating range measurements into the SLAM framework. The system's design and performance are evaluated through simulations and virtual experiments, demonstrating its effectiveness in addressing challenges commonly encountered in GPS-denied navigation.

Keywords: monocular-based SLAM, GPS-denied, MAVs, range-to-base, observability

1. Introduction

Navigating micro aerial vehicles (MAVs) in GPS-denied environments remains a significant challenge in robotics, where high precision and robustness are essential for autonomous operation. Applications in search and rescue, environmental monitoring, and infrastructure inspection increasingly demand effective solutions for localization and mapping under such challenging conditions. In scenarios where GPS is unreliable or unavailable, Simultaneous Localization and Mapping (SLAM) becomes an essential tool for enabling navigation autonomy in real-time. Visual-based SLAM, particularly monocular SLAM (MonoSLAM), is widely used due to its lightweight nature and compatibility with MAV platforms. However, monocular SLAM inherently faces limitations, particularly related to scale and depth ambiguity as well as drift, which are exacerbated over time in complex environments.

Recent research in visual SLAM has led to substantial advancements. Systems such as ORB-SLAM [1] and its extension ORB-SLAM3 [2] have become foundational approaches, offering robust monocular SLAM solutions with capabilities for large-scale environments. ORB-SLAM3, in particular, incorporates multi-map support and inertial measurement unit (IMU) integration, enhancing system robustness and adaptability to various scenarios. Other works, such as VINS-Mono [3], take a tightly coupled approach, fusing visual data with inertial measurements for improved scale estimation and error minimization, demonstrating significant improvements in performance over long-duration missions.

In addition to advancements in pure visual SLAM, recent research has focused on enhancing SLAM systems through sensor fusion methods. Visual-inertial SLAM (VI-SLAM) systems [4, 5] use IMUs to compensate for the limitations of monocular systems, such as scale drift and sensitivity to rapid motion. Multi-sensor fusion methods [6, 7] incorporate additional sensors like lidar or stereo cameras, further improving accuracy and robustness in complex, GPS-denied environments.

Theoretical work on observability analysis also provides critical insights into SLAM performance and stability. For example, Luo et al. [8] and Forster et al. [9] analyze the conditions under which visual-inertial systems are fully observable, guiding the design of SLAM systems with improved state estimation capabilities. Hartley et al. [10] extend these findings by investigating hybrid approaches, where a combination of different sensors contributes to observability and error resilience.

Another critical area of development is in algorithms optimized for MAVs applications in GPS-denied environments. Brossard et al. [11] propose an AI-assisted SLAM system that leverages deep learning to handle complex visual features in dynamic environments, while Karrer et al. [7] utilize dense SLAM techniques that improve map detail and accuracy by leveraging depth information. Li et al. [12] focus specifically on the integration of visual and inertial data for small MAVs, highlighting the potential for achieving high-accuracy localization and mapping in constrained environments.

Given this context, this work proposes enhancing monocular-based SLAM with attitude, altitude and range-to-base measurements, offering a novel approach to mitigate drift by improving system observability. By incorporating range measurements relative to a known base location, the MAV can reduce accumulated errors, maintain spatial consistency, and navigate more robustly in GPS-denied environments, enabling long-term autonomous navigation with minimal drift. This approach is grounded in nonlinear observability analysis, which theoretically justifies integrating range data into the monocular SLAM framework. The design is validated through simulations and virtual experiments, demonstrating its effectiveness in challenging scenarios.

This chapter contributes to the growing body of research on SLAM in GPS-denied environments, offering a framework for improved MAV visual-based navigation through integrated sensor fusion. The proposed monocular-based enhancement represents a significant advancement toward resilient and scalable navigation solutions for real-world applications, addressing both the theoretical and practical aspects of SLAM-based navigation.

The remainder of this chapter is organized as follows: Section 2 presents the observability analysis that supports the proposed approach. Section 3 describes the design of the proposed system. Experimental results are discussed in Section 4, and Section 5 concludes the chapter with directions for future research.

2. Observability analysis

This section presents a study on how the observability property of a bearing-only SLAM system is affected when different aiding measurements, such as attitude, altitude, and range-to-base measurements, are fused into the system. The theoretical findings from this analysis support the design of the monocular-based SLAM method proposed in this work.

The property of *observability* plays a critical role in the performance and reliability of a SLAM (Simultaneous Localization and Mapping) system. A system is said to be observable if its initial state $\mathbf{x}_0$, defined at any initial time t_0, can be uniquely determined using the state transition model $\dot{\mathbf{x}} = \mathbf{f}(\mathbf{x}, \mathbf{u})$, the observation model $\mathbf{y} = \mathbf{h}(\mathbf{x})$, and a finite set of measurements $\mathbf{y}[t_0, t]$ taken from time t_0 to a finite time t.

When a system is fully observable, the minimum achievable error in state estimation depends only on the noise characteristics of the system and is independent of any prior knowledge about the initial state. This property is fundamental for ensuring robust and consistent state estimation in SLAM.

To simplify the analysis, two simplified 3-DOF models will be employed. The first model represents the basic longitudinal dynamics (x-z plane) of a camera mounted on a MAV (See **Figure 1** left plot). The second model captures the basic lateral dynamics (x-y plane) of the camera (See **Figure 1** right plot).

For the longitudinal dynamics, the system is defined as:

$$\{ \quad \dot{x}_r = v_x, \quad \dot{z}_r = v_z, \quad \dot{\theta}_r = \omega_\theta, \quad \dot{v}_x = V_x, \quad \dot{v}_z = V_z, \quad \dot{\omega}_\theta = \Omega_\theta., \tag{1}$$

Here, $\mathbf{x}_r = [x_r, z_r, \theta_r, v_x, v_z, \omega_\theta]^T$ represents the state vector of the camera-robot, where $[x_r, z_r, \theta_r]^T$ and $[v_x, v_z, \omega_\theta]^T$ denote the position and orientation of the camera-robot and their corresponding time derivatives, respectively. In the model described by (1), the system is assumed to be influenced by an unknown input $\mathbf{u} = [V_x, V_z, \Omega_\theta]^T$, representing linear and angular accelerations. These inputs are modeled as zero-mean Gaussian processes with known covariance.

For the lateral dynamics, the system is defined as:

$$\{ \quad \dot{x}_r = v_x \quad \dot{y}_r = v_y \quad \dot{\psi}_r = \omega_\psi \quad \dot{v}_x = V_x \quad \dot{v}_y = V_y \quad \dot{\omega}_\psi = \Omega_\psi \tag{2}$$

Here, $\mathbf{x}_r = [x_r, y_r, \psi_r, v_x, v_y, \omega_\psi]^T$ represents the state vector of the camera-robot, where $[x_r, y_r, \psi_r]^T$ and $[v_x, v_y, \omega_\psi]^T$ denote the position and orientation of the camera-robot and their corresponding time derivatives, respectively. In the model described

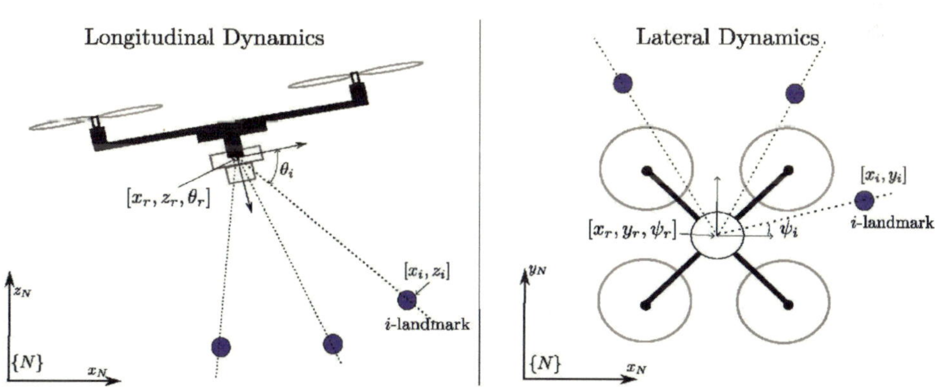

Figure 1.
The observability analysis was performed using two simplified 3-DOF models: one for longitudinal dynamics (left plot) and another for lateral dynamics (right plot).

by (2), the system is assumed to be influenced by an unknown input $\mathbf{u} = \left[V_x, V_y, \Omega_\psi\right]^T$, representing linear and angular accelerations. These inputs are modeled as zero-mean Gaussian processes with known covariance.

It is assumed that angular (bearing) measurements from a set of 2D feature points, which constitute the map of the camera-robot's environment, are available.

For the longitudinal dynamics described in (1), the bearing measurement model is given by:

$$\mathbf{h}_{\theta i}(\mathbf{x}) = \arctan 2\left(\frac{z_r - z_i}{x_r - x_i}\right) - \theta_r, \tag{3}$$

where $\mathbf{y}_i = [x_i, z_i]^T$ represents the position of the ith feature point.

For the lateral dynamics described in (2), the bearing measurement model is expressed as:

$$\mathbf{h}_{\psi i}(\mathbf{x}) = \arctan 2\left(\frac{y_r - y_i}{x_r - x_i}\right) - \psi_r, \tag{4}$$

where $\mathbf{y}_i = \left[x_i, y_i\right]^T$ denotes the position of the i-th feature point.

For both the system dynamics in (1) and (2), the complete state vector $\mathbf{x}$, which is to be estimated for each corresponding SLAM system, consists of the camera-robot state $\mathbf{x}_r$ and the n states $\mathbf{y}_i$ representing all the map features:

$$\mathbf{x} = \left[\mathbf{x}_r \quad \mathbf{y}_1 \quad \mathbf{y}_2 \quad \cdots \quad \mathbf{y}_n\right]^T \tag{5}$$

In the SLAM system with the state vector $\mathbf{x}$, it is assumed that the map features $\mathbf{y}_i$ are static, that is, $\dot{\mathbf{y}}_i = 0$.

Given the above, the objective is to investigate how the observability properties of each SLAM system—one defined by the longitudinal dynamics and the other by the lateral dynamics—are affected when additional types of measurements are incorporated into the system, beyond the bearing measurements.

For the longitudinal system, three types of aiding measurements are considered: (i) attitude (pitch), (ii) altitude, and (iii) range-to-base measurements. It is worth noting that attitude and altitude-aiding measurements are commonly employed in navigation systems, as they are readily available from most onboard hardware of MAVs. In contrast, the use of range-to-base measurements has been significantly less explored in the literature.

The attitude (pitch) measurement model is:

$$\mathbf{h}_\theta(\mathbf{x}) = \theta_r \tag{6}$$

The altitude measurement model is:

$$\mathbf{h}_{z_r}(\mathbf{x}) = z_r \tag{7}$$

The range-to-base measurement model is:

$$\mathbf{h}_{r_1}(\mathbf{x}) = \sqrt{x_r^2 + z_r^2} \tag{8}$$

For the lateral system, two types of aiding measurements are considered: (i) attitude (yaw) and (ii) range-to-base measurements.

The attitude (yaw) measurement model is:

$$\mathbf{h}_{\psi}(\mathbf{x}) = \psi_r \tag{9}$$

The range-to-base measurement model is:

$$\mathbf{h}_{r_2}(\mathbf{x}) = \sqrt{x_r^2 + y_r^2} \tag{10}$$

2.1 Observability of longitudinal system

A nonlinear system is said to be *locally weakly observable* if the *observability rank condition* is satisfied, that is, $\text{rank}(\mathcal{O}) = \dim(\mathbf{x})$ [13], where $\mathcal{O}$ represents the observability matrix. In this context, $\mathcal{L}_f^i(\mathbf{h})$ denotes the ith order Lie derivative [14] of the scalar field $\mathbf{h}$ (which represents a measurement) with respect to the vector field $\mathbf{f}$.

For the longitudinal system, four configurations are defined. The first configuration considers only bearing (angular) measurements, $\mathbf{h}_{\theta i}(\mathbf{x})$, as specified in (3). For this configuration, the observability matrix $\mathcal{O}_{lon}^1$ is constructed for n angular measurements as follows:

$$\mathcal{O}_{lon}^1 = \left[\frac{\partial \mathcal{L}_f^0(\mathbf{h}_\theta^1)}{\partial \mathbf{x}}^T \quad \frac{\partial \mathcal{L}_f^1(\mathbf{h}_\theta^1)}{\partial \mathbf{x}}^T \quad \cdots \quad \frac{\partial \mathcal{L}_f^0(\mathbf{h}_\theta^n)}{\partial \mathbf{x}}^T \quad \frac{\partial \mathcal{L}_f^1(\mathbf{h}_\theta^n)}{\partial \mathbf{x}}^T \right]^T, \tag{11}$$

The second configuration, in addition to bearing measurements, also considers attitude (pitch) measurements $\mathbf{h}_\theta(\mathbf{x})$ (6). For this configuration, the observability matrix $\mathcal{O}_{lon}^2$ is constructed by augmenting the observability matrix $\mathcal{O}_{lon}^1$ with the derivatives of the attitude measurement function, as follows:

$$\mathcal{O}_{lon}^2 = \left[\mathcal{O}_{lon}^1 \left| \frac{\mathcal{L}_f^0(\mathbf{h}_\theta)}{\partial \mathbf{x}}^T \frac{\mathcal{L}_f^1(\mathbf{h}_\theta)}{\partial \mathbf{x}}^T \right. \right]^T \tag{12}$$

The third configuration adds altitude measurements $\mathbf{h}_{z_r}(\mathbf{x})$ (7) to the previous ones. Consequently, the observability matrix $\mathcal{O}_{lon}^3$ is constructed as follows:

$$\mathcal{O}_{lon}^3 = \left[\mathcal{O}_{lon}^2 \left| \frac{\mathcal{L}_f^0(\mathbf{h}_{z_r})}{\partial \mathbf{x}}^T \frac{\mathcal{L}_f^1(\mathbf{h}_{z_r})}{\partial \mathbf{x}}^T \right. \right]^T \tag{13}$$

Finally, the fourth configuration is constructed by adding base-to-range measurements $\mathbf{h}_{r_1}(\mathbf{x})$ (8) to all the previous ones. Therefore, the observability matrix $\mathcal{O}_{lon}^4$ is constructed as follows:

$$\mathcal{O}_{lon}^4 = \left[\mathcal{O}_{lon}^3 \left| \frac{\mathcal{L}_f^0(\mathbf{h}_{r_1})}{\partial \mathbf{x}}^T \frac{\mathcal{L}_f^1(\mathbf{h}_{r_1})}{\partial \mathbf{x}}^T \right. \right]^T \tag{14}$$

Note that there are no strict rules regarding the order of Lie derivatives used to construct the observability matrix $\mathcal{O}$. In this case, only zero-order and first-order Lie derivatives were employed to construct the observability matrices, as higher-order derivatives do not significantly affect the results. Furthermore, derivatives

System configuration	Unobservable modes	Observable states
$\mathcal{O}^1_{lon}$	6	—
$\mathcal{O}^2_{lon}$	4	θ_r, ω_θ
$\mathcal{O}^3_{lon}$	2	$y_r, \theta_r, v_y, \omega_\theta$
$\mathcal{O}^3_{lon}$	0	$\mathbf{x}$ (all)

Table 1.
Observability results for the longitudinal SLAM system.

corresponding to four map features were used to compose the observability matrices, resulting in $\dim(\mathbf{x}) = 14$. Increasing this number does not improve the results. The observability matrices were computed numerically using MATLAB's symbolic toolbox.

Table 1 presents the results of the observability analysis for the longitudinal SLAM system. As expected, the observability of the system improves as more sensory information is fused into it. Notably, full observability is achieved when range-to-base measurements are included in the system.

2.2 Observability of lateral system

For the lateral system, three configurations are defined. The first configuration considers only bearing (angular) measurements, $\mathbf{h}_{\psi i}(\mathbf{x})$, as specified in (4). For this configuration, the observability matrix $\mathcal{O}^1_{lat}$ is constructed for n angular measurements as follows:

$$\mathcal{O}^1_{lat} = \left[\frac{\partial \mathcal{L}^0_f(\mathbf{h}^1_\psi)}{\partial \mathbf{x}}^T \quad \frac{\partial \mathcal{L}^1_f(\mathbf{h}^1_\psi)}{\partial \mathbf{x}}^T \quad \dots \quad \frac{\partial \mathcal{L}^0_f(\mathbf{h}^n_\psi)}{\partial \mathbf{x}}^T \quad \frac{\partial \mathcal{L}^1_f(\mathbf{h}^n_\psi)}{\partial \mathbf{x}}^T \right]^T, \tag{15}$$

For the second configuration, the observability matrix $\mathcal{O}^2_{lat}$ is constructed by augmenting the observability matrix $\mathcal{O}^1_{lat}$ with the derivatives of the attitude measurement model $\mathbf{h}_\psi(\mathbf{x})$ given in (9), as follows:

$$\mathcal{O}^2_{lat} = \left[\mathcal{O}^1_{lat} \middle| \frac{\partial \mathcal{L}^0_f(\mathbf{h}_\psi)}{\partial \mathbf{x}}^T, \frac{\partial \mathcal{L}^1_f(\mathbf{h}_\psi)}{\partial \mathbf{x}}^T \right]^T. \tag{16}$$

Finally, the third configuration is constructed by adding base-to-range measurements $\mathbf{h}_{r_2}(\mathbf{x})$, as defined in (10), to all previous ones. Thus, the observability matrix $\mathcal{O}^3_{lat}$ is constructed as follows:

$$\mathcal{O}^3_{lat} = \left[\mathcal{O}^2_{lat} \middle| \frac{\partial \mathcal{L}^0_f(\mathbf{h}_{r_2})}{\partial \mathbf{x}}^T, \frac{\partial \mathcal{L}^1_f(\mathbf{h}_{r_2})}{\partial \mathbf{x}}^T \right]^T. \tag{17}$$

The same conditions used to construct and compute the observability matrices for the longitudinal system are applied in this case as well.

Table 2 presents the results of the observability analysis for the lateral SLAM system. Similar to the longitudinal system, the observability of the lateral system improves as more sensory information is fused. In this case, full observability is not entirely achieved even when range-to-base measurements are included. However, it is important to note that the robot's pose becomes observable with this configuration.

System configuration	Unobservable modes	Observable states
$\mathcal{O}_{lat}^{1}$	6	—
$\mathcal{O}_{lat}^{2}$	4	θ_r, ω_θ
$\mathcal{O}_{lat}^{3}$	1	x_r, y_r, θ_r, ω_θ[1]

[1]*This result is obtained using small values for xr and yr. However, this does not pose a problem due to the translational invariance of the system.*

Table 2.
Observability results for the lateral SLAM system.

2.3 Simulation results

To validate the theoretical findings obtained from the observability analysis, both 2DOF SLAM systems—longitudinal and lateral—were implemented in MATLAB and simulated in environments similar to those illustrated in **Figure 2**. In these simulations, the positions of the landmarks were randomly generated for each run of the algorithm, and the robot was programmed to follow a predefined trajectory.

Using the simulation environment described earlier (**Figure 2**, left plot), the four system configurations of the longitudinal SLAM system ($\mathcal{O}_{lon}^{1}$, $\mathcal{O}_{lon}^{2}$, $\mathcal{O}_{lon}^{3}$, and $\mathcal{O}_{lon}^{4}$) were evaluated. For each configuration, the Mean Absolute Error (MAE) for x_r, z_r, and θ_r was calculated based on 20 Monte Carlo simulations. The results are shown in **Figure 3**. As anticipated, improvements in the observability of the SLAM system led to a reduction in MAE.

Similarly, for the lateral SLAM system (**Figure 2**, right plot), its three system configurations ($\mathcal{O}_{lat}^{1}$, $\mathcal{O}_{lat}^{2}$, and $\mathcal{O}_{lat}^{3}$) were evaluated. For each configuration, the MAE for x_r, y_r, and θ_r was calculated. The results are presented in **Figure 4**. As with the longitudinal system, improvements in the observability of the lateral SLAM system resulted in a reduction in MAE.

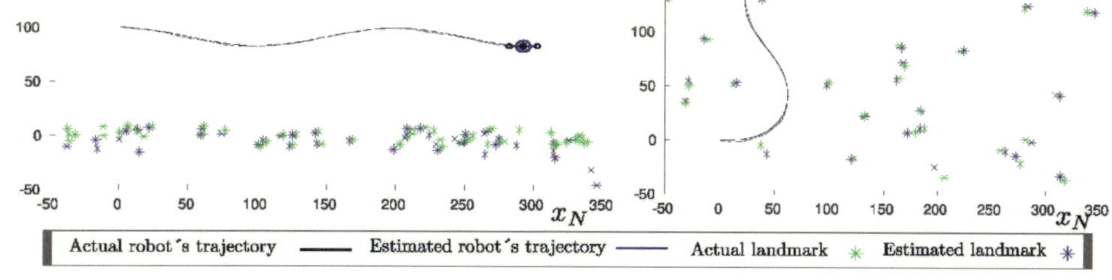

Figure 2.
3-DOF simulation environments used to test the observability results for the longitudinal SLAM system (left plot) and the lateral SLAM system (right plot).

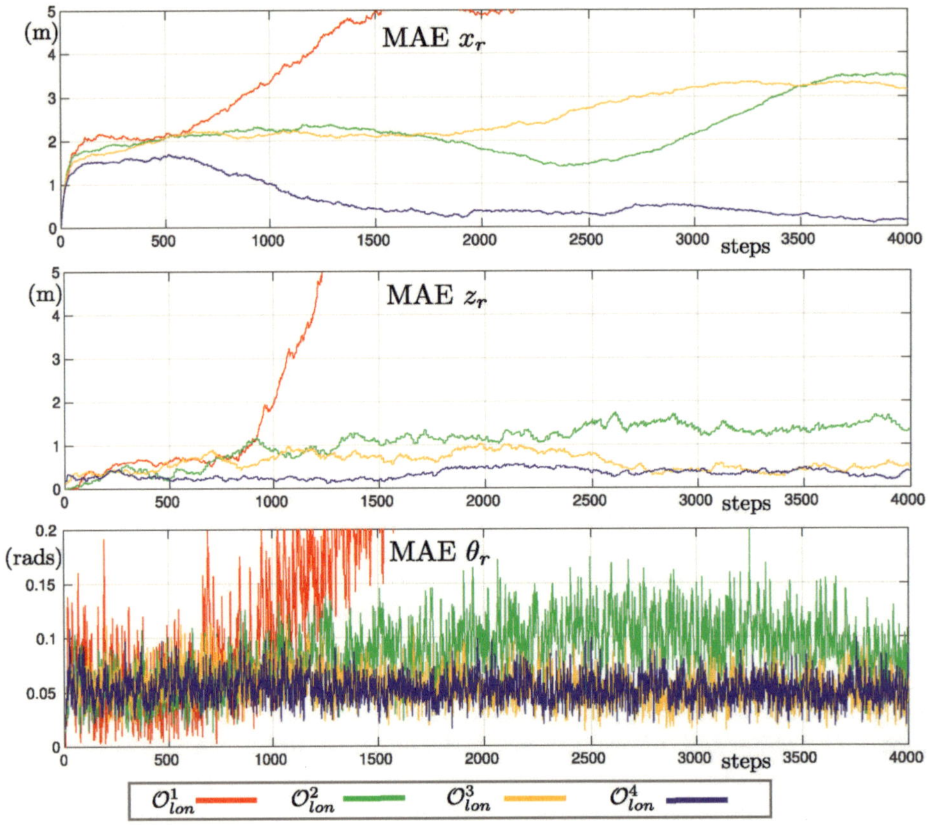

Figure 3.
Longitudinal SLAM system: Comparison of the MAE for the MAV state across the four tested system configurations.

3. Method description

3.1 Architecture and system specification

In the previous section, it was demonstrated that incorporating range-to-base measurements can significantly enhance the observability properties of bearing-based SLAM systems. Improved observability, in turn, leads to a reduction in estimation errors. Building on these findings, this section presents a complete 6DOF monocular-based SLAM system for MAV navigation, which integrates range-to-base measurements as a key component.

3.1.1 MAV's state vector

The 6DOF state vector of the MAV is defined as $\mathbf{x}_r$:

$$\mathbf{x}_r = \begin{bmatrix} \mathbf{e}^{NR} & \omega^R & \mathbf{r}^N & \mathbf{v}^R \end{bmatrix}^T \tag{18}$$

The components of the state vector $\mathbf{x}_r$ are described as follows: The vector $\mathbf{e}^{NR} = [\theta, \phi, \psi]$ represents the robot's orientation relative to the navigation frame $(^N)$. Here, θ,

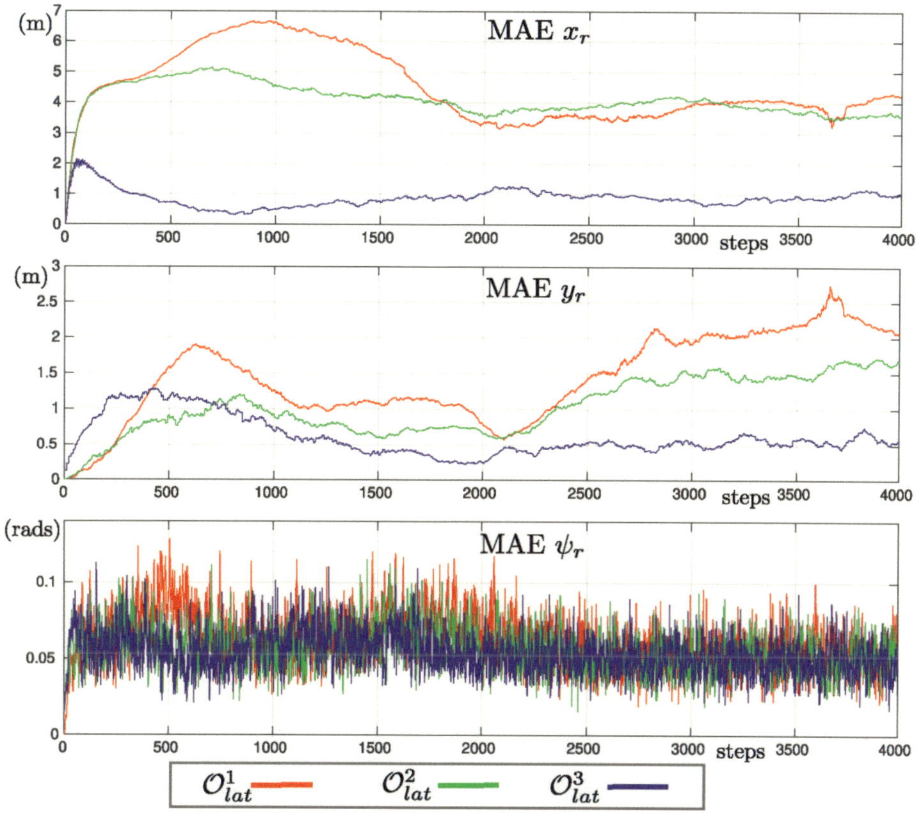

Figure 4.
Lateral SLAM system: Comparison of the MAE for the MAV state across the three tested system configurations.

ϕ, and ψ correspond to the Tait-Bryan (Euler) angles, commonly referred to as *roll*, *pitch*, and *yaw*, respectively. The intrinsic rotation sequence employed in this work is $\psi - \phi - \theta$. The vector $\omega^R = [\omega_x, \omega_y, \omega_z]$ defines the robot's angular velocity along the axes x_R, y_R, and z_R, as expressed in the robot's coordinate frame $(^R)$. The vector $\mathbf{r}^N = [x_r, y_r, z_r]$ specifies the robot's position in the navigation frame $(^N)$. The vector $\mathbf{v}^R = [v_x, v_y, v_z]$ captures the robot's linear velocity along the x_R, y_R, and z_R axes, expressed in the robot frame $(^R)$.

For autonomous navigation in local environments, the system adopts a local tangent frame as the navigation frame, denoted $(^N)$. This navigation frame adheres to the NED (north-east-down) convention, with its origin defined by the robot's initial position. All coordinate systems employed in this work are right-handed. Magnitudes are expressed in the navigation frame $(^N)$, robot frame $(^R)$, or camera frame $(^C)$, as indicated by the respective superscripts (see **Figure 5**).

3.1.2 Visual measurements

To estimate the robot state vector defined in Eq. 18, it is assumed that the robot is equipped with a standard monocular camera. At each frame, the camera provides a set of visual measurements $\{\mathbf{z}_{uv_1}, \mathbf{z}_{uv_2}, \ldots, \mathbf{z}_{uv_n}\}$ corresponding to n static 3D points in the robot's environment. The i-th visual measurement is modeled as:

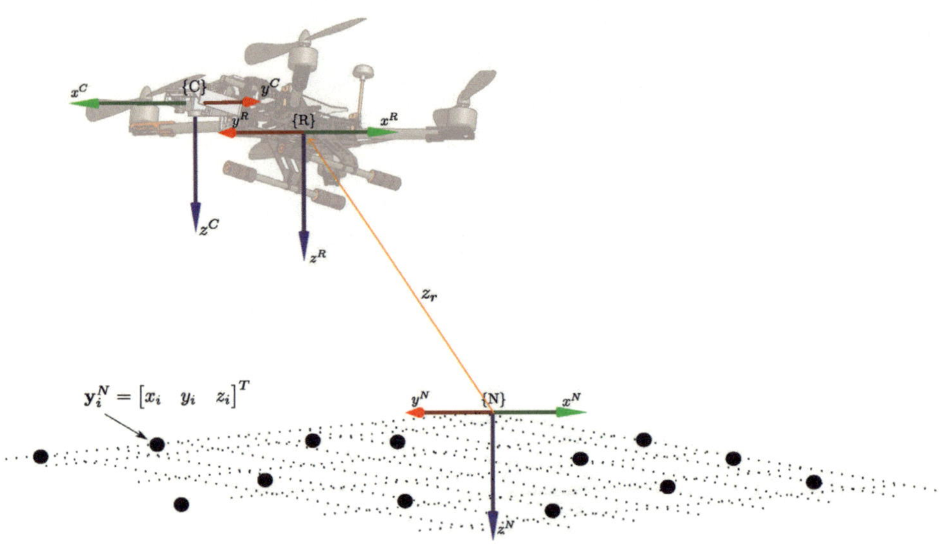

Figure 5.
6-DOF system parameterization.

$$\mathbf{z}_{uv_i} = \begin{bmatrix} u_i^* \\ v_i^* \end{bmatrix} + \xi_{uv} \tag{19}$$

where $[u_i^*, v_i^*]^T$ represents the true position in the image plane of the projection of the static 3D points, and ξ_{uv} denotes the measurement noise (uncertainty) associated with the visual observations.

The position of a static 3D point, referred to as the ith landmark in the robot's environment, is expressed in the navigation frame $(^N)$ by the vector $\mathbf{y}_i^N$ (see **Figure 5**):

$$\mathbf{y}_i^N = \begin{bmatrix} x_i & y_i & z_i \end{bmatrix}^T \tag{20}$$

The visual model $\mathbf{h}_{uv}(\mathbf{x})$ describes the projective transformation that maps a 3D point $\mathbf{y}_i^N = [x_i, y_i, z_i]$ in the navigation frame $(^N)$ to its corresponding 2D image plane coordinates $[u_i, v_i]$ and is defined as:

$$\mathbf{h}_{uv}(\mathbf{x}) = \begin{bmatrix} u_i \\ v_i \end{bmatrix} = \mathbf{f}_d(u', v', k_1, \dots, k_n) \tag{21}$$

with:

$$s \begin{bmatrix} u_i' \\ v_i' \\ 1 \end{bmatrix} = \begin{bmatrix} f & 0 & u_0 \\ 0 & f & v_0 \\ 0 & 0 & 1 \end{bmatrix} \begin{bmatrix} r_{11} & r_{12} & r_{13} & x_c \\ r_{21} & r_{22} & r_{23} & y_c \\ r_{31} & r_{32} & r_{33} & z_c \end{bmatrix} \begin{bmatrix} x_i \\ y_i \\ z_i \\ 1 \end{bmatrix} \tag{22}$$

Here, the camera distortion model $\mathbf{f}_d$ depends on the undistorted point coordinates $[u_i', v_i']$ and the distortion parameters $k_1, \dots, k_n$. The camera's focal length and principal point are represented by f and $[u_0, v_0]$, respectively. These parameters, along with the distortion coefficients, are assumed to be known through prior calibration. This work utilizes the distortion model proposed in [15].

In Eq. 22, the rotation matrix $\mathbf{R}^{NC} = (\mathbf{R}^{RC}\mathbf{R}^{NR})$ transforms coordinates from the navigation frame $(^N)$ to the camera frame $(^C)$. $\mathbf{R}^{NR}(\theta, \phi, \psi)$ is the rotation matrix that maps the navigation frame $(^N)$ to the robot frame ^{R} and is derived from the state vector's orientation parameters in $\mathbf{e}^{NR}$. $\mathbf{R}^{RC}$ defines the rotation from the robot frame $(^R)$ to the camera frame $(^C)$, which is assumed to be known.

The camera's position in the navigation frame $(^N)$ is denoted by $\mathbf{c}^N = [x_c, y_c, z_c]^T$, where:

$$\mathbf{c}^N = \mathbf{r}^N + \mathbf{R}^{RN}\mathbf{t}_c^R, \quad \text{and} \quad \mathbf{R}^{RN} = (\mathbf{R}^{NR})^T.$$

The vector $\mathbf{t}_c^R$ represents the camera's position expressed in the robot frame $(^R)$ and is assumed to be known.

3.1.3 Attitude measurements

Attitude measurements $\mathbf{z}_e$ are defined as:

$$\mathbf{z}_e = \begin{bmatrix} \theta^* \\ \phi^* \\ \psi^* \end{bmatrix} + \xi_e \tag{23}$$

where $[\theta^*, \phi^*, \psi^*]^T$ represents the true attitude of the robot, and ξ_e denotes the measurement noise (uncertainty) associated with the attitude observations. These measurements are directly obtained from the robot's Attitude and Heading Reference System (AHRS). In this case, the measurement model is given by:

$$\mathbf{h}_e(\mathbf{x}) = \begin{bmatrix} \theta \\ \phi \\ \psi \end{bmatrix} \tag{24}$$

3.1.4 Altitude measurements

It is assumed that altitude measurements, expressed in the navigation frame $(^N)$, can be obtained from an altitude sensor, which is typically a barometer. Altitude measurements, denoted as $\mathbf{z}_z$, are defined as:

$$\mathbf{z}_{z_r} = z_r^* + \xi_z \tag{25}$$

where z_r^* represents the actual altitude of the MAV, expressed in the $(^N)$ frame, and ξ_z is the measurement noise (or uncertainty) associated with the altitude observations. The measurement model is simply given by:

$$\mathbf{h}_{z_r}(\mathbf{x}) = z_r \tag{26}$$

3.1.5 Range-to-base measurements

As discussed in Section 2, measurements of the range from the home position (base) to the MAV can significantly enhance the observability of the SLAM system. However, unlike other types of aiding measurements, which are typically obtained from onboard sensors commonly available on most MAV platforms, range-to-base measurements may require the implementation of an ad-hoc solution. For this purpose, Radio Frequency (RF) ranging techniques can be employed to compute range-to-base measurements. These methods exploit RF signal properties such as signal propagation time (Time of Flight, ToF), signal phase (Phase-Based Ranging), or signal strength (Received Signal Strength Indicator, RSSI). Examples of applications of this technology can be found in [16, 17].

Range-to-base measurements, denoted as $\mathbf{z}_R$, are defined as:

$$\mathbf{z}_R = r^* + \xi_R \tag{27}$$

where r^* represents the actual range from the base to the MAV, expressed in the $(^N)$ frame, and ξ_R is the measurement noise (or uncertainty) associated with these observations.

The measurement model is given by:

$$\mathbf{h}_R(\mathbf{x}) = \sqrt{x_r^2 + y_r^2 + z_r^2} \tag{28}$$

3.2 EKF-SLAM

In this study, the local SLAM process is implemented using an Extended Kalman Filter (EKF). However, alternative stochastic filtering techniques can also be employed. The implementation follows the standard EKF-SLAM framework, characterized by the iterative cycle of prediction and update steps, as detailed in [18, 19].

To implement EKF-SLAM, the robot state vector $\mathbf{x}_r$, as defined in Eq. 18, is extended by augmenting it with the states of n map features $\mathbf{y}_i$, where $i \in \{1, \dots, n\}$. These features correspond to the visual landmarks observed by the camera as the MAV explores previously uncharted areas of its environment.

The augmented system state, $\mathbf{x}$, is expressed as:

$$\mathbf{x} = \begin{bmatrix} \mathbf{x}_r^T & \mathbf{y}_1^T & \cdots & \mathbf{y}_n^T \end{bmatrix}^T \tag{29}$$

In the SLAM literature, this augmentation of the system state is commonly referred to as *feature initialization*, which is further elaborated in Section 3.2.3.

Consequently, given the set of measurements $\mathbf{z}_{(\bullet)}$ outlined in Section 3.1, the primary objective of the proposed monocular-based SLAM method is to estimate the augmented state vector $\mathbf{x}$.

3.2.1 Prediction step

The estimate of the state vector, $\hat{\mathbf{x}} = \mathbb{E}\{\mathbf{x}\}$, along with its covariance matrix, $\mathbf{P} = cov(\mathbf{x}, \mathbf{x}) = \mathbb{E}\left\{(\mathbf{x} - \hat{\mathbf{x}})(\mathbf{x} - \hat{\mathbf{x}})^T\right\}$, is propagated over time using the EKF prediction equations:

$$\begin{aligned} \dot{\hat{\mathbf{x}}}^{-} &= \mathbf{f}(\hat{\mathbf{x}}^{\pm}, \mathbf{u}) \\ \dot{\mathbf{P}}^{-} &= \mathbf{A}\mathbf{P}^{\pm} + \mathbf{P}^{\pm}\mathbf{A}^{T} + \mathbf{G}\mathbf{Q}\mathbf{G}^{T} \end{aligned} \tag{30}$$

Here, $\mathbf{f}(\hat{\mathbf{x}}^{\pm}, \mathbf{u})$ represents the robot's dynamic or kinematic model, $\mathbf{u}$ is the input vector, $\mathbf{A} = \frac{\partial \mathbf{f}}{\partial \mathbf{x}}(\hat{\mathbf{x}}^{\pm}, \mathbf{u})$ is the Jacobian of $\mathbf{f}$ with respect to the state, and $\mathbf{G} = \frac{\partial \mathbf{f}}{\partial \mathbf{u}}(\hat{\mathbf{x}}^{\pm}, \mathbf{u})$ is the Jacobian of $\mathbf{f}$ with respect to the input. The noise vector $\mathbf{n}_k \sim \mathcal{N}(\mathbf{0}, \mathbf{Q})$ models the process noise affecting the state.

In the EKF equations, the following notations are used: $(-)$ for *a priori* values, $(+)$ for *a posteriori* values, and $(\pm)$ for the "last available value." In practice, the propagation described by Eq. 30 can be implemented using simple Euler integration.

The discretized kinematic model of the MAV is represented by $\hat{\mathbf{x}}_{k+1} = \mathbf{f}(\hat{\mathbf{x}}_k, \mathbf{u}_k)$ and is defined as follows:

$$\begin{cases} \mathbf{e}^{NR}_{k+1} = \mathbf{e}^{NR}_{k} + \mathbf{R}^{\omega e}\omega^{R}_{k}\Delta t \\ \omega^{R}_{k+1} = \omega^{R}_{k}(\mathbf{I} - \mathbf{I}k_{\omega}\Delta t) \\ \mathbf{r}^{N}_{k+1} = \mathbf{r}^{N}_{k} + \mathbf{R}^{RN}\mathbf{v}^{N}_{k}\Delta t \\ \mathbf{v}^{R}_{k+1} = \mathbf{v}^{R}_{k}(\mathbf{I} - \mathbf{I}k_{v}\Delta t) \\ \mathbf{y}_{1[k+1]} = \mathbf{y}_{1[k]} \\ \vdots \\ \mathbf{y}_{n[k+1]} = \mathbf{y}_{n[k]} \end{cases} \tag{31}$$

For this unconstrained constant acceleration model, the process noise covariance matrix is given by $\mathbf{Q} = \text{diag}(\Omega^{R}, \mathbf{V}^{R})$, where $\Omega^{R} = \mathbf{I}\sigma_{\omega}^{2}\Delta t$ and $\mathbf{V}^{R} = \mathbf{I}\sigma_{v}^{2}\Delta t$. These represent unknown angular and linear velocity impulses modeled as zero-mean Gaussian processes with known covariances σ_{ω} and σ_{v}. The parameters k_{ω} and k_{v} are correlation time factors that model how quickly the angular and linear velocities decay to zero in the absence of sensor measurements.

Additionally, the matrix $\mathbf{R}^{\omega e}$ establishes the relationship between the angular positions (θ, ϕ, ψ) and the angular rates $(\omega_x, \omega_y, \omega_z)$:

$$\mathbf{R}^{\omega e} = [1 \quad \sin\phi\tan\theta\cos\phi\tan\theta 0\cos\phi - \sin\phi 0\sin\phi/\cos\theta\cos\phi/\cos\theta] \tag{32}$$

3.2.2 Update step

Whenever a measurement $\mathbf{z}_{\{s\}_k}$ becomes available at step k from a sensor $\{s\}$, with a measurement model $\mathbf{h}_{\{s\}}(\hat{\mathbf{x}}_k^{-})$, the state estimate $\hat{\mathbf{x}}$ and its covariance matrix $\mathbf{P}$ are updated using the EKF update equations:

$$\begin{aligned} \hat{\mathbf{x}}_k &= \hat{\mathbf{x}}_k^{-} + \mathbf{K}_k\left(\mathbf{z}_{\{s\}_k} - \mathbf{h}_{\{s\}}(\hat{\mathbf{x}}_k^{-})\right) \\ \mathbf{P}_k &= (\mathbf{I} - \mathbf{K}_k\mathbf{C}_{\{s\}_k})\mathbf{P}_k^{-} \\ \mathbf{K}_k &= \mathbf{P}_k^{-}\mathbf{C}_{\{s\}_k}^{T}\left(\mathbf{C}_{\{s\}_k}\mathbf{P}_k^{-}\mathbf{C}_{\{s\}_k}^{T} + \mathbf{R}_{\{s\}}\right)^{-1} \end{aligned} \tag{33}$$

Here, $\mathbf{K}_k$ is the Kalman gain, and $\mathbf{C}_{\{s\}_k} = \frac{\partial \mathbf{h}_{\{s\}}}{\partial \mathbf{x}}(\hat{\mathbf{x}}_k^{-})$ represents the Jacobian of the measurement model $\mathbf{h}_{\{s\}}$ with respect to the state $\hat{\mathbf{x}}_k^{-}$. Additionally, $\mathbf{R}_{\{s\}}$ is the measurement noise covariance matrix associated with sensor $\{s\}$.

Measurement type	Measurement $\mathbf{z}_{\{s\}_k}$	Model $\mathbf{h}_{\{s\}}(\hat{\mathbf{x}}_k^-)$
Visual	$\mathbf{z}_{uv_i} = [u_i^* \quad v_i^*]^T + \xi_{uv}$	$\mathbf{h}_{uv}(\mathbf{x}) = \mathbf{f}_d(u', v', k_1, \ldots, k_n)$
Attitude	$\mathbf{z}_e = [\theta^* \quad \phi^* \quad \psi^*]^T + \xi_e$	$\mathbf{h}_e(\mathbf{x}) = [\theta \quad \phi \quad \psi]^T$
Altitude	$\mathbf{z}_{z_r} = z_r^* + \xi_z$	$\mathbf{h}_{z_r}(\mathbf{x}) = z_r$
Range-to-base	$\mathbf{z}_R = r^* + \xi_R$	$\mathbf{h}_R(\mathbf{x}) = \sqrt{x_r^2 + y_r^2 + z_r^2}$

Table 3.
Summary of measurements and corresponding models used in the update equations.

Table 3 provides a summary of the measurements $\mathbf{z}_{\{s\}_k}$ and their corresponding measurement models $\mathbf{h}_{\{s\}}(\hat{\mathbf{x}}_k^-)$ used to update the estimated system state $\hat{\mathbf{x}}_k$ and its covariance matrix $\mathbf{P}_k$, as described by the update equations in (33). A complete description of these measurements and models can be found in Section 3.1.

3.2.3 Features initialization

For initializing new map features $\mathbf{y}_{new}^N = [x_i, y_i, z_i]^T$ into the system state $\hat{\mathbf{x}}$, an initialization function $\mathbf{y}_{new}^N = \mathbf{g}(\hat{\mathbf{x}}, \mathbf{z}_{uv_i})$ must be defined. Here, $\mathbf{z}_{uv_i}$ represents the ith visual measurement used by $\mathbf{g}(.)$ to compute the pose of $\mathbf{y}_{new}^N$.

Once $\mathbf{y}_{new}^N$ is computed, the system state and covariance matrix are updated as follows:

$$\begin{aligned}\hat{\mathbf{x}}_{new} &= \left[\hat{\mathbf{x}}_{old}^T \quad ; \quad \left(\mathbf{y}_{new}^N\right)^T\right]^T, \\ \mathbf{P}_{new} &= \mathbf{J}\begin{bmatrix}\mathbf{P}_{old} & 0 \\ 0 & \mathbf{R}_g\end{bmatrix}\mathbf{J}^T,\end{aligned} \tag{34}$$

where $\mathbf{J} = \frac{\partial \mathbf{g}}{\partial(\hat{\mathbf{x}}, \mathbf{z}_{uv_i})}(\hat{\mathbf{x}}, \mathbf{z}_{uv_i})$ is the Jacobian matrix, and $\mathbf{R}_g$ represents the measurement noise covariance associated with the measurements $\mathbf{z}_{uv_i}$.

The undelayed initialization technique described in [20] is used to compute new features $\mathbf{y}_{new}^N$. This technique leverages monocular visual measurements and range measurements obtained from an ultrasonic sensor.

3.2.4 Map management

To ensure a stable computational cost, the system removes outdated or low-quality visual features from its state. A feature is considered "weak" if it exhibits a high ratio of failed matches relative to the number of times it was expected to be detected by the camera. Similarly, a feature is deemed "old" if it has been absent from camera observations for a significant number of instances.

4. Virtual experiments

The proposed visual-based SLAM system was developed using C++. For testing, the Webots simulation platform was employed [21]. Webots is a widely recognized tool in

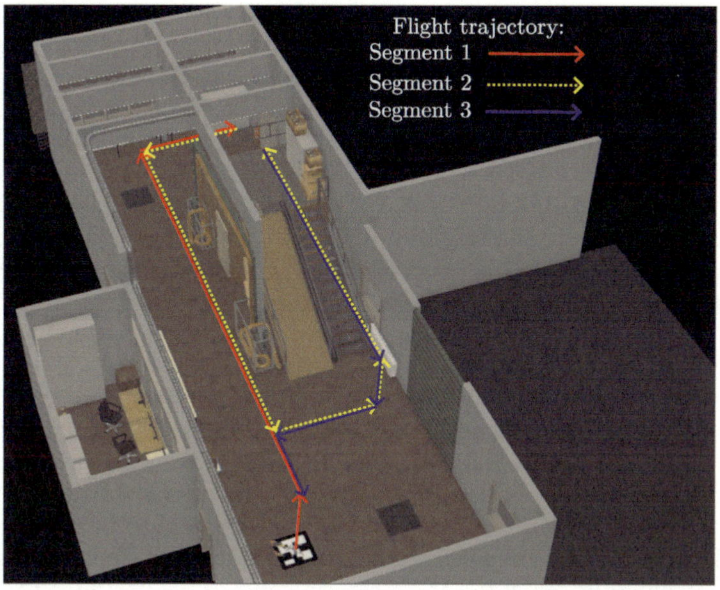

Figure 6.
Virtual experiments were conducted using the Webots simulator in an indoor factory-like environment. The flight trajectory is depicted in three distinct color segments for easier interpretation.

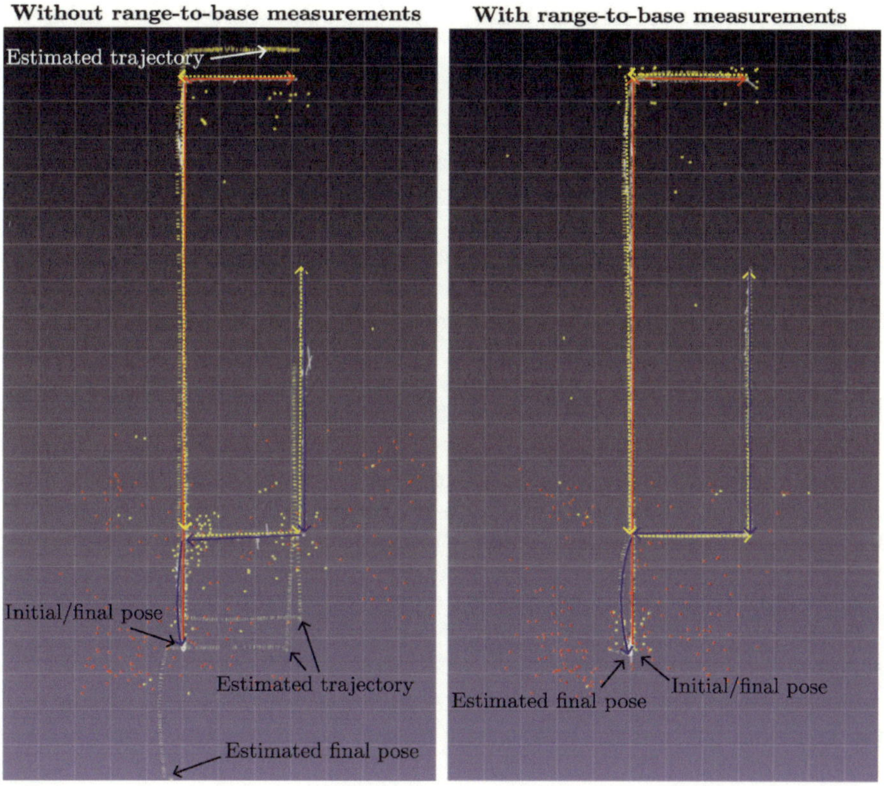

Figure 7.
Comparison of the results obtained without range-to-base measurements (left plot) and those obtained with their inclusion (right plot). In the latter case, it is worth noting how the estimation error is minimized.

research, education, and industry, providing a virtual environment for prototyping and validating robotic algorithms before deploying them in real-world scenarios.

Figure 6 depicts the indoor factory-like environment utilized for the virtual experiments. Additionally, the flight trajectory employed in the experiments is shown. To enhance the clarity of the experimental results, the trajectory is divided into three segments, each represented by a distinct color. The flying robot employed in the virtual experiments is a DJI Mavic 2 Pro. For analysis, image frames are captured from its front monocular camera at a resolution of 400×240 pixels and a rate of 30 frames per second. Furthermore, as detailed in Section 3, attitude and altitude measurements are incorporated from the IMU and altimeter, respectively.

The main objective of experiments were to investigate the effect of including range-to-base measurements into the SLAM system. To emulate range-to-base measurements the model defined in (27) is used, in this case, the measurement uncertainty ξ_R is modeled as Gaussian white noise with PSD $\sigma_{\xi R}^2 = 0.2m$.

Figure 7 presents a comparison between the results from one run of the experiment without range-to-base measurements (left plot) and those from one run of the experiment with range-to-base measurements included (right plot). In the first case, the accumulated error drift between the actual and estimated flight trajectories is clearly evident. Notably, when the MAV returns to its initial position at the end of the trajectory, the final estimated pose exhibits a significant error. Conversely, when range-to-base measurements are fused into the SLAM system, the error drift in the estimated trajectory is noticeably minimized.

5. Conclusions

This work presented a monocular-based EKF-SLAM system for MAVs operating in GPS-denied environments. The main contribution was to demonstrate that incorporating range-to-base measurements into the SLAM system significantly enhances its performance. Specifically, based on the results of virtual experiments, it was shown that the pose estimation error along the MAV's flight trajectory is minimized, even when older map features are removed from the system to maintain real-time operation.

The inclusion of range-to-base measurements in the SLAM system is supported by the theoretical findings from the nonlinear observability study presented in Section 2. This study demonstrated that observability is considerably improved with the addition of this type of measurement. Observability is a critical property with significant implications for the performance and reliability of a SLAM system. For example, in an unobservable system, errors can accumulate over time without bounds. Observability ensures that such errors are corrected as new measurements are incorporated.

While numerous methods in the literature address the problem of UAV navigation in GPS-denied environments (e.g., [22–24]), most rely on closing-the-loop actions to minimize accumulated error drift or merely aim to reduce the rate of error growth. In contrast, the proposed method is designed to keep the error bounded throughout the entire trajectory.

Although incorporating range-to-base measurements into SLAM systems offers substantial benefits, it is important to note that, unlike other commonly available aiding sensors such as AHRS and altimeters—which are standard on most MAV platforms—integrating range-to-base measurements often requires custom solutions using technologies that are less explored in the context of MAV navigation systems. Consequently, while these preliminary results are highly promising, further research

DOI: http://dx.doi.org/10.5772/intechopen.1009895

is necessary to explore the practical implications of the proposed approach in real-world scenarios.

Acknowledgements

The authors would like to thank Juan Carlos Trujillo for bringing forward the idea of using range-to-base measurements in the context of monocular SLAM.

The authors acknowledges the use of ChatGPT for language polishing of the manuscript.

Abbreviations

SLAM	simultaneous localization and mapping
MAV	micro aerial vehicle
GPS	global positioning system
IMU	inertial measurement unit
AHRS	attitude and heading reference system
MAE	mean absolute error
NED	north-east-down
RF	radio frequency
ToF	phase-based ranging
RSSI	received signal strength indicator
EKF	extended Kalman filter

Author details

Rodrigo Munguia[1*†] and Antoni Grau[2†]

1 Department of Computer Science (CUCEI), University of Guadalajara, Guadalajara, Mexico

2 Department of Automatic Control, Technical University of Catalonia UPC, Barcelona, Spain

*Address all correspondence to: rodrigo.munguia@academicos.udg.mx

† These authors contributed equally.

References

[1] Mur-Artal R, Tardos JD. ORB-SLAM2: An Open-Source SLAM System for Monocular, Stereo, and RGB-D Cameras. IEEE Transactions on Robotics. 2017;**33**(5):1255-1262. DOI: 10.1109/TRO.2017.2705103

[2] Campos C, Elvira R, Gómez Rodríguez JJ, Montiel JMM, Tardós JD. ORB-SLAM3: An Accurate Open-Source Library for Visual, Visual-Inertial and Multi-Map SLAM. IEEE Transactions on Robotics. Dec. 2021;**37**(6):1874-1890. DOI: 10.1109/TRO.2021.3075644

[3] Qin T, Li P, Shen S. VINS-Mono: A Robust and Versatile Monocular Visual-Inertial State Estimator. IEEE Transactions on Robotics. Aug. 2018;**34**(4):1004-1020. DOI: 10.1109/TRO.2018.2853729

[4] Jiang H, Cang N, Lin Y, Li Z. LR-SLAM: Visual Inertial SLAM System with Redundant Line Feature Elimination. Journal of Intelligent & Robotic Systems. 2024;**110**(1):169-183. DOI: 10.1007/s10846-024-02184-2

[5] Cadena C, Carlone L, Carrillo H, Latif Y, Scaramuzza D, Neira J, Reid I, Leonard JJ. Past, Present, and Future of Simultaneous Localization and Mapping: Toward the Robust-Perception Age. IEEE Transactions on Robotics. 2016;**32**(6):1309-1332. DOI: 10.1109/TRO.2016.2624754

[6] Zhuang Y, Sun X, Li Y, Huai J, Hua L, Yang X, Chen R. Multi-sensor integrated navigation/positioning systems using data fusion: From analytics-based to learning-based approaches. Information Fusion. 2023;**95**:62-90. DOI: 10.1016/j.inffus.2023.01.025

[7] Laidlow T, Bloesch M, Li W, Leutenegger S. Dense RGB-D-Inertial SLAM with Map Deformations. arXiv. 2022;abs/2207.10940. DOI: 10.48550/arXiv.2207.10940

[8] Hashim HA. Guaranteed Performance Nonlinear Observer for Simultaneous Localization and Mapping. arXiv. 2020;abs/2006.11858. DOI: 10.48550/arXiv.2006.11858

[9] Forster C, Carlone L, Dellaert F, Scaramuzza D. On-Manifold Preintegration for Real-Time Visual-Inertial Odometry. IEEE Transactions on Robotics. 2017;**33**(1):1-21. DOI: 10.1109/TRO.2016.2597321

[10] Cremona J, Civera J, Kofman E, Pire T. GNSS-stereo-inertial SLAM for arable farming. Journal of Field Robotics. Oct. 2024;**41**(7):2215-2225. DOI: 10.1002/rob.22232

[11] Abdelaziz N, El-Rabbany A. INS/LIDAR/Stereo SLAM Integration for Precision Navigation in GNSS-Denied Environments. Sensors. Aug. 2023;**23**(17):7424. DOI: 10.3390/s23177424

[12] Elamin A, El-Rabbany A, Jacob S. Event-Based Visual/Inertial Odometry for UAV Indoor Navigation. Sensors. Dec. 2024;**25**(1):61. DOI: 10.3390/s25010061

[13] Hermann R, Krener AJ. Nonlinear Controllability and Observability. IEEE Transactions on Automatic Control. Oct. 1977;**22**(5):728-740. DOI: 10.1109/TAC.1977.1101601

[14] Slotine JE, Li W. Applied Nonlinear Control. Englewood Cliffs, NJ: Prentice-Hall; 1991

[15] Bouguet JY. Camera Calibration Toolbox for MATLAB. Online. 2008. [Online]. Available from: https://www.vision.caltech.edu/bouguetj/calib_doc/

[16] Wu D, Bao L, Li R. UWB-Based Localization in Wireless Sensor Networks. International Journal of Communications, Network and System Sciences. Aug. 2009;**2**(5):407-421. DOI: 10.4236/ijcns.2009.25046

[17] Xu H, Zhang W, Yang L. Wireless localization and ranging with ultra-wideband signals. In: Proceedings of the 2011 IEEE International Conference on Ultra-Wideband (ICUWB); 2011 Sep 14-16; Bologna, Italy. IEEE; 2011. p. 580-584. DOI: 10.1109/ICUWB.2011.6058913

[18] Durrant-Whyte H, Bailey T. Simultaneous localization and mapping: Part I. IEEE Robotics Automation Magazine. 2006;**13**(2):99-110. DOI: 10.1109/MRA.2006.1638022

[19] Bailey T, Durrant-Whyte H. Simultaneous localization and mapping (slam): Part II. IEEE Robotics Automation Magazine. 2006;**13**(3): 108-117. DOI: 10.1109/MRA.2006.1678144

[20] Urzua S, Munguía R, Grau A. Vision-based slam system for MAVs in GPS-denied environments. International Journal of Micro Air Vehicles. 2017;**9**(4): 283-296. DOI: 10.1177/1756829317705325

[21] Cyberbotics Ltd., Webots: Professional Mobile Robot Simulation Software, Lausanne, Switzerland, 2023. [Online]. Available from: https://www.cyberbotics.com [Accessed: 2024 October 3]

[22] Bry A, Bachrach A, Roy N. State Estimation for Aggressive Flight in GPS-Denied Environments Using Onboard Sensing. In: Proceedings of the 2012 IEEE International Conference on Robotics and Automation (ICRA). St. Paul, MN, USA: IEEE; May 2012. pp. 1–8. DOI: 10.1109/ICRA.2012.6225295

[23] Yin Y, Wang Z, Zheng L, Su Q, Guo Y. Autonomous UAV Navigation with Adaptive Control Based on Deep Reinforcement Learning. Electronics. 2024;**13**(13):2432. DOI: 10.3390/electronics13132432

[24] Balamurugan G, Valarmathi J, Naidu VPS. Survey on UAV Navigation in GPS Denied Environments. In: Proceedings of the 2016 International Conference on Signal Processing, Communication, Power and Embedded System (SCOPES). Paralakhemundi, India: IEEE; Oct. 2016. pp. 198-204. DOI: 10.1109/SCOPES.2016.7955827

Chapter 3

Ground Control Points Positioning with PPP-AR Method for UAV-Based Block Adjustment

Burhaneddin Bilgen, Sercan Bülbül and Hasan Bilgehan Makineci

Abstract

Unmanned aerial vehicles (UAVs) have become a prevalent tool for large-scale mapping, offering efficient and cost-effective solutions. This study examines the position accuracy of photogrammetric outcomes generated from UAV imagery when ground control point (GCP) coordinates are derived using Precise Point Positioning with Ambiguity Resolution (PPP-AR). Utilizing a Parrot ANAFI UAV, 10-minute GNSS measurements at six GCPs were processed with open-source PPP-AR software, including Pride PPP-AR, PPP-Arisen, and raPPPid. To evaluate the impact of session durations, the 10-minute data were divided into 7- and 5-minute intervals. Accuracy analysis was conducted by comparing the coordinates and distance differences of six pillars, determined through static GNSS sessions, with those derived from photogrammetric models. Results indicate that photogrammetric outcomes based on 10-minute GNSS observations provide optimal position accuracy, particularly in flat terrains, meeting practical mapping requirements but proving insufficient for high-precision geodetic applications. The study found that 5- and 7-minute observations produced greater errors, especially with raPPPid software. However, all solutions achieved sub-meter accuracy levels, with no statistically significant differences in accuracy between the tested software for 10-minute durations. These findings highlight the importance of session duration and terrain characteristics in achieving accurate photogrammetric outcomes.

Keywords: PPP-Arisen, pride PPP-AR, raPPPid, photogrammetric block adjustment, UAV product accuracy

1. Introduction

Unmanned aerial vehicles (UAVs) provide users with significant speed in large-scale map generation projects and are preferred for their advantages, such as ease of access to hard-to-reach environments. Despite these advantages, when the spatial accuracy of the generated maps is examined, they tend to show weaknesses compared to geodetic methods [1–3]. Particularly for final outcomes such as digital elevation models (DEM) and orthomosaics generated without ground control points (GCPs), horizontal and vertical spatial accuracy generally cannot exceed the meter level [4]. However, studies utilizing GCPs indicate that results with sufficient accuracy for large-scale map generation can be achieved. Within this context, research has discussed the impacts of methods used to determine the absolute positions of GCPs on the final outcomes [5]. Recently, methods such as Post-Processed Kinematic (PPK) and Network RTK (CORS) have become prominent in discussions of the geodetic accuracy of UAV-generated outcomes [6, 7]. However, an alternative known as Precise Point Positioning (PPP) has also attracted the attention of researchers in recent years [8–10].

The PPP method, one of the absolute positioning techniques, was first introduced by Zumberge et al. [11]. This method aims to obtain precise positioning information using a single GNSS receiver. The most significant disadvantage of PPP is its long convergence time [12, 13]. To address this, improvements have been made over time, transitioning from the traditional PPP algorithm to the Precise Point Positioning with Ambiguity Resolution (PPP-AR) algorithm. Unlike the traditional PPP method, where ambiguities are treated as fractional values, the PPP-AR algorithm estimates them as integer values [14]. This advancement has led to the emergence of various alternative systems and software offering high position accuracy with the PPP-AR technique, contributing to its increasing popularity in recent discussions [15].

To process GNSS data with the PPP method, several online services such as APPS, CSRS-PPP, magicGNSS, and Trimble RTX, as well as open-source software like GAMP, PPPH, Pride PPP-AR, PPPLib, PPP-Arisen, and raPPPid, are available. Among these, Pride PPP-AR, PPP-Arisen, and raPPPid implement the PPP-AR algorithm [16–19].

Statistical methods are used to evaluate the accuracy of outcomes generated from photogrammetric blocks adjusted using GCP coordinates obtained from different software. Root mean square error (RMSE) analysis, two-population variance test, Student's *t*-test, and Bartlett's test are among the methods applicable for this purpose. RMSE is a reliable sensitivity parameter, especially for measurement groups containing extreme numerical values, and is the most used method in the literature. Additionally, the two-population variance test is preferred for comparing the variances of two normally distributed measurement groups [20, 21].

The aim of this study is to investigate the horizontal and vertical position accuracy of large-scale maps generated through photogrammetric block adjustment using images acquired from UAV-based photogrammetry flight planning and GCPs with positions determined through 10-, 7-, and 5-minute sessions processed *via* free PPP-AR software (Pride PPP-AR, PPP-Arisen, and raPPPid). One of the objectives is to identify the optimal measurement duration for the PPP-AR method. In a test area with slight slopes, the coordinates and horizontal-vertical distances of six pillars previously established and determined through static sessions over multiple periods were compared with those derived from the photogrammetric model, and biases were calculated. Six GCPs placed in the field for use in photogrammetric block adjustment were measured in 10-minute sessions to determine their coordinates using three open-source PPP-AR software. The session durations were also reduced to 5 and 7 minutes, and GCP coordinates were determined separately for each software. Seven different scenarios were employed in the photogrammetric block adjustment, producing seven orthomosaics and DEMs, and their accuracy analyses were conducted. The RMSE analysis in this study revealed the accuracies of the generated photogrammetric outcomes, while the two-population variance test was used for pairwise statistical comparisons between different photogrammetric outcomes.

2. Methods and data

The code and carrier phase observation equations of dual-frequency GNSS data can be expressed in terms of the distance between station i and satellite k as follows [15, 22].

$$P_{i,1}^k = \rho_i^k + c\left(\delta t_i - \delta t^k\right) + \frac{A}{f_1^2} + d_{i,1} - d_1^k \tag{1}$$

$$L_{i,1}^k = \rho_i^k + c\left(\delta t_i - \delta t^k\right) - \frac{A}{f_1^2} + \lambda_1 N_{i,1}^k + b_{i,1} - b_1^k \tag{2}$$

$$P_{i,2}^k = \rho_i^k + c\left(\delta t_i - \delta t^k\right) + \frac{A}{f_2^2} + d_{i,2} - d_2^k \tag{3}$$

$$L_{i,2}^k = \rho_i^k + c\left(\delta t_i - \delta t^k\right) - \frac{A}{f_2^2} + \lambda_2 N_{i,2}^k + b_{i,2} - b_2^k \tag{4}$$

Where $P_{i,1}^k$ represents the phase pseudorange observations; $L_{i,1}^k$ denotes the carrier phase observations; ρ_i^k is the geometric distance between the station and the satellite; c is the speed of light in a vacuum; δt_i and δt^k are the receiver and satellite clock errors, respectively; $\frac{A}{f_1^2}$ indicates the effect of first-order ionospheric delays; f_1 and f_2 are L_1 and L_2 frequencies; λ_1 and λ_2 are the corresponding wavelengths; $N_{i,1}^k$ and $N_{i,2}^k$ are the integer ambiguities; $d_{i,1}$ and d_1^k represent the pseudorange bias of the first frequency caused by hardware delays in the receiver and satellite, respectively; and $b_{i,1}$ and b_1^k indicate the phase bias of the first frequency due to hardware delays in the receiver and satellite, respectively. For simplicity, higher-order ionospheric delays, tropospheric delays, multipath effects, and random noise are omitted.

Accordingly, the ionosphere-free GPS pseudorange and carrier-phase observations take the following form [9, 23]:

$$P_{i,0}^k = \alpha P_{i,1}^k - \beta P_{i,2}^k = \rho_i^k + c\left(\delta t_i - \delta t^k\right) + d_{i,0} - d_0^k \tag{5}$$

$$L_{i,0}^k = \alpha L_{i,1}^k - \beta L_{i,2}^k = \rho_i^k + c\left(\delta t_i - \delta t^k\right) + \alpha\lambda_1 N_{i,1}^k - \beta\lambda_2 N_{i,2}^k + b_{i,0} - b_0^k \tag{6}$$

where

$$\alpha = \frac{f_1^2}{f_1^2 - f_2^2} \tag{7}$$

$$\beta = \frac{f_2^2}{f_1^2 - f_2^2} \tag{8}$$

$$\alpha - \beta = 1 \tag{9}$$

and

$$d_{i,0} = \alpha d_{i,1} - \beta d_{i,2} \tag{10}$$

$$d_0^k = \alpha d_1^k - \beta d_2^k \tag{11}$$

$$b_{i,0} = \alpha b_{i,1} - \beta b_{i,2} \tag{12}$$

$$b_0^k = \alpha b_1^k - \beta b_2^k \tag{13}$$

$P_{i,0}^k$ and $L_{i,0}^k$ are the ionosphere-free pseudorange observation and carrier-phase observation, respectively. Correspondingly, $d_{i,0}$ and d_0^k are the ionosphere-free pseudorange bias at the receiver and the satellite, and $b_{i,0}$ and b_0^k are the ionosphere-free combination phase bias at the receiver and the satellite, respectively.

Meanwhile, we have the Melbourne–Wübbena (MW) combination observable:

$$L_{i,m}^k = \lambda_w \left(\frac{L_{i,1}^k}{\lambda_1} - \frac{L_{i,2}^k}{\lambda_2} \right) - \lambda_n \left(\frac{P_{i,1}^k}{\lambda_1} - \frac{P_{i,2}^k}{\lambda_2} \right) = \lambda_w \left(N_{i,w}^k + \frac{b_{i,1} - b_1^k}{\lambda_1} - \frac{b_{i,2} - b_2^k}{\lambda_2} \right) - \lambda_n \left(\frac{d_{i,1} - d_1^k}{\lambda_1} + \frac{d_{i,2} - d_2^k}{\lambda_2} \right) \tag{14}$$

λ_w and λ_n are the wide-lane (WL) wavelength and narrow-lane (NL) wavelength; $N_{i,w}^k = N_{i,1}^k - N_{i,2}^k$ is the WL ambiguity. The MW combination eliminates ionospheric delay, the geometric distance from the satellite to the receiver, the satellite clock, and the receiver clock. It is only affected by multipath, measurement noise, and hardware delays. Since the WL wavelength λ_w can reach up to 86 cm, determining the integer ambiguity becomes easier. In other words, the WL ambiguity is resolved using the MW combination $L_{i,m}^k$. The corresponding receiver phase bias and satellite phase bias:

$$b_{i,w} = \lambda_w \left(\frac{b_{i,1}}{\lambda_1} - \frac{b_{i,2}}{\lambda_2} \right) - \lambda_n \left(\frac{d_{i,1}}{\lambda_1} + \frac{d_{i,2}}{\lambda_2} \right) \tag{15}$$

$$b_w^s = \lambda_w \left(\frac{b_1^k}{\lambda_1} - \frac{b_2^k}{\lambda_2} \right) - \lambda_n \left(\frac{d_1^k}{\lambda_1} + \frac{d_2^k}{\lambda_2} \right) \tag{16}$$

After resolving the WL ambiguity with the MW combination, the equation $N_{i,2}^k = N_{i,1}^k - \check{N}_{i,w}^k$ can be transformed into the ionosphere-free combination equation as follows:

$$P_{i,0}^k = \alpha P_{i,1}^k - \beta P_{i,2}^k = \rho_i^k + c\left(\delta t_i - \delta t^k\right) + d_{i,0} - d_0^k \tag{17}$$

$$\overline{L}_{i,0}^k = L_{i,0}^k - \beta \lambda_2 \check{N}_{i,w}^k = \rho_i^k + c\left(\delta t_i - \delta t^k\right) + \lambda_n N_{i,1}^k + b_{i,0} - b_0^k \tag{18}$$

Where $\check{N}_{i,w}^k$ represents the resolved WL ambiguity; $N_{i,1}^k$ denotes the NL ambiguity; and $\overline{L}_{i,0}^k$ represents the ionosphere-free combined carrier phase observation after resolving the WL ambiguity.

The pseudorange and phase biases in Eqs. (17) and (18) depend linearly on the clock and ambiguity parameters. In this way, the ambiguity parameter absorbs the constant part of the hardware delay, and the clock parameter absorbs the time-varying part. Therefore, whether the hardware delay is constant or time-varying, the effect on the ambiguity is to introduce a constant bias. The key to correcting the undifferentiated ambiguity is to separate the constant bias from the integer ambiguity. There are methods to correct the undifferentiated ambiguity, such as the integer clock

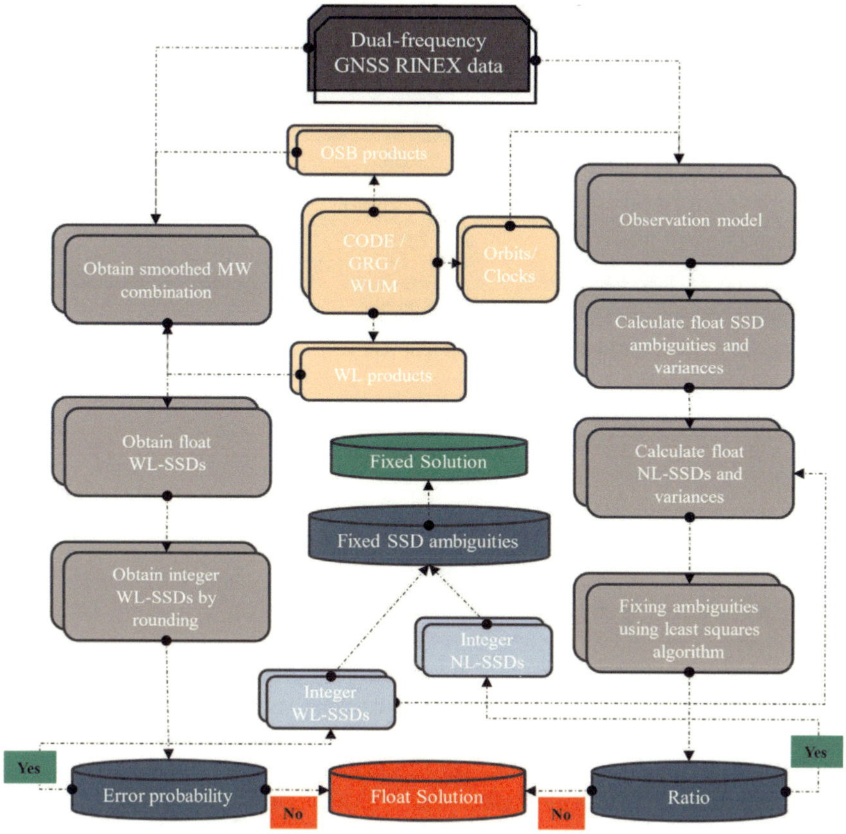

Figure 1.
The workflow scheme of the PPP-AR solution [24].

model, the decoupled clock model, the uncalibrated phase delay (UPD) model, and the phase clock/bias model. The workflow scheme of the PPP-AR solution is presented in **Figure 1**.

2.1 Data process

This study used Pride PPP-AR, PPP-Arisen, and raPPPid software to process GNSS data. The common feature of all three software is that they can solve using the PPP-AR algorithm. Pride PPP-AR is a software package developed by Wuhan University GNSS Research Center. The software package aims to post-process multiple GNSS data for the scientific community, such as geodesy, seismology, photogrammetry, gravimetry. It has multi-GNSS data processing with GPS, GLONASS, Galileo, BDS-2/3, and QZSS features [18, 19]. PPP-Arisen is a cross-platform open-source PPP toolbox that is compatible with both CODE and CNES products and performs ambiguity resolution based on the Integer Phase Clock (IPC) method with a satellite-to-satellite single difference (SSD) strategy [19, 22, 25]. raPPPid can evaluate GPS, GLONASS, Galileo, and BeiDou data with both traditional PPP and PPP-AR models. The software allows the combination of all GNSS signals, the processing of different frequencies for each GNSS, and the processing of static and kinematic observation data at any recording interval [16]. The parameters used to process the data in this study are given in **Table 1**.

Software	Pride PPP-AR	PPP-Arisen	raPPPid
Observations	GPS: L1 + L2 GLONASS: L1 + L2	GPS: L1 + L2 GLONASS: L1 + L2	GPS: L1+ L2 GLONASS: L1 + L2
Sampling rate	5 seconds	5 seconds	5 seconds
Process algorithm	Static, PPP-AR	Static PPP-AR	Static, PPP-AR
GNSS products	WUM MGEX	CODE	WUM MGEX
Ionospheric correction	Iono-free solution	Iono-free solution	Iono-free solution
Tropospheric correction	VMF3 + GRAD	VMF3 + GRAD	VMF3 + GRAD
Adjustment	Least squares algorithm (LAMBDA)	Kalman filter	Least squares algorithm (integer ambiguity resolution)

Table 1.
The parameters used to process GNSS data.

2.2 UAV's path planning and image acquisition

The fundamental way to produce a large-scale map using UAV is to use a flight plan based on photogrammetry. The photogrammetry technique is a plan that includes overlapped (forward and side) image acquisition and flight height determination according to the determined Ground Sampling Distance (GSD) value. In this research article, the photogrammetric flight plan was operated by Parrot ANAFI, a rotary-wing, compact, integrated camera UAV. The flight planning determined GSD as ~1.5 cm/px (flight height 45 m above ground level), with 80% forward and 70% side overlap. Since the integrated camera of the ANAFI UAV is non-metric, paying attention to the calibration stage in the image processing section after using it for photogrammetric image acquisition is necessary (**Table 2**). In addition, the Pix4Dcapture application, which allows autonomous flight, was used for flight planning. There is no option to make flight planning according to the DEM (fixed GSD) in this software. For this reason, the flight was performed at a fixed height. Because the terrain is slightly sloping, images were taken with GSD differences not exceeding 10%.

UAV	Parrot ANAFI
Type	Rotary wing (quadcopter)
Flight weight	~450 gr (with battery and payload)
Controller	Remote with smart device
Max. horizontal and vertical speed	~15 & 4 m/s
Payload	RGB camera (21 MP)
Camera	4608 × 3456 pixel
Focal lenght	4 mm
Pixel size	1.34 μm

Table 2.
The specifications of ANAFI UAV.

2.3 Photogrammetric processing of digital images

Photogrammetric process steps are generally completed in three stages. The first step is known as image matching and block balancing. At this stage, overlapped image coordinates and generic preselection are preferred. For UAV image alignment, distinguishable points in the images we call "Key Points" are matched with multiple images that can be matched. These points are also called "tie points." The point cluster produced with tie points is called a sparse cloud. GCPs marked on sparse cloud (GCP midpoints are found individually from the images and marked by the operator) are optimized together with camera calibration values, and block balancing is completed. In the second stage, a mathematical interpolation method makes the sparse cloud obtained from balanced coordinates and aligned images very dense. New coordinated points are produced to obtain a dense cloud. After these two steps are performed with image processing techniques, Triangulated Irregular Networks (TIN) are applied to the dense cloud, and the second stage is finalized by producing a mesh model. In the last stage, a high-resolution DEM and orthomosaic are produced using the meshed model. These two data are typically accepted as the final products of the photogrammetric process. In addition, contours (2- and 5-m intervals) were produced using DEM within the scope of this study, and all final products were exported and used in large-scale maps.

2.4 Statistical analysis and two population variance test

In this study, the differences between the terrain coordinates obtained as a result of the static GNSS session and the coordinates obtained from the photogrammetric model were calculated, and an accuracy analysis was performed to determine the spatial accuracy (horizontal and vertical) of the generated outputs. Root mean square error (RMSE) analysis, which is the most commonly used statistical method in accuracy determination, was preferred.

$$RMSE = \sqrt{\frac{\sum_{1}^{n}(X_{Mi} - X_{Gi})^2}{n}} \tag{19}$$

In Eq. (19), X_{Gi} denotes the absolute terrain coordinates, and X_{Mi} denotes the coordinates obtained from the photogrammetrically produced 3D model or orthomosaics. A two-population variance test is performed to determine whether a significant difference exists between the accuracies obtained from different models. If there is no statistical difference between the models, the optimal PPP-AR software is the one with the minimum RMSE. A two-population variance test is used to statistically compare the variances calculated for different software with current session durations. The null hypothesis for the test is as follows.

$$H_0 : E(RMSE_1^2) = E(RMSE_2^2) = \sigma_0^2 \tag{20}$$

The test statistic:

$$F_{test} = \frac{RMSE_1^2}{RMSE_2^2} \tag{21}$$

where the bigger variance value must be written in denumerator. If $F_{test} < F_{\alpha, f_1, f_2}$ equation is achieved, the null hypothesis is accepted. Thus, it is concluded that the variances of measurement groups are equal [21].

2.5 General workflow of the study

The study's general process steps consist of four stages. The field stage consists of geodetic and photogrammetric operations to obtain data. The workflow was carried out by processing the obtained coordinate data and editing the UAV images, followed by large-scale map production and accuracy analysis of the results (**Figure 2**).

3. Results and discussion

Within the study area located in the Selçuk University Campus, six control points in the form of precisely positioned pillars with high 3D position accuracy have been established (**Figure 3**). Additionally, six GCPs were set up to uniformly cover the application area for photogrammetric block adjustment. At the GCPs, 10-minute measurements were conducted with a 5-second recording interval using Javad Triumph1 and SOKKIA GCX3 GNSS receivers (**Figure 4**). The characteristics of the GNSS receivers used in the study are given in **Table 3**. A total of 381 images were captured in two separate flights (fixed GSD) covering the study area using a low-cost compact UAV with an integrated camera (ANAFI).

The 10-minute GNSS measurements conducted at the GCPs were divided into three segments of 5, 7, and 10 minutes. The 5-, 7-, and 10-minute measurements were processed using the PPP-AR algorithm described in Eqs. (1)–(18) with the open-source software tools PPP-Arisen, Pride PPP-AR, and raPPPid. Due to the inherent nature of the Pride PPP-AR software, it could not process observations shorter than 10 minutes, so the 5- and 7-minute datasets could not be processed using this software. The three-dimensional photogrammetric models and two-dimensional orthomosaic

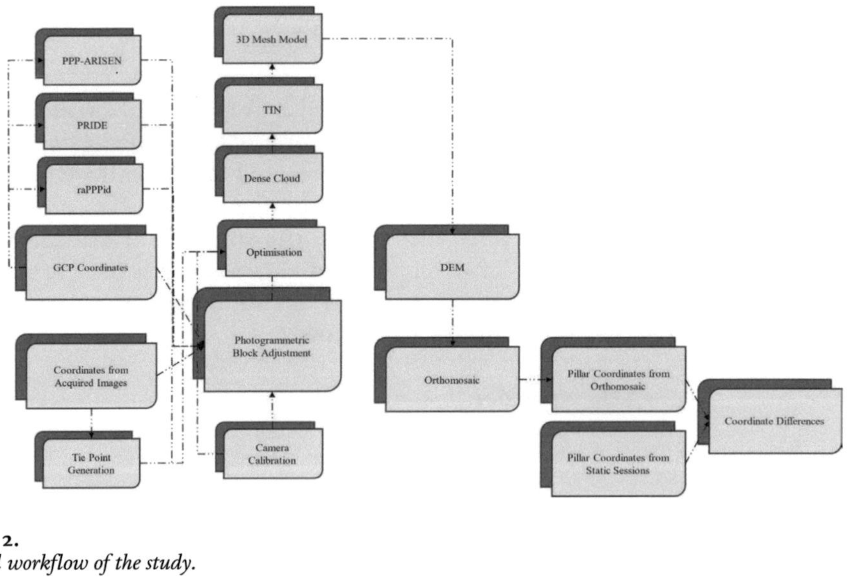

Figure 2.
General workflow of the study.

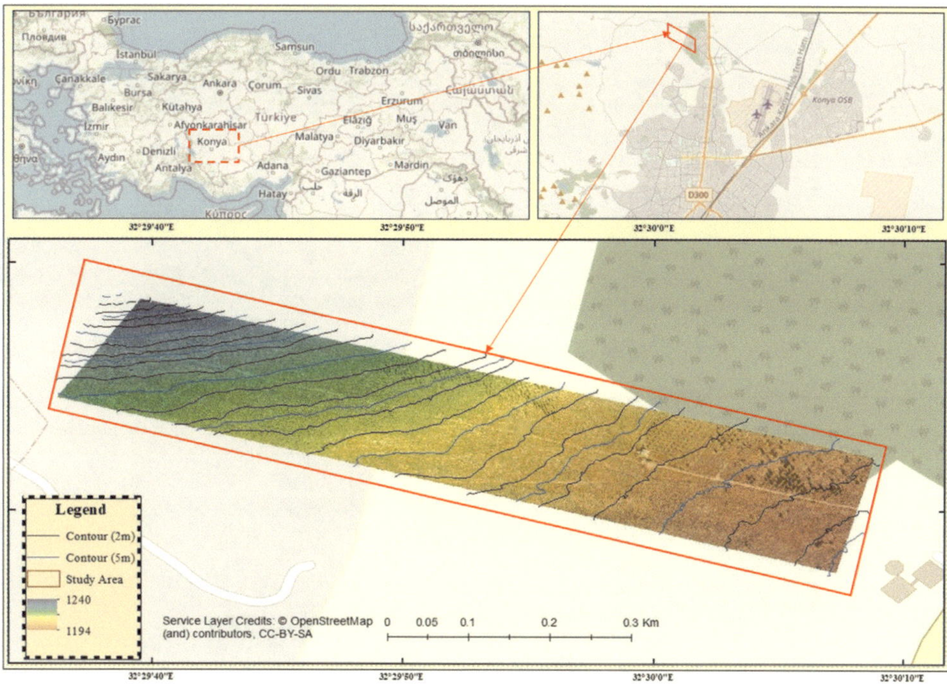

Figure 3.
Study area.

data of the study area were generated in seven different scenarios using six GCPs (**Figures 5** and **6**).

The coordinates of the pillars, visible in green in **Figures 5** and **6**, were extracted from the generated orthomosaics, and the differences between these coordinates and the true benchmark coordinates determined through static sessions were calculated. These differences were used to compute the horizontal position errors (**Figure 7**).

When **Figure 7** is examined, the horizontal position of pillar 1 was determined with a minimum error of 6.4 cm for 5- and 10-minute session durations using orthomosaics generated with PPP-Arisen-derived GCPs. The orthomosaic produced with Pride PPP-AR-derived GCPs resulted in a position error of 12.4 cm for a 10-minute session duration. In contrast, the orthomosaic generated with raPPPid-derived GCPs yielded position errors for pillar 1 of 42.4, 13.6, and 21.5 cm for 5-, 7-, and 10-minute observation durations, respectively. For pillar 2, the horizontal position was determined with a minimum error of 6.3 cm for a 10 minute session duration using models generated from both PPP-Arisen-derived and Pride PPP-AR-derived GCPs. However, for orthomosaics generated with raPPPid-derived GCPs, the position errors for pillar 2 were 32.8, 20.4, and 13.7 cm for 5-, 7-, and 10-minute session durations, respectively. The horizontal position of pillar 3 was obtained with an error of 17.1 cm using raPPPid-derived GCPs for a 10-minute session duration. The largest errors for pillars 1, 2, and 3 were 42.4, 32.8, and 35.1 cm, respectively, and were observed when using raPPPid-derived GCPs. For pillar 4, the best result was achieved using raPPPid-derived GCPs with a 10-minute session duration; for pillar 5, the best result was obtained using PPP-Arisen-derived GCPs with a 5-minute session duration; and for pillar 6, the best result was achieved using raPPPid-derived GCPs with a 7-minute session duration. The minimum errors for pillars 4, 5, and 6 were 35.2, 38.9, and

Figure 4.
Samples from GCPs and pillars.

44.0 cm, respectively, while the maximum errors were 47.7, 63.3, and 82.6 cm, respectively. It should be noted that the errors mentioned here are also influenced by the transformation of GNSS coordinates into the projection system.

Figure 8 shows the vertical position errors of pillars. When **Figure 8** is examined, the vertical position of pillar 1 was determined with a minimum error of 10.6 cm for 10-minute session duration using orthomosaics generated with raPPPid-derived GCPs. The orthomosaic generated with PPP-Arisen-derived GCPs resulted in a vertical error of 15.7 cm for a 10-minute session duration. In contrast, the orthomosaic generated with raPPPid-derived GCPs yielded position errors for pillar 1 of 87.0 cm, and 80.8 cm for 5-, and 7-minute session durations, respectively. For pillar 2, the vertical position was determined with a minimum error of 16.1 cm for a 7-minute session duration using models generated from raPPPid-derived GCPs. However, for orthomosaics generated with other raPPPid-derived GCPs, the vertical errors for pillar 2 were 73.4 cm, and 23.1 cm for 5-, and 10-minute session durations, respectively. The vertical position of pillar 3 was obtained with an error of 39.6 cm using

Receiver Specifications		 **Javad Triumph-1**	 **Sokkia GCX3**
Static accuracy	Horizontal	0.3 cm + 0.1 ppm	0.3 cm + 0.4 ppm
	Vertical	0.35 cm + 0.4 ppm	0.5 cm + 0.6 ppm
Signals tracked	GPS	C/A, P1, P2, L2C (L + M), L5 (I + Q)	L1 C/A, L1C, L2P, L2C
	GLONASS	C/A, P1, P2, L2C, L3 (I + Q)	L1 C/A, L1P, L2 C/A, L2P
	SBAS	L1, L5	L1 C/A, WAAS/MSAS/ EGNOS/ GAGAN
	GALILEO	—	E1
	Beidou	—	B1, B2
	QZSS	—	—
Antenna type		Integrated	Integrated

Table 3.
The specifications of GNSS receivers.

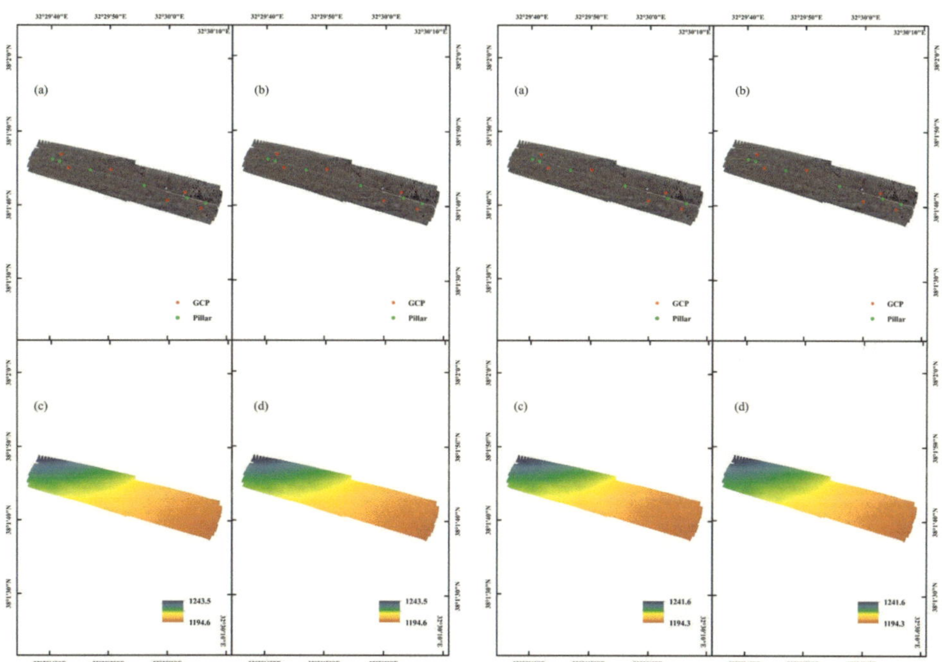

Figure 5.
Outputs generated using 5-minute (left side) and 7-minute (right side) GNSS observations: (a) orthomosaic generated using PPP-Arisen GCP coordinates, (b) orthomosaic generated using raPPPid GCP coordinates, (c) DEM generated using PPP-Arisen GCP coordinates, (d) DEM generated using raPPPid GCP coordinates.

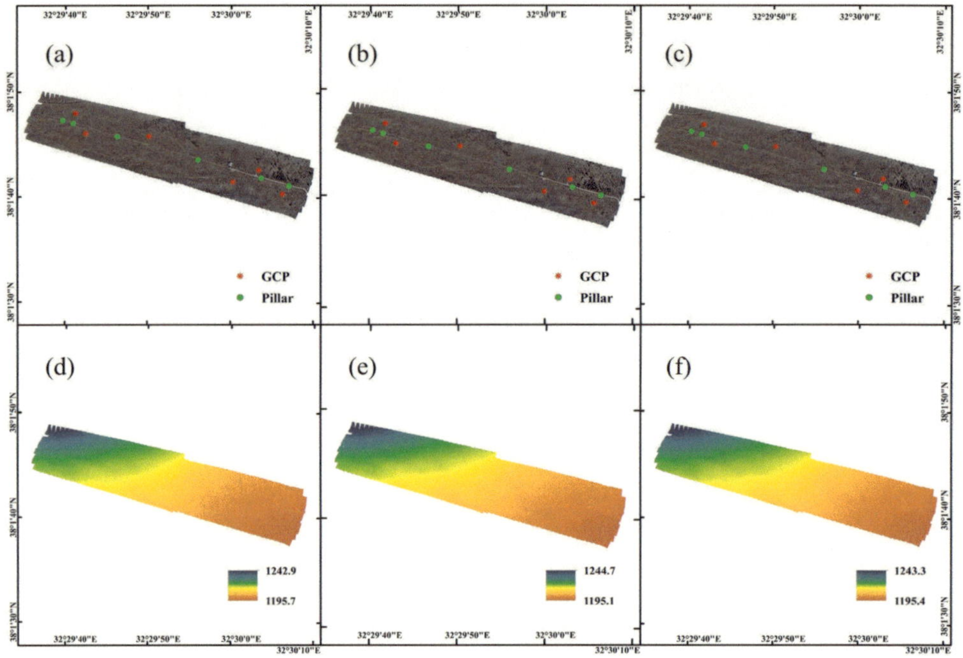

Figure 6.
Outputs generated using 10-minute GNSS observations: (a) orthomosaic generated using Pride PPP-AR GCP coordinates, (b) orthomosaic generated using PPP-Arisen GCP coordinates, (c) orthomosaic generated using raPPPid GCP coordinates, (d) DEM generated using Pride PPP-AR GCP coordinates, (e) DEM generated using PPP-Arisen GCP coordinates, (f) DEM generated using raPPPid GCP coordinates.

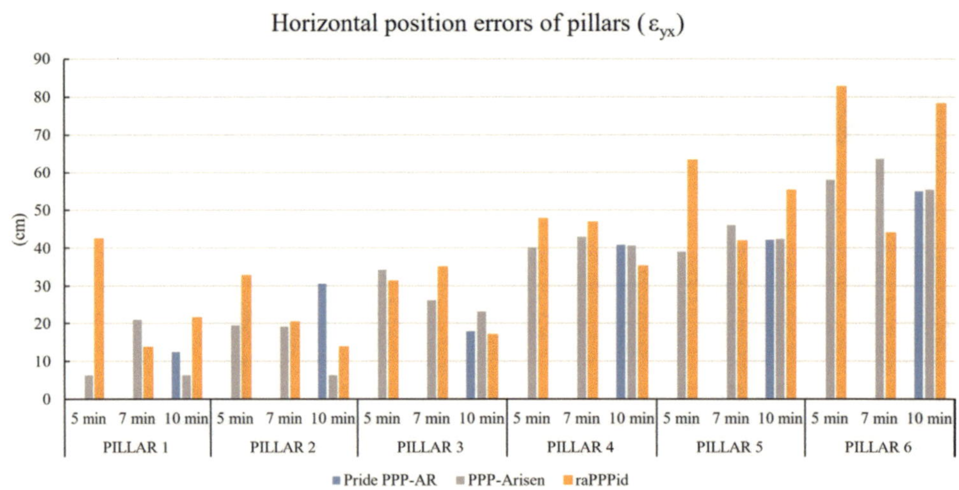

Figure 7.
Horizontal position errors of pillars.

raPPPid-derived GCPs for a 10-minute session duration. The largest errors for pillars 1, 2, and 3 were 87.0 cm, 73.4 cm, and 76.9 cm, respectively, and were observed when using raPPPid-, and Pride PPP-AR-derived GCPs. For pillar 4, the best result was achieved using raPPPid-derived GCPs with a 5-minute session duration; for pillar 5, the best result was obtained using raPPPid-derived GCPs with a 7-minute session

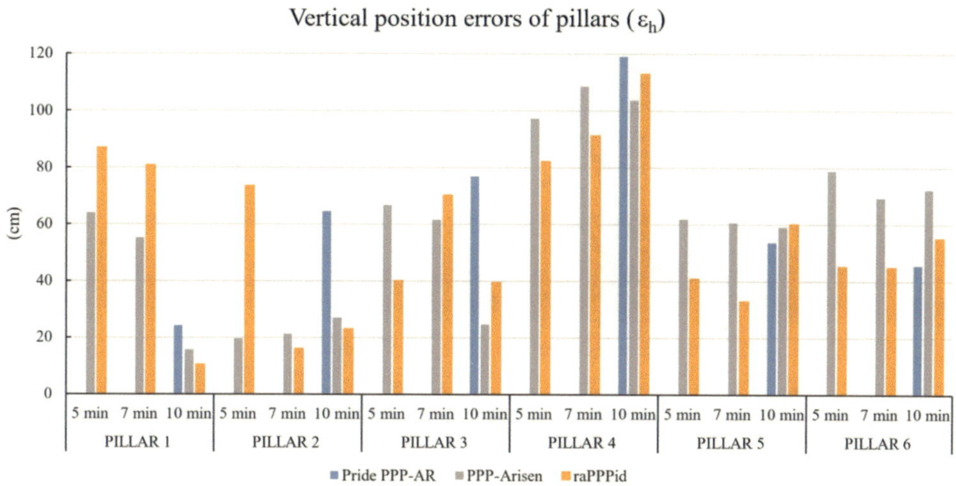

Figure 8.
Vertical position errors of pillars.

duration; and for pillar 6, the best result was achieved using raPPPid-derived GCPs with a 7-minute session duration. The minimum errors for pillars 4, 5, and 6 were 82.2 cm, 33.1 cm, and 44.9 cm, respectively, while the maximum errors were 119.1 cm, 61.9 cm, and 79.0 cm, respectively.

The biases of the horizontal distances calculated using the coordinates extracted from the model from the known horizontal distances between the pillars are presented in **Figure 9**.

In **Figure 9**, the differences between the horizontal distances calculated from the coordinates extracted from the generated orthomosaic and the horizontal distances calculated from the coordinates obtained from the static GNSS sessions are shown. For Pride PPP-AR, PPP-Arisen, and raPPPid, these differences range from −30.5 to 18.5 cm, −21.8 to 31.5 cm, and − 35.7 to 60 cm, respectively. The biases in the horizontal distances (1–2, 1–3, 2–3) where pillars 4, 5, and 6 are not involved in the combination are less than 15.6 cm. In the remaining horizontal distances, the biases are less than 30.5 cm when the session duration is 10 minutes. In both cases, very good results were obtained. However, in the remaining horizontal distances, when the session durations drop to 5 and 7 minutes, the biases increase up to 60 cm. This situation is believed to be due to the location of pillars 4, 5, and 6 in a more sloped part of the terrain. Since the pillar heights are greater in that region, the projection plane reduction error also increases when obtaining the orthomosaic. For the 4–5 horizontal distance with a 7-minute session duration, PPP-Arisen and raPPPid show biases of −21.5 and − 35.7 cm, respectively. For the 3–6 horizontal distance with a 5-minute session duration, PPP-Arisen and raPPPid show biases of 25.4 and 36.5 cm, respectively. For the 3–4 horizontal distance with a 5-minute session duration, raPPPid shows a bias of 45.5 cm. For the 2–6 horizontal distance with a 5-minute session duration, raPPPid shows a bias of 35.5 cm. For the 2–4 horizontal distance with a 5-minute session duration, raPPPid shows a bias of 44.5 cm. For the 1–4, 1–5, and 1–6 horizontal distances with a 5-minute session duration, raPPPid shows biases of 60.0, 36.7, and 51.0 cm, respectively. These findings indicate that the coordinates and, consequently, the horizontal distances obtained from orthomosaics generated with

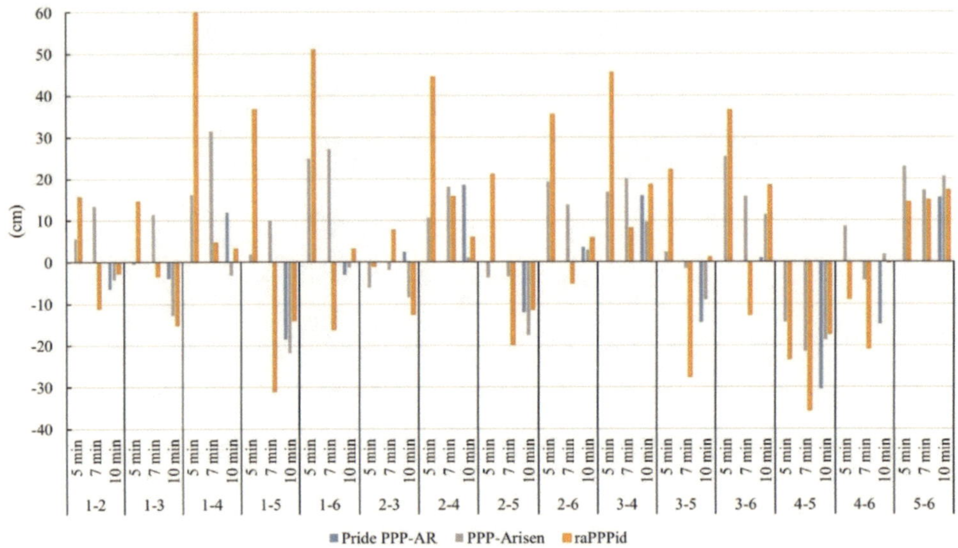

Figure 9.
Biases from known distances.

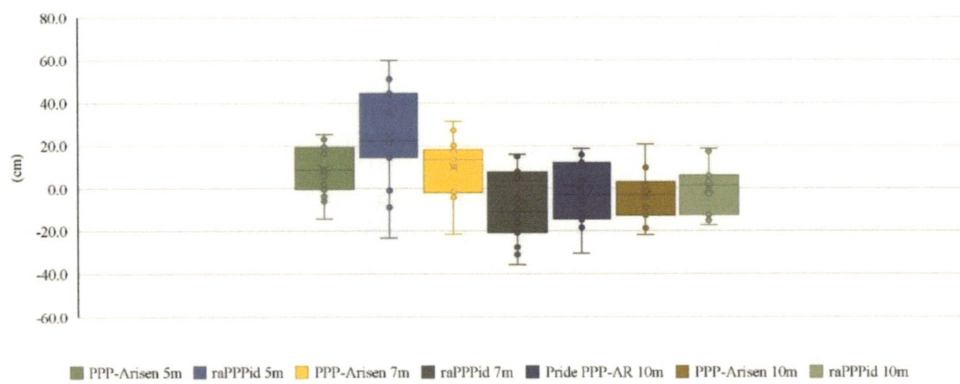

Figure 10.
Box plots for biases from known distances.

GCP coordinates derived from 5- and 7-minute solutions based on raPPPid show larger errors. A box plot of these differences is presented in **Figure 10**.

When the box plot in **Figure 10** is examined, it can be seen that the errors in the distance differences for orthomosaics generated with GCP coordinates based on PPP-Arisen 5 m, raPPPid 7 m, and Pride PPP-AR 10 m are closest to a normal distribution. Additionally, no outliers were observed in any of the scenarios. Among them, the raPPPid 5 m scenario has the widest range of variation, from −23.3 to 60.0 cm. The median values of the deviations are 8.6 cm for PPP-Arisen 5 m, 22.2 cm for raPPPid 5 m, 13.5 cm for PPP-Arisen 7 m, −11.1 cm for raPPPid 7 m, −2.9 cm for Pride PPP-AR 10 m, −3.1 cm for PPP-Arisen 10 m, and 1.2 cm for raPPPid 10 m. The box plot graphs demonstrate that meaningful and accurate statistical inferences can be made about the biasess from the known horizontal distances. **Figure 11** presents the biases between

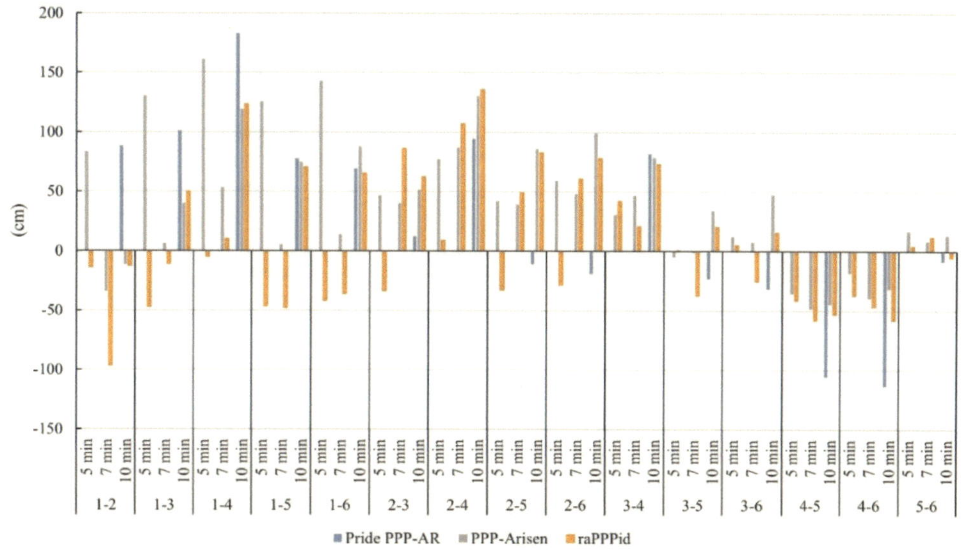

Figure 11.
Biases from known height differences.

the height differences calculated from the coordinates extracted from the orthomosaic and the height differences calculated from the geodetic coordinates.

Figure 11 shows the biases between the height differences calculated from the coordinates extracted from the generated DEM and the height differences calculated from the coordinates obtained from the static GNSS sessions. The biases range from −113.6 to 183.2 cm for Pride PPP-AR, −48.0 to 161.2 cm for PPP-Arisen, and − 96.9 to 136.0 cm for raPPPid. The biases in the height differences (1–2, 1–3, 2–3) where pillars 4, 5, and 6 are not involved in the combination are less than 130.7 cm. In the remaining height differences, the biases increase up to 183.2 cm. In both cases, the results show that it is difficult to obtain accurate height information from the generated photogrammetric outcomes. For the 4–5 height difference, the bias is −105.5 cm with a 10-minute session duration for Pride PPP-AR. For the 4–6 height difference, the bias is −113.6 cm with a 10-minute session duration for Pride PPP-AR. For the 2–4 height difference, the biases are 94.6, 130.6, and 136.0 cm for Pride PPP-AR, PPP-Arisen, and raPPPid, respectively, with a 10-minute session duration. For the 1–6 height difference, the bias is 142.9 cm with a 5-minute session duration for PPP-Arisen. For the 1–5 height difference, the bias is 125.9 cm with a 5-minute session duration for PPP-Arisen. For the 1–4 height difference, the biases are 183.2, 119.3, and 123.5 cm for Pride PPP-AR, PPP-Arisen, and raPPPid, respectively, with a 10-minute session duration. These findings indicate that the coordinates and, consequently, the heights obtained from the DEMs generated with GCP coordinates calculated using Pride PPP-AR and PPP-Arisen-based solutions often show larger errors. A box plot of these differences is presented in **Figure 12**.

The box plots in **Figure 12** show that the biases in the height differences for the DEMs generated with raPPPid 7 m, Pride PPP-AR 10 m, and PPP-Arisen 10 m-based GCP coordinates are closest to a normal distribution. Additionally, no outliers were observed in any of the scenarios. The main issue here is the very wide range of biases in the Pride PPP-AR 10 m-based DEMs. The range of the Pride PPP-AR 10 m scenario is from −113.6 to 183.2 cm, which is the widest range. The median values of the biases

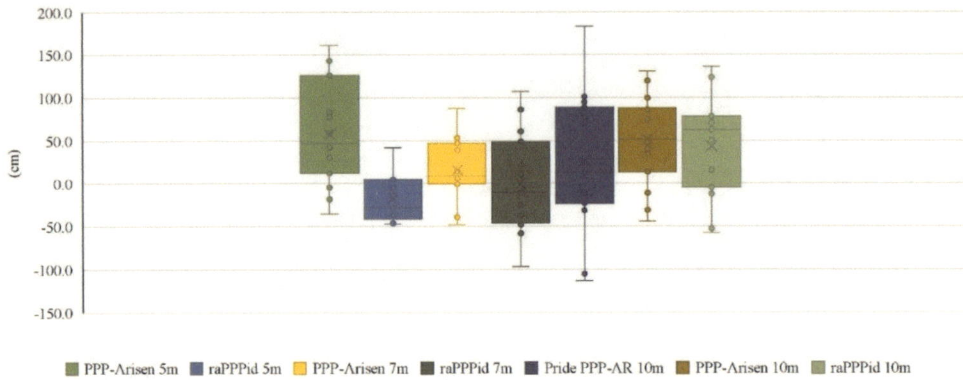

Figure 12.
Box plots for biases from known height differences.

	Horizontal statistical analysis (F-Test)		
	Session	**PPP-Arisen**	**raPPPid**
Pride PPP-AR	5 m	—	—
	7 m	—	—
	10 m	1.11	1.44
PPP-Arisen	5 m	—	2.22
	7 m	—	1.23
	10 m	—	1.59

Table 4.
Horizontal statistical comparison.

are 47.1 cm for PPP-Arisen 5 m, −28.2 cm for raPPPid 5 m, 8.7 cm for PPP-Arisen 7 m, −10.6 cm for raPPPid 7 m, 12.4 cm for Pride PPP-AR 10 m, 51.6 cm for PPP-Arisen 10 m, and 62.6 cm for raPPPid 10 m. The box plot graphs demonstrate that meaningful and accurate statistical inferences can be made about the biases from the known height differences. Utilizing Eqs. (19)–(21), a two-population variance test is performed to determine whether there is a significant difference between the accuracies obtained from different PPP software-based models. In the statistical analysis, since the degrees of freedom for the critical value calculation of RMSEs is 6, $F_{table} = F_{0.05,6,6} = 4.28$ is used. Separate comparisons were made for horizontal and vertical variances, and the results of the analysis are provided in **Tables 4** and **5**.

In **Table 4**, all test values are smaller than the critical value of 4.28. The accuracies provided by Pride PPP-AR and PPP-Arisen are statistically equal. Similarly, there is no significant difference between the photogrammetric products based on Pride PPP-AR and raPPPid. Therefore, all three software can be used interchangeably for GCP positioning with a 10-minute session duration. Furthermore, no significant differences exist between PPP-Arisen and raPPPid software for 5-, 7-, and 10-minute session durations. This means that, within the specified measurement durations, both software can be used interchangeably to produce photogrammetric products with optimal accuracy.

	Vertical statistical analysis (F-Test)		
	Session	**PPP-Arisen**	**raPPPid**
Pride PPP-AR	5 min	—	—
	7 min	—	—
	10 min	1.95	1.89
PPP-Arisen	5 min	—	1.14
	7 min	—	1.19
	10 min	—	1.03

Table 5.
Vertical statistical comparison.

Table 5 statistically compares the vertical accuracies of the photogrammetric outcomes based on all three software-based GCP coordinates. All test values in the table are smaller than the critical value of 4.28. There is no significant difference in vertical accuracy between using PPP-Arisen or raPPPid instead of Pride PPP-AR with a 10-minute session duration. Similarly, for 5-, 7-, and 10-minute session durations, there is no significant difference in vertical accuracy when using raPPPid instead of PPP-Arisen. Therefore, these two software can be used interchangeably to produce photogrammetric products with optimal vertical accuracy.

4. Conclusions

In recent years, the production of large-scale maps from UAV images has become quite common in photogrammetry. For UAV image-based map generation to be considered advantageous, it is essential to generate maps with optimal position accuracy in a practical and economical way, according to the defined generation objectives. In this study, the position accuracy of models, which can be generated using the PPP-AR method to determine GCP coordinates from a low-cost UAV, has been investigated. For this purpose, seven different DEMs and orthomosaics produced from UAV images in the selected study area within the campus of Selçuk University were evaluated in terms of position accuracy. The coordinates obtained from static GNSS sessions of six pillars in the study area were compared with the coordinates obtained from photogrammetric block adjustment results, and then, the accuracies of horizontal distances and heights derived from the model coordinates were examined.

According to the findings obtained in the study, 10-minute session durations yielded better results in terms of both horizontal and vertical accuracies for all software. In the 5- and 7-minute session durations, larger errors were particularly observed in the models based on the raPPPid software. PPP-Arisen and Pride PPP-AR generally provided similar accuracies and were statistically proven to be interchangeable. It can be stated that raPPPid software has wider error ranges compared to the other software, but in certain situations (e.g., vertical accuracy of Pillar 1), it performed well. In terms of horizontal accuracy, the lowest errors were obtained with PPP-Arisen and Pride PPP-AR software, especially for pillars 1 and 2. The biases in horizontal distances were influenced by the slope of the terrain and the height differences where the pillars were located. Vertical accuracies were characterized by larger errors compared to horizontal accuracies. It was observed that the variation ranges of DEMs based on Pride PPP-AR were wider. Looking at the statistical test results, no significant difference was found between PPP-Arisen and Pride PPP-AR software in terms of horizontal and vertical variances. All three software provided comparable accuracies during the 10-minute session durations.

For optimal horizontal accuracy of photogrammetric outcomes, any of the Pride PPP-AR, PPP-Arisen, or raPPPid software can be preferred. However, since raPPPid software exhibits larger error rates at shorter session durations, it is recommended to use it only during 10-minute observation periods. In this study, it is advised that the session duration be at least 10 minutes in situations where horizontal and vertical accuracy are critical. Additionally, the impact of the software used on accuracy should be considered, especially during short-duration measurements (5–7 minutes). In sloping areas, where accuracy losses may occur, it is also suggested to establish additional GCPs. To minimize errors caused by height differences, projection plane transformations should be carefully performed. The fact that the errors and variances follow a normal distribution suggests that statistical modeling should be used in similar future studies. In conclusion, for projects requiring precise height information, the adequacy of DEMs obtained using the current software should be questioned, and additional validation methods should be employed.

There were some limitations in this research. One of these limitations, the most important one, is the stereo-planar view difference. Even if we created orthomosaic and DEM from stereo data, outcomes could be viewed in a planar environment. For this reason, the result of the research includes operator-based choice errors. Also, UAV-based orthorectification was another error source. Because we used a non-metric camera, the outcomes could have been poorer 3D coordinate accuracy. If those limitations reduced, it would be more useful results.

Acknowledgements

The authors thank the developers of Pride PPP-AR, PPP-Arisen, and raPPPid open-source software package for Precise Point Positioning with Ambiguity Resolution (PPP-AR).

Conflict of interest

The authors declare no conflict of interest.

Author details

Burhaneddin Bilgen[1], Sercan Bülbül[2] and Hasan Bilgehan Makineci[2*]

1 Ankara Hacı Bayram Veli University, Ankara, Türkiye

2 Konya Teknik University, Konya, Türkiye

*Address all correspondence to: hbmakineci@ktun.edu.tr

References

[1] Makineci HB, Karabörk H, Durdu A. Comparison of digital elevation models produced with photogrammetric usage of UAV by geodetic techniques. Türkiye Uzaktan Algılama Dergisi. 2020;**2**(2): 58-69

[2] Balázsik V, Tóth Z, Abdurahmanov I. Analysis of data acquisition accuracy with UAV. International Journal of Geoinformatics. 2021;**17**:1-10

[3] Paneque-Gálvez J, McCall MK, Napoletano BM, Wich SA, Koh LP. Small drones for community-based forest monitoring: An assessment of their feasibility and potential in tropical areas. Forests. 2014;**5**:1481-1507. DOI: 10.3390/f5061481

[4] Ferrer-González E, Agüera-Vega F, Carvajal-Ramírez F, Martínez-Carricondo P. UAV photogrammetry accuracy assessment for corridor mapping based on the number and distribution of ground control points. Remote Sensing. 2020;**12**(15):2447

[5] Szypuła B. Accuracy of UAV-based DEMs without ground control points. GeoInformatica. 2024;**28**(1):1-28

[6] Famiglietti NA, Cecere G, Grasso C, Memmolo A, Vicari A. A test on the potential of a low cost unmanned aerial vehicle RTK/PPK solution for precision positioning. Sensors. 2021;**21**(11):3882

[7] Eker R, Alkan E, Aydın A. A comparative analysis of UAV-RTK and UAV-PPK methods in mapping different surface types. European Journal of Forest Engineering. 2021;**7**(1):12-25

[8] Ocalan T, Turk T, Tunalioglu N, Gurturk M. Investigation of accuracy of PPP and PPP-AR methods for direct georeferencing in UAV photogrammetry. Earth Science Informatics. 2022;**15**(4):2231-2238

[9] Makineci HB, Bilgen B, Bulbul S. A new precise point positioning with ambiguity resolution (PPP-AR) approach for ground control point positioning for photogrammetric generation with unmanned aerial vehicles. Drones. 2024;**8**(9):456. DOI: 10.3390/drones8090456

[10] Erol B, Turan E, Erol S, Kuçak RA. Comparative performance analysis of precise point positioning technique in the UAV– based mapping. Measurement. 2024;**233**:114768

[11] Zumberge JF, Heflin MB, Jefferson DC, Watkins MM, Webb FH. Precise point positioning for the efficient and robust analysis of GPS data from large networks. Journal of Geophysical Research - Solid Earth. 1997;**102**(B3): 5005-5017. DOI: 10.1029/96JB03860

[12] Héroux P, Kouba J. GPS precise point positioning using IGS orbit products. Physics and Chemistry of the Earth, Part A: Solid Earth and Geodesy. 2001;**26**: 573-578. DOI: 10.1016/S1464-1895(01)00103-X

[13] Kouba J, Héroux P. Precise point positioning using IGS orbit and clock products. GPS Solutions. 2001;**5**:12-28. DOI: 10.1007/PL00012883

[14] Mu X, Wang L, Shu B, Tian Y, Li X, Lei T, et al. Performance analysis of multi-GNSS real-time PPP-AR positioning considering SSR delay. Remote Sensing. 2024;**16**:1213

[15] Geng J, Chen X, Pan Y, Zhao Q. A modified phase clock/bias model to improve PPP ambiguity resolution at Wuhan University. Journal of Geodesy.

2019;**93**(10):2053-2067. DOI: 10.1007/s00190-019-01301-6

[16] Glaner MF, Weber R. An open-source software package for precise point positioning: raPPPid. GPS Solutions. 2023;**27**:174. DOI: 10.1007/s10291-023-01488-4

[17] Zhang C, Guo A, Ni S, et al. PPP-ARISEN: An open-source precise point positioning software with ambiguity resolution for interdisciplinary research of seismology, geodesy and geodynamics. GPS Solutions. 2023;**27**:45. DOI: 10.1007/s10291-022-01380-7

[18] Geng J, Zhang Q, Li G, et al. Observable-specific phase biases of Wuhan multi-GNSS experiment analysis center's rapid satellite products. Satellite Navigation. 2022;**3**(1):1-15. DOI: 10.1186/s43020-022-00084-0

[19] Zeng J, Geng J, Li G, et al. Improving cycle slip detection in ambiguity-fixed precise point positioning for kinematic LEO orbit determination. GPS Solutions. 2024;**28**:135. DOI: 10.1007/s10291-024-01639-1

[20] Bilgen B, Bulbul S, Inal C. Statistical comparison on accuracies of web-based online PPP services. Journal of Surveying Engineering. 2022;**148**(4):04022009. DOI: 10.1061/(ASCE)SU.1943-5428.0000403

[21] Ghilani CD, Wolf PR. Adjustment Computations: Spatial Data Analysis. USA: Wiley; 2006

[22] Ayso E, Kahveci M. GNSS kod (pseudorange) ölçüleri ile tek nokta konum belirleme yazilimi: ktun_spp. Konjes. 2022;**10**(3):578-598. DOI: 10.36306/konjes.1112955

[23] Loyer S, Perosanz F, Mercier F, et al. Zero-difference GPS ambiguity resolution at CNES–CLS IGS analysis Center. Journal of Geodesy. 2012;**86**: 991-1003. DOI: 10.1007/s00190-012-0559-2

[24] Georgia K, Loyer S, Perosanz F. PPP and PPP-AR kinematic post-processed performance of GPS-only, Galileo-only and multi-GNSS. Remote Sensing. 2019; **11**(21):2477. DOI: 10.3390/rs11212477

[25] Schaer S, Villiger A, Arnold D, et al. The CODE ambiguity-fixed clock and phase bias analysis products: Generation, properties, and performance. Journal of Geodesy. 2021;**95**:81. DOI: 10.1007/s00190-021-01521-9

Chapter 4

Cybersecurity Issues in UAV Control and Network System: A Systematic Review

Desh Deepak Sharma

Abstract

Cybersecurity threats in Unmanned Aerial Vehicle (UAV) control and networks are becoming increasingly significant as UAVs are employed in critical applications such as surveillance, disaster response, logistics, and military operations. These threats often target the communication, control, and data transmission layers, posing risks to the confidentiality, integrity, and availability of UAV systems. This book chapter reviews the various intrusion detection techniques to be implemented as countermeasures to cyber threats in UAV control and communication networks. The advantages, limitations, and applications of these techniques are highlighted. The emerging areas for future research in threat detection are outlined. Various case studies of cybersecurity in UAV control and networks are presented. STRIDE Threat Modeling is discussed with pseudocode for cyber threat detection and needed intrusion detection techniques.

Keywords: cyber security in UAV, intrusion detection system, threat actor, threat modeling, UAV

1. Introduction

The global positioning system, barometer, accelerometer, magnetometer, and gyroscopic are among the sensors installed on the UAVS. These sensors gather data on position, altitude, and surrounding circumstances. The UAV is equipped with optical sensors, ultrasonic detectors, and infrared detectors to detect obstructions and prevent collisions. The computational part includes task allocation, path planning, and navigation. The UAV framework comprises the control, communication, and computation parts, so networked drones can be considered a cyber-physical system. In networked drones, the control and computation parts should be capable of executing joint path planning, cooperative control, monitoring and diagnostic, collision avoidable, and tackling interoperable data (**Figure 1**).

Security threats affect the safe and reliable performance of UAVs in cyber-physical systems. The open wireless communication channel and nonstandard application of drones make the framework vulnerable to attack, consequently, the physical system may reach an unwanted state and perform critical malfunctions. The different security threats in networked UAV systems must be

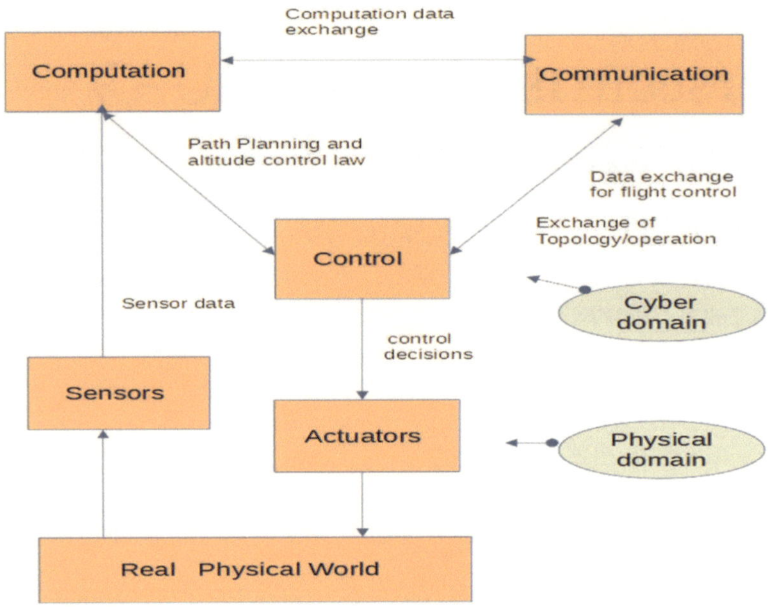

Figure 1.
A framework of networked drone.

analyzed, and a security threat model should be developed focusing on various system vulnerabilities [1].

Cyber-physical threats pertain to manipulating control and sensor data through malevolent activities that can be carried out by unmanned aerial vehicles (UAVs). From the perspective of cyberspace security, security risks and assaults are examined and grouped. These include replies, spoofing, jamming, Denial of Service (DoS), eavesdropping, side-channel, manipulation, and system infiltration attacks, **Figure 2** [2]. The research on privacy impacts resulting from the physical loss of UAVs has not given enough attention. For safe communication between UAVs, a key agreement protocol and authentication should be created [3].

Multi-input, multi-output technology is used to secure UAVs' physical layers and preserve the UAV network's confidentiality [4]. An attempt at a cyberattack on the information system has been detected using a stochastic model technique with a confusion matrix [5]. A blockchain-based multi-UAV task processing system for situation awareness and real-time decision-making is proposed in the research work, which also applies blockchain technology to multi-UAV tasks [6]. To provide secure communication and meet physical tamper-proof criteria, a lightweight UAV-assisted authentication and key agreement protocol is suggested for unattended Internet of Things (IoT) devices [7].

There is a major challenge to encourage UAV participation and optimize UAV trajectory for online job offloading without jeopardizing user equipment privacy [8]. A two-factor authentication scheme with fuzzy verifiers is presented for a UAV-assisted vehicular *ad-hoc* network based on chaotic maps [9]. To avoid attacks on the UAV system, the original security system depends on an expert knowledge base [10]. Due to risks resulting from operating on open wireless channels and having limited onboard processing resources, security and privacy concerns are also growing as UAV systems are becoming more vulnerable [11]. A UAV works as a relay or a jammer in a dual UAV-assisted edge computing system [12].

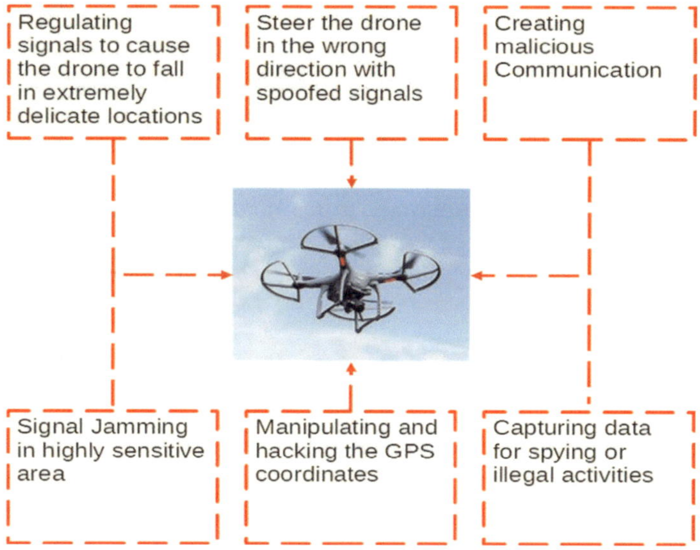

Figure 2.
Possible cyber threats on UAV control and network.

In the case of eavesdropping, Attackers can fetch unencrypted messages and modify them. The jamming attack is related to a range of jamming among the UAVs, and it corresponds to jamming the network of the UAV. In the Man in the Middle (MITM) case, a malicious UAV is capable of interrupting an original communication channel. This malicious UAV can modify, drop, or send fake messages.

In the case of replay, a malicious UAV tries to fly near a swarm of UAVs, intends to listen to encrypted messages, and tries to modify and send these modified messages to another UAV. In the case of a Sybil attack, a malicious UAV generates virtual identities termed Sybil nodes. The actual UAV falsely detects these Sybil nodes as actual nodes in the system [13].

Security issues are highly considered to be tackled in cyber-physical systems considering confidentiality, integrity, and availability. The new innovative technologies have to be developed for UAV software designs. The cybersecurity issues are to be considered in composition structure and different applications. An analysis has to be done on the effects on cyber domain and security of the industrial, commercial, and personal data. The malicious use of the UAV platform has to be identified [14].

1.1 UAV communication network

5G mobile network, WLAN, WSN, and *ad-hoc* networks are examples of possible communication networks in cyber-physical systems secure data sharing and privacy issues are major concerns in the communication being held among UAVs. In real-time, the location of UAVs needs to be broadcasted to the control center. In a networked UAV system, the control techniques and communication network are vulnerable to threats such as eavesdropping, spoofing, jamming. MITM, replay, and Sybil. The freely accessible drones, also known as invader drones, are causing the fuzzing and invading scenario. The UAV remains silent and stealthy and has the capability to fly at low altitudes. UAVs can steal sensitive and private data because of their cautious and covert movements.

There has been a huge technological advancement in the field of wireless communication in the last few decades. Technology has revolutionized from voice communication to interactive multimedia applications. A tremendous increase in high data rate and connectivity demanding user equipment is observed. There is an immense need for new technological trends to satisfy the cutting-edge requirements of 5G and beyond wireless communication networks. Mobility, maneuverability, low cost, and Line of sight (LOS) communication make unmanned aerial vehicles (UAV) a promising candidate for future wireless communication networks. Despite the numerous benefits of UAV's UAV-assisted wireless networks several challenges also exist, which need to be addressed [15, 16].

1.2 UAV control network

The cyber threats exploit vulnerabilities in control software to inject malicious commands, impact unauthorized UAV control, and target ground control interfaces or remote systems. The attacker impersonates a legitimate UAV or ground control system. An attacker relays legitimate communication between UAVs and ground control to appear authentic. Malicious UAVs operated by attackers can target legitimate UAV systems, consequently, there are possible collision or swarming attacks. Threat actors overwhelm the UAV control network with excessive traffic, leading to service disruption, which prevents the UAV from receiving commands. These threat actors intercept and manipulate communication between the UAV and its control station for the alteration of commands [17, 18].

2. Intrusion detection system

The identification of cyberattacks that may be launched at various network nodes is the primary goal of the intrusion detection system (IDS). The several types of intrusion detection strategies include anomaly, rule, and signature-based systems. To identify unknown threats, a creative intrusion detection system has to be created. To prevent harmful actions and suspicious attacks that could threaten drone cyber-physical systems, a creative intrusion detection system (IDS) needs to be created [19].

The identification of cyberattacks that may be launched at various network nodes is the primary goal of the intrusion detection system (IDS). The several types of intrusion detection strategies include anomaly, rule, and signature-based systems. It is necessary to create a novel intrusion detection system to identify unidentified attacks. Rule-based intrusion detection has been created to secure the communication infrastructure between flying objects and ground stations by quickly identifying hostile activities [20].

The behavior rule-based attack models are designed with care to account for impulsive, coincidental, and opportunistic attacks. For malevolent UAVs in the aerial system with a higher detection rate, the adaptive behavior-rule-based intrusion detection scheme specification is designed [21].

To determine the GPS position of an object in flight, the signature-based intrusion detection approach is recommended. A bioinspired detection method can identify cyberattacks in aircraft networks. Rule-based and signature-based intrusion detection systems, however, are unable to identify unknown threats or attacks with dynamic signatures [22].

Intrusion detection techniques for Unmanned Aerial Vehicle (UAV) systems are critical to ensuring their operational security, safety, and reliability. UAV systems are vulnerable to various threats, including spoofing, jamming, malware, and unauthorized access to communication links. Below are key intrusion detection techniques for UAV systems:

2.1 Types of intrusion detection techniques

The identification of cyberattacks that may be launched at various network nodes is the primary goal of the intrusion detection system (IDS). Rule-based, signature-based, and anomaly-based are some of the different intrusion detection techniques. It is necessary to create a novel intrusion detection system in order to identify unidentified attacks.

Techniques for countering UAV cyber threats and enhancing drone security are presented in a comprehensive review [23–26]. When dealing with unidentified timeline-based hacks, the IDS systems listed below may be employed:

2.1.1 Signature-based intrusion detection systems (SIDS)

Signature intrusion detection systems (SIDS), often referred to as knowledge-based detection or misuse detection, use pattern-matching approaches to identify known attacks. Matching techniques are employed in SIDS to locate a prior intrusion. Put another way, an alarm is raised when an intrusion signature matches the signature of an earlier incursion that is already recorded in the signature database.

This method detects known attack patterns by matching them with pre-stored signatures in a database.

2.1.2 Behavior-based intrusion detection

Beyond identifying specific attack fingerprints, a behavior- or anomaly-based intrusion detection system (IDS) can discover and examine odd or malicious patterns of behavior. This kind of technology analyzes massive volumes of data and network traffic using machine learning, artificial intelligence, and statistics to identify anomalies. To identify these timeline-based assaults, this class of behavior-based intrusion prevention systems examines how technological systems behave, as well as the types of traffic requests that are made. This *technique* monitors UAV actions and compares them with expected behavioral models to detect malicious activity.

2.1.3 Game theory-based approaches

This technique, which has a proactive approach to security, models interactions between attackers and defenders as a strategic game to predict and counteract intrusions.

2.1.4 Blockchain-based intrusion detection

This technique uses blockchain to ensure secure, immutable, and decentralized logging of UAV communication and activities. The technique enhances data integrity and prevents unauthorized tampering. However, it overheads in terms of computation and communication.

2.1.5 Physical intrusion detection

This technique detects physical interference, such as attempts to capture or damage the UAV, applies anti-tampering mechanisms and accelerometer anomaly detection, and provides an additional layer of security for physical threats. This approach is unable to detect cyber intrusions.

2.1.6 Hybrid intrusion detection systems

This technique, which has broader coverage and robustness, combines multiple detection techniques (e.g., signature-based and anomaly-based) to improve detection accuracy and reduce false positives.

2.1.7 Machine learning and AI-based techniques

This technique uses supervised, unsupervised, or reinforcement learning to identify patterns and predict potential threats. This is real-time attack detection and response, and adaptable to complex and evolving threats. The large datasets are required for training and significant computational resources. This technique implements statistical methods (e.g., Z-score analysis) and machine learning algorithms (e.g., Random Forest, SVM, or Neural Networks).

2.1.8 Network-based intrusion detection

This technique monitors communication traffic between the UAV and ground control stations for signs of intrusion. This technique is capable of detecting unusual traffic patterns, such as Denial of Service (DoS) attacks or Man in the Middle (MitM) attacks.

2.1.9 Host-based intrusion detection

This technique focuses on monitoring the UAV's onboard systems, including its operating system, firmware, and software. It can detect local compromises and malware.

2.1.10 Anomaly-based detection

This technique detects deviations from normal behavior, such as unusual network traffic, sensor readings, or flight paths, and is capable of identifying unknown or novel attacks. The comparative study of different intrusion detection techniques is shown in **Table 1**.

3. Cyber threats on UAV control and network system

Cyber-physical threats pertain to manipulating control and sensor data through malevolent activities that can be carried out by unmanned aerial vehicles (UAVs). In terms of metrics and statistical models, the model has profiles that describe how subjects behave around objects. It also contains rules that gather information about this behavior from audit records and identify unusual behavior.

Sr. no.	Techniques	Description	Advantages	Disadvantages	Applications
1.	Signature-Based IDS	Detects known attack patterns or signatures by matching system activity against a database	High accuracy for known attacks, Easy to implement	Cannot detect zero-day attacks Needs regular updates of signature database	Protecting Communication links Detection of malware of protocol-based attack
2.	Anomaly-Based IDS	Learns normal UAV behavior patterns and flags deviations as potential intrusions	Able to detect unknown attacks	Computationally Intensive because of the use of machine learning algorithms	GPS spoofing or jamming detection, Identification of abnormal navigation patterns
3.	Behavior-Based IDS	Monitors UAV operations to identify deviations in specific behaviors like navigation or communication	Specific application threat scenarios	Limited to predefined behavior patterns	Control and command hijacking detection
4	Heuristic-Based IDS	Uses heuristic algorithms to detect suspicious activities based on predefined rules or experiences.	Effective against known variations of attacks and faster than signature-based IDS	Risk of false positives if heuristics are inaccurate	Malware detection in UAV firmware
5.	Host-Based IDS (HIDS)	Runs directly on the UAV to monitor its internal systems	Immediate detection of onboard intrusion	Vulnerable to insider manipulation	Detecting unauthorized software changes

Table 1.
Comparative summary of various intrusion detection techniques.

The UAV control and network system comprises components like command and control (C2) links, flight controllers, navigation systems, and onboard sensors. These systems are critical to UAV operation but are vulnerable to a range of cyberattack vectors, **Table 2**.

The secure and dependable operation of UAVs in cyber-physical systems is impacted by security risks. The framework is susceptible to assault because of the open wireless communication channel and nonstandard drone application. As a result, the physical system may enter an undesired condition or experience serious faults. It is necessary to assess the numerous security threats in networked UAV systems and to design a security threat model that focuses on different system weaknesses.

The UAV is equipped with infrared, ultrasonic, and vision sensors to identify obstructions and prevent collisions, among other crucial duties. It is necessary to assess the numerous security threats in networked UAV systems and to design a security threat model that focuses on different system weaknesses. Various major security threats on UAV control and communication are described as shown below.

Sr. no.	Attack vector	Descriptions	Targets	Consequences
1	Jamming Attacks	Disrupting the communication signals between the UAV and its ground control station (GCS) or GPS satellites	• Interference with uplink/downlink signals • Blocking satellite signals disrupts navigation	• Loss of control or navigation failure • Forced landing or crashes
2.	Spoofing attacks	injecting false signals to deceive the UAV's sensors or communication systems	• Providing fake location data to mislead the UAV • Impersonating a legitimate controller to hijack the UAV	• Mission Deviation • Redirection of UAVs to hostile areas
3.	Hijacking	Exploiting vulnerabilities in authentication or encryption to take unauthorized control of the UAV	• Weak Control and Command (C2) Links • Unsecured Control Software	• Unauthorized missions • Theft of sensitive data or UAV payloads
4.	Malware Injection	Introduction of malicious code into the UAV's firmware or control software	• Tampering with flight parameters • Corrupting mission objectives	• Erratic behavior or crashes • Extraction of sensitive mission data
5.	Replay Attacks	Capturing legitimate command sequences and replaying them to disrupt UAV operations	• C2 Links • Authentication Mechanisms	• Duplication of commands • Unauthorized execution of previous instructions
6.	Denial of Service Attacks (DoS)	Flooding the C2 link or onboard systems with excessive requests, rendering them unresponsive	• C2 communication Channel • Onboard Computational Resources	• Communication Breakdown • Inability to execute commands
7.	Sensor manipulation	Targeting onboard sensors to feed false or corrupted data to the flight controller	• GPS receivers: for false positioning • Inertial Measurement Units: for incorrect orientation or speed data • Environmental Sensors: Manipulation data for specific applications	• Navigation Errors • Payload mission inaccuracies
8.	Physical Access attacks	Gaining physical access to the UAV to tamper with its hardware or software	• Flight controllers • Communication modules	• Extraction of sensitive data
9.	Side-Channel Attacks	Exploiting non-primary information (e.g., power consumption, electromagnetic emissions) to infer sensitive data	• Encryption Key • Control system states	• The decryption of secure communication • Insights into UAV operations
10.	Supply Chain Attacks	Compromising UAV components or software during development or delivery	• Embedded hardware chips • Third-party software libraries	• Backdoor access to UAVs • Potential control compromise during operations

Table 2.
Attack vectors on UAV control and network system.

3.1 Man in the middle (MITM)

Attackers who are eavesdropping have the ability to obtain unencrypted messages and alter them. The jamming attack correlates to jamming the UAV network and is related to the range of jamming among UAVs. An initial communication channel can be interrupted by a malevolent unmanned aerial vehicle (UAV) in a Man in the Middle (MITM) scenario. Malicious UAVs can alter, drop, or send false messages. A hostile UAV attempting to fly close to a group of other UAVs to listen in on encrypted signals attempts to change them before sending them again to another UAV in a repeat scenario. A malevolent UAV creates virtual identities known as Sybil nodes in the event of a Sybil assault. These Sybil nodes are mistakenly detected by the real UAV as real nodes.

3.2 Password cracking attack

A malware attack against a commercially operated UAV that was remotely controlled revealed multiple security flaws. In the attack, they gain access to the device through weaknesses in the communication mechanism and use the Robot Operating System (ROS) control tools. The entire goal of this attack was to seize control of the UAV. Identity spoofing is an attack that involves breaking into a device's password, which is classified as an authentication incursion.

3.3 Spoofing GPS

GPS spoofing is a significant cybersecurity threat to Unmanned Aerial Vehicle (UAV) control and communication systems. It involves transmitting fake GPS signals to deceive a UAV into believing false positional or timing information. This can lead to disruptions, misdirection, or even the complete capture of the UAV. An attacker generates a stronger GPS signal than the legitimate one, tricking the UAV into locking onto the spoofed signal. The attacker gradually modifies the spoofed signal's parameters (position or time) to subtly alter the UAV's trajectory without triggering alarms.

3.4 Maldrone

It is a software flaw created specifically with UAVs in mind. Maldrone was deployed by Drone 2.0 when the drone was in midair during the whole assault. With that, threat actor can take command of the drone launch location and make it malfunction whenever he wants.

3.5 Signal blocking (jamming)

As the name suggests, it completely blocks the GPS signal, rendering a receiver and any device that depends on it useless.

3.6 MITM attack

Attackers who are eavesdropping have the ability to obtain non-encrypted messages and alter them. An initial communication channel can be interrupted by a malevolent unmanned aerial vehicle (UAV) in a Man in the Middle (MITM) scenario. Malicious UAVs can alter, drop, or send false messages. A hostile UAV attempting to fly close to a group of other UAVs to listen in on encrypted signals attempts to change them before sending them again to another UAV in a repeat scenario.

3.7 Sybil attack

When a malevolent UAV launches a Sybil attack, it creates virtual identities known as Sybil nodes. These Sybil nodes are mistakenly identified by the real UAV as genuine system nodes. When it comes to availability, confidentiality, and integrity, cyber-physical systems security concerns are highly regarded and must be addressed. It is necessary to build new and novel technologies for UAV software designs. It is necessary to take into account the composition structure and various applications of cyber security issues.

4. Research gap and future direction

4.1 Research gap

Cybersecurity in drones is a critical area of research with numerous gaps that need to be addressed due to the increasing adoption of drones in commercial, military, and recreational applications (**Table 3**).

4.2 Emerging areas for future research

The future research areas of cyber security issues are shown in **Table 4**.

Sr. no.	Key areas	Research gaps
1	Communication Security	Developing robust, lightweight encryption protocols suitable for drones with limited computational resources
2	GPS Spoofing and Navigation Interference	Develop solutions for resilient navigation systems.
3	Firmware and Software Vulnerabilities	Create Techniques for secure firmware updates (e.g., blockchain-based update mechanisms or digital signatures) and real-time vulnerability detection.
4	Malware and Ransomware Targeting Drones	Design of effective detection mechanisms for drone-specific malware and developing immune systems against such attacks
5	Autonomous Operation Security	Securing AI/ML models in drones against adversarial inputs and ensuring robust decision-making
6	Physical Hijacking and Unauthorized Access	Physical tamper-proofing and biometric or secure key-based access controls for drones
7	DDoS and Swarm Attacks	Create mechanisms to detect and mitigate such attacks in real-time.
8	Legal and Ethical Frameworks	Identification and implementation of standards for drones and ethical frameworks for their operation.

Table 3.
Potential research gaps.

Sr. no.	Areas
1	*Quantum-resistant Encryption protocols* for Drones to Prepare for post-quantum Security Challenges
2	*Blockchain Communication systems* to ensure trust and transparency in drone networks
3	*AI-driven threat detection* for anomaly and intrusion detection in real-time drone operations

Table 4.
Future cyber threat detection areas in UAV control and network.

5. Security threat model

A security threat model for an Unmanned Aerial Vehicle (UAV) system identifies potential vulnerabilities, attack vectors, and the corresponding mitigation for ensuring the security of the system. UAV systems face a range of threats due to their reliance on wireless communication, onboard sensors, and autonomy. Creating a security threat model algorithm for an unmanned aerial vehicle (UAV) system involves identifying potential threats, analyzing vulnerabilities, and implementing countermeasures. Common threat actors are shown in **Table 5**.

Sr. no.	Threat actors	Motives	Techniques
1	Cybercriminals	• Financial gain (e.g., ransom, data theft, or selling stolen UAVs or data) • Disruption of business operations	• Ransomware attacks on UAV control systems. • Intercepting and stealing sensitive data from UAV-Ground Control Station (GCS) communications. • Exploiting software vulnerabilities for unauthorized access
2	Hackers	• Testing skills or gaining notoriety	• Political or social activism • GPS or signal spoofing to misdirect UAVs • Malware injection to alter UAV functionality
3	Nation-State Actors	• Espionage: Collecting intelligence on military or commercial operations • Sabotage: Disrupting critical infrastructure or missions • Strategic dominance in conflicts or rivalries	• Advanced Persistent Threats (APTs) targeting UAV networks • Cyber-physical attacks to hijack drones mid-flight • Exploiting supply chain vulnerabilities to implant backdoors
4	Terrorist Organizations	• Using UAVs for surveillance, attacks, or propaganda • Disrupting public safety and security	• GPS spoofing or signal jamming to capture or redirect UAV • Weaponizing drones for attacks (e.g., deploying explosives or chemical agents) • Exploiting UAV systems for reconnaissance
5	Insider Threats	• Financial incentives (e.g., selling proprietary information) • Personal grievances or ideological differences	• Tampering with UAV software or hardware • Leaking sensitive operational data • Facilitating unauthorized access to systems

Sr. no.	Threat actors	Motives	Techniques
6	Industrial Competitors	• Gaining competitive advantage • Sabotage rival companies	• Espionage to steal intellectual property (e.g., UAV designs, algorithms) • Disrupting drone services through cyberattacks • Using UAVs to gather sensitive data about competitors
7	Rogue UAV Operators	• Personal gain or mischief • Testing UAV vulnerabilities	• Deploying rogue drones to intercept data or disrupt legitimate UAV operations • Overloading airspace with unauthorized UAVs creates confusion
8	AI-Based Adversaries	• Exploiting vulnerabilities in AI-powered UAV systems • Using adversarial attacks to manipulate or deceive AI algorithms	• Adversarial inputs to mislead AI decision-making in UAVs • Spoofing AI-driven sensors for reconnaissance or sabotage • Using swarm attacks powered by AI

Table 5.
Threat actors in UAV system.

5.1 STRIDE-based threat modeling for UAVs

A threat model for UAVs helps to identify potential security risks, vulnerabilities, and attack vectors that could compromise the integrity, availability, or confidentiality of the drone and its operations. The threat landscape for drones is complex due to their reliance on software and hardware. The STRIDE threat modeling framework is a systematic approach used to identify security threats, shown in **Table 6**, in a system

Sr. no	Stride category	Threat	Impact	Mitigation
1.	Spoofing	• GPS Spoofing • Command spoofing	Loss of navigation accuracy	GPS anti-spoofing authentication, encryption
2.	Tampering	• Firmware modification • Physical hardware tempering	• Malware injection • Sensor manipulation	• Secure boot, code signing • Tamper-proof hardware
3.	Repudiation	Denial of command or action	Lack of accountability	Lack of a Secure logging digital signature
4.	Information Disclosure	• Interception of UAV telemetry • Exposure of encryption key	• Data breach • Loss of confidentiality	• Encrypt communication and onboard data • Secure Key storage
5.	Denial of Service	• GPS or communication jamming • DDoS on the ground station	• Mission Disruption • Control System Unavailability	• Anti-jamming technologies • Firewalls, rate limiting
6.	Elevation of Privilege	Root access to the UAV system	• Full control by an attacker	• Patch vulnerabilities, strict access controls

Table 6.
Various threats on UAV control and network system.

by categorizing them into six main threat types: *Spoofing, Tampering, Repudiation, Information Disclosure, Denial of Service (DoS)*, and *Elevation of Privilege*. In order to create a suitable Drone as a Service (DaaS) threat model, the research work prioritizes the desired attributes of the updated STRIDE threat model, which include authenticity, integrity, non-reputability, confidentiality, availability, and authorization [27]. Using STRIDE threat modeling procedures to classify cyberattacks, the threat model for unmanned aerial vehicles (UAVs), along with the threats and vulnerabilities have been presented [28]. A cybersecurity threat analysis of multi-UAV systems based on the STRIDE model has been offered to aid in the security design process [29, 30].

The goal of this effort is to promote more study and research in order to create strong security features for UAV communication systems [31].

5.2 Pseudocode of threat model to UAV system

```
STRIDE threat_model (UAV system).
Define enum SRTIDE (threats) {.
SPOOFING.
TAMPERING.
REPUDIATION.
DENIAL_OF_SERVICE.
JAMMING.
ELEVATION of PRIVILEGE.
DENIAL of SERVICE.
}
//Define system components.
//Sample system components.
Class components(UAV system) = {components 1, components 2}.
[
Components1 = [UAV 3D flight coordinates].
Components1 = [yaw, roll, pitch].
]
Class component {.
string component 1, component 2.
list<STRIDE> Potential Threats.
list<stings >IDS technique.
}

Initiate threat_model.
identify_threats →(UAV system).
analyze_vulnerabilities →(UAV system, threats).
assess_risks →(threats, vulnerabilities)
develop_countermeasures→ (risks)
implement_countermeasures→ (UAV system, countermeasures).
monitor_and_update→ (UAV system).
return threat model.
```

5.3 Explanation of STRIDE threat modeling for UAV system

Below is a *point-wise explanation* of the *pseudocode for the STRIDE threat model* applied to a *UAV system*.

5.3.1 Input: UAV system details

Define the UAV system components: *sensors, communication links, control unit, and actuators*.
Identify the *data flow* between these components.

5.3.2 Define STRIDE threat categories

- *S*poofing: The Attacker impersonates an entity.
- *T*ampering: Unauthorized modification of data.
- *R*epudiation: Denying an action.
- *I*nformation disclosure: Unauthorized access to data.
- *D*enial of Service (DoS): Disrupting UAV operations.
- *E*levation of privilege: Gaining unauthorized access.

5.3.3 Identify threats for each component

Iterate over *each component* (e.g., GPS, IMU, Controller, Wireless Communication).
Check for potential threats under each *STRIDE category*.
Assign risk levels.
For each identified threat, *evaluate impact and likelihood*.
Assign a *risk score* (e.g., High, Medium, Low).

5.3.4 Mitigation strategies

- If *Spoofing detected* → Use cryptographic authentication.
- If Tampering detected → Use data integrity checks (hashing, encryption).
- If *Repudiation detected* → Use logging and non-repudiation mechanisms.
- If *Information Disclosure detected* → Encrypt communication channels.
- If *Denial of Service detected* → Implement intrusion detection and redundancy.
- If *Elevation of Privilege detected* → Enforce access control policies.

5.3.5 Output: Threat assessment report

- Generate a threat matrix mapping components to SRTIDE categories.
- Summarize risk levels and recommended mitigation actions.

6. Case studies

Here are notable *case studies* of cybersecurity issues and solutions in UAV (Unmanned Aerial Vehicle) control and networks [32]. These examples highlight the vulnerabilities, attack methods, and mitigation strategies:

6.1 GPS spoofing attack on UAVs

Case Study

- *Incident*: In 2011, a U.S. RQ-170 Sentinel stealth drone was captured by Iranian forces. The attackers allegedly used GPS spoofing to manipulate the drone into landing in a hostile location.
- *Attack method*: Fake GPS signals were transmitted to the drone, tricking it into believing it was in a different location and guiding it to land in enemy territory.

Key Lessons

- *Vulnerability*: GPS reliance without verification mechanisms.
- *Mitigation*:
    - *Anti-spoofing mechanisms*: Use of encrypted GPS signals or multi-factor location verification (e.g., integrating GPS with inertial navigation systems).
    - *AI-based detection*: AI models can identify anomalies in GPS data, such as sudden or improbable shifts in location.

6.2 Communication link jamming

Case Study

- *Incident*: In 2019, during military exercises, adversaries successfully jammed the communication channels of UAVs, disrupting their operations.
- *Attack method*: Radio Frequency (RF) jamming was used to overload the UAV's communication channels with noise, preventing command and control signals from being transmitted.

Key Lessons

- *Vulnerability*: Lack of robust communication protocols to counter RF interference.
- *Mitigation*:
    - *Frequency Hopping Spread Spectrum (FHSS)*: Switches communication frequencies dynamically to avoid jamming.
    - *AI-based signal analysis*: AI systems can detect and counteract jamming attempts by identifying clean signal paths.

6.3 Malware insertion into UAV firmware

Case Study

- *Incident*: In 2018, researchers demonstrated how a malware-infected firmware update could allow attackers to hijack drones. This proof-of-concept attack showed the risks of unsecured update mechanisms.
- *Attack method*: Attackers inject malicious code into the firmware, granting unauthorized control over UAV systems.

Key Lessons

- *Vulnerability*: Unsecured software update mechanisms.
- *Mitigation*:
    - *Secure boot*: Ensures that only authenticated firmware is executed.
    - *Code signing*: Digitally sign firmware updates to verify authenticity.
    - *AI for malware detection*: Employ AI to analyze firmware for malicious patterns before deployment.

6.4 Denial of service (DoS) on UAV swarm

Case Study

- *Incident*: A simulated attack in 2020 demonstrated how a DoS attack on a UAV swarm disrupted communication between drones, leading to mission failure.
- *Attack method*: Flooding the communication network with excessive traffic to overwhelm the UAV's processors and communication modules.

Key Lessons

- *Vulnerability*: Centralized communication systems for swarm coordination.

- *Mitigation*:
  - *Decentralized control*: Use blockchain or distributed systems for swarm communication.
  - *AI traffic management*: AI models can filter out malicious traffic and prioritize legitimate commands.

6.5 Data interception during UAV missions

Case Study

- *Incident*: In 2021, attackers intercepted sensitive data transmitted between UAVs and ground stations during a reconnaissance mission.
- *Attack method*: Man in the middle (MitM) attack, exploiting weak encryption in the communication link.

Key Lessons

- *Vulnerability*: Lack of strong encryption for UAV data transmissions.
- *Mitigation*:
  - *End-to-end encryption*: Use robust encryption protocols like AES-256 and TLS.
  - *AI-enhanced intrusion detection*: AI models can detect MitM attacks by monitoring unusual communication patterns or delays.

6.6 Insider threat leading to UAV system breach

Case Study

- *Incident*: An insider at a UAV manufacturing firm leaked critical control software, allowing attackers to exploit vulnerabilities and hijack drones.
- *Attack method*: Exploitation of insider access to obtain proprietary information.

Key Lessons

- *Vulnerability*: Insider access without monitoring or restrictions.
- *Mitigation*:
  - *Access control*: Implement role-based access controls and limit access to critical systems.
  - *AI behavior analytics*: Monitor user behavior to detect unusual activities that may indicate insider threats.

6.7 Drone hijacking *via* weak authentication

Case Study

- *Incident*: In 2020, security researchers successfully hijacked a commercial drone by exploiting weak password authentication mechanisms in the drone's control app.
- *Attack method*: Brute-forcing the weak password and gaining control over the UAV.

Key Lessons

- *Vulnerability*: Weak authentication mechanisms in consumer drones.
- *Mitigation*:
    - *Strong authentication*: Require multi-factor authentication for accessing UAV controls.
    - *AI-based user authentication*: Use AI to detect unauthorized login attempts and enforce adaptive security measures.

6.8 Swarm AI adversarial attack

Case Study

- *Incident*: In a research study, adversaries used adversarial machine learning to disrupt the coordination of AI-powered UAV swarms.
- *Attack method*: Feeding adversarial inputs into the swarm's AI models to confuse their decision-making processes.

Key Lessons

- *Vulnerability*: Lack of robustness in AI models against adversarial attacks.
- *Mitigation*:
    - *Robust AI training*: Train AI systems with adversarial examples to improve resilience.
    - *Real-time AI monitoring*: Deploy secondary AI models to monitor and validate decisions made by the primary AI.

7. Conclusion

This book chapter summarizes the various intrusion detection techniques with advantages and disadvantages. The summaries have been presented for the identification of threat actors, and to highlight the descriptions of different IDS techniques, their target points and impacts on UAV control and network. Different case studies of cybersecurity on UAV control and communication networks with attack methods and mitigation schemes are outlined.

Acknowledgements

This work is supported by the research project (project Id 3246) awarded by the Council of Science and Technology, U.P., India.

Author details

Desh Deepak Sharma
Department of Electrical Engineering, MJP Rohilkhand University, Bareilly, India

*Address all correspondence to: desh.sharma@mjpru.ac.in

References

[1] Javaid AY, Sun W, Devabhaktuni VK, Alam M. Cyber security threat analysis and modeling of an unmanned aerial vehicle system. In: 2012 IEEE Conference on Technologies for Homeland Security (HST), Waltham, MA, USA. 2012. pp. 585-590. DOI: 10.1109/THS.2012.6459914

[2] Wei X, Ma J, Sun C. A survey on security of unmanned aerial vehicle systems: Attacks and countermeasures. IEEE Internet of Things Journal. 2024; **11**(21):34826-34847. DOI: 10.1109/JIOT.2024.3429111

[3] Wang D, Cao Y, Lam K-Y, Hu Y, Kaiwartya O. Authentication and key agreement based on three factors and PUF for UAV-assisted post-disaster emergency communication. IEEE Internet of Things Journal. 2024;**11**(11): 20457-20472. DOI: 10.1109/JIOT.2024.3371101

[4] Ji Y, Yu K, Qiu J, Yu J. Massive MIMO and secrecy guard zone based improving physical layer security in UAV-enabled uRLLC networks. IEEE Transactions on Vehicular Technology. 2023;**72**(4): 4553-4567. DOI: 10.1109/TVT.2022.3221866

[5] Lee S, Kang D. Designing simulation logic of UAV cyber operation using cyber security framework. IEEE Access. 2024;**12**:3488-3498. DOI: 10.1109/ACCESS.2023.3349131

[6] Xie H, Zheng J, He T, Wei S, Shan C, Hu C. B-UAVM: A Blockchain-supported secure multi-UAV task management scheme. IEEE Internet of Things Journal. 2023;**10**(24): 21240-21253. DOI: 10.1109/JIOT.2023.3279923

[7] Tian C, Ma J, Li T, Zhang J, Ma C, Xi N. Provably and physically secure UAV-assisted authentication protocol for IoT devices in unattended settings. IEEE Transactions on Information Forensics and Security. 2024;**19**: 4448-4463. DOI: 10.1109/TIFS.2024.3379861

[8] Zhang R, Zhou R, Wang Y, Tan H, He K. Incentive mechanisms for online task offloading with privacy-preserving in UAV-assisted Mobile edge computing. IEEE/ACM Transactions on Networking. 2024;**32**(3):2646-2661. DOI: 10.1109/TNET.2024.3364141

[9] Cui J et al. A practical and provably secure authentication and key agreement scheme for UAV-assisted VANETs for emergency rescue. IEEE Transactions on Network Science and Engineering. 2024; **11**(2):1454-1468. DOI: 10.1109/TNSE.2023.3323972

[10] Li H, Li X, Zhang Z, Hu C, Dunkin F, Ge SS. ESUAV-NI: Endogenous security framework for UAV perception system based on neural immunity. IEEE Transactions on Industrial Informatics. 2024;**20**(1): 732-743. DOI: 10.1109/TII.2023.3271443

[11] Khan MA, Javaid S, Mohsan SAH, Tanveer M, Ullah I. Future-proofing security for UAVs with post-quantum cryptography: A review. IEEE Open Journal of the Communications Society. 2024;**5**:6849-6871. DOI: 10.1109/OJCOMS.2024.3486649

[12] Zhong L, Liu Y, Deng X, Wu C, Liu S, Yang LT. Distributed optimization of multi-role UAV functionality switching and trajectory for security task offloading in UAV-assisted MEC. IEEE Transactions on Vehicular Technology. 2024;**73**(12):19432-19447. DOI: 10.1109/TVT.2024.3434354

[13] Zhi Y, Fu Z, Sun X, et al. Security and privacy issues of UAV: A survey. Mobile Network Application. 2020;**25**: 95-101. DOI: 10.1007/s11036-018-1193-x

[14] Jing HD, Xiao D, Rong QY, et al. A survey on cyber security of unmanned aerial vehicles. Chinese Journal of Computers. 2019;**42**(5):1076-1094

[15] Shahzadi R, Ali M, Khan HZ, Muhammad Naeem. UAV assisted 5G and beyond wireless networks: A survey. Journal of Network and Computer Applications. 2021;**189**:103114, ISSN 1084-8045. DOI: 10.1016/j.jnca.2021.103114

[16] Tang D, Zhang Q. UAV 5G: Enabled wireless communications using enhanced deep learning for edge devices. Wireless Networks. 2024;**30**: 7126-7136. DOI: 10.1007/s11276-023-03589-x

[17] Bai N, Hu X, Wang S. A survey on unmanned aerial systems cybersecurity. Journal of Systems Architecture. 2024; **156**:103282. DOI: 10.1016/j.sysarc.2024.103282. ISSN 1383-7621

[18] Tsao K-Y, Girdler T, Vassilakis VG. A survey of cyber security threats and solutions for UAV communications and flying ad-hoc networks. Ad Hoc Networks. 2022;**133**:102894, ISSN 1570-8705. DOI: 10.1016/j.adhoc.2022.102894

[19] Yaacoub J-PA et al. Cyber-physical systems security: Limitations, issues, and future trends. Microprocessors and Microsystems. 2020;**77**:103201

[20] Strohmeier M, Lenders V, Martinovic I. Intrusion detection for airborne communication using PHY-layer information. In: Almgren M, Gulisano V, Maggi F, editors. Detection of Intrusions and Malware, and Vulnerability Assessment. DIMVA 2015. Lecture Notes in Computer Science(). Vol. 9148. Cham: Springer; 2015. DOI: 10.1007/978-3-319-20550-2_4

[21] Mitchell R, Chen R. Adaptive intrusion detection of malicious unmanned air vehicles using behavior rule specifications. IEEE Transactions on Systems, Man, and Cybernetics. 2014; **44**(5):593-604

[22] Man M, Chen Y, Cai N, Ma G, Wei M. Bio-inspired electrostatic detection method for threat perception in autonomous platforms. IEEE Robotics and Automation Letters. Apr 2025;**10**(4): 3692-3699. DOI: 10.1109/LRA.2025.3539548

[23] Dina AS, Manivannan D. Intrusion detection based on machine learning techniques in computer networks. Internet of Things. 2021;**16**:100462. DOI: 10.1016/j.iot.2021.100462

[24] Mohammed AB, Fourati LC, Fakhrudeen AM. Comprehensive systematic review of intelligent approaches in UAV-based intrusion detection, blockchain, and network security. Computer Networks. 2024;**239**: 110140, ISSN 1389-1286. DOI: 10.1016/j.comnet.2023.110140

[25] Choudhary G, Sharma V, You I, Yim K, Chen I-R, Cho J-H. Intrusion detection Systems for Networked Unmanned Aerial Vehicles: A survey. In: 2018 14th International Wireless Communications & Mobile Computing Conference (IWCMC), Limassol, Cyprus. 2018. pp. 560-565. DOI: 10.1109/IWCMC.2018.8450305

[26] Di B, Gao J, Yi W, Zhu YY, Han Z. Intrusion detection for unmanned aerial systems: A survey. In: Advances in Guidance, Navigation, and Control

ICGNC 2022, Lecture Notes in Electrical Engineering. Singapore: Springer; 2023. p. 845. DOI: 10.1007/978-981-19-6613-2_461

[27] Salamh Fahad E, Umit K, Marcus R. A constructive DIREST security threat modeling for drone as a service. Journal of Digital Forensics, Security and Law. 2021;**16**:2. DOI: 10.15394/jdfsl.2021.1695

[28] Alluhybi WI, Alhazmi OH. Towards a threat model for unmanned aerial vehicles. In: Peng SL, Hsieh SY, Gopalakrishnan S, Duraisamy B, editors. Intelligent Computing and Innovation on Data Science, Lecture Notes in Networks and Systems. Vol. 248. Singapore: Springer; 2021. DOI: 10.1007/978-981-16-3153-5_35

[29] Tufekci B, Tunc C. Vulnerability and threat analysis of UAVs. In: 2021 IEEE/ACS 18th international conference on computer systems and applications (AICCSA), Tangier, Morocco. 2021. pp. 1-2. DOI: 10.1109/AICCSA53542.2021.9686826

[30] Jacobsen RH, Marandi A. Security threats analysis of the unmanned aerial vehicle system. In: MILCOM 2021–2021 IEEE Military Communications Conference (MILCOM), San Diego, CA, USA. 2021. pp. 316-322. DOI: 10.1109/MILCOM52596.2021.9652900

[31] Ficco M, Granata D, Palmieri F, Massimiliano Rak A. Systematic approach for threat and vulnerability analysis of unmanned aerial vehicles. Internet of Things. 2024;**26**:101180, ISSN 2542-6605. DOI: 10.1016/j.iot.2024.101180

[32] Shafik W. Cyber security perspectives in public spaces: Drone case study. In: Cybersecurity Risk in Contemporary Business Systems. IGI Global; 2023. p. 19. DOI: 10.4018/978-1-6684-7207-1.ch004

Chapter 5

Readiness of the Technological Innovation Ecosystem of Medium Altitude Long Endurance Unmanned Aerial Vehicle in Indonesia

Agus Krisnowo, Adhi Dharma Permana, Bagus Anang Nugroho, Mochamad Taufik, Fauzie Dahmir, Guntur Haryanto, Agus Dwiono, Jonathan Prabowo, Irfan Pratama Putra and Jumain Appe

Abstract

Indonesia is currently developing a Medium Altitude Long Endurance Unmanned Aerial Vehicle (MALE UAV). This vehicle is used as a platform to meet the growing need for aerial surveillance in response to increased threats in border areas, terrorism, and the theft of natural resources, such as illegal logging and illegal fishing. This book chapter will discuss the readiness of the technology innovation ecosystem assessed using a national innovation system concept approach, technology innovation readiness, and efforts to increase the local content level (TKDN) of the MALE UAV. The results indicate that several framework conditions still need to be developed, including establishing certification testing institutions. For technology innovation readiness, the findings show that the domestic manufacturing industry is sufficiently prepared for the airframe component, while the Flight Control System (FCS), Ground Control System (GCS), Communication System (CS), and Weapon System (WS) components still require strengthening. Efforts to increase the local content can be pursued by strengthening the industrial structure and engineering design capabilities.

Keywords: ecosystem, innovation, technology, TKDN, MALE UAV

1. Introduction

The use of unmanned aerial vehicles (UAVs) has surged over the past two decades, making them a popular instrument for a wide range of applications. This is evident from numerous publications discussing the development of unmanned aerial vehicles for specific uses and applications, both in terms of onboard hardware and data processing strategies utilizing UAV data. Examples of UAV applications for specific uses include those used in agriculture and forestry [1–3], disaster response [4], building inspections for improved productivity and speed [5–8], structural damage assessment [9], mining areas [10], and geoscience and remote sensing engineering [11]. In the construction industry, UAVs can monitor construction progress and quality control [12–14]. Additionally, there has been development in UAV data processing techniques and specific hardware for UAV spectroscopy [15], path planning [16], and power supply efficiency [17].

Aside from civilian applications, UAVs are also widely used for military purposes. Up until 2015, only the United States, the United Kingdom, and Israel were developing UAVs for military needs, both for defense and attack purposes. However, with rapid technological advances, between 2016 and 2020, other countries successfully developed UAVs for their military needs, including Russia, China, Iran, Azerbaijan, France, Pakistan, Saudi Arabia, the United Arab Emirates, Egypt, Nigeria, and Turkey [18]. Military UAVs are used for surveillance and reconnaissance missions, combat support, troop protection, electronic warfare, precision strikes, training, and testing. Recently, UAVs have evolved from basic reconnaissance tools into versatile and deadly weapons, equipped with sensors and weaponry. The integration of artificial intelligence (AI) and machine learning (ML), enhanced navigation systems, anti-jamming capabilities, and advanced satellite communications allows modern UAVs to conduct precise, silent, radar-evading attack missions like never before. The UAV industry is now valued at several billion dollars per year, with a promising trend for the future, though the largest market share is still in military applications [19].

One type of unmanned aerial vehicle is the Medium Altitude Long Endurance (MALE) type. MALE UAVs are unmanned aerial vehicles that can fly at medium altitudes and remain airborne for extended periods. MALE UAVs serve various functions, such as area surveillance, intelligence gathering, and attack missions [20]. MALE UAVs have several advantages, including carrying larger payloads and flying for extended hours or even days continuously. **Table 1** shows several types of UAVs.

Type of UAV	Altitude	Range
Hand held	<600 m	<2 km
Close	<1500 m	<10 km
NATO	<3000 m	<50 km
Tactical	<5500 m	<160 km
Medium altitude long range	< 9100 m	<200 km
High altitude long range	<9100 m	NA
Hypersonic	<15,200 m	>200 km

Table 1.
Classification of UAV based on altitude and range [20].

In Indonesia, the development of the MALE UAV since 2017 is carried out in collaboration with various agencies, such as the Agency for the Assessment and Application of Technology (BPPT), the Ministry of Defense, the Indonesian Air Force, ITB (Bandung Institute of Technology), PT. Dirgantara Indonesia (PTDI) and PT. LEN Industry. The development of the Medium Altitude Long Endurance Unmanned Aerial Vehicle (MALE UAV) in Indonesia aims to meet the needs for air surveillance and warfare tools. Its existence is increasingly prioritized due to rising threats in border areas, terrorism, smuggling, piracy, and natural resource theft (such as illegal logging and illegal fishing). Several engineering processes have been undertaken, including design, model testing, structural testing, and the maiden flight test. Ideally, Elang Hitam (EH1) was targeted to receive type certification (TC) in 2022 and become a combat-ready version by 2024. However, due to several factors, this target has not yet been achieved.

To accelerate and foster its ecosystem, the design and engineering of the MALE UAV Elang Hitam involve various research and industry institutions according to the required competencies in a consortium. At the time, BPPT was appointed as the coordinator of the consortium, whose members included the Ministry of Defense's R&D, National Institute of Aeronautics and Space (LAPAN), and ITB. In the industry, PT. Dirgantara Indonesia (PTDI) and PT. LEN Industry were involved. PT. Dirgantara Indonesia, as an aircraft manufacturing industry, was chosen as the lead integrator [21]. The main user of the MALE Combat UAV product is the Indonesian Air Force, with plans to incorporate it into Squadron 51 [22]. Another primary user is the Indonesian Navy, which needs it to secure Indonesia's Archipelagic Sea Lanes (ALKI). Aside from defense, the MALE UAV can also be used for Surveillance, Targeting, and Reconnaissance. The operational concept of the Combat MALE UAV can be seen in **Figure 1**. The operation of the MALE UAV involves the MALE UAV vehicle, a Mobile Ground Control, and a UAV Control Console, with communication via Line of Sight (LOS) or Beyond Line of Sight (BLOS).

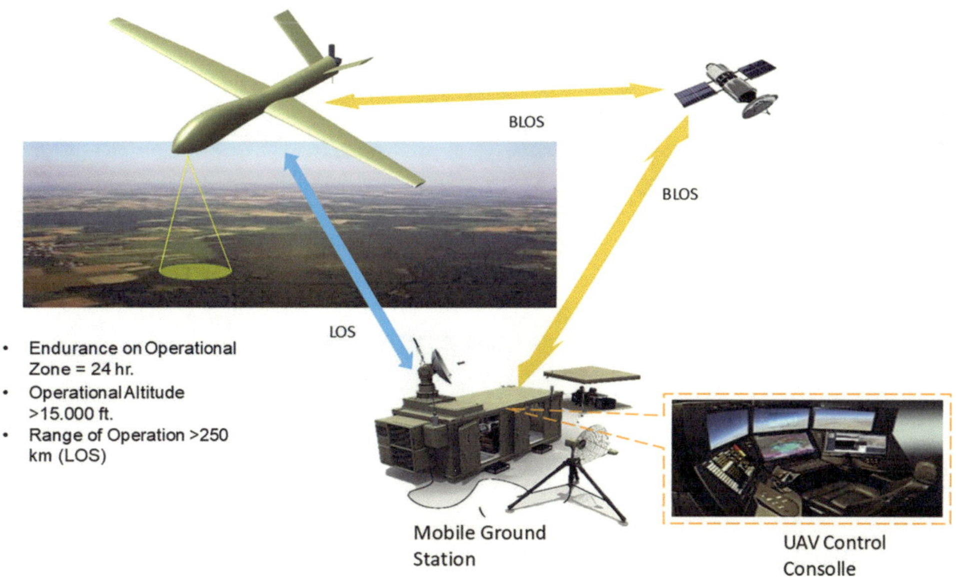

Figure 1.
Operational concept of the MALE UAV.

To master Combat MALE UAV technology, several key technologies must be acquired. It is known that the design and engineering of the Combat MALE UAV are based on operational requirements provided by the Ministry of Defense. Thus, the technical specifications of the Combat MALE UAV are made in Ref. to these operational requirements, which include a weight of up to 1.3 tons, the ability to take off and land on a short 700-meter runway, fly at an altitude of up to 20,000 feet (6000 meters), reach a maximum speed of 235 kilometers per hour, stay airborne for up to 30 hours, and carry a payload of up to 300 kg [23].

1.1 Product breakdown structure (PBS)

The Product Breakdown Structure (PBS) is a diagram that describes a tree of components and subcomponents for the Combat MALE UAV. PBS is used as a tool to analyze the design and engineering process based on the product. The approach taken to develop a PBS may vary between different industries. One reference used in creating the Combat MALE UAV PBS is MIL-STD-881D, which is based on the Work Breakdown Structure (WBS). The differences in PBS are usually only related to the placement of components/subcomponents at different tiers. However, they integrate to form a complete Combat MALE UAV. According to MIL-STD-881D, the PBS for the MALE UAV can be arranged, as shown in **Figure 2** [24].

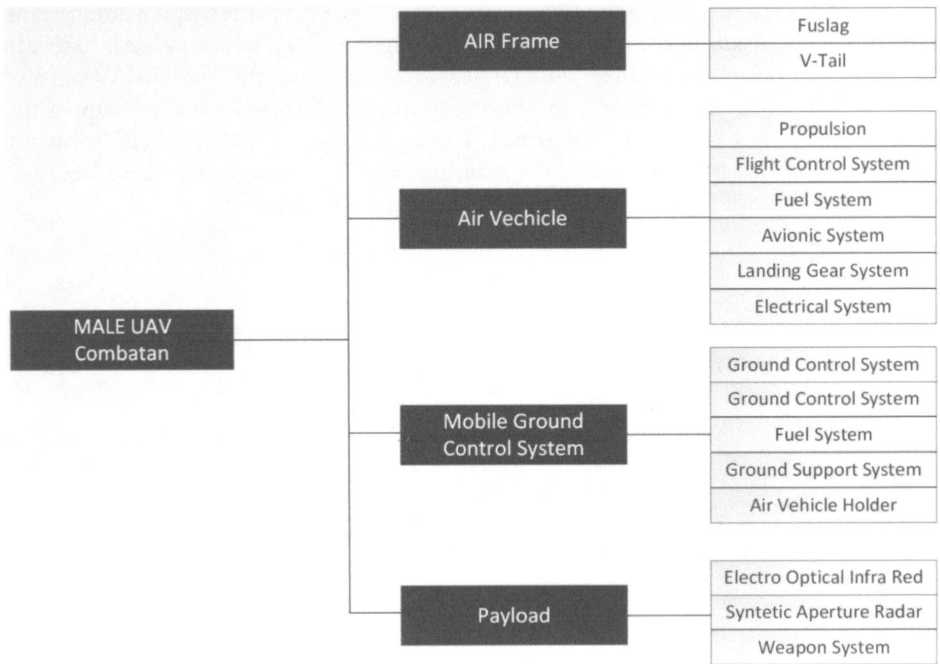

Figure 2.
Product breakdown structure of the combat MALE UAV.

1.2 Critical technology elements (CTEs)

Critical Technology Elements are technologies that significantly influence the success of the development or production of a platform or system that meets operational standard requirements. The Critical Technology Elements of the MALE UAV consist of the following:

1.2.1 Vehicle/air frame

It is the overall structure of the aircraft itself, consisting of the fuselage, wings, and tail. The MALE UAV is generally made from composite materials, with parts that may be detachable or integrated as a single unit. The main components of the vehicle are as follows: fuselage, wing, and *Tail.* The part of the air frame that is critical relates to the composite materials (carbon composite) used in the primary structure, the aerodynamic design of the wing, fuselage, and V-tail to meet operational requirements.

1.2.2 Propulsion system

The propulsion system/motor is also one of the Critical Technology Elements (CTEs) of the MALE UAV. The engine in this case serves as the power source for the aircraft, allowing it to fly at a certain speed. For MALE UAVs, there are several types of propulsion systems, including piston engines, both reciprocating piston engines and rotary piston engines (Wankel) for propeller drive, as well as small turbofan engines adapted to the size of the MALE UAV.

1.2.3 Payload

The payload that the MALE UAV will carry is determined by the mission it is assigned. The payload on the MALE UAV is located in one of the compartments in the fuselage, usually positioned at the front. The type or kind of payload is adapted to the UAV's flight mission, including electronic warfare equipment, electronic reconnaissance equipment, TV/photo cameras, or missiles containing explosive materials. For the Combat MALE UAV, the total allowable payload is 300 kg.

1.2.4 Flight control computer

The flight control computer is the control system located on board the vehicle. This system connects to the Ground Control Station via Line of Sight (LOS) or Beyond Line of Sight (BLOS). Essentially, the MALE UAV is an unmanned vehicle that is controlled remotely through a control system. In this case, the control is carried out by the pilot to manage the movements of the MALE UAV in the air.

1.2.5 Ground control station

The operation of the UAV, whether for launch, flight control, or monitoring all activities related to its mission until it returns and lands, is managed from the ground control station.

1.2.6 Landing gear system

The landing gear system is used during takeoff and landing. The landing gear must be able to support the total weight of the aircraft during parking, taxiing, takeoff, and landing.

1.2.7 Avionic system

Avionics encompasses all electronic flight systems used within the aircraft. Its main systems consist of communication, navigation, and overall system indicators.

1.2.8 Fuel system

The fuel system includes all components related to supplying aviation fuel to the propulsion system/engine.

2. Readiness of the technology innovation ecosystem for MALE UAV

2.1 Innovation ecosystem

Innovation in this context is defined as the result of a process that possesses a degree of novelty and a level of usefulness or success in applying something new. The term 'new' can refer to something that is new to the world, new to a country/nation, or new to a company. In other words, the concept of the innovation system can be defined as a network of institutions in the public and private sectors whose interactions generate new technologies [25]. The innovation system comprises a set of actors who collectively play an important role in influencing innovative performance [26]. The innovation system is also associated with the scope or area of work, such as the national innovation system [27] or sectoral innovation system [28]. Additionally, the term national research and innovation system has emerged [29, 30], which refers to all actors and activities in the economy that are necessary for the occurrence of industrial and commercial innovations leading to economic development. Thus, the innovation ecosystem can be defined as a series of actors, activities, artifacts, institutions, and relationships, including complementary and substitutive relationships, which are crucial for the innovative performance of an actor or a population of actors [31].

The discussion of the innovation system in this chapter will focus more on the national innovation system with a Triple Helix approach [32]. The Triple Helix concept illustrates the importance of interaction among three main actors: Academia, Industry, and Government. The OECD (Organization for Economic Cooperation and Development) defines the national innovation system (NIS) as a network of various institutions in the public and private sectors whose interactions shape a country's ability to disseminate knowledge and technology innovations and influence the overall innovative performance of the country [33]. Companies, such as Boeing, Airbus, and Apple, practice innovation through an open system approach that combines upstream and downstream organizational knowledge resources within their supply chains [34]. It is believed that innovation has evolved from a linear university-based knowledge model (Mode 1) to a non-university-industry knowledge model (Mode 2) [35]. In addition to their supply chain partners, governments, industry associations, universities, and the broader community can also actively participate, collectively forming an innovation ecosystem characterized by multi-level, multi-modal, multi-nodal, multi-lateral features, as well as coexistence, co-evolution, co-specialization, and co-opetition. Mode 3 is known as the university-industry-government-civil society model, or 'quadruple helix' [36]. By involving civil society, the concept of sustainable innovation begins to emerge, in this case, a complex dynamic ecosystem.

In relation to the ecosystem, the technology innovation ecosystem is a collaborative environment that fosters technology-based innovation by integrating various components and stakeholders. This ecosystem encourages the exchange of knowledge and ideas and the development of complementary technologies [37]. It involves many actors, including businesses, research organizations, and end-users, who contribute to achieving purpose-driven innovations [38]. The evolution of the innovation ecosystem benefits from the support of research organizations and the use of specific tools and methods to facilitate service innovation activities [39]. However, successful innovation within this ecosystem requires careful consideration of various risks, including initiative risks, interdependencies, and integration. Companies must assess these risks holistically to develop strong innovation strategies and ensure effective implementation [40]. Technology is vital in driving innovation in this ecosystem, influencing decision-making processes, and enabling mechanisms for knowledge transformation. The concept of the 'innovation ecosystem' is increasingly used to describe a collective of heterogeneous yet complementary organizational actors that together create system-level outputs, similar to 'ecosystem services' facilitated by natural ecosystems and services that transcend the outputs and activities of each individual participant within the ecosystem [41].

In this book chapter, the discussion of the MALE UAV innovation ecosystem will be conducted using the Triple Helix approach, plus end-users. With the Triple Helix approach, the readiness of various elements within the unmanned aerial vehicle (PTTA)/MALE UAV ecosystem, including industrial actors in Indonesia, can be illustrated within the framework of the ecosystem, as shown in **Figure 3**. Recent Triple Helix theory investigates the non-linear relationships between universities, industry, and government for the creation and sharing of knowledge, where industry acts as a source of production, government provides regulations, stability, and ground rules, and universities/research institutions supply new knowledge and technology [43]. The use of the Quadruple Helix approach in the case of the MALE UAV is less appropriate because the understanding of soft issues in the Quadruple Helix ecosystem, such as trust relationships and development, is still limited [44]. These soft factors are considered an integral part of partnership and collaboration strategies that can facilitate the sharing of fundamental resources in the context of a truly open innovation ecosystem, such as Smart City [45].

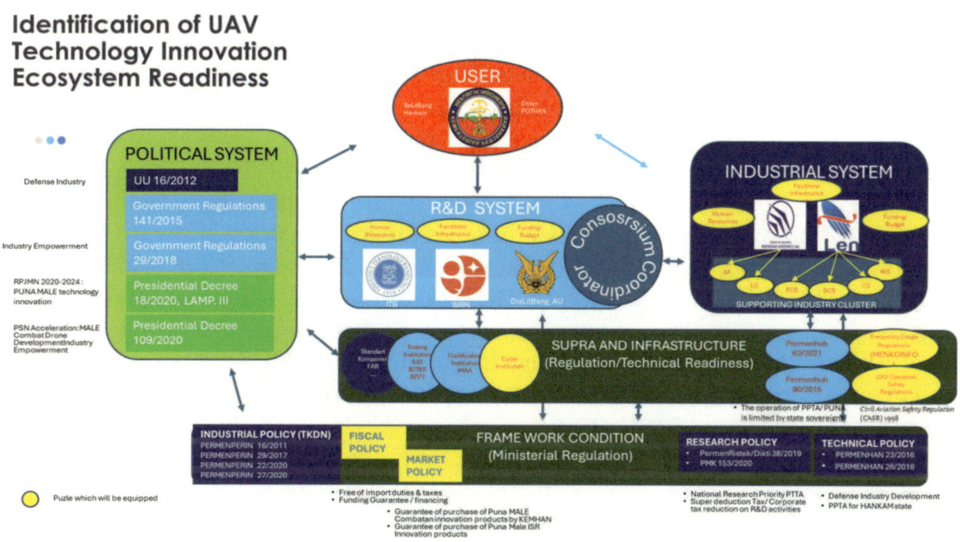

Figure 3.
Readiness of the MALE UAV ecosystem. Source: Agus Krisnowo et al., 2021, Adapted [42].

The Triple Helix innovation system approach, supplemented by the end-user (Customer) component for MALE UAV as illustrated in **Figure 4**, can be outlined as follows:

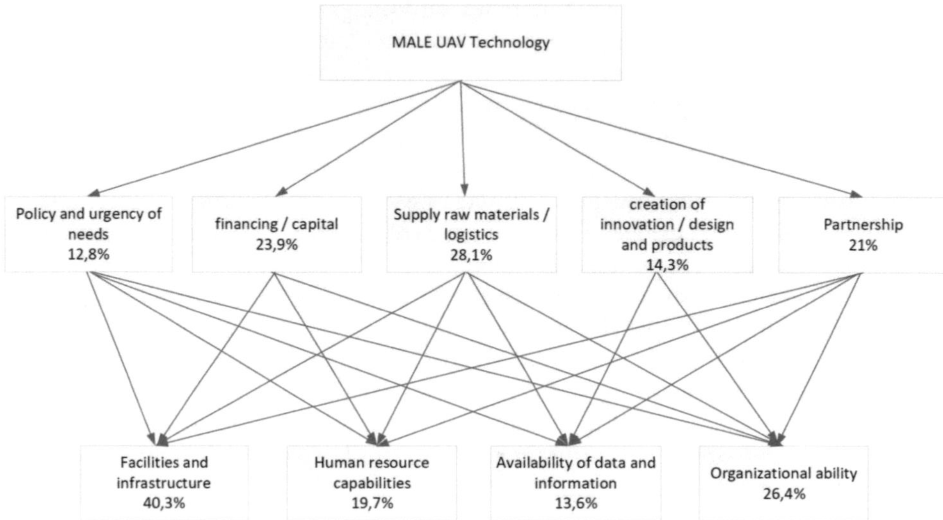

Figure 4.
Hierarchy of priority for MALE UAV technology development.

The Academia (A) component comprises a single or a group of academics/universities/research institutions. In this component, the members consist of the Bandung Institute of Technology (ITB), the Agency for the Assessment and Application of Technology (BPPT), the National Institute of Aeronautics and Space (LAPAN), and the Air Force Research and Development Agency, along with the Defense and Security Research and Development Agency. The two institutions, BPPT and LAPAN, have now merged into the National Research and Innovation Agency (BRIN) [46].

The Business (B) component comprises the industrial system, whose members include PT. Dirgantara Indonesia and PT. LEN Industry.

The Government (G) component consists of various institutions within the political system in the framework of both a super- and infrastructure. In the political system, regulations at the highest levels of government are issued in the form of laws, government regulations, and presidential regulations. The regulations within the Framework Condition are derived from the regulations in the political system and are at the ministerial regulation level, covering aspects of industrial policy, research policy, fiscal policy, and technical policy. In the super- and infrastructure categories, the regulations are at the ministerial or agency level, containing regulations that govern more detailed scopes.

An additional component, the End-User/Customer (C), in this case, is represented by the Ministry of Defense, specifically by the Director-General of Defense Potential. The inclusion of the end-user element here indicates that the innovative products of the MALE UAV must have a market/user to ensure the sustainability of the innovative product continues. To accelerate the achievement of the MALE UAV, goals are accelerated by linking and coordinating all existing sub-ecosystems into a consortium among user institutions, research institutions, and industries. The division of tasks and roles in the development of the Combat MALE UAV is carried out by breaking down the work structure (Work Breakdown Structure), so that all tasks are completely divided into work packages carried out by the relevant units within the consortium.

2.2 Readiness of the innovation ecosystem

The analysis of the innovation ecosystem readiness using the ABG-C (Aeronautical, Biological, Geological, and Chemical) approach indicates that most of the subsystems are sufficiently fulfilled, although some subsystems that still require further study regarding their readiness (indicated by yellow circular blocks in **Figure 3**). Some of these subsystems include the framework condition, where there are still no specific market policy regulations concerning innovative product outcomes. This will impact the economic scale of product development. Several elements that support the readiness of the MALE UAV technology innovation ecosystem are identified, including the following: (i) Political System (Governance), (ii) Academic Research System, (iii) Industrial System, (iv) Framework Condition, (v) Supra- and Infrastructure, and (vi) End-User/Customers. They can be described as follows:

2.2.1 Political system (governance)

The sustainability of a research and innovation program is heavily influenced by government/state policies. In relation to MALE UAVs, the government has generally issued several regulations that support the development of unmanned aircraft. Based on the existing legal framework, there is currently Law No. 16/2012 concerning Defense Industry, Government Regulation (PP) 147/2015 on the Management of the Defense Industry and PP 29/2018 on Empowerment of the Industry. These three pieces of legislation generally encourage the empowerment of the national industry in the procurement of goods and services, including procurement for the national defense system [47–49].

Reflecting on the experience of U.S. arms embargoes in 1991 and 1999 and the European Union (EU) in 1999, which paralyzed Indonesia's armament system [50], the importance of self-reliance in the defense industry, including the MALE Combat UAV industry, has become evident. Self-reliance in the defense industry in Indonesia refers to the Minister of Defense's Decision No. KEP/104/M/I/2020, as a derivative of Law No. 16 of 2012 and Government Regulation (PP) No. 141 of 2015, aimed at achieving a strong, independent, and highly competitive national defense industry that can support advancements in defense and security technology in accordance with contemporary developments.

The priority for the development of the MALE UAV defense industry is reflected in several regulations, such as Presidential Regulation No. 109 of 2020 regarding the Acceleration of Strategic Project Implementation, the Minister of Defense's Decision No. KEP/104/M/I/2020 on National Defense Policy, and the Minister of Research, Technology, and Higher Education Regulation No. 38 of 2019 on National Research Priorities 2020–2024. Industry self-reliance is achieved through industrial empowerment as provided by PP No. 29 of 2018, which increases the use of domestic products (Article 54) with indicators for increasing the Domestic Component Level (TKDN) (Article 56). This was followed by the issuance of Presidential Regulation 18/2020, LAMP III related to the 2020–2024 National Medium-Term Development Plan (RPJMN) regarding MALE UAV technology innovation and Presidential Regulation 109/2020 on the Acceleration of the National Strategic Project for the Development of MALE Combat Drones. Thus, politically, the regulatory readiness is quite strong; however, the current study hypothesis suggests that additional regulations related to budgetary political systems are needed [51–55].

2.2.2 Academic-research system

The definition of 'research and experimental development' (R&D) according to the OECD is: creative work undertaken systematically to increase knowledge and use that knowledge to devise new applications [56]. It also recommends promoting technology transfer between companies and research institutions carried out to enhance and expand knowledge—including knowledge about humanity, culture, and society—and to create new ways to apply the available knowledge. As stated by Ankrah et al. [57], companies should be encouraged to build close relationships with academic institutions to gain various benefits, including technology transfer. In Indonesia, regulations related to research and development are included in the National Science and Technology System Law, which positions science and technology as assets that serve as the foundation for national development investment (Articles 5 and 6). This new law establishes the formation of a National Endowment Fund for Research, Development, Assessment, and Application (Article 62). The National Science and Technology System Law also includes several new provisions, including those regarding the Master Plan for Advancing Science and Technology (Article 8); concerning Inventions and Innovations (Articles 34–38); and provides tax incentives for businesses that allocate part of their income for research and development activities (Article 89) [58]. In relation to the development of MALE UAVs, several research collaborations have been carried out between universities and research institutions. Each has specific roles and contributions according to their core competencies and coordinates when discussing systematically. This is in line with the knowledge system model as a holistic conceptualization that establishes, for a country, a collection of institutions and knowledge actors and describes the interconnections among them [59].

The research and development institutions currently involved in the consortium are LAPAN, ITB, the Air Force Research and Development Agency, and BPPT, which also serves as the consortium's coordinator. As of September 1st of 2021, the institutions LAPAN and BPPT (along with two other institutions such as LIPI (Indonesian Institute of Sciences) and BATAN (National Nuclear Energy Agency)) are merged into the National Research and Innovation Agency (BRIN) by Presidential Decree No. 78/2021. As previously stated, the development activities are carried out using the Work Breakdown Structure (WBS) concept, so all tasks will be fully allocated among all elements of the Work Packages (WPs), in accordance with the roles and responsibilities of the consortium members and/or through external parties. The needs for Human Resources (HR) and budget in the development of the MALE UAV are addressed through the structure of the WBS. The extent of HR availability within research institutions to support the MALE Combat UAV program is currently under verification, and initial identification of HR needs using the WBS approach will be discussed in the subsection on developing and strengthening the MALE UAV innovation ecosystem.

2.2.3 Industrial system

Broadly speaking, the product breakdown structure for the MALE UAV consists of six subsystems, namely Air Frame Design & Analysis (AF), Landing Gear (LG), Flight Control System (FCS), Mobile Ground Control Station (GCS), Communication System (CS), and Weapon System (WS).

The industries currently involved in the consortium include PT. Dirgantara Indonesia and PT. LEN Industry. PT. Dirgantara Indonesia serves as the lead integrator for the MALE UAV, as well as the manufacturer of the airframe components, including design and analysis, in collaboration with ITB and BPPT. It is known that PT. Dirgantara Indonesia has more than 40 years of experience in:

- Engineering work packages for new product development, product testing and certification, reverse engineering development, etc.

- Designing and manufacturing tools and jigs.

- Detailed part manufacturing, metal forming/fabricated parts, composite components, bonding components, etc.

- Subassembly, major assembly, and final assembly.

In addition, PT. Dirgantara Indonesia has successfully developed the Wulung UAV, which is remotely controlled both manually and automatically. It uses composite materials and is powered by a pusher-type single-piston engine, equipped with a single Ground Control Station as central control. Wulung UAV is capable of performing ISR (Intelligence, Surveillance, and Reconnaissance), with a maximum endurance of 4 hours and a radius of operation of 120 km.

Meanwhile, PT. LEN Industry is tasked with developing and producing the Flight Control System (FCS), Ground Control Station (GCS), and communication systems. PT. LEN Industry, a defense electronic industry, mainly focuses on C4ISR (Command, Control, Communications, Computer, Intelligence, Surveillance, and Reconnaissance). PT. LEN Industry independently develops defense products and collaborates with strategic partners to meet the needs of Indonesia's primary weapon systems (alutsista). However, due to limitations in human resources and budget, as well as the target for the maiden flight, the development of the Flight Control Computer (FCC), GCS, and communication/avionic systems will be carried out in stages, initially through technology transfer. This equipment will temporarily be procured/imported. In parallel, PT. LEN Industry is also working on technology transfer for the Flight Control Computer. Open innovation is considered an effective way to achieve sustainable innovation through collaboration and stakeholder engagement. Open innovation is built on well-defined industry sectors or products. From industry observations, open platforms can be initiated by large companies with established resources, such as recognized brands and markets. They can easily attract potential external partners for knowledge exchange. Therefore, to accelerate the technology transfer process in the FCC, GCS, communication systems, avionics, payload systems, and combat systems, steps need to be taken to strengthen the industrial structure. One important step is to build industrial clusters that can support the design and manufacturing processes of the MALE COMBAT UAV. Discussions regarding potential industries expected to support the development program of the MALE UAV will be addressed in the subsection on strategies to increase the domestic content level (TKDN).

2.2.4 Framework condition (microregulations that can facilitate the MALE UAV program)

The initial identification of regulations related to the development of MALE UAVs includes regulations for unmanned aircraft for national defense through Minister of Defense Regulation No. 26/2016 on the Unmanned Aircraft System for National

Defense and Security Tasks, which includes classifications of Unmanned Aircraft Systems (micro, mini, small, medium, and large). This regulation can serve as a basis for developing combat MALE UAVs [60].

Minister of Industry Regulation No. 16/2011 on Domestic Component Level (TKDN) contains the provisions and procedures for calculating the Domestic Component Level, and Minister of Industry Regulation No. 22/2020 on the provisions and procedures for calculating TKDN for digital products. Both of these regulations can be used as references in reviewing the strategy for calculating TKDN, specifically for MALE UAV products [61, 62].

Regulation PMK No. 153/PMK.010/2020 concerns the Granting of Gross Income Reductions for Research and Development Activities, Super Deduction Tax [63]. This regulation aims to encourage taxpayers to engage in R&D activities, as the R&D budget has mostly been funded by the government through the state budget (APBN). Article 2 states: Taxpayers conducting certain research and development activities in Indonesia may be granted a reduction in gross income of up to 300% of the amount spent on certain research and development activities in Indonesia that are charged over a specified period. Therefore, industries involved in the development of MALE UAVs are recommended to utilize the Super Deduction Tax for R&D, in accordance with the provisions of Government Regulation (PP) No. 45/2019. This facility is granted to domestic corporate taxpayers.

Analysis of the framework condition shows that several existing regulations can be used to promote the development of MALE UAVs. However, further examination is needed to determine whether additional regulations are required to facilitate the MALE UAV program and address other existing obstacles.

2.2.5 Supra- and infrastructure (other supporting institutions or technical regulations)

Support from supra- and infrastructure, relating to the readiness of technical regulations or technical institutions, is crucial, starting from the design process to product certification and even during product marketing. Some institutions involved include:

2.2.5.1 Testing institutions for MALE UAV

Testing institutions can conduct component subsystem and system testing, ranging from model scale to prototype scale. Aerodynamic model testing can be carried out at the Indonesia Low-Speed Tunnel (ILST) BRIN, while structural testing can be done at the BRIN construction testing laboratory. Additional testing institutions, such as those related to the security of MALE UAV communication systems (Cybersecurity), may be needed. The security of UAV communication systems is critical because if communication uses insecure channels, the transmitted data can be intercepted or even manipulated. Therefore, a reliable and secure communication channel is necessary. This regulation does not seem to be specifically regulated in Indonesia. Two types of standards need to be considered for the safety and security of UAVs, including Process Standards and Coding Standards.

Process standards describe the development process that must be followed to ensure that the final product is written in a safe manner (DO-178) or in a guaranteed manner (ISO 14508). Coding standards describe a subset of high-level programming languages that ensure the software is written as securely as possible (MISRA C) and as safely as possible (CERT C).

Safety is particularly essential in UAV development, but a UAV can only be considered safe if it cannot be controlled by hostile intruders. ISO 14508 (also known as the 'Common Criteria' referring to the source document) is an international process-oriented standard that defines the requirements for information technology security. These requirements are categorized according to seven Evaluation Assurance Levels (EALs). Functional security requirements include auditing, communication, cryptography, data protection, authentication, security management, privacy, and Target of Evaluation (TOE) protection.

2.2.5.2 Product certification institutions

Many countries have enacted laws to regulate the use of UAVs for various types of users. These regulations have evolved alongside advances in UAV technology. Some countries have established certification bodies to certify the use of UAVs in their airspace. Certification for Manned or Unmanned Aircraft is required in aviation regulations. This certification also indicates that the developed aircraft meets the standards and is fit for production. Airplane certificates are issued by the airworthiness regulatory bodies, which is called the Directorate of Airworthiness and Aircraft Operations (DKPPU) in Indonesia. In the United States, the corresponding body is the Federal Aviation Administration (FAA); in the UK, the Civil Aviation Authority (CAA); and in Germany, the Luftfahrt Bundesamt (LBA). Currently, unmanned aircraft certification can only be conducted by the Indonesian Military Airworthiness Authority (IMAA). This is due to DKPPU's lack of experience in certifying unmanned aircraft and its greater focus on certifying transport aircraft [64].

2.2.5.3 Regulations related to UAV safety and operations

Most countries are currently grappling with regulatory issues related to unmanned aerial vehicles concerning public safety. When an aircraft is designed, built, and certified for flight, it must comply with applicable regulations, such as those regarding the existing airspace. This depends on the aircraft's certification type and the equipment it contains. The equipment requirements in an aircraft are intended to assist air traffic controllers in directing and separating aircraft from one another. Along with the required equipment, there are regulations that pilots of those vehicles must adhere to. Any aircraft wishing to fly in controlled airspace must be airworthy and must comply with the design, safety, maintenance, and operational regulations applicable in that country. A lack of guidelines, policies, standards, and published regulations will affect UAV operations in civil airspace.

For UAVs to be allowed to take off and land at manned airfields in populated areas, safety and reliability evidence must be provided by the UAV manufacturer. Therefore, manufacturers must avoid taking off overpopulated areas during test flights and look for suitable and commonly used takeoff and landing locations for experimental UAVs. The airfield must be selected so that the takeoff flight path is free from human habitation over the sea or uninhabited areas. Once operations are proven safe and airworthiness certification is granted, UAVs can then operate from other airfields.

The Chicago Convention 25 is a foundation that has been updated and translated through various editions. Although the Chicago Convention 25 does not specifically refer to UAVs, it does make provisions for unmanned aircraft [65]. The FAA is the leading authority in the world regarding the regulation of aircraft and airspace, and many countries base their regulations on FAR. The FAA Flight Plan 2004–200,830 states that one of its goals is to develop policies, procedures, and approval processes to allow the operation of unmanned aerial vehicles. Indonesia currently has regulations related to the operation of unmanned aerial vehicles, namely Minister of Transportation Regulation No. PM 63 of 2021 concerning Civil Aviation Safety Regulation Part 107 on Small Unmanned Aircraft Systems and Minister of Transportation Regulation No. 37 of 2020. These regulations govern the operation of unmanned aircraft (drones) in Indonesia. These regulations replace Minister of Transportation Regulation No. 47 of 2016 and No. 180 of 2015 [66].

2.2.6 End-users/customers

The current users of Combat MALE UAVs are the Ministry of Defense, specifically the Air Force, which is responsible for securing the territory of the Republic of Indonesia through air routes. Other agencies or institutions may also use combat MALE UAVs for territorial security or specific purposes.

2.3 Development and strengthening of the MALE UAV innovation ecosystem

To strengthen the current innovation ecosystem and recommend planning for the development of MALE UAV technology in the future, steps need to be taken based on priority scales. The analysis will use the Analytic Hierarchy Process (AHP) method, involving respondents selected from experts who are knowledgeable and understand the capabilities for the development of MALE UAV technology. There are four aspects of technology components used: Facilities and Infrastructure (Technoware), Human Resource Capabilities (Humanware), Availability of Data and Information (Infoware), and Organizational Capability (Orgaware), which are compared with five variables that serve as important alternative choices: Policy and urgency of needs, financing/capital, logistics/supply of raw materials, creation of innovations (design and products), and partnership networks.

The AHP decision-making method breaks down a complex problem into a hierarchical structure with multiple levels consisting of objectives, criteria, subcriteria, and alternative strategies. The AHP method was first developed by Saaty [67] to measure the relative priorities of a given set according to an appropriate scale of values. The assessment scale is set from values of 1–9, as shown in **Table 2**. Decisions are usually based on individual perceptions that should make the final decision and assess priorities, emphasizing the importance of consistency and the correlation of alternatives that have been compared throughout the decision-making process. The intensity of the

Comparison	Rating scale
A is equally important as B	1
A is slightly more important than B	3
A is more important than B	5
A is significantly more important than B	7
A is absolutely more important than B	9
Value in between two adjacent opinions	2, 4, 6, 8

Table 2.
Guidelines for assessment in the AHP method.

contribution of technology components is obtained from the respondents' assumptions regarding the importance level of the Technoware, Humanware, Infoware, and Orgaware components. For weighting the research results, the Pairwise Comparison Scale (AHP) will be used to assess the comparison of the importance level of one element with another [68]. The assessment of the intensity of contribution for each technology component is facilitated using Expert Choice Software. Expert Choice is a Decision Support System (DSS) application that can assist in making decisions with multiple criteria and evaluating alternative preferences using the AHP method.

The assessment of the intensity of contribution is used to determine the priority for developing technology components. Determining the priority for developing technology components is based on objectives, criteria, and subcriteria arranged in an AHP hierarchical structure. The four technology components are:

- Technoware is defined as physical facilities that enhance human strength and capability in producing products and services.
- Humanware is defined as the individuals who possess skills or expertise, without which technoware would be useless.
- Infoware is defined as written or electronic documents that enable humanware to acquire information and learn more quickly.
- Orgaware is defined as implemented procedures and organizational structures that coordinate resources and activities to achieve objectives.

By using the Expert Choice tools, the weighting process for criteria and subcriteria in the technology components yields the following graph of priority for the development of domestically produced MALE UAV technology:

Table 3 shows that based on the five criteria, the order of criteria from the lowest to the highest in the development of MALE UAV is the Urgency of Need factor (12.8%), the Innovation Creation factor (14.3%), the Partnership factor (21%), the Financial/Funding factor (23.9%), and the highest factor is the Supply of Raw Materials (28.1%). **Table 4** reflects the ranking based on the priority of components, considering all the selected criteria. Among the four technological components, the priority of technological components from the lowest to the highest is the Availability of Data and Information (Infoware), Human Resource Capability (Humanware), Organizational Capability (Orgaware), and the Capability of Facilities and Infrastructure (Technoware). The Technoware component remains the top priority at 40.3%. In conclusion, the results of the hierarchical diagram, along with the weight values of the criteria obtained from the priority of MALE UAV technology development, are presented.

Supply of raw materials	**28,1%**
Financial/funding factor	23,9%
Partnership factor	21,0%
Innovation creation factor	14,3%
Urgency of need factor	12,8%

Table 3.
The order of criteria.

Facilities and infrastructure	**40,3%**
Organizational capability	26,4%
Human resource capability	19,7%
Availability of data and information	13,6%

Table 4.
The priority of components.

Based on the criteria of policy and urgency of needs, financing/capitalization, supply of raw materials, innovation creation, and partnership, the overall priority of components from the highest to the lowest is as follows: the capability of facilities and infrastructure (40.3%), organizational capability (26.4%), human resource capability (19.7%), and availability of data and information (13.6%). Thus, the facilities and infrastructure capability component is the primary and foremost priority in the current development of MALE UAV. **Figure 4** shows the Priority Hierarchy of MALE UAV Technology Development.

3. Readiness of MALE UAV technology and key technology acquisition strategies

Technology readiness is the level of maturity or readiness of a technology to be adopted by users. The technology readiness level is measured using a measurement system known as the Technology Readiness Level (TRL). It is well known that unmanned aircraft integrate various advanced technologies, requiring interdisciplinary approaches in their development process. Even today, the technology continues to evolve for meeting civilian and military needs. This is evident from the many innovative developments in unmanned vehicles, whether they are still in the conceptual or testing phases or have already been directly applied in the field, including military applications.

Many components in the design and engineering process of current combat MALE UAVs still rely on foreign technologies. Therefore, technology transfer is necessary, especially for key technologies, so that Indonesia can become more self-reliant in developing combat MALE UAVs in the future. The importance of self-sufficiency in the defense industry is illustrated by Turkey, where the combat MALE drone Bayraktar TB2 has proven successful in battles against Armenia, leading to supply embargoes on its production components. For instance, the Canadian company Rotax announced in October 2020 that it would halt engine supplies, and Andair Ltd., a UK company that has been supplying fuel systems, would also stop shipments of its components to Turkey [69]. According to the same source, the production phase of the Bayraktar TB2 reportedly continues to run normally post-embargo, with the Bayraktar TB2 now using domestically produced engines, specifically the PD170 made by TEI (Tusaş Engine Industries Inc.) and utilizing similar domestic fuel system components. It has been reported that Baykar Savunma has designed a much more advanced check valve.

Therefore, it is essential to implement a phased strategy for the acquisition and development of key technologies for combat MALE UAVs in Indonesia. Identifying technology readiness and industrial readiness can be conducted using the Technology Readiness Level (TRL) and Manufacturer Readiness Level (MRL) approaches. The results of TRL and MRL measurements can serve as criteria for analyzing technology acquisition stages. The initial preliminary technology and industry readiness identification for combat MALE UAVs can be seen in **Figure 5**.

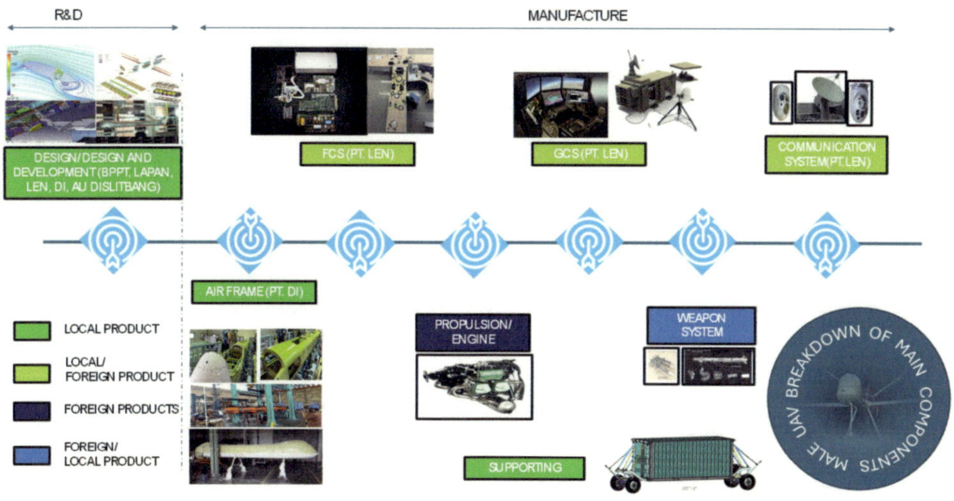

Figure 5.
Identification of technology and industry readiness for combat MALE UAVs. Source: Agus Krisnowo et al. 2021, Adapted [42, 70].

Based on the results of the technology readiness identification, along with several criteria that will be determined (for example, the security of the component supply chain/embargo), the sequence/stages of key technologies that must be mastered first can be established. Determining the order of technology acquisition stages has not yet been carried out due to human resources and budget limitations. One of the analyses for determining the sequence can use the AHP (Analytic Hierarchy Process) method to select the priority scale of which key technologies will be acquired first.

4. Domestic content level/local content (TKDN)

Domestic content is calculated based on the value/cost used in the production of a product based on labor/materials/components/services that will be utilized [71].

$$Local\ Content\,(\%) = \frac{(Total\ Product\ Value - Imported\ Content)}{Total\ Product\ Value} x\, 100\% \quad (1)$$

This calculation will be based on the products (goods, services, and works) according to the components/materials/services where the country has a comparative advantage. The factors influencing the ability to meet domestic content policy objectives can be characterized in four categories: (i) Market size and stability, (ii) Policy design and coherence, (iii) Limitations of domestic content requirements, and (iv) Depth of industrial structure, size, and stability, which will affect the continuity of the production process of domestic producers [72]. Suppose the domestic market is small or unstable and cannot absorb the products produced by domestic producers. In that case, they risk going out of business, thus undermining job creation or technology transfer objectives. Regulatory design and policy coherence must also be aligned to avoid contradictions and overlaps that could cause confusion during implementation. Similarly, if there are no credible domestic industries and the industrial structure is weak, any domestic content policy will not be able to sustain the existence of such industries.

Therefore, policymakers must deeply understand the resource supply chains and domestic capacity to supply the industry [73]. This deep understanding includes the ability to have deep knowledge of whether domestic suppliers can provide competitive materials and components, whether domestic skills are available to perform the tasks needed by the industry, the size of the procurement market (and at what stage of the project life cycle), and the accessibility of project locations. Thus, every domestic content policy must be based on information regarding domestic resource readiness, so it can provide useful support to achieve development goals. The components considered in assessing the achievement of domestic content, or what is better known as the Domestic Content Level (TKDN) of a product, are currently still limited to components related to production costs in the production process of a product. These components are Raw Material & Component Cost, Raw Material Related Service Cost, Direct Labor Cost, Direct Labor Related Service Cost, Indirect Labor Cost, Direct Factory Cost, Indirect Factory Cost, and Indirect Factory Service Cost [61].

4.1 Local content MALE UAV (EH1B)

As stated earlier, most components of the MALE Combat UAV are sourced from imports, including the technology. The current method of calculating the Domestic Content Level (TKDN) still uses a 'cost-based' concept, where all components are calculated based on the costs incurred. Therefore, if the TKDN value of the MALE Combat UAV (EH1) is calculated based on the existing regulations (Ministry of Industry Regulation 16/2011), the results can be seen in **Table 5** (Self-assessment).

Supplier of good and services	:	**PT. DIRGANTARA INDONESIA**
Address	:	JL. PAJAJARAN NO 154 BANDUNG
Production result	:	MALE UAV
Product type	:	EH 1 B

Description		**Cost (USD)**			**Local Content level %**
		Local content %	**Foreign content %**	**Total %**	
I. Direct Material					
1	Raw materials for direct materials	8.25%	91.75%	100%	8.25%
2	Raw material for other related costs	100%	0%	100%	100%
II. Direct labor					
1	Direct labor	100%	0%	100%	100%
2	Direct labor for other related costs	100%	0%	100%	100%
III. Factory overhead					
1	Indirect labor	100%	0%	100%	100%
2	Owned machines	0%	0%	0%	0%
3	Rented machines	0%	0%	0%	0%
4	Other related indirect costs	100%	0%	100%	100%
Production cost		38.34%	61.66%	100%	**38.34%**

Table 5.
Self-assessment of domestic local content MALE UAV.

This self-assessment calculation shows that the raw material inputs are still predominantly sourced from foreign sources, with a value of 92%. Overall, this contributes 61.66% to the total MALE UAV product. As a result, the TKDN of the MALE UAV is only about 38.34%. Efforts to increase TKDN can be implemented through two strategies: first, by changing the calculation method, and second, by strengthening the industrial structure.

4.1.1 Strategy I

4.1.1.1 Intangible products are assessed

Currently, the calculation of TKDN products is still based on cost, so that intangible research and development products, such as design engineering, intellectual property rights, and innovation products, have not been assessed. If the TKDN calculation includes elements of brainware/intangible research and development products, then the TKDN value of the MALE combat UAV is predicted to increase by approximately 50%.

4.1.2 Strategy II

4.1.2.1 Building an industrial cluster system

From the technology innovation ecosystem diagram shown in **Figure 4**, it can be seen that there are core industries in the industrial system section, namely PT. Dirgantara Indonesia and PT. LEN Industry. Below them, there are components of the MALE combat UAV that can be supported by domestic supporting industries. Potential local industries that are expected to contribute include:

1. PT. CMI Teknologi Bandung

   PT. CMI Teknologi Bandung operates in the field of Radio frequency (RF) and Microwave technology, including Radar, Satellite Communication, and Terrestrial Radio, along with its derivatives. Specifically, PT. CMI Teknologi Bandung develops products, such as satellite telecommunications, terrestrial radio products for both civilian and military use, and information technology (IT) products for control systems. The proposed involvement of PT. CMI in the MALE Combat UAV Program is for the development of the communication system.

2. PT. Hariff Daya Tunggal engineering Bandung

   PT. Hariff (HDTE) operates in the fields of electronic engineering, hardware, and software for defense systems, telecommunications technology, and energy systems. PT. Hariff positions itself as a telecommunication turnkey solution provider; thus, most of Hariff's business is project-based. Currently, HDTE has become one of the largest supporters for all telecommunications providers in Indonesia and has expanded into several new businesses, such as Power Systems (Solar Panels, Generators, Rectifiers, Batteries), and Defense & Military Systems in joint projects with Pindad and the Indonesian National Armed Forces (Radar Systems, BMS (Building Management Systems), Drones, etc.). The proposed involvement of PT. Hariff in the MALE Combat UAV Program is for the development of the Weapon System.

3. PT. Infoglobal Teknologi Semesta Surabaya Indonesia

   PT. Infoglobal Teknologi Semesta, a technology-based state-owned enterprise Privately Owned Enterprise (Badan Usaha Milik Swasta/BUMS), operates in the field of electronics engineering, specifically in data processing for avionics systems (electronic systems covering Communication, Navigation, and Indicators/Radar, C2, and aircraft system management). PT. Infoglobal has obtained Defense Industry Licenses and Defense Equipment Production Licenses from the Indonesian Ministry of Defense sequentially through License Letter No: SP/32/VIII/2016/DJ POT and License Letter No: SI PROD/13/VIII/2016/DJ POT. Specifically, PT. Infoglobal develops products, such as military aircraft telecommunications (avionics) and information technology (IT) for C2 (Command & Control) systems. The proposed involvement of PT. Infoglobal in the MALE Combat UAV Program is for the development of an avionic system.

5. Anticipated future applications of MALE UAVs by Indonesia

In 2019, Indonesia imported six medium altitude long endurance (MALE) UAVs from China Aerospace Science and Technology Corporation (CASC). Its operational radius ranges from 1500 to 2000 km and can be controlled via SatCom. Indonesia then armed the Unmanned Aerial Combat System (UACS) with Chinese-made AR-2 air-to-surface precision-guided ammunition with a 1.5–8 km range [74]. The six MALE-type CH4 aircraft are currently stationed in two locations, namely Pontianak and the Natuna Islands. All MALE-type UAVs are operated under the control of the Indonesian Air Force. With the addition of the MALE CH4 UAV, the Indonesian Air Force has two squadrons of MALE UAVs. The first is the 51st Air Squadron at Supadio Pontianak Air Base, West Kalimantan, which operates Aerostar drones. Second, the 52nd Air Squadron at Raden Sadjad Air Base, Natuna Islands, which operates CH4 drones [75]. If Indonesia succeeds in developing the MALE UAV, this innovative product will be combined to support Squadron 51 of CH4 UAVs.

With the advancement of technology, UAV operating systems can now be equipped with satellite technology, allowing pilots to control the aircraft even beyond the horizon. This capability is known as Beyond Visual Line of Sight (BVLOS). UAVs utilizing BVLOS technology have the ability to fly outside the pilot's direct line of sight [76]. Currently, the Indonesian government is ordering several Medium Altitude Long Endurance (MALE) UAVs equipped with BLOS technology to enhance the country's defense system. Two Turkish-made drones, the ANKA produced by Turkish Aerospace and the Bayraktar TB2 manufactured by Baykar, are expected to strengthen the Indonesian Air Force. The Turkish drones are scheduled to be stationed in Natuna, where they will replace the CH4 UAV, which will be relocated to Pontianak. In Pontianak, the aircraft will be repurposed for training [75].

The acquisition of various MALE UAVs is anticipated to accelerate technology transfer through the Offsets (OFSET) scheme, which requires compensation related to the purchase of products. This scheme allows for the establishment of a Technology Transfer Agreement (TOT) as a condition for purchasing UAV products. Indonesia is leveraging this scheme, with PT. Dirgantara Indonesia (PTDI) designated as the domestic industry responsible for producing UAVs [74].

An important outcome of this preliminary study is the need for intensive coordination among consortium members regarding potential industries that can contribute to supplying some of the needed materials and components of the male combat UAV. This can be done by collaborating in developing male combat UAVs in Indonesia. Intensive coordination among consortium team members is essential in optimizing and synergizing all available resources in Indonesia.

6. Conclusion

In conclusion, the following can be summarized from this discussion:

1. From the perspective of the national innovation system, the government's UAV MALE program is quite strong due to regulatory support from the law, government regulations, presidential regulations, and ministerial regulations.

2. From the academic side, UAV development has involved universities and several research institutions. However, the involvement of universities needs to be increased, especially to support FCS, GCS, CS, and WS. Each has different tasks and roles but supports one another.

3. The business/industry side is currently not very strong because, based on PBS, the participation of domestic industry in the development of MALE UAV Combat parts has not been clearly identified.

4. Equally important is the existence of customers/users of UAVs that can be utilized for surveillance, targeting, and reconnaissance. UAV users for these purposes are not only the Ministry of Defense but also other ministries responsible for territorial surveillance, natural resources, and disaster management. Mapping potential users is crucial as it relates to the sustainability of the program and the economic value of the UAVs to be produced.

5. In addition to ABG + C, UAV development is also supported by a robust framework condition through derivative regulations, such as Ministerial Regulation No. 38/2019 on the National Research Priorities for Combat MALE UAVs, Ministerial Regulation No. 23/2016 on Defense Industry Development, and Ministerial Regulation No. 26/2016 regarding unmanned aerial vehicles for national defense.

6. The calculation of the Domestic Content Level (TKDN) for MALE UAV using the Cost Base method according to Ministerial Regulation No. 16/2011 resulted in a self-assessment showing a TKDN value of approximately 38% for the Combat MALE UAV EH1B.

7. Potential domestic industries ready to support include: PT CMI Indonesia for the Communication System, PT Hariff DTE for the Weapon System, and PT Infoglobal for the Avionics System.

8. In the future, UAVs will move toward autonomy, with reduced human intervention and increased operational efficiency. The use of artificial intelligence algorithms will enhance the ability to analyse data in real time, make decisions, and adapt to highly contested environments.

9. These advancements, along with ongoing improvements in drone technology, will be crucial for the Indonesian Armed forces to maintain an edge in modern warfare.

Conflict of interest

The authors declare no conflicts of interest.

Author details

Agus Krisnowo[1,2]*, Adhi Dharma Permana[3], Bagus Anang Nugroho[3], Mochamad Taufik[2], Fauzie Dahmir[2], Guntur Haryanto[1,2], Agus Dwiono[2], Jonathan Prabowo[2], Irfan Pratama Putra[2] and Jumain Appe[2]

1 Interdisciplinary School of Management and Technology, Sepuluh Nopember Institute of Technology, Surabaya, Indonesia

2 Research Center for Process and Manufacturing Industry Technology-National Research and Innovation Agency, Jakarta, Indonesia

3 Research Center for Transportation Technology-National Research and Innovation Agency, Jakarta, Indonesia

*Address all correspondence to: aguskrisnowo@yahoo.com; agus023@brin.go.id

References

[1] Adao T, Hruˇska J, P´adua L, Bessa J, Peres E, Morais R, et al. Hyperspectral imaging: A review on UAV-based sensors, data processing and applications for agriculture and forestry. Remote Sensing. 2017;**9**:1110. DOI: 10.3390/rs9111110

[2] Torresan C, Berton A, Carotenuto F, Di Gennaro SF, Gioli B, Matese A, et al. Forestry applications of UAVs in Europe: A review. International Journal of Remote Sensing. 2017;**38**:2427-2447. DOI: 10.1080/01431161.2016.1252477

[3] Tsouros DC, Bibi S, Sarigiannidis PG. A review on UAV-based applications for precision agriculture. Information. 2019;**10**(11):349. DOI: 10.3390/info10110349

[4] Giordan D, Hayakawa Y, Nex F, Remondino F, Tarolli P. Review article: The use of remotely piloted aircraft systems (RPASs) for natural hazards monitoring and management. Natural Hazards and Earth System Sciences. 2018;**18**:1079-1096. DOI: 10.5194/nhess-18-1079-2018

[5] Rakha T. Review of unmanned aerial system (UAS) applications in the built environment - Towards automated building inspection procedures using drones. Automation in Construction. 2018;**93**:252-264. DOI: 10.1016/j.autcon.2018.05.002

[6] Nugroho ASB. Kajian Pemanfaatan Drone Untuk Pekerjaan Pengawasan Konstruksi. 2016. Available from: http://e-journal.uajy.ac.id/id/eprint/10544

[7] Szóstak M, Nowobilski T, Mahamadu AM, Pérez DC. Unmanned aerial vehicles in the construction industry - Towards a protocol for safe preparation and flight of drones. International Journal of Intelligent Unmanned Systems. 2022;**11**(2):296-316. DOI: 10.1108/IJIUS-05-2022-0063

[8] Mary N, Shafiyia S, Ben Maaouia M. Applications of drone technology in construction projects: A systematic literature review. International Journal of Research - GRANTHAALAYAH. 2022;**10**(10):1-14. DOI: 10.29121/granthaalayah.v10.i10.2022.4810

[9] Kerle N, Nex F, Gerke M, Duarte D, Vetrivel A. UAV-based structural damage mapping: A review. ISPRS International Journal of Geo-Information. 2019;**9**:14. DOI: 10.3390/ijgi9010014

[10] Ren H, Zhao Y, Xiao W, Hu Z. A review of UAV monitoring in mining areas: Current status and future perspectives. International Journal of Coal Science & Technology. 2019;**6**:320-333. DOI: 10.1007/s40789-019-00264-5 [11]

[11] Nexa* F, Armenakisb C, Cramerc M, Cuccid DA, Gerkee M, Honkavaaraf E, et al. UAV in the advent of the twenties: Where we stand and what is next. ISPRS Journal of Photogrammetry and Remote Sensing. 2022;**103**:215-242. DOI: 10.1016/j.isprsjprs.2021.12.006

[12] Jacob Loyola N, Muñoz La Rivera F, Herrera RF, Atencio E. Unmanned aerial vehicles (UAVs) for physical progress monitoring of construction. Sensors (Switzerland). 2021;**21**(4227):1-27

[13] Israr A, Mustafa Abro GE, Khan MSA, Farhan M, Zulkifli S. Internet of Things (IoT)-enabled unmanned aerial vehicles for the inspection of construction sites: A vision and future directions. Vol. 2021. Mathematical Problems in Engineering: Article ID 9825281. 15p. Article ID 9931112. DOI: 10.1155/2021/9931112

[14] Tjandra K, D, Irawan FG, Nugraha P, Sunindijo RY. Drone readiness in the Indonesian construction industry. Construction Economics and Building. 2022;**22**(4):36-58. DOI: 10.5130/AJCEB.v22i4.8161

[15] Aasen H, Honkavaara E, Lucieer A, Zarco-Tejada P. Quantitative remote sensing at ultra-high resolution with UAV spectroscopy: A review of sensor technology, measurement procedures, and data correction workflows. Remote Sensing. 2018;**10**:1091. DOI: 10.3390/rs10071091

[16] Aggarwal S, Kumar N. Path planning techniques for unmanned aerial vehicles: A review, solutions, and challenges. Computer Communications. 2020;**149**:270-299. DOI: 10.1016/j.comcom.2019.10.014

[17] Boukoberine MN, Zhou Z, Benbouzid M. A critical review on unmanned aerial vehicles power supply and energy management: Solutions, strategies, and prospects. Applied Energy. 2019;**255**:113823. DOI: 10.1016/j.apenergy.2019.113823

[18] Cole C. Webinar Watch: 'Drone Warfare: Today, Tomorrow, Forever? 2020. Available from: https://dronewars.net/2020/10/30/watch-drone-warfare-today-tomorrow-forever/

[19] Cohn P, Green A, Langstaff M, Roller M. Commercial Drones are Here: The Future of Unmanned Aerial Systems, Article. 2017. Available from: http://www.mckinsey.com/industries/travellogisticsandinfrastructure/our-insights/commercial-drones-are-here-the-future-of-unmanned-aerial-systems

[20] Chamola V, Kotesh P, Agarwal A, Naren NG, Guizani M. A comprehensive review of unmanned aerial vehicle attacks and neutralization techniques. Ad Hoc Networks. 2021;**111**:1-20. DOI: 10.1016/j.adhoc.2020.102324

[21] Budiyanto A. iNews.ID. 2021. Available from: https://jabar.inews.id/berita/hebat-indonesia-produksi-drone-berdaya-jelajah-250-km-dengan-misi-intai-24-jam; iNews.ID, 31 Agustus 2021

[22] Sawiyya RB. TNI AU Salah Satu Pengguna Drone Serang Terkuat di Kawasan. 2023. Available from: https://www.airspace-review.com/2023/04/27/tniausalahsatupenggunadroneserang terkuatdikawasan/

[23] Fikri A. Drone Asli Indonesia Elang Hitam, Mirip MQ-9 AS dan CH-4 Cina? 2019. Available from: https://tekno.tempo.co/read/1289457/drone-asli-indonesia-elang-hitam-mirip-mq-9-as-dan-ch-4-cina

[24] Mill STD-881D. Work Breakdown Structures for Defense Materiel Items, Department Of Defense Standard Practice. US Government Computer and software, ASSIST, Revision D; 2018

[25] Freeman C. Technology Policy and Economic Performance: Lessons from Japan. London: Frances Pinter; 1987

[26] Nelson Resenbeg RR. National Innovation Systems: A Comparative Study. Oxford: Oxford University Press; 1993

[27] Lundvall B-A. National Innovation Systems: Towards a Theory of Innovation and Interactive Learning. London: Pinter Publishers; 1992

[28] Breschi S, Malerba F. Sectoral innovation systems: Technological regimes, schumpeterian dynamics and spatial boundaries. In: Alfonso G, Malerba F, editors. The Organisation of Economic Innovation in Europe. Cambridge: Cambridge University Press; 1999. pp. 88-102

[29] Arnold E, Boekholt P, Deiaco E, McKibbin S, de la Mothe J, Simmonds P, et al. Research and Innovation Governance in Eight Countries: A Meta-Analysis of Work Funded by EZ (Netherlands) and RCN (Norway). Technopolish, Canada: University of Ottawa; 2003

[30] Arnold E, Kuhlmann S, van der Meulen B. A Singular Council: Evaluation of the Research Council of Norway. Technopolis Group. Enschede, The Netherlands: University of Twente Research Information; 2001

[31] Granstrand O, Holgersson M. Innovation Ecosystems: A Conceptual Review and a New Definition. Technovation. Vol. 90-91. UK: Elsevier Ltd; 2020. p. 102098. DOI: 10.1016/j.technovation.2019.102098

[32] Etxkowitz H, Leydesdorff L. The dynamics of innovation: From national systems and "mode 2" to a triple helix of university–industry–government relations. Research Policy. 2000;**19**(2):109-123

[33] Jin C. Reflections on the construction of a new national innovation system [J]. Proceedings of the Chinese Academy of Sciences. 2018;**33**(05):479-483

[34] Zeng D, Hu J, Ouyang T. Managing innovation paradox in the sustainable innovation ecosystem: A case study of ambidextrous capability in a focal firm. Sustainability. 2017;**9**:2091

[35] Gibbons M, Limoges C, Nowotny H, Schwartzman S, Scott P, Trow M. The New Production of Knowledge, the Dynamics of Science and Research in Contemporary Societies. London, UK: Sage; 1994. [Google Scholar]

[36] Carayannis EG, Campbell DFJ. Mode 3: Meaning and implications from a knowledge systems perspective', in knowledge creation, diffusion, and use in innovation networks and knowledge clusters. In: Elias GC, Campbell DFJ, editors. A Comparative Systems Approach across the United States, Europe and Asia. Westport, CT, USA: Praeger; 2016. pp. 1-25. [Google Scholar]

[37] Thompson V, Hardash JA, Decker B, Summers RO. NASA (In) novation ecosystem: Taking technology innovation from buzz to reality. In: 2012 IEEE Aerospace Conference. Big Sky, MT, USA: IEEE; 2012. pp. 1-9. DOI: 10.1109/AERO.2012.6187447

[38] Amitrano CC et al. On technology in innovation systems and innovation-ecosystem perspectives: A cross-linking analysis. Sustainability. 2018;**10**(10):3744. DOI: 10.3390/su10103744

[39] Annanperä E, Liukkunen K, Markkula J. Innovation in evolving business ecosystems: A case study of information technology-based future health and exercise service. International Journal of Innovation and Technology Management. 2015;**4**:12

[40] Adner. Match Your Innovation Strategy to Your Innovation Ecosystem. Harvard Business Review; 2006. Available from: https://hbr.org/2006/04/match-your-innovation-strategy-to-your-innovation-ecosystem

[41] Thomas L, DW, Autio E. Innovation ecosystem. "Innovation ecosystems", Oxford Research Encyclopaedia of Business and Management. In: Aldag R editor. Social Science Research Network. UK: Oxford University Press; 2019. pp. 1-37. DOI: 10.2139/ssrn.3476925

[42] Krisnowo A, Nugroho BA, Budiyanto D. Technical Document, Assessment of TKDN and Supply Chain of Combatant MALE UAVs. 2021

[43] Etzkowitz H, Leydesdorff L. The triple helix - university - industry-government relations: A laboratory for knowledge based economic development. EASST Review. 1995;**14**:11-19. [Google Scholar]

[44] Miller K, McAdam R, McAdam M. A systematic literature review of university technology transfer from a quadruple helix perspective: Toward a research agenda. R&D Management. 2018;**48**(1):7-24

[45] Schaffers H. Smart Cities and the Future Internet: Towards Cooperation Frameworks for Open Innovation. 2011. Available from: https://link.springer.com/chapter/10.1007/978-3-642-20898-0_31

[46] Presidential Regulation (Perpres) 78/2021 Concerning the National Research and Innovation Agency

[47] Law No. 16/2012. About the Defense Industry

[48] Government Regulation (PP) 147/2015 Concerning Defense Industry Management

[49] Government Regulation (PP) No. 29/2018 Concerning Industrial Empowerment

[50] Kusumadewi A, Armenia R, Maret. Kisah Embargo AS dan Sukhoi Rusia di Balik Jet Tempur RI. 2016. Available from: https://www.cnnindonesia.com/nasional/20160301150059-20-114600/kisah-embargo-as-dan-sukhoi-rusia-di-balik-jet-tempur-ri

[51] Minister of Defense Decree Number: KEP/104/M/I/2020 concerning National Defense Policy

[52] Presidential Regulation of the Republic of Indonesia Number: 109 of 2020 Concerning the Acceleration of Strategic Project Implementation

[53] Regulation of the Minister of Research, Technology and Higher Education Number: 38 of 2019 Concerning National Research Priorities 2020-2024

[54] Presidential Regulation 18/2020, LAMP. III is related to the 2020-2024 RPJMN Concerning MALE UAV Technology Innovation

[55] Presidential Regulation 109/2020 Concerning the Acceleration of National Strategic Projects for the Development of MALE COMBATAN Drones

[56] Wyckoff A, Ziarko W, Nas SO. OECD. Frascati Manual 2015: Guidelines for Collecting and Reporting Data on Research and Experimental Development, The Measurement of Scientific, Technological and Innovation Activities. Paris: OECD Publishing; 2015. DOI: 10.1787/9789264239012-en

[57] Ankrah SN, Burgess TF, Grimshaw P, Shaw NE. Asking both university and industry actors about their engagement in knowledge transfer: What single group studies of motive omit. Technovation. 2013;**33**:50-65. DOI: 10.1016/j.technovation.2012.11.001

[58] Law Number 11 of 2019 Concerning the National System of Science and Technology

[59] Hertz JC, Brinkerhoff DW, Bush R, Karetji P. Knowledge Systems: Evidence to Policy Concepts in Practice. 2020. Available from: https://rtipress.scholasticahq.com/article/16981

[60] Minister of Defense Regulation 26/2016, Concerning Unmanned Aircraft Systems for National Defense and Security Tasks

[61] Minister of Industry Regulation No. 16/M-IND/PER/2/2011 Concerning Provisions and Procedures for Calculating Domestic Component Levels

[62] Minister of Industry Regulation 22/2020 TKDN Which is the TKDN Calculation for Digital Products

[63] Regulation of the Minister of Finance No. 153/PMK.010/2020 Concerning the Provision of Gross Income Reduction for Research and Development Activities (Super Deduction Tax)

[64] Rohman A, Aziz A, Awang Rahmadi N, Hartono, Muzayadah NL, Kusumoaji D, et al. Kajian Perencanaan Sertifikasi Militer Pesawat Tanpa Awak LSU05NG dengan Metode WBS dan CPM. In: Seminar Nasional Kebijakan Penerbangan dan Antariksa IV (SINAS 08 KPA–IV). Bogor: In Media; 2019. pp. 45-57

[65] Ingham LA. Considerations for a roadmap for the operation of unmanned aerial vehicles (UAV). In: South African Airspace, Doctor of Philosophy at Stellenbosch University. Aeronautical Journal-New. UK: Cambridge University Press; 2008;**Series 110**(1112):695-701

[66] Minister of Transportation Regulation No PM 63 of 2021 Concerning Civil Aviation Safety Regulations

[67] Saaty TL. Decision making with the analytical hierarchy process. International Journal of Services Sciences. 2008;**1**(1):83-98

[68] Leal JA. AHP-express: A simplified version of the analytical hierarchy process method. MethodX. 2020;**7**:100748

[69] Adjie H. Drone Kombatan Asal Turki, Bayraktar TB2 Terkena Embargo Komponen Vital dari Kanada. 2020. Available from: https://www.indomiliter.com/drone-kombatan-asal-turki-bayraktar-tb2-terkena-embargo-komponen-vital-dari-kanada/

[70] Muksin. Penyelesaian PSN Drone Male Kombatan Untuk Perkuat Kedaulatan Indonesia. 2021. Available from: https://www.ekon.go.id/publikasi/detail/%203403/%20penyelesaian-psn-drone-male-kombatan-untuk-perkuat-kedaulatan-indonesia

[71] Maryati S. Calculation Method & TKDN Process for Goods/Services Products. 2024. Available from: https://www.ijintender.co.id/tkdn

[72] dan Stern K. The Impact of Local Content Policies on South Africa: Drawing Lessons from Foreign Investors' Experience of the PPPFA and REIP4. 2021. Available from: http://forum.tips.org.za/images/Paper_The_impact_of_local_contentPolicies_on_South_Africa_Drawing_lessons_from_foreign_investorsexperience.pdf

[73] Ramdo. Local Content: Key Characteristics, Designing Local Content Policies in Mineral-Rich Countries. 2018. Available from: https://www.jstor.org/stable/resrep21957.4

[74] Harjono T. TUSAŞ to Deliver ANKA-S to Indonesia by October 2025. 2025. Available from: https://turdef.com/article/tusas-to-deliver-anka-s-to-indonesia-by-october-2025

[75] Irawan G. TNI AU Proyeksikan Drone Buatan Turki Beroperasi di Natuna Utara Gantikan Buatan China. 2024. Available from: https://m.tribunnews.com/nasional/2024/12/30/tni-au-proyeksikan-drone-buatan-turki-beroperasi-di-natuna-utara-gantikan-buatan-china?page=all

[76] Wills I et al. The Difference between BVLOS, VLOS, and EVLOS, 2023. Available from: https://coastaldrone.co/the-difference-between-bvlos-vlos-and-evlos/

Section 2

Environmental Applications

Chapter 6

Drones Applied to Cetacean Research: A Case Study of Fin Whales

Eduard Degollada, Beatriu Tort and Dorottya Mészáros

Abstract

The fin whale is the only whale species regularly found in the Mediterranean Sea, with a year around presence. However, the aquatic environment and the whale's diving behavior have posed challenges to studying this marine mammal. The increasing use of drones in cetacean research has significantly enhanced our understanding of the species. Drones provide the ability to quickly and discreetly fly over the whales, minimizing the disturbance, while capturing high-quality footage that enables the observation of their behavior and characteristic features used for identification, as well as supporting morphometric analysis. Additionally, drones can assist in collecting blow samples and guiding research vessels for closer, more effective approaches to conduct biopsies, collect fecal samples, or deploy tagging devices. This technological advancement has greatly contributed to a deeper understanding of fin whales, offering valuable insights into the health of the population.

Keywords: drones, cetacean, fin whale, identification, behavior, health, morphometrics, sampling, population

1. Introduction

The study of cetaceans has always faced difficulties due to the aquatic environment in which these animals are found. The use of Unmanned Aerial Vehicles (UAVs) commonly known as "drones" has been a breakthrough in cetacean research [1–3]. This new technology has allowed researchers to continuously record cetaceans not only at the surface but also a few meters below [3–5], allowing to obtain valuable data in non-expensive and user-friendly manner [2, 6, 7]. For this reason, the popularity of the use of drones has increased exponentially in the last years, with studies on a diverse research field, such as population studies, behavioral studies, photo-identification, morphometrics and the determination of health status. Furthermore, UAVs are also used as a tool to collect blow samples, and to deploy devices such as behavior monitoring D-TAGs.

Line transect surveys have been conducted with drones in order to assess the abundance and distribution of cetacean populations in coastal areas [8]. For this kind of study, fixed-wing drones seem to be the best option due to their longer flight time [7].

However, population studies have also been conducted with multi-rotor drones [8, 9]. On the other hand, drones have proven to be a good tool to better measure the number of individuals in a sighting, being able to accurately count the animals that are at or near the surface at that moment [8, 9].

Drone photo-identification has been performed in some baleen whales such as southern right whale (*Eubalaena australis*), by its unique and identifiable callosities patterns on their head [10], bowhead whales (*Balaena mysticetus*) where the animals were identified focusing on different scars and pigmentation marks along the body [11], and fin whales (*Balaenoptera physalus*) which can be recognized by their characteristic white pigmentation of chevron and blazer positioned right after the blow hole [12, 13]. Odontocete species, such as sperm whales [14] and killer whales [15] have also been identified by drone photo-identification techniques.

In contrast to boat-based observations, the aerial perspective from a drone allows a series of images to be obtained that enable the description of different types of behavior, such as feeding, socializing and mating, making it one of the tools that have provided the greatest advances in the study of cetacean behavior. Therefore, it has been possible to determine feeding strategies on resident Byde's whales in New Zealand [16] gray whales in the USA [4], humpback whales in the Gulf of Alaska [17], fin whales in the Antarctic Peninsula [18] and blue whales in New Zealand [19]. Social behavior in nursery areas has been studied in humpback whales, where social interactions between adults and between mother and calf have been documented [20, 21], and on southern right whales, with described calf behavior development [22]. Additionally, such studies were carried out at mating grounds for northern right whales [23] and on mating behaviors in gray whales [5]. Disruptive tourism activities have also been evaluated such as the swimming with humpback whales in the Pacific Tonge Breeding ground [24]. Several similar behavior studies have been conducted for odontocetes such as Risso's dolphin [25], dusky dolphins [5, 26, 27] and killer whales [15].

No UAV disturbance reactions were described in studies of either humpback whale breeding ground in Tonga when flying at 30 m above sea level [6, 20], or gray whales in the west coast of the USA when flying 25 m above sea level [4]. In addition, Domínguez-Sánchez et al. [1], on blue whales was only able to discern one individual whale reaction. But it has been described in odontocete species such as bottlenose dolphins [28, 29] and common dolphins [29].

Early methods of morphological measures were rudimentary, relying on physical measurements taken from dead specimens often on whaling ships or from stranded animals [30, 31]. Later on, small manned aircraft were used to perform observations and collect aerial photographs for photogrammetry [32]; however, this method is not cost-effective. Today, with technological advancement, cetacean aerial photogrammetry is a method that involves the usage of a UAV equipped with high-resolution cameras and sensors, to capture aerial-vertical footage of the whales from a known height. Zenithal images of the animals, when coming close to the surface to breathe, enable us to obtain images of closely straight-positioned animals, which allows morphological and volumetric analysis [33]. Photogrammetric and body condition studies have been performed in many baleen whales such as blue whales [34, 35], gray whales [36–39], humpback whales [40, 41] and fin whales [35]. There are also studies on odontocetes such as sperm whales [42], killer whales [43] and short-finned pilot whales [44].

With these images, it is also possible to study whale entanglements, such as the study done by Ramp et al. [12] on blue, fin and humpback whales. As well as whale injuries or malformations, mainly caused by ship strikes, as presented in Tort et al. [45] a study on fin whale collision risk.

Blow samples are a useful way to determine the health status of whale and dolphin populations by analyzing their compounds found in the respiratory tract. Little is known about whale respiratory microbiome [46]; consequently, several studies are being performed to study possible pathogens. Furthermore, these samples might provide genetic material from the sampled individual. The utilization of drones for the collection of blow samples is becoming more widespread, as it provides a more efficient means of approaching the animals while potentially reducing disturbance to a minimal level. This method of data collection has been performed in studies involving humpback whales [46] and fin whales [47].

For over 10 years, a research project has been conducted to study fin whale aggregations in the Catalan coast, north-western Mediterranean Sea, in springtime. The main goal of the project (called Fin Whale Project) is to determine fin whale presence, habitat use and threats in the study area. Throughout the project it has also been possible to monitor the migration of fin whales from the Catalan coast toward the North Atlantic area, *via* the east coast of the Iberian Peninsula and the Strait of Gibraltar. One of the main results obtained until now is the identification of the Catalan coast as a spring-feeding ground for fin whales [48].

Since the inception of the project, drones have been used as a main tool to complement the research performed from the research vessel. Over time, with technological advances and enhanced expertise, drones have evolved into one of the key research instruments; performing behavioral and photo-identification analysis, as well as morphometric and body condition studies, blow sampling and boat guidance.

Fin whales are fast migratory cosmopolitan offshore species with undocumented traveling routes and unknown breeding grounds. A significant knowledge gap exists in fin whale research, which could be addressed through the implementation of drone-assisted studies. This study seeks to contribute to the understanding and conservation of fin whales while establishing the best practices for utilizing drones in various research objectives. It emphasizes the importance of standardizing protocols for the different techniques to facilitate data sharing and result comparison between researchers and to minimize disturbances to cetaceans.

2. Drones insight and flight methodology

The protocols followed during the study will be explained below. Focusing on the use of drones from boats, the techniques for locating and approaching the fin whales and the protocols for obtaining images for photo-identification, behavioral and morphometric studies.

2.1 Use of drones from the vessel

The limited flight time of most commercial drones requires the use of cetacean research vessels, particularly for studies involving offshore species. Vertical take-off drones or multi-rotor drones, are the only models capable of precise positioning while hovering over the target, allowing close proximity to the animal therefore, enabling the acquisition of detailed imagery. There are many drone models; however, boat-based marine mammal research prioritizes small, versatile drones with superior control and imaging technologies. These UAVs should weigh no more than 1 kg and offer a favorable quality-to-price ratio, as they will be used in high-risk aquatic environment. For the presented study, different models of the DJI brand (Phantom 2 and

3 pro, Mavic 2 pro and Mavic 3) have been used over the years. In general, the flight time is limited by the size and the proportional energy consumption, with the latest models currently capable of remaining airborne for approximately 35 minutes in real time. The duration will largely depend on various conditions, such as the drone's operational activity, movement and environmental conditions, including wind speed. The limited battery time also means that this technology is not practical for searching for animals. Thus, the drone will take off once the whale is in sight or hover in the air a few minutes before the animal is expected to resurface from a dive.

The launching method from the boat depends on the type of the vessel. Flights from motorboats or inflatable boats can be performed as there are no outstanding structures to take into consideration. But in the case of sailing boats, with all the superstructure of the mast, rigging and antennae, it is recommended to take off from the stern without having the need to reduce speed. However, landing is most successfully executed from the bow or the side, while reducing the ship's movement as much as possible. In both cases, it is essential to perform the task manually, with the necessary care and protection.

One of the main obstacles when recording at sea is the lighting and reflections, posing a significant challenget to see the screens where the images from the drone camera are received. It is therefore important to achieve maximum darkness in order to see them in good conditions.

The enhancement of video quality of drones, with capabilities of recording up to 5 K and 60 frames per second, renders video footage an excellent tool for detailed observation of the animals. At the same time, the resolution of the images transmitted during the flight makes it necessary to have a screen of equivalent capacity to show the image in real-time without cuts or loss of quality. Nowadays, some drone commands have high-quality integrated cameras, but they are usually small which makes it difficult to detect details. For this reason, it is preferable to use larger screens, as long as they are of adequate quality to support the data transmission. This will facilitate the detection of fine details that will allow us to locate the fin whales promptly in order to approach and film them before a new dive.

As long as there is no animal on the surface, it is advisable to have the boat in the image as a reference, otherwise it is very easy to lose orientation. As for the altitude, for a better detectability of blows or movement indicating the presence of the whale, it is suggested to place the device between 50 and 100 m. Simultaneously, it is essential to consider the brightness, which will depend on the inclination of the sun, or the presence of clouds and the movement of the surface with waves; therefore, when the sun is higher, there tends to be more generalized reflections. Whereas when the sun is low, it will be the quadrant in which it is located that will prevent a good view, and the drone will have to be oriented toward the opposite side.

As for the wind, multicopters can withstand sufficiently high speeds above which it is no longer feasible to continue the survey search as sea conditions become more difficult, such as Beaufort 4 or the equivalent of around 16 knots. Higher wind speeds would require time and experience for a proper landing. Adjusting the boat's course to a downwind direction can help to reduce apparent wind and bow pitching.

2.2 Technique for locating and approaching fin whales. Reaction of fin whales to the drone presence

Under normal conditions, the sighting of a fin whale is initially done visually by the research team on board, which can be approximately up to about 2 miles away. When the animal is closer, around 500 m, but not yet close enough for conventional photography, the drone is launched. Although, it is recommended to first observe the whale breathing intervals, behavior, speed and direction, in order to maximize the likelihood of the drone reaching the correct location at the optimal time.

Once in the air, and with the whale in sight by onboard observers, it requires good directional guidance to steer the drone toward the whale until it can be visualized on the screen. The approach should be made as quickly as possible, according to the instructions of a guide, while the pilot concentrates on detecting the whale in the image. It is important to consider that the whales will breathe several times, with the frequency depending on the activity being performed, before diving again for a few minutes. This provides limited time to approach and capture high-quality footage. Once the target is located and focused, the descent is made with the animal centered on the screen, and the drone is positioned as zenith as possible. Taking into account the sun and the brightness, as previously mentioned, placing it between the sun and the animal.

In our 10-year project, we have filmed over 2.400 minutes of fin whale images. By analyzing those videos, it is possible to state that this species does not show an apparent reaction when using small drones. By contrast, we have observed in odontocetes a clear reaction with behavioral change, such as turning and swimming laterally with one eye pointing toward the drone, in the following species: sperm whales, striped dolphins, Risso's dolphins, Cuvier's beaked whale, common pilot whale and also as reported by Fettermann et al. [28] in bottlenose dolphin. This effect has been linked to the frequencies produced by the drones and their visual and shadow detection [6, 49]. In whales, evasive reactions have only been observed in response to larger and noisier multicopters that rapidly change position over the whale. These drones not only generate acoustic noise but also vibration on the water surface when approaching within a few meters, potentially making them more detectable by the animals.

2.3 Obtaining suitable images for identification, behavior and morphometric studies

The objective of the aerial filming and the type of drone will determine the protocols for obtaining images. We consider that the main or most immediate purposes are to identify the animal, to observe its behavior and to have graphic material to study morphometric data. The high resolution of filming on today's drones allows frames to be used for these purposes.

Therefore, depending on the image quality of the drone, it will be necessary to film at greater or lesser proximity and, if possible, to obtain full-body images first. Considering the brightness and the density of the blow that may cover the chevron and the blaze, it is advisable to lower down to frame the head, positioning the drone at the most suitable angle to observe the characteristic pigmentation.

Complimentarily, these images can be further analyzed to study animal behavior, provided that the whales are not influenced by the presence of the device.

2.4 Vessel guidance for approaching and obtaining biological samples

One of the most valuable applications of drones in fin whale research is serving as an auxiliary guide for the boat. As the drone is able to track the animal while it is submerged between breaths, the UAV can maintain observation even when the whale is out of sight from the vessel. Consequently, the behavior and position of the whale are continuously reported to the team by the drone pilot. The anticipation of whale surfacing enhances the team's preparedness, thereby improving the efficiency of photographic documentation and data collection. Simultaneously, it allows the vessel to approach the whale with a precise description of its movements underwater, allowing the skipper to steer the boat for a smooth and less intrusive approach. This greatly facilitates biopsies and the deployment of tagging devices. In addition, filming the whale and the boat within a single frame enables subsequent morphometric studies by providing a basis for comparison, as well as insight into behavioral responses to the research vessel. Another area where UAVs can play a critical role is in the detection and localization of feces. Defecation in fin whales usually occurs in the last breath before diving. When this happens at some distance from the boat, it is difficult to observe and even more challenging to locate it. Detection while filming the animal allows hovering over the defecated material and indicating the position for sample collection.

There are different strategies for approaching, tracking and guiding the vessel with the use of a drone. On the one hand, the drone can fly low as a direct visual indicator for the ship, marking the position of the whale. On the other hand, it can fly high, with the pilot having both whale and vessel in the picture and thus giving indications to the helmsman and the team.

3. Research lines

The following section deals with the importance and advances in knowledge about photo-identification studies, behavior, morphometry, health status and sample collection of fin whales.

3.1 Photo-identification

The identification of individuals in cetacean research is of utmost importance in many studies, from population through behavioral and to habitat studies. In fin whales, photo-identification by dorsal fin and dorsal pigmentation has historically been used. The challenge in differentiating between highly similar fins, coupled with the slight variation over time (nicks, scars, etc.), as well as the diverse light conditions and angles of the photographs, suggest that this technique may not enable satisfactory cataloging for global application or consistent identification of individuals across various regions.

The appearance of UAVs allowing zenithal observation has revolutionized the technique of photo-identification in cetaceans and specifically with fin whales considering the difficulties of the conventional technique mentioned above. The characteristic pigmentation and facial asymmetry, consisting of blaze and chevron marks, demonstrate the clear differences between each individual. The blaze is a light spot widening from the eye and extending posteriorly to the spiracle in a rounded form to about the midline on the right side only, as a continuation of the white right mandible characteristic of the asymmetry of this species. The chevron is a white W-shaped line centered on the dorsum caudal to the chevron and the blaze. The central area or V with the cranial vertex and where the central pattern of the chevron is formed can be clearly seen and distinguished. At this junction, characteristic drawings of each individual are generated, which facilitate their cataloging by means of classification by similar shapes: straight lines, curved lines, letter shapes, lack of union between the branches of the chevron, etc. [13]. Finally, from each of the orifices of the spiracles,

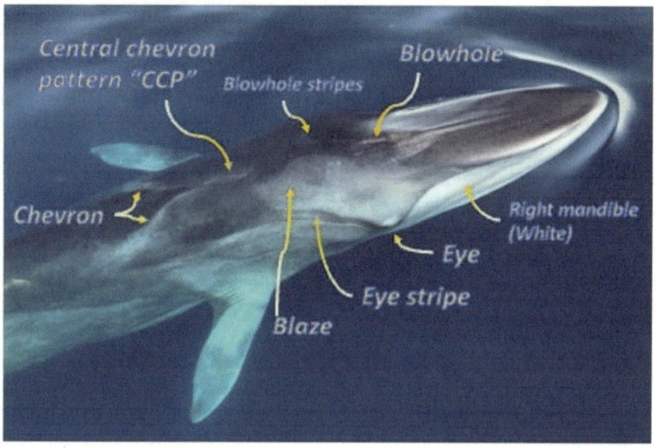

Figure 1.
Fin whale head pigmentation adapted from Degollada et al. [13].

white lines emerge in a posterior direction, generally curved, following the dorsal profile of the blaze (**Figure 1**).

Subsequently, the pigmentations described above imply that even if two individuals share similarities in one of these characteristics, for example, the chevron, they almost certainly differ in the others. Moreover, even if the image fails to capture all of the pigmentations clearly due to water conditions (e.g., steam from the blow), the angle or changes in lighting, the exact match of one feature will still confirm the identification of the same animal. Thus, the shape and profile are sufficiently varied and extensive in detail to facilitate the unequivocal identification of the individual. Although still, images provide greater detail, the whale's speed and the brief time it surfaces makes it exceedingly difficult to obtain high-quality images. As a result, video footage is prioritized. By considering the resolution and the number of frames per second of the drone videos, it becomes possible to obtain sufficient frames for identification. Consequently, in all cases it is advisable to use the video mode rather than the photographic mode.

Another practical detail to take into account when obtaining adequate footage for identification by drone is the weather conditions. It can influence the presence of water on the body, distorting the image in case of waves or the density and direction of the blow masking the identifiable area.

3.2 Behavioral study

Fin whales, as well as most mysticetes, display most of their behaviors underwater. For this reason, little was known about fin whale behavior before the use of technology such as D-Tags or drones. Drones are the best tool to study near-surface behavior in detail.

The study of fin whale behavior was the primary goal of the project regarding drone usage. In the Catalan coast, five different behaviors have been recorded: feeding, foraging, socializing, resting and traveling (**Table 1**).

In this case study, drone footage has been key to considering the Catalan coast as a feeding ground for fin whales in spring. Feeding behavior has been the most recorded event in the area over the years (**Figure 2**), being also reinforced by the foraging behavior monitored from the boat.

	Description	Video attached
Foraging	It is defined as the active search for prey. During this behavior, the animals perform zigzag movements and large circles. While maintaining a constant breathing pattern, when performed in medium to deep water and irregular when it is close to the surface. This behavior is also characterized by abrupt changes in direction. Foraging is often followed by feeding; therefore, these two behaviors are closely related.	Video 1, https://edmaktub.org/en/drones-applied-to-cetacean-research/#Video%201
Feeding	The feeding events can be determined either by observing all the feeding sequences (**Figure 2**) or by observing the animal emerging from the deep with a full mouth. Fin whale feeding dynamics often consist of accelerating and turning to the right and opening the mouth to engulf a large amount of water and prey, which is later filtered through the baleens. Vertical feeding events have also been reported. Vertical feeding events have been recorded as well, but less frequently. Defecation is also an indicator of this type of behavior, but it is not a feeding event itself.	Video 2, https://edmaktub.org/en/drones-applied-to-cetacean-research/#Video%202
Traveling	It is described as a behavior in which the animal is moving diligently to another area. This behavior is characterized by a pretty straight-line track and constant speed, which can usually be five knots or more.	Video 3, https://edmaktub.org/en/drones-applied-to-cetacean-research/#Video%203
Resting	It is described as a behavior in which the animal is very relaxed, swimming slowly a few meters below the surface and going up to breath in a very smooth and relaxed way. With a relatively long breathing interval. When the fin whales are with this behavior a lower reaction to external inputs has been noticed.	Video 4, https://edmaktub.org/en/drones-applied-to-cetacean-research/#Video%204
Socializing	Is a behavior resulting from the interaction between two or more animals. This social activity can be motivated by mating interests, group and feeding associations or mother-calf relationships. Intraspecies interactions are most commonly observed; however, interspecies interactions are also present. On the Catalan coast, the predominant social behavior has been mother-calf interactions. However, sporadically, interactions between adults have also been recorded.	Video 5, https://edmaktub.org/en/drones-applied-to-cetacean-research/#Video%205

Table 1.
Description of the different fin whale behaviors recorded on the Catalan coast. The total percentage exceeds 100 as the socializing and feeding behaviors are identified in sightings where other main behaviors are also counted.

Figure 2.
Fin whale feeding sequence.

Figure 3.
Three fin whales emerge to breath with full mouths while some striped dolphins are leaping in front of them.

In Catalan waters, fin whales are usually solitary, occasional small groups are encountered, of two to four individuals (**Figure 3**). Larger aggregations are relatively rare in this area. However, groups of up to 10 individuals have been sporadically observed, seemingly linked to krill abundance peaks in the study area. Notably, no cooperative feeding strategies have been documented when individuals are feeding concurrently within the same area.

An opposite dynamic was observed in Galicia, where the animals were regularly seen feeding in large aggregations of 8–15 individuals.

The documentation of surface and near-surface feeding activity has not only provided insight into feeding dynamics of fin whales but also helped to illuminate seasonal variation in feeding success (**Figure 3**).

Feeding events per sighting can be stabilized and standardized based on the drone's flight time, allowing average comparisons between seasons. Always bear in mind that only near-surface events can be observed by the drone. Monitoring from the boat together with the observation of defecation is what gives us the information on feeding at depth.

Few social interactions, such as turning under each other, have been observed. Over the 10 years, five solitary mother-calf encounters have also been recorded in which calves swim close together around the mother. The aerial image makes it possible to clearly distinguish between a calf and a small animal in terms of behavior and proportional sizes (**Figure 4**, Video 5, https://edmaktub.org/en/drones-applied-to-cetacean-research/#Video%205).

Traveling behavior has been observed in varying frequency depending on the season. During favorable feeding seasons, when the food availability was high in the area, traveling behavior was rarely documented. However, in seasons characterized by lower resource availability, traveling behavior was more prevalent. Observations of this behavior became more conspicuous when following the whales southwards to the Atlantic, where aggregations of 2 to 4 animals were frequently recorded.

Resting patterns have been described as the moment when the whale is more vulnerable to ship strikes (**Figure 5**). During this behavior, the animal typically swims only a few meters below the surface at a slow pace, a depth insufficient to evade most collisions, particularly with large vessels. However, it is deep enough for the whale

Figure 4.
Mother and calf swimming side by side in the Catalan coast.

Figure 5.
A fin whale coming to the surface to breathe with a big cargo ship crossing on their back.

to remain unseen. As an example, in 2022, while monitoring a fin whale exhibiting resting behavior, the whale appeared to be on a collision course with a cargo ship. The drone captured footage of the cargo ship passing within 100 m of the animal. No behavioral reaction from the animal has been observed. During the boat's approach to the whale's location, only a few blows were observed. But the whale remained only a few meters from the surface all the time, making it very difficult for the merchant vessel to spot (Video 6, https://edmaktub.org/en/drones-applied-to-cetacean-research/#Video%206). This example explains the vulnerability of these animals in the area as well as the difficulty of implementing sufficient conservation measures.

Interactions between fin whales and other cetacean species have occasionally been encountered. In the Mediterranean Sea, the most frequent interaction occurs with striped dolphins (**Figure 6**), although observations with common and bottlenose dolphins have also been documented. Dolphins typically appear to engage in playful behavior, swimming around the head of the whales, similar to bow-riding behavior exhibited when accompanying boats.

Figure 6.
Fin whale feeding with many stripe dolphins in front of her mouth.

In the Atlantic, aggregations of fin whales have been observed with blue whales, humpback whales and minke whales. However, no true social interactions have been documented; rather, instances of occasional aggregation appear to be driven primarily by feeding possibilities.

To effectively record fin whale behavior, the drone flew at altitudes ranging from 25 to 40 m, allowing it to record both the whale and its surroundings. This height is especially important when there is more than one animal in the sighting. At times, lower flights were required to have better details of feeding strategies. The recording of diving intervals by researchers onboard proved highly valuable for flight planning and battery optimization, particularly in the case of deep dives. The drone takes off 1 or 2 minutes prior to the predicted surfacing time, allowing sufficient time to position it optimally in order to easily locate the animal surfaces again.

3.3 Morphometrics and body condition

As mentioned in the introduction, thanks to technological advancement, UAVs are a tool to be used to get high-quality footage to study whale morphology and body condition. By combining the existing photogrammetrical and morphological methods (described by: [32, 33, 43, 50–56]) and adjusting them to the species under study (fin whale). To obtain adequate footage, the UAV must be positioned above the whale, with the camera pointing down at the animal at a 90° angle, while keeping the whole body of the whale in the center of the field of view. The aim is to document the animal in a straight horizontal body position while breaking through the surface ("sample point"). With UAVs, the acquisition of large amounts of accurate and reliable data for precise morphometric analysis is possible.

The collected footage then undergoes a visual inspection and still images of the "sample points" are extracted in full resolution for morphological measurements, with the intention to obtain at least three pictures of an individual from one sighting to minimize future precision errors to minimize future precision errors. The obtained images undergo a second visual inspection where pictures of whales with arched or curved body position and more than 20% masked by environmental factors are rejected from further analysis. The remaining images are matched to the exact altitude of the UAV from the flight records or in case of the use of LIDAR (a laser scanning system with higher accuracy in altitude measurement than the barometer) from the sensor's metadata. Thereafter, the adequate still images are imported into a morphometric software called MorphomeriX from 55, where the body parameters are measured manually (**Figure 7**). These pixel-based measures from aerial-vertical images are scaled to real-life units (meter) with a known-sized calibration object to obtain the best estimate, the most accurate size of the whales.

Developmental changes in the body can be monitored using these measurements, both at the individual level for recaptured individuals and at the population level over time. These measurements encompass size, growth, and the accompanying proportional variations, as well as the allometric relationships between body parameters. Additionally, seasonal fluctuations in volume and body condition offer valuable insights into foraging success, which corresponds to the productivity of the foraging grounds (**Figure 8**).

This way the analysis of body volume is useful information to determine fin whale nutritional condition and therefore an open door to assess health status.

The visual indicators of most relevance to health can be classified as cachexia or emaciation, deformities, lesions and the presence of ectoparasites.

Loss of body mass is one of the main indicators as external signs of weight reduction and poor body condition. Extreme thinness in whales, *emaciation* and, in extreme cases, *cachexia* is an important indicator of long-term lack of food, whether or not related to an associated pathological process.

The main causes may be lack of food due to habitat disturbance or impediments to finding and ingesting food due to external physical factors, such as entanglement in fishing gear or materials that restrict mobility, trauma from non-lethal collisions or amputations, and pathological processes.

In all these cases, as they are resistant animals with large energy reserves, prepared to withstand periods of starvation, the process is slow and long in time, which leads them to this situation of loss of body mass.

The main sign of wasting is the reduction of the epaxial muscle mass, the longitudinal muscles that are located dorsolaterally to the spine, which causes a concave

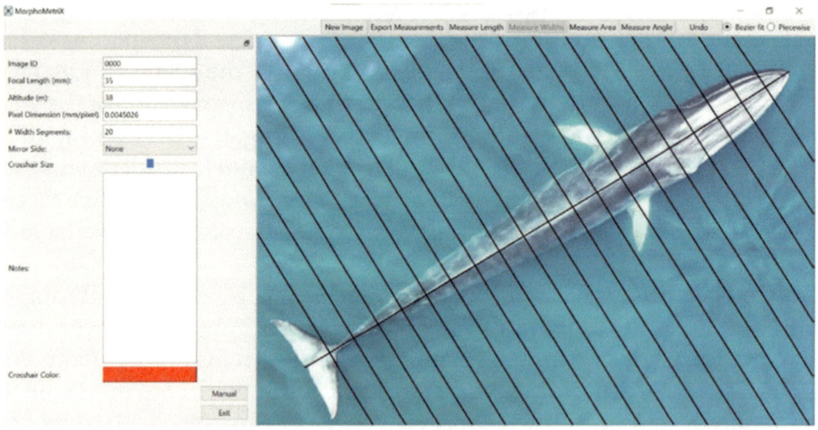

Figure 7.
A fin whale being analyzed with MorphometriX.

Figure 8.
An animal sighted two times with different body volume.

contour with two concavities on both sides of the spine that is marked forming a ridge, the neck and ribs are also visible.

Deformities are those alterations of the normal morphology corresponding to the species in question. Thus, deformities are understood as those alterations of the anatomical structure that have been created outside of development in a more or less abrupt manner (**Figure 9**). They could be caused by a disease involving degenerative processes that directly or indirectly affect the musculoskeletal system and/or the integument or, above all, trauma.

Considering only deformities of considerable size and that affect motility, the most relevant cases found have been column bendings at the level of the caudal peduncle associated with ship strikes. The probability of survival of these animals makes them a small proportion of the possible number of collisions and of the existing risk.

Lesions, in isolation, do not serve as direct indicators of health problems unless they are extensive or suggestive of severe pathological conditions. Instead, they primarily reflect the risk of exposure to factors responsible for their formation, whether those are pathological or anthropogenic, such as human-induced injuries.

Figure 9.
Fin whale with scoliosis.

Within this category, we could consider that the most worrying and most prominent indicators of this type of risk are anthropogenic injuries, especially due to interaction with ships, such as injuries caused by impact with the hull or by cuts from propellers.

The *ectoparasites* found in cetaceans in general and in the fin whale in particular do not tend to represent a serious health problem for the host. Their presence is mostly a reflection of other processes present or of an individual predisposition. Under normal conditions, it will be influenced by factors such as temperature, salinity and water flow [57]. Normally, cases of massive infestation are accompanied by some serious health problems, which, among other consequences, results in reduced swimming speed and a potential decline in immune function, thereby facilitating colonization, attachment and growth.

Among the different species of parasitic epibionts, the one that may represent a higher risk to health is the copepod *Penella balaenoptera*, as it anchors through the epidermis, going through the blubber and deepening to the dermis and subcutaneous tissue (**Figure 10**) [58, 59]. In this manner, it interrupts the integrity of the integument as a foreign body and allows the possible entry of pathogenic microorganisms [60].

The drone perspective also provided enhanced insights into fin whale interaction with vessels. The Catalan coast study area is a high-transited area, having two main harbors: Barcelona and Tarragona. There is a huge number of merchant vessels moving on an average speed of 15 knots, up to 25 knots for the ferries. The interactions with merchant vessels usually lead to the death of the animal with a small chance of survival (**Figure 9**, Video 7, https://edmaktub.org/en/drones-applied-to-cetacean-research/#Video%207).

Interaction with recreational vessels has also been reported on fin whales in the area, observing cuts and contusions in some of the animals. Most of the lesions reported are located close to the dorsal fin or peduncle, probably because it is the region of the body more exposed while performing an elusive dive (**Figure 11**).

To conclude, with this indirect measuring method, the body parameters can be assessed; furthermore, temporal and permanent changes in the body morphology can be followed over time by remeasuring individuals and controlling the visual health indicators, which gives information on growth tendencies, proportional changes, allometric relationships, volumetric changes, sex-based variation, and health status. These morphological attributes are essential for monitoring the local population to

Figure 10.
Fin whale head full of parasites Penella balaenoptera.

Figure 11.
Images obtained with the drone of the individual Bp_193. (A) Image from May 2021. (B) Image of April 2022. (C) Image from April 2022 of an injury in front of the dorsal fin.

determine the population status and health and for the implementation of proper conservation and population management actions.

The wide range of results arising from our morphological studies further represent the extensive utility of UAVs in the field of cetacean science.

3.4 Blow sampling

Traditionally, exhaled air samples were collected using a long pole or rod from a boat. Drones, however, offer a less intrusive approach to getting closer to large cetaceans compared to boats. The ability to fly directly over the animal at the moment of the powerful exhalation enables the collection of these samples. This has become one of the primary objectives of the use of drones in cetacean research.

The speed at which the fin whale moves, compared to other species, significantly complicates this task. However, extensive experience and a thorough understanding of the individual's behavior facilitate successful sampling. After observing the whale's movements and breathing patterns, the drone is positioned several meters above the animal, ensuring that the front half of its body is captured within the frame for reference. At the moment the whale is about to exhale, the drone is maneuvered toward the blowhole, aligning its speed with that of the animal, ensuring the device is exposed to the jet of air, thereby allowing the sampling plate to be impregnated (Video 8, https://edmaktub.org/en/drones-applied-to-cetacean-research/#Video%208). The drone should be positioned downwind of the blow during sampling, which can be determined by the direction of the vapor cloud.

The sample will be collected in structures adapted to the drone, such as Petri dishes, alone or with absorbent materials or culture medium, depending on the purpose of the analysis to be carried out. The placement of the plates on the drone varies according to the type of drone [47, 61].

When considering the placement of sampling material on the drone, aerodynamics and the existence of sensors must be taken into account. Improvements in sensor-based anti-collision systems prevent the positioning of any object within range. It is therefore practical to use flat structures oriented vertically underneath the drone or horizontally on the upper surface. The forced circulation by the propellers a priori facilitates sample collection above the drone.

4. Discussion

When using drones for cetacean research, there are several aspects to take into account: the project aims, the budget and the platforms from which the flights will be performed. From our experience, small drones are the best option with a reasonable quality-price ratio, recording nowadays at 5 K 60 fps definition. These drones also have a high versatility and are easy to maneuver, requiring just one expert drone pilot and initial guidance from researchers aboard the vessel.

On the other hand, fixed-wing and large drones are more challenging and specific to utilize. In the case of fixed-wing drones, they are mainly used for population studies, by performing line transects. Large drones present significant challenges in terms of take-off, maneuverability, and landing. These types of drones have extended battery lifespans; however, due to the logistical requirements, these instruments must be launched from land or large research vessels. This complicates their management and necessitates additional personnel to carry out the transect. Moreover, large multicopters face similar issues. The cost of these large drones is significantly higher than that of small UAVs, the maneuver and control of the device is more complicated and charging the batteries needed to fly can be a big issue depending on the type of vessel used for the research. Being bigger allows these drones to deploy monitoring devices such as D-Tags, but in general, they are less versatile and less accessible for some of the researchers working on this field [62–64].

As discussed above, drones give an aerial perspective which is extremely useful to capture footage for different research fields, being able to film the same animal several times and obtain an extensive amount of information about the target research lines. By multiplying the effort carried out at sea with the help of drones, a wide array of data is acquired that can be implemented and analyzed with various methods for different scientific purposes. This data was priorly difficult and costly to obtain before the introduction of this new technology.

One of the most significant improvements that drones have achieved in case of fin whales is the identification of individuals. The use of drones has enhanced the accuracy of fin whale identification, as the distinctive patterns of the chevron and the blazer provide a clear and reliable means of identification. These patterns are characteristic due to their unique shapes and pigmentation, which appear to remain consistent over time, further supporting the effectiveness in distinguishing individual fin whales [13]. Standardizing this photo-identification technique around the globe could bring a huge amount of data regarding population aggregations and migratory movements still unknown on this species.

Moreover, this method of identification could be applied to other species of the family Balaenopteridae that also have chevrons, such as the sei whale and the Bryde's whale (personal communication).

Although the quality of the video is very high, the detail obtained is still not close to the quality of a good photo taken with a reflex camera with the appropriate lens, so small details that could be interesting to determine, for example, a skin condition, will be lost.

From our experience in drone research, the knowledge gained can be applied to improve the conservation and protection of marine mammals, with the aim of mitigating the risks associated with anthropogenic pressures and human-induced threats. Vessel collisions are a primary cause of mortality among fin whales. By systematically gathering and sharing data on population dynamics through aerial monitoring and morphological studies, as well as habitat use from behavioral studies, it becomes possible to inform policymakers and support the establishment of protected areas. Additionally, to reduce collision risks, modifications to shipping routes and/or the implementation of speed restrictions in regions with well-established whale movement patterns should be considered.

Finally, while the drone is an extraordinarily valuable tool, it is crucial to understand both its capabilities and limitations to maximize the quality of the collected data. Furthermore, it is essential to conduct further analysis of the animal's reactions to the drones in order to develop appropriate protocols that minimize any potential discomfort. Establishing standardized protocols for different species is vital to ensure a consistent approach for various research objectives. Thereby, contributing to the global advancement of accumulating knowledge of different species from all over the globe.

5. Conclusions

In conclusion, drones have proven to be a highly effective tool in advancing fin whale research across multiple domains. Their ability to capture high-quality images has significantly enhanced photo-identification efforts and therefore increased the probability of recapturing individuals over time. Furthermore, drones offer a non-invasive means of studying whale behavior, providing valuable insights into their feeding patterns, social interactions and movement dynamics without disturbing the animals. In terms of morphological studies, drones enable precise aerial measurements, which help assess growth rates, body condition, and health indicators. Additionally, drones play a crucial role in collecting biological samples, such as whale blow, allowing for the analysis of hormones, genetic material, and other biomarkers. All the above-mentioned research lines can be directly applied to inform conservation strategies and enhance the protection of these marine species. Overall, the integration of drone technology into fin whale research has revolutionized the way we study these magnificent creatures, offering safer, more efficient, and less intrusive methods for monitoring their populations, health, and behaviors. Giving the opportunity to researchers to standardize protocols to be able to easily share and compare the data.

Acknowledgements

We would like to express our heartfelt appreciation to the dedicated volunteers and interns who contributed to the field seasons of the Fin Whale Project. Our sincere gratitude also goes to the generous donors whose support made this project a reality.

A special thank you to Club Nautic de Vilanova, the primary administrator of this initiative, for their continued partnership and logistical assistance.

Conflict of interest

The authors declare no conflict of interest.

Author details

Eduard Degollada[1*], Beatriu Tort[1,2] and Dorottya Mészáros[1]

1 EDMAKTUB Association, Barcelona, Spain

2 Polytechnical University of Catalonia, Barcelona, Spain

*Address all correspondence to: edmaktub@edmaktub.org

References

[1] Domínguez-Sánchez CA, Acevedo-Whitehouse KA, Gendron D. Effect of drone-based blow sampling on blue whale (*Balaenoptera musculus*) behavior. Marine Mammal Science. 2018;**38**:841-850. DOI: 10.1111/mms.12482

[2] Raoult V, Colefax AP, Allan BM, Cagnazzi D, Castelblanco-Martínez N, Ierdiaconou D, et al. Operational protocols for the use of drones in marine animal research. Drones. 2020;**4**:64. DOI: 10.3390/drones4040064

[3] King SL, Jensen FH. Rise of the machines: Integrating technology with playback experiments to study cetacean social cognition in the wild. Methods in Ecology and Evolution. 2023;**14**:1873-1886. DOI: 10.1111/2041-210X.13935

[4] Torres LG, Nieukirk SL, Lemos L, Chandler TE. Drone up! Quantifying whale behavior from a new perspective improves observational capacity. Frontiers in Marine Science. 2018;**5**:319. DOI: 10.3389/fmars.2018.00319

[5] Ramos EA, Hartman KL, Baird RW, Lerma JK, Rodríguez-González FM, Orbach DN. Drone perspectives on cetacean mating and sex. In: Würsig B, Orbach DN, editors. Sex in Cetaceans. Morphology, Behavior, and the Evolution of Sexual Strategies. Berlin, Germany: Springer; 2023. pp. 225-249. DOI: 10.1007/978-3-031-35651-3_11

[6] Christensen F, Dujon AM, Sprogis KR, Arnould JPY, Bejder L. Noninvasive unmanned aerial vehicle provides estimates of the energetic cost of reproduction in humpback whales. Ecosphere. 2016;7(10):e01468. DOI: 10.1002/ecs2.1468

[7] Álvarez-González M, Suarez-Bregua P, Pierce GJ, Saavedra C. Unmanned aerial vehicles (UAVs) in marine mammal research: A review of current applications and challenges. Drones. 2023;**7**:667. DOI: 10.3390/drones7110667

[8] Kelaher BP, Colefax AP, Tagliafico A, Bishop MJ, Giles A, Butcher PA. Assessing variation in assemblages of large marine fauna off ocean beaches using drones. Marine and Freshwater Research. 2019;**71**:68-77. DOI: 10.1071/MF18375

[9] Fettermann T, Fiori L, Gillman L, Stockin KA, Bollard B. Drone surveys are more accurate than boat-based surveys of bottlenose dolphins (*Tursiops truncatus*). Drones. 2022;**6**:82. DOI: 10.3390/drones6040082

[10] Salgado Kent, CP, Burton C, Giroud M, Elsdon B. A photo-identification study of southern right whales to update aggregation area classification in the southwest of Australia. Report to the National Environmental Science Program. Sydney, Australia: Edith Cowan University; 2022

[11] Young BG, Kioski WR, Kilabuk R, Watt CA, Ryan KP, Ferguson SH. Collaborative field research using drones for whale photo-identification studies in Cumberland Sound, Nunavut. Drone Systems and Applications. 2022;**10**:256-265. DOI: 10.1139/dsa-2021-0026

[12] Ramp C, Gaspard D, Gavrilchuk K, Unger M, Schleimer A, Delarue J, et al. Up in the air: Drone images reveal underestimation of entanglement rates in large rorqual whales. Endangered Species Research. 2021;**44**:33-44. DOI: 10.3354/esr01084

[13] Degollada E, Amigó N, O'Callaghan SA, Varola M, Ruggero K,

Tort B. A novel technique for photo-identification of the fin whale, *Balaenoptera physalus*, as determined by drone aerial images. Drones. 2023;7(3):220. DOI: 10.3390/drones7030220

[14] O'Callaghan SA, Al Abbar F, Costa H, Prieto R, Gammell M, O'Brien J. Aerial photo-identification of sperm whales (*Physeter macrocephalus*). Aquatic Mammals. 2024;**50**(6):479-494. DOI: 10.1578/AM.50.6.2024.479

[15] Weiss MN, Franks DW, Giles DA, Youngstrom S, Wasser SK, Balcomb KC, et al. Age and sex influence social interactions, but not associations, within a killer whale pod. Proceedings of the Royal Society. 2021;**B 288**:20210617. DOI: 10.1098/rspb.2021.0617

[16] Izadi S, Aguilar de Soto N, Constantine R, Johnson M. Feeding tactics of resident Bryde's whales in New Zealand. Marine Mammal Science. 2022;**38**:1104-1117. DOI: 10.1111/mms.12918

[17] Werth AJ, Kosma MM, Chenoweth EM, Straley JM. New views of humpback whale flow dynamics and oral morphology during prey engulfment. Marine Mammal Science. 2019;**35**:1556-1578. DOI: 10.1111/mms.12614

[18] Herr H, Viquerat S, Devas F, Lees A, Wells L, Gregory B, et al. Return of large fin whale feeding aggregations to historical whaling grounds in the Southern Ocean. Scientific Reports. 2022;**12**:9458. DOI: 10.1038/s41598-022-13798-7

[19] Torres LG, Barlow DR, Chandler TE, Burnett JD. Insight into the kinematics of blue whale surface foraging through drone observations and prey data. PeerJ. 2020;**8**:e8906. DOI: 10.7717/peerj.8906

[20] Fiori L, Martinez E, Bader MF-K, Orams MB, Bollard B. Insights into the use of an unmanned aerial vehicle (UAV) to investigate the behavior of humpback whales (Megaptera novaeangliae) in Vava'u, Kingdom of Tonga. Marine Mammal Science. 2020;**36**:209-223. DOI: 10.1111/mms.12637

[21] Jones SL, Stephenson TA, Zoidis AM, Todd SK. Drone observations of a mother–calf humpback whale (*Megaptera novaeangliae*) pair synchronous feeding in the Bay of Fundy, Canada. Aquatic Mammals. 2022;**48**(6):716-719. DOI: 10.1578/AM.48.6.2022.716

[22] Nielsen MLK, Sprogis KR, Bejder L, Madsen PT, Christiansen F. Behavioural development in southern right whale calves. Marine Ecology Progress Series. 2019;**629**:219-234. DOI: 10.3354/meps13125

[23] Cole TVN, Hamilton P, Henry AG, Duley P, Pace RM III, White BN, et al. Evidence of a North Atlantic right whale Eubalaena glacialis mating ground. Endangered Species Research. 2013;**21**:55-64. DOI: 10.3354/esr00507

[24] Fiori L, Martinez E, Orams MB, Bollard B. Using Unmanned Aerial Vehicles (UAVs) to assess humpback whale behavioral responses to swim-with interactions in Vava'u, Kingdom of Tonga. Journal of Sustainable Tourism. 2020;**28**:1743-1761. DOI: 10.1080/09669582.2020.1758706

[25] Hartman K, van der Harst P, Vilela R. Continuous focal group follows operated by a drone enable analysis of the relation between sociality and position in a Group of Male Risso's Dolphins (*Grampus griseus*). Frontiers in Marine Science. 2020;7:283. DOI: 10.3389/fmars.2020.00283

[26] Weir JS, Fiori L, Orbach DN, Piwetz S, Protheroe C, Würsig B. Dusky dolphin (*Lagenorhynchus obscurus*) mother—Calf pairs: An aerial perspective. Aquatic Mammals. 2018;**44**(6):603-607. DOI: 10.1578/AM.44.6.2018.603

[27] Orbach DN, Eaton J, Fiori L, Piwetz S, Weir JS, Würsig M, et al. Mating patterns of dusky dolphins (*Lagenorhynchus obscurus*) explored using an unmanned aerial vehicle. Marine Mammal Science. 2020;**36**:1097-1110. DOI: 10.1111/mms.12695

[28] Fettermann T, Fiori L, Bader M, Doshi A, Breen D, Stockin KA, et al. Behaviour reactions of bottlenose dolphins (*Tursiops truncatus*) to multirotor Unmanned Aerial Vehicles (UAVs). Scientific Reports. 2019;**9**:8558. DOI: 10.1038/s41598-019-44976-9

[29] Castro J, Borges FO, Cid A, Laborde MI, Rosa R, Pearson HC. Assessing the behavioural responses of small cetaceans to unmanned aerial vehicles. Remote Sensing. 2021;**13**:156. DOI: 10.3390/rs13010156

[30] Fujino K. On the body proportion of the Fin Whales (*Balaenoptera physalus* (L)) caught in the North Pacific Ocean. Scientific Reports of the Whales Research Institute. 1954;**9**:121-163

[31] Ohsumi S. Yearly change in age and body length at sexual maturity of fin whale stock in the eastern north pacific. Scientific Reports of the Whales Research Institute. 1986;**37**:1-16

[32] Best PB, Ruther D. Aerial photogrammetry of southern right whales, *Eubalaena australis*. Journal of Zoology. 1992;**228**:595-614. DOI: 10.1111/j.1469-7998.1992.tb04458.x

[33] Bierlich K, Schick S, Hewitt J, Dale J. A Bayesian approach for predicting photogrammetric uncertainty in morphometric measurements derived from UAS. Marine Ecology Progress Series. 2021;**673**:193-210. DOI: 10.3354/meps13814

[34] Durban J, Moore MJ, Chiang G, Hickmott LS, Bocconcelli A, Howes G, et al. Photogrammetry of blue whales with an unmanned hexacopter. Marine Mammal Science. 2016;**32**:151-1515. DOI: 10.1111/mms.12328

[35] Gough WT, Smith HJ, Savoca MS, Czapanskiy MF, Fish FE, Potvin J, et al. Scaling of oscillatory kinematics and Froude efficiency in baleen whales. Journal of Experimental Biology. 2021;**224**:jeb237586. DOI: 10.1242/jeb.237586

[36] Torres LG, Bird CN, Rodríguez-González F, Christiansen F, Bejder L, Lemos L, et al. Range-wide comparison of gray whale body condition reveals contrasting sub-population health characteristics and vulnerability to environmental change. Frontiers in Marine Science;**9**:867258. DOI: 10.3389/fmars.2022.867258

[37] Fernandez Ajó A, Pirotta E, Bierlich KC, Hildebrand L, Bird CN, Hunt KE, et al. Assessment of a non-invasive approach to pregnancy diagnosis in gray whales through drone-based photogrammetry and faecal hormone analysis. Royal Society Open Science. 2023;**10**:230452. DOI: 10.1098/rsos.230452

[38] Pirotta E, Bierlich KC, New L, Hildebrand L, Bird CN, Fernandez Ajó A, et al. Modeling individual growth reveals decreasing gray whale body length and correlations with ocean climate indices at multiple scales. Global Change Biology. 2024;**30**:e17366. DOI: 10.1111/gcb.17366

[39] Bierlich KC, Karki S, Bird CN, Fern A, Torres LG. Automated body

length and body condition measurements of whales from drone videos for rapid assessment of population health. Marine Mammal Science. 2024;**40**:e13137. DOI: 10.1111/mms.13137

[40] Bierlich KC, Hewitt J, Schick RS, Pallin L, Dale J, Friedlaender AS, et al. Seasonal gain in body condition of foraging humpback whales along the Western Antarctic Peninsula. Frontiers in Marine Science. 2022;**9**:1036860. DOI: 10.3389/fmars.2022.1036860

[41] Napoli C, Hirtle N, Stepanuk J, Christiansen F, Heywood EI, Grove TJ, et al. Drone-based photogrammetry reveals differences in humpback whale body condition and mass across North Atlantic foraging grounds. Frontiers in Marine Science. 2024;**11**:1336455. DOI: 10.3389/fmars.2024.1336455

[42] Dickson T, Rayment W, Dawson SM. Drone photogrammetry allows refinement of acoustically derived length estimation for male sperm whales. Marine Mammal Science. 2021;**37**:1150-1158. DOI: 10.1111/mms.12795

[43] Durban J, Fearnbach H, Paredes A, Hickmott L, LeRoi D. Size and body condition of sympatric killer whale ecotypes around the Antarctic Peninsula. Marine Ecology Progress Series. 2021;**677**:209-217. DOI: 10.3354/meps13866

[44] Arranz P, Christiansen FO, Sprogis K, Gero S, Glarou M, Visser F, et al. Free Ranging Short-Finned Pilot Whales Morphometric Measurements from Aerial Photographs (North Atlantic). Vol. V1. Spain: University of La Laguna, Santa Cruz de Tenerife; 2022. DOI: 10.17632/5nhx7tgrxc.1

[45] Tort B, Prieto R, O'Callaghan SA, Dominguez P, Degollada E. Ship strike risk for fin whales (*Balaenoptera physalus*) off the Garraf coast, Northwest Mediterranean Sea. Frontiers in Marine Science. 2022;**9**:867287. DOI: 10.3389/fmars.2022.867287

[46] Apprill A, Miller CA, Moore MJ, Durban JW, Fearnbach H, Barrett-Lennard LG. Extensive core microbiome in drone-captured whale blow supports a framework for health monitoring. mSystems;**2**:e00119-17. DOI: 10.1128/mSystems.00119-17

[47] O'Mahony EN, Sremba AL, Keen EM, Robinson N, Dundas A, Steel D, et al. Collecting baleen whale blow samples by drone: A minimally intrusive tool for conservation genetics. Molecular Ecology Resources. 2024;**24**:e13957. DOI: 10.1111/1755-0998.13957

[48] Tort B, Degollada E. Results of the study of the fin whales on its route around the Iberian Peninsula. Barcelona, Spain: Fin Whale Project Report; 2024

[49] Smith CE, Sykora-Bodie ST, Bloodworth B, Pack SM, Spradlin TR, LeBoeuf NR. Assessment of known impacts of unmanned aerial systems (UAS) on marine mammals: Data gaps and recommendations for researchers in the United States. Unmanned Vehicle System. 2016;**4**:31-44. DOI: 10.1139/juvs-2015-0017

[50] Dawson S, Bowman M, Leunissen E, Sirguey P. Inexpensive aerial photogrammetry of studies of whale and large marine animals. Frontiers in Marine Science. 2017;**4**:366-373. DOI: 10.3389/fmars.2017.00366

[51] Christiansen F, Sironi M, Moore M, Ricciardi M, Warick H, Irschick D, et al. Estimating body mass of free-living whales using aerial photogrammetry and 3D volumetrics. Methods in Ecology

and Evolution. 2019;**10**:2034-2044. DOI: 10:2034-2044

[52] Gray P, Bierlich K, Mantell S. Drones and convolutional neural networks facilitate automated and accurate cetacean species identification and photogrammetry. Methods in Ecology and Evolution. 2019;**10**:1490-1500. DOI: 10.1111/2041-210X.13246

[53] Castrillon J, Bengtson NS. Evaluating cetacean body condition; a review of traditional approaches and new developments. Ecology and Evolution. 2020;**10**:6144-6162. DOI: 10.1002/ece3.6301

[54] Soledade L, Burnett JD, Chandler TE, Sumich JL, Torres LG. Intra- and inter-annual variation in gray whale body condition on a foraging ground. Ecosphere. 2020;**11**:e03094. DOI: 10.1002/ecs2.3094

[55] Torres WI, Bierlich KC. MorphoMetriX: A photogrammetric measurement GUI for morphometric analysis of megafauna. Journal of Open Source Software. 2020;**5**:1825. DOI: 10.21105/joss.01825

[56] Cheney B, Dale J, Thompson P, Quick N. Spy in the sky: A method to identify pregnant small cetaceans. Remote Sensing in Ecology and Conservation. 2022;**8**:492-505

[57] Carrillo JM, Overstreet RM, Raga JA, Aznar FJ. Living on the edge: Settlement patterns by the symbiotic barnacle *Xenobalanus globicipitis* on small cetaceans. PLoS ONE. 2015;**10**(6):e0127367. DOI: 10.1371/journal.pone.0127367

[58] Fraija-Fernández N, Hernández-Hortelano A, Ahuir-Baraja AE, Raga JA, Aznar FJ. Taxonomic status and epidemiology of the mesoparasitic copepod *Pennella balaenoptera* in cetaceans from the western Mediterranean. Diseases of Aquatic Organisms. 2018;**128**:249-258. DOI: 10.3354/dao03226

[59] Oren S, Edery N, Yasur Landau D, King R, Mazuz M, Bari S, et al. First report of *Pennella balaenopterae* infestation in a fin whale (*Balaenoptera physalus*) carcass washed ashore on the Israeli Coastline. Israel Journal of Veterinary Medicine. 2023;**78**:4-8

[60] Mazzariol S, Di Guardo G, Petrella A, Marsili L, Fossi CM, Leonzio C, et al. Sometimes sperm whales (*Physeter macrocephalus*) cannot find their way back to the high seas: A multidisciplinary study on a mass stranding. PLoS ONE. 2011;**6**(5):e19417. DOI: 10.1371/journal.pone.0019417. Epub May 18

[61] Pirotta V, Smith A, Ostrowski M, Russell D, Jonsen I, Grech A, et al. An economical custom-built drone for assessing whale health. Frontiers in Marine Science. 2017;**4**:425

[62] Parham E, Meiselman H, Yu J, Morris D. Drone Tagging. University of Michigan, Michigen, United States of America. 2023. DOI: 10.7302/8019

[63] Wiley DN, Zadra CJ, Friedlaender AS, Parks SE, Pensarosa A, Rogan A, et al. Deployment of biologging tags on free swimming large whales using uncrewed aerial systems. Royal Society Open Science. 2023;**10**:221376. DOI: 10.1098/rsos.221376

[64] Quian C, Krishnan M, Otterbach C, Hancock A. Improving Flight Stability of Remote Biologging Tag-Deployment Systems. Michigen, United States of America: University of Michigan; 2024. DOI: 10.7302/2337

Chapter 7

Environmental Monitoring in the Oil and Gas Industry Using Machine Vision Associated with Robotics and AI

Navid Nasiri, Ahmed Al-Maashri, Hadj Bourdoucen, Said Al-Abri and Nabil Aouf

Abstract

Emerging technologies such as artificial intelligence and unmanned vehicle systems present promising opportunities for enhancing environmental monitoring in the oil and gas industry. Traditional methods often fall short in delivering real-time data, broad spatial coverage, and rapid response. This chapter focuses on AI-powered multi-drone systems designed to detect oil contamination in marine environments. To understand their function, the chapter first outlines the essential components of unmanned systems, highlighting recent advances in machine vision that have significantly improved detection, navigation, and obstacle avoidance in harsh settings. Deploying unmanned aerial vehicle(s) offers advantages such as broader area coverage, reduced mission duration, and increased reliability. However, coordinating these systems introduces complexities, especially in communication, data exchange, real-time decision-making, power management, and collision avoidance. For instance, as per communication, wireless telecommunication is emphasized as a cornerstone of successful multi-drone operations. The chapter presents relevant simulation scenarios alongside field experiment insights to validate not only the communication but also system capabilities. Given the intricacy of multi-drone operations, the integration of subsystems often involves tradeoffs, which necessitates the use of optimization techniques. Through a balanced exploration of system modeling, analytical methods, and hardware prototyping, the chapter addresses common misconceptions surrounding the effectiveness of AI-integrated drone/swarm drones. Ultimately, readers will gain a comprehensive understanding of how intelligent, cooperative unmanned systems can revolutionize environmental monitoring in demanding industrial environments.

Keywords: environmental monitoring, machine vision, unmanned vehicle systems, artificial intelligence, multi-drone systems, oil contamination detection, real-world experiments

1. Introduction

Oil spills pose significant environmental concerns, presenting serious risks to marine ecosystems, coastal economies, and public health. A notable incident occurred in 2010 when nearly 750,000 cubic meters of crude oil leaked into the Gulf of Mexico [1]. This catastrophic event had devastating consequences for marine life and the surrounding coastal areas, leading to long-term ecological damage. Currently, the methods used for detecting and containing oil spills are not only costly but also often slow to respond, requiring intervention by specialized teams with specific skills. Additionally, inaccurate information about the locations and sizes of spills can severely disrupt cleanup operations. These traditional methods for detecting and cleaning up oil spills typically involve manual monitoring and extensive resource usage, which can result in delayed responses and significant environmental damage.

In recent years, technological advancements have opened new avenues for improving the efficiency of oil spill detection and response efforts [2]. Among these innovations, AI-enhanced multi-drone systems have emerged as transformative solutions. Multi-drone systems enable real-time monitoring of vast geographical areas, aiding in the rapid identification of incidents and enhancing overall situational awareness [3]. The use of unmanned aerial vehicles (UAVs) allows for the quick deployment of multiple drones to cover larger areas more effectively than single-unit operations. This collaborative approach not only accelerates detection but also improves the accuracy of assessing oil contamination [4]. Emerging research indicates that coordinated drone operations, equipped with advanced imaging technologies and sensors, can significantly enhance environmental monitoring and the efficiency of response strategies.

Concurrent advancements in machine vision further bolster the capabilities of multi-drone systems. By utilizing advanced algorithms and image processing techniques, these systems can automatically identify and analyze oil spills with greater accuracy. This integration of technology not only reduces the workload on human operators but also minimizes the likelihood of human error, ensuring a more reliable detection process. Studies show that the deployment of machine vision alongside multi-drone frameworks leads to efficient monitoring of oil spills, enabling timely interventions that mitigate environmental impacts [2].

Traditional monitoring methods for oil spill detection in marine environments, such as visual inspections and satellite imagery, have long been the cornerstone of environmental management. However, with the increasing complexity of maritime operations and the urgency of environmental protection, these methods reveal significant shortcomings that necessitate the exploration of innovative solutions. Among these challenges are limited coverage, high costs, and inflexibility, all of which have encouraged researchers to seek new ways to address these issues. We further elaborate on these limitations:

- Limited Coverage and Response Time: One of the most critical limitations of traditional monitoring techniques is their restricted coverage area and response time. Ground-based monitoring often relies on manual observations that can only cover limited geographical regions. This can lead to delayed detection of spills, particularly in vast oceanic areas where immediate human presence is challenging. Furthermore, satellite imagery, although advantageous for wide-area surveillance, suffers from time delays due to revisit times and cloud cover, which can obscure detection efforts. As a result, the lag in identifying spills can exacerbate environmental damage and complicate response efforts.

- Human Errors: Another significant drawback of traditional monitoring methods is their reliance on human assessment, which is inherently prone to error. Visual inspections can suffer from inaccuracies, as human observers may misidentify substances or overlook critical details, leading to false negatives and problematic outcomes. These subjective evaluations can hinder effective decision-making during oil spill responses, resulting in inefficient allocation of resources and delayed interventions [3].

- High Operational Costs: Traditional methods like manual inspections and boat-based patrols require substantial manpower and logistical support, leading to high operational costs. These costs are particularly elevated in remote or hard-to-reach locations. The heavy financial burden associated with deploying search teams or vessels naturally limits the frequency and thoroughness of monitoring efforts. This underscores the need for more cost-effective strategies [2].

- Inefficiency in Harsh Environments: Traditional monitoring methods exhibit low efficiency when faced with harsh environmental conditions. Changes in weather, sea state, or surface moisture can significantly affect both the visibility of spills and the effectiveness of monitoring techniques. These environmental and marine limitations reduce the efficiency of traditional methods and highlight the need for adaptable systems capable of operating under varying conditions [1].

How can emerging technologies help?

As our understanding of environmental management evolves and the shortcomings of traditional methods become apparent, there is an urgent need to adopt more effective strategies that prioritize timely detection and response to oil spills. As previously mentioned, detecting and containing oil spills is both slow and involves significant financial costs. This process is often prolonged by slow and inefficient coordination among the various parties involved in response efforts. The involvement of specialized teams adds another layer of complexity to the situation, making it more difficult to assess the necessary resources. This complexity can lead to worsening environmental damage, especially when data related to spills are inaccurate or incomplete [5].

Given the inefficiencies of traditional monitoring methods, there is an immediate need for innovation. The concept of integrating advanced technologies, such as AI-enhanced multi-drone systems, presents a compelling alternative to traditional methods. These modern and enhanced approaches offer not only faster response times and greater accuracy but also address many of the limitations associated with conventional approaches. Recent advancements in artificial intelligence and UAVs promise significant improvements in oil spill detection and containment. In the process of detecting and containing oil spills, the timely and accurate exchange of data is crucial to reducing the harmful impacts on the environment. Intelligent systems, in addition to timely detection, can also play a crucial role in the accurate exchange of data with minimal errors [6].

At the core of our exploration is the *multi-drone system*, illustrated in **Figure 1**, which serves as the central platform for automated monitoring in environmental contexts, particularly for detecting oil contamination in marine environments. This system is enhanced by several interconnected components and technologies that contribute to its overall efficacy.

The *autonomous control systems* are integral to the operation of the multi-drone system. These systems leverage advanced algorithms that enable drones to operate

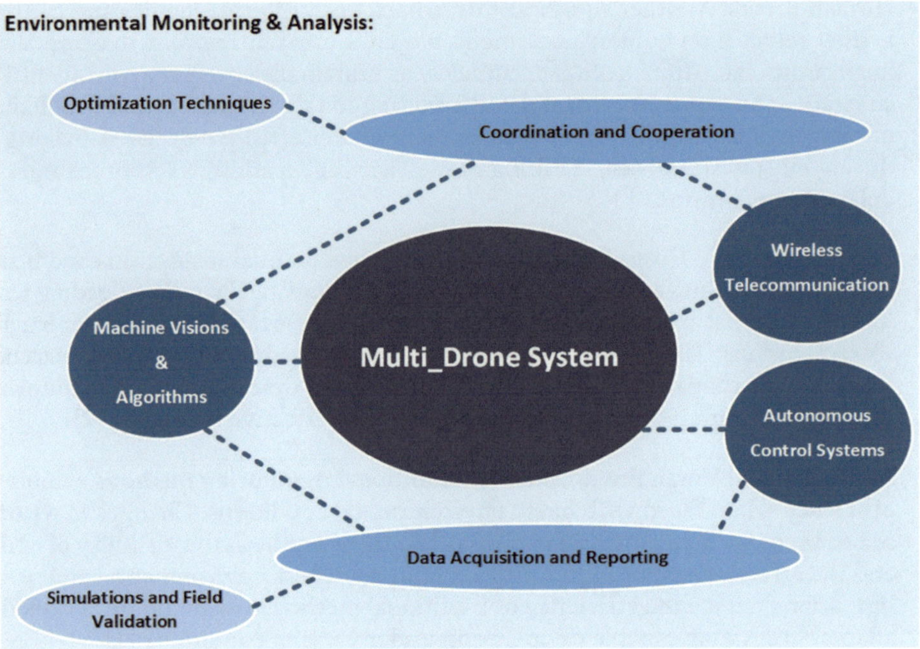

Figure 1.
Book chapter structure.

independently, making real-time decisions based on environmental data. The ability to autonomously navigate harsh conditions significantly improves operational efficiency in monitoring scenarios.

Critical to the multi-drone system's capabilities are *machine vision and algorithms*. Recent breakthroughs in machine vision technologies empower drones to detect and identify oil spills with high accuracy. These algorithms facilitate advanced functionalities such as navigation and obstacle avoidance, which are essential for operating in complex marine environments.

Effective *wireless telecommunication* is paramount for the success of the multi-drone system. Robust communication networks enable seamless coordination and data sharing among multiple drones, ensuring that they work in harmony to cover extensive areas efficiently. This coordination enhances the reliability and responsiveness of the system during monitoring missions.

To facilitate informed decision-making, the system incorporates comprehensive *data acquisition and reporting* mechanisms. These systems collect, analyze, and disseminate real-time data about environmental conditions, allowing for timely responses to detected contaminants.

In a multi-drone environment, *coordination and cooperation* among drones are essential. This ensures that missions are conducted efficiently and comprehensively, with drones strategically positioned to maximize coverage and reduce mission times.

The complexity of multi-drone systems may lead to conflicting subsystem requirements, necessitating the application of *optimization techniques*. These methods help to balance trade-offs between performance factors, such as speed and coverage, ensuring that the system functions optimally under varying conditions.

The effectiveness of the multi-drone system is rigorously tested through *simulation and field validation*. Simulations provide a cost-effective means to evaluate system performance, while field tests confirm the reliability of the technologies in real-world applications.

Ultimately, the integration of these components within the multi-drone system facilitates comprehensive *environmental monitoring and analysis*. By harnessing the capabilities of AI-driven technologies, this system aims to enhance the detection of oil spills and improve response times, significantly contributing to environmental protection efforts.

2. Multi-drone systems

The multi-drone configurations enhance the efficiency of detecting and estimating the dimensions and locations of oil spills through collaborative tracking and broader coverage. One key advantage is the ability of drones to share data in real time, facilitating a comprehensive understanding of spill dynamics and promoting coordinated monitoring. This collaborative approach ensures that essential information is not isolated, allowing remaining drones to redistribute tasks in case of battery depletion or malfunctions, thereby maintaining coverage over the affected area.

Moreover, the integration of advanced algorithms augments the collective intelligence of the drone fleet, leading to improved operational efficiency and quicker detection and response times. This rapid reaction capability is crucial for minimizing environmental damage and safeguarding marine ecosystems. By accumulating data from multiple drones, the system can also predict oil spill trajectories, providing decision-makers with valuable insights for implementing swift response measures [7].

The deployment of multiple drones significantly enhances monitoring capabilities by covering larger geographic areas more efficiently than a single UAV. Coordinated movements enable the creation of comprehensive aerial maps and extensive sensor data collection, which are vital in maritime environments prone to rapidly spreading spills. By scaling multi-drone systems, surveillance operations across vast oceanic regions become markedly more efficient, facilitating timely identification of oil spills and supporting rapid response initiatives to mitigate potential environmental damage [8].

In conclusion, multi-drone systems are poised to transform the monitoring processes for oil spills through collaborative tracking and expanded coverage capabilities. These advancements not only enhance the effectiveness of response strategies during environmental crises but also promote sustainable and responsible environmental management practices [9].

3. Autonomous control systems

The integration of autonomous control systems in drone technology has ushered in a new era of operational efficiency and effectiveness across various applications. Specifically, this section will delve into three critical aspects: *path optimization*, which focuses on optimizing flight routes to minimize travel time and energy consumption; *safety*, which emphasizes the implementation of protocols and technologies designed to mitigate risks and enhance the safety of drone operations; and *coverage area maximization*, which addresses strategies to ensure comprehensive surveillance and monitoring over extensive regions. Together, these subsections highlight the multifaceted benefits of autonomous control systems, demonstrating their pivotal role in transforming drone operations into sophisticated, reliable solutions for diverse environmental and industrial challenges.

3.1 Path optimization

Path optimization in unmanned aerial vehicles (UAVs) refers to the strategic calculation of efficient trajectories for tasks such as oil spill detection. This process considers factors such as energy consumption, coverage area, and obstacle avoidance to ensure high operational efficiency. A key equation that underpins this optimization is the dynamic model of UAVs:

$$x(t) = Ax(t) + Bu(t) \tag{1}$$

where (x(t)) represents the state vector (position, velocity, etc.), (u(t)) signifies control input (thrust, pitch, roll), and (A) and (B) are system matrices reflecting the UAV's dynamics. This equation enables precise predictive modeling of UAV behavior across various environmental conditions, which is foundational for efficient path planning.

Refs. [7, 10] are both widely used in fields requiring route optimization. Based on their studies, two essential parameters under path optimization are *efficient area coverage* and *energy-efficient operations*. Efficient area coverage employs advanced algorithms allowing drones to navigate their designated environments strategically, thereby maximizing the surveillance of regions prone to oil spills. By applying dynamic models and real-time data, UAVs can adaptively modify their trajectories, enhancing coverage and operational efficiency. The area coverage equation can be expressed as:

$$f(n) = g(n) + h(n) \tag{2}$$

Where f(n) is the total estimated cost, g(n) is the cost to reach node n, and h(n) is the estimated cost from node n to the goal. This optimization ensures comprehensive coverage, reducing the likelihood of neglected areas, which is vital for timely intervention during spill incidents.

The second important parameter, *energy-efficient operations*, is pivotal for extending UAV operational capabilities, particularly in extensive missions. By optimizing flight paths for both speed and energy efficiency, UAVs can maintain prolonged operational durations. Key strategies include dynamic throttle control that adjusts engine power according to flight phases, and enhancing energy conservation during cruising or descending. These adjustments not only maximize coverage but also minimize the frequency of battery replacements or refueling, crucial in remote applications.

In conclusion, improving path optimization in UAVs relies on leveraging advanced algorithms for efficient area coverage and energy conservation. Methods such as dynamic modeling, real-time data processing, and adaptive trajectory planning significantly enhance the reliability and efficiency of UAV operations, ensuring swift responses to environmental monitoring tasks such as oil spill detection. The integration of high-resolution imaging and machine learning further augments these capabilities, facilitating accurate and timely interventions in pollution management.

3.2 Safety

In the flight path, there is a possibility of obstacles like ships or other drones in the same mission. These large vessels can pose significant risks to aircraft, especially during takeoff and landing phases when altitude is limited. To mitigate such dangers, air traffic control systems are designed to monitor maritime traffic closely and provide pilots with real-time updates. Therefore, navigation systems must anticipate certain actions in the presence of obstacles. This predictive capability is essential for ensuring the safety and efficiency of autonomous vehicles. By utilizing advanced algorithms and machine learning techniques, these systems can analyze real-time data from various sensors, such as cameras, to identify potential hazards in the environment.

Autonomous control systems empower drones to safely navigate around obstacles. Their advanced algorithms allow them to maintain stability and adjust their paths as needed, which is crucial in avoiding potential collisions in cluttered or uncertain environments. Ref. [3] emphasizes the capability of drones to maneuver around obstacles safely, revealing their methods to ensure operational safety during experiments.

The control systems, on the other hand, are designed to handle turbulence and other challenging atmospheric conditions. This stability ensures that drones can continue to operate effectively even in adverse weather, maintaining the integrity of their monitoring tasks. These advanced control systems utilize a combination of sensors, algorithms, and real-time data processing to adapt to changing conditions. By continuously analyzing factors such as wind speed, temperature fluctuations, and humidity levels, the drones can make instantaneous adjustments to their flight paths. This capability not only enhances their operational efficiency but also extends their range and duration of missions. Ref. [4] discusses the robustness of the control systems in maintaining stability and operational effectiveness during flight, particularly in turbulent conditions [4, 11].

Finally, autonomous control systems integrated into drones not only enhance efficiency through path optimization but also ensure safety during operations. These advancements are critical in facilitating effective monitoring and detection of oil spills, thereby contributing significantly to environmental management in the oil and gas industry [1, 4].

3.3 Coverage area maximization

The effective coverage of target areas is paramount for UAV operations, particularly in applications such as environmental monitoring, search and rescue, and disaster response. To achieve optimal coverage, several innovative strategies have emerged, each addressing specific operational challenges and enhancing overall efficiency. This section will explore three key subsections: *grid-based approaches*, which systematically divide the area into manageable sections for thorough exploration; *adaptive flight patterns*, which leverage real-time data to adjust flight trajectories dynamically based on environmental conditions and target requirements; and *safety enhancements*, which focus on improving operational integrity and minimizing risks associated with UAV missions. Together, these strategies contribute to maximizing coverage area, ensuring that UAVs can operate effectively and efficiently in varying contexts.

3.3.1 Grid-based approaches

Grid partitioning is a highly effective method for ensuring complete coverage of an operational area during UAV missions. By dividing the area into a structured grid, UAVs can methodically scan each sector, eliminating the risk of overlapping and ensuring no section is missed. This organized approach maximizes the efficiency of the flight, especially when combined with energy-efficient operations such as throttle control. Algorithms used for trajectory planning consider the UAV's energy consumption profile, optimizing flight paths to balance speed with fuel or battery efficiency, further enhancing operational duration. Throttle control dynamically adjusts the engine settings, allowing the UAV to conserve energy during less critical phases of the mission, leading to extended flight times and increased survey coverage. Together, these strategies ensure that UAVs operate efficiently while covering vast areas in a systematic and energy-conscious manner.

$$Coverage = \sum_{grid} A_{cell} \tag{3}$$

Where A_{cell} is the area of each grid cell.

3.3.2 Adaptive flight patterns

Grid partitioning and dynamic adjustments work together to optimize UAV operations, especially in scenarios that require comprehensive coverage, such as oil spill monitoring. By dividing the operational area into a grid, UAVs can methodically scan each sector without overlapping, ensuring every section is covered efficiently. This structured approach can be enhanced through real-time data and environmental feedback, allowing for dynamic adjustments to flight patterns as new information on oil spill dynamics is collected. These adaptive changes improve the overall efficiency of coverage by responding to shifting conditions, ensuring that the UAVs remain focused on the most critical areas.

3.3.3 Safety enhancements

Autonomous UAV control systems rely on a combination of advanced sensor integration and robust control strategies to ensure smooth and efficient operations, particularly in dynamic or challenging environments. To detect and avoid obstacles in real time, these systems use onboard sensors such as LiDAR and cameras. These sensors feed data into algorithms like Rapidly-exploring Random Trees (RRT), which allow for quick re-planning of the UAV's flight path when obstacles are detected. By continuously scanning the environment, the UAV can avoid collisions and dynamically adjust its route to ensure safe navigation through complex environments.

In addition to obstacle detection, stability during flight is maintained through the use of robust control strategies. These strategies are essential for keeping the UAV steady, especially when facing adverse conditions such as wind gusts or turbulence. By leveraging feedback loops from the onboard sensors, the UAV is able to dynamically adjust its flight parameters in real time, including speed and orientation. This continuous adaptation helps maintain optimal flight performance, ensuring the UAV can handle unexpected environmental challenges while preserving its planned trajectory and mission objectives.

$$\tau = K_p e + K_d \frac{de}{dt} + K_i \int edt \tag{4}$$

Where τ is control thrust, e is an error in position or attitude, and K_p, K_d, K_i are proportional, derivative, and integral gains [9].

Example: An illustrative example of path optimization can be seen in the implementation of a zigzag trajectory mission for the drone during oil spill detection in the experimental arena. The autonomous drone's navigation system was meticulously programmed to follow this predefined path while maintaining a 25% overlap between successive flight lines. This strategic approach was designed to guarantee comprehensive area coverage, ultimately enhancing the optimization of the search pattern.

As a result of this tailored zigzag pattern, the drone successfully navigated the defined area and consistently detected oil spills with closed contours, thus demonstrating the effectiveness of the path optimization strategy. The trials conducted revealed a remarkable achievement: the drone reduced the search time by approximately 30% compared to conventional random flight patterns. This improvement not only illustrates the advantages of employing systematic trajectory planning but also underscores the potential for increased operational efficiency in real-world oil spill detection scenarios. The incorporation of such optimized paths can significantly enhance the responsiveness and effectiveness of environmental monitoring efforts.

4. Autonomous path planning

Autonomous path planning is a key aspect of using unmanned aerial vehicles (UAVs) for efficient oil spill detection and response. By utilizing artificial intelligence (AI) algorithms, UAVs can optimize their operations and ensure comprehensive coverage and effective interventions. This path planning process includes four major phases, as shown in **Figure 2**. In the following sections, we will first address the

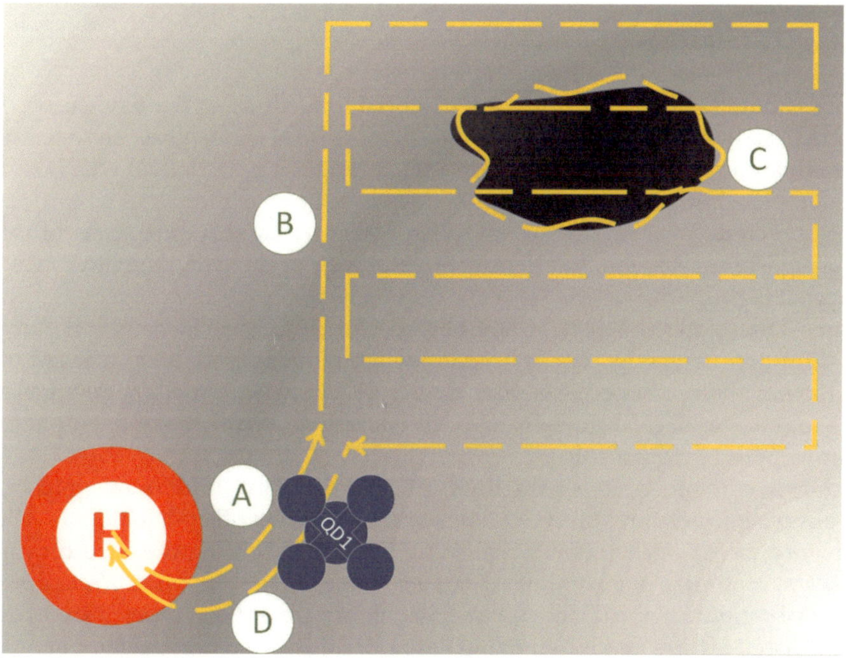

Figure 2.
The main phases of path planning: A: After taking off and heading to the start point, B: scanning, C: skimming, and D: back to the landing point.

characteristics of these four phases, followed by an examination of the common parameters and key considerations shared across all stages.

4.1 Path planning

The initial phase, path A, encompasses the time frame that begins with the takeoff of the unmanned aerial vehicle (UAV) and extends until it reaches the area where an oil spill is suspected to have occurred. During this period, the geographical coordinates of the suspected site are transmitted to the detection system, which can be accomplished through satellite communication or by gathering information from local fishermen who may have observed the spill.

The subsequent phase, path B, is characterized by a comprehensive patrol operation aimed at locating the oil spill with a higher degree of accuracy compared to the initial stage. During this phase, the unmanned aerial vehicles (UAVs) utilize a range of sophisticated algorithms specifically designed to detect and identify any indications of oil spills present on the surface of the sea within a designated and confined area.

Once the UAVs successfully delineate the boundaries of the oil spill, they proceed to create a detailed map of the spill. This process, path C, represents the third phase of their autonomous operational movement. Following the generation of the oil spill map or in response to other factors such as the depletion of battery power, the fourth phase is initiated.

In this phase, path D, the UAVs are programmed to return to their designated landing site, where they will execute an automated landing procedure at the appropriate location. Upon reaching this location, they will execute an automated landing procedure at the correct and suitable spot.

4.2 Optimal navigation

Artificial intelligence algorithms are essential in facilitating the navigation of unmanned aerial vehicles (UAVs) through intricate and challenging environments. These sophisticated algorithms consider a wide range of parameters, which encompass geographical information systems (GIS), current environmental conditions, and previously recorded data related to oil spills. By analyzing this diverse set of information, the algorithms are able to effectively determine and outline the most efficient and optimal flight paths for the UAVs to follow.

Figure 3 illustrates the distribution of importance among the common parameters essential for optimal navigation in unmanned aerial vehicles (UAVs) utilized in oil spill detection and response. The chart clearly delineates how each parameter contributes to the overall effectiveness of UAV operations, with a notable emphasis on efficient response mechanisms.

As shown, *efficient response* constitutes 60% of the chart, underscoring its critical role in ensuring timely and effective interventions during oil spill incidents. Within this category, *timely interventions* account for 50%, highlighting the need for rapid responses to minimize environmental impact. Integration with *multi-drone operations* and *resource optimization* each comprise 25%, showcasing their importance in enhancing coordinated efforts and maximizing resources during spill management.

In contrast, *optimal navigation* is represented at 40%, pointing to its significant impact on the overall operation of UAVs. Both *route assessment* and *adaptive flight planning* share equal weight at 50% each, indicating their fundamental roles in

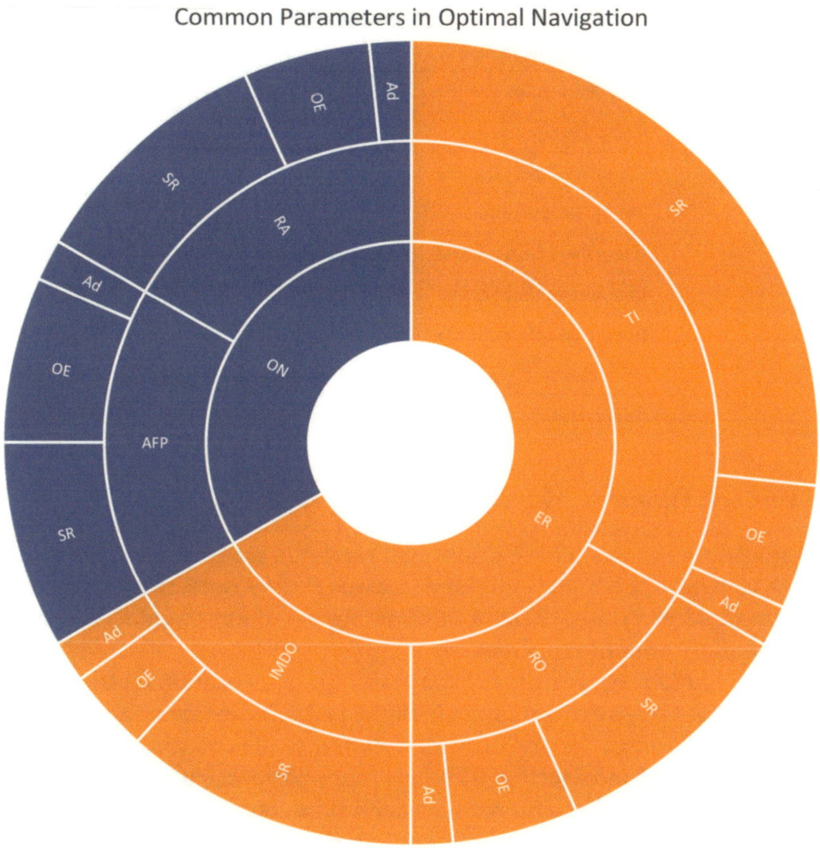

	Explanation	Abreaction
1	***Optimal Navigation***	ON
2	***Efficient Response***	ER
3	***Route Assessment***	RA
4	***Adaptive Flight Planning***	AFP
5	***Timely Interventions***	TI
6	***Integration with Multi-Drone Operations***	IMDO
7	***Resource Optimization***	RO
8	***Impact on Spill Response***	SR
9	***Operational Efficiency***	OE
10	***Adaptability***	Ad

Figure 3.
Distribution of significance among the key parameters crucial for optimal navigation in UAVs employed in oil spill detection and response.

determining effective flight paths and adjusting to dynamic conditions throughout the mission [8, 12, 13].

Overall, the pie chart not only visualizes the relative importance of these parameters but also emphasizes the interdependence between optimal navigation and efficient response capabilities in achieving the primary goals of oil spill detection and environmental protection.

Route Assessment enables UAVs to analyze multiple navigation options based on environmental conditions, obstacles, and previous spill incidents. This capability is critical for thorough surveys, enhancing spill detection effectiveness, particularly in

	Explanation	Abbreviation
1	Optimal navigation	ON
2	Efficient response	ER
3	Route assessment	RA
4	Adaptive flight planning	AFP
5	Timely interventions	TI
6	Integration with multi-drone operations	IMDO
7	Resource optimization	RO
8	Impact on spill response	SR
9	Operational efficiency	OE
10	Adaptability	Ad

Table 1.
Abbreviation and explanation of common parameters in optimal navigation.

extensive maritime regions where traditional methods are inadequate. By evaluating factors such as wind speeds and potential hazards, UAVs determine optimal routes that facilitate rapid response, thereby minimizing detection-to-intervention time and reducing potential contaminants' spread.

Adaptive flight planning is essential for maintaining operational effectiveness as conditions change. UAVs can adjust their flight paths in real time, allowing them to navigate unforeseen obstacles and adverse weather while ensuring continuous data acquisition during spill monitoring. Efficient flight paths calculated by advanced autonomous systems significantly reduce travel time, enabling UAVs to respond swiftly to spills, which is vital for implementing effective interventions (**Table 1**).

The *integration with multi-drone operations* enhances coverage and responsiveness during spill response efforts. By coordinating multiple UAVs, each can cover unique areas while retaining adaptability to emerging challenges. This collaborative approach maximizes monitoring efficiency and streamlines operations in complex and time-sensitive scenarios.

Resource optimization is paramount in spill response operations, focusing on how effectively UAVs deploy necessary technologies and personnel. By enhancing flight operation efficiency, UAVs strategically manage resources, reducing costs while maximizing operational effectiveness.

In summary, advancements in autonomous path planning have established UAVs as indispensable tools for oil spill monitoring and environmental management. The integration of artificial intelligence in navigation systems and response strategies significantly improves monitoring and intervention efforts, paving the way for more effective ecological protection and risk mitigation.

5. Machine vision for oil spill detection

Artificial intelligence (AI) refers to the simulation of human intelligence processes by machines, particularly computer systems, enabling the ability to analyze data, learn from experiences, and make informed decisions. Within this realm, machine vision has emerged as a pivotal technology that allows computers to interpret and understand visual information from the world through images and videos. By leveraging AI-driven machine vision, multi-drone systems can significantly enhance a variety of areas, including the detection and monitoring of oil spills, offering rapid and accurate analysis in real time while overcoming the limitations of traditional monitoring methods.

Several studies, such as Refs. [14–18], have shown that machine vision techniques substantially improve the detection of oil spills in aerial imagery. The application of advanced algorithms not only enhances detection accuracy but also minimizes the time necessary for analysis, thereby facilitating more rapid response strategies in environmental management. Future research should prioritize the refinement of machine vision algorithms to improve object recognition capabilities across diverse environmental conditions. The incorporation of machine learning methodologies could further enhance the system's performance and adaptability to dynamic marine environments.

This study demonstrates that real-time oil spill detection utilizing machine vision can deliver prompt notifications to environmental response teams. The efficacy of the applied image processing techniques substantiates their viability for operational implementation in the surveillance of marine ecosystems. Collaboration among researchers, environmental agencies, and technology developers is essential for refining these machine vision systems. By standardizing methodologies and facilitating data sharing, the academic community can improve detection capabilities and enhance the effectiveness of spill management operations.

In the exploration of machine vision for oil spill detection, this section will delve into several critical subsections that underscore the technology's transformative impact on environmental monitoring. First, *real-time analysis* highlights the capability of machine vision systems to process aerial imagery as it is captured, allowing for immediate identification and assessment of oil spills. Next, the focus will shift to *processing efficiency*, examining how advanced algorithms streamline data analysis, significantly reducing the time required for detection and response. The subsection on *application in studies* will provide insight into various research efforts and case studies demonstrating successful implementations of machine vision techniques in real-world scenarios. Lastly, we will discuss the importance of *adaptation to environmental conditions*, addressing the challenges posed by diverse marine environments and illustrating how machine vision algorithms can be fine-tuned to maintain high accuracy under varying conditions. Together, these subsections elucidate the multifaceted advantages of machine vision in combating oil spill incidents effectively.

5.1 Real-time analysis and processing efficiency

Real-time analysis is a critical feature of machine vision systems utilized in unmanned aerial vehicles (UAVs) for detecting oil spills. These systems leverage advanced algorithms and high-resolution imaging sensors to efficiently monitor large water bodies. By processing visual data in real time, UAVs can promptly identify anomalies indicative of oil spills, facilitating timely intervention and remediation. The integration of machine learning enhances predictive accuracy by distinguishing oil from other substances, thus reducing false positives that could lead to misallocation of resources.

UAVs equipped with machine vision capabilities can analyze video streams in real time using specialized algorithms. These algorithms employ adaptive edge detection techniques to continuously evaluate visual input, focusing on important indicators such as color variations and texture details characteristic of oil spills. The unique color profiles of oil allow for effective detection; algorithms may convert images to grayscale to enhance the focus on significant color differences. Additionally, texture analysis provides insights into the interaction between oil and water, enabling the identification of distinctive patterns formed on affected surfaces.

As these technologies advance, they not only improve immediate response strategies but also contribute to preventative measures. By analyzing environmental data and identifying patterns related to potential spills, policymakers can allocate resources more effectively and implement targeted interventions, ultimately enhancing overall environmental protection efforts.

5.2 Application in studies

Research illustrates that drones equipped with advanced machine vision algorithms, such as the Canny edge detection method, can effectively delineate oil spill boundaries. This method enhances edge visualization in captured images through various stages, including noise reduction and gradient calculation, allowing for precise assessments of spill size and shape. Moreover, the integration of machine learning enhances the system's capability to distinguish oil spills from other surface phenomena by recognizing unique patterns associated with different types of spills in varied environmental conditions [2].

The reliability of real-time detection systems has been affirmed through extensive trials, demonstrating high accuracy in identifying spill locations and dimensions in diverse environments. These systems utilize algorithms that analyze satellite imagery and aerial data, enabling real-time monitoring during spill incidents [19]. Additionally, the adaptability of machine vision algorithms to varying environmental conditions ensures consistent detection accuracy, even under challenging scenarios like low light or adverse weather. Advancements in deep learning and convolutional neural networks have improved these algorithms' robustness, allowing them to interpret visual information with greater precision [20].

For dependable detection across challenging circumstances, machine vision algorithms are engineered to adapt to factors like weather conditions, object appearance variations, and scene dynamics. Techniques such as image preprocessing and feature extraction enhance their reliability in various applications, including oil spill detection from satellite imagery [20]. Advanced algorithms counteract the effects of weather by adjusting image processing parameters, while high-sensitivity sensors improve performance in low-light conditions, facilitating UAV operations during dawn, dusk, and overcast scenarios.

Additionally, the use of multispectral and hyperspectral sensors allows UAVs to detect and monitor marine contamination more effectively. Integrating machine learning with remote sensing enhances data analysis capabilities, enabling rapid responses to contamination events and supporting regulatory compliance. Experimental setups simulating oil spills validate the effectiveness of adaptive algorithms in identifying spills under realistic conditions, with continuous learning from previous incidents enhancing their performance over time [2].

In conclusion, the integration of machine vision technologies with UAVs provides a robust framework for detecting and evaluating oil spills in marine environments. This capacity for real-time processing supports prompt intervention, while algorithm adaptability ensures accuracy in complex conditions. Anticipated advancements in remote sensing and processing techniques are expected to further enhance these systems, solidifying their role in effective environmental monitoring and response strategies.

5.3 Adaptation to environmental conditions

The ability of machine vision algorithms to adjust and adapt effectively to a wide range of environmental conditions is of paramount importance for ensuring that detection accuracy is consistently maintained across different scenarios and situations. This adaptability allows these algorithms to perform well in varying lighting conditions, weather patterns, and even in the presence of occlusions or obstructions. For instance, advancements in deep learning techniques have enabled machine vision systems to learn from vast datasets, improving their robustness and generalization capabilities. As a result, these systems can recognize and interpret visual information with greater precision, even when faced with unexpected changes in their surroundings. This adaptability is particularly crucial in dynamic environments, such as autonomous driving or industrial automation, where conditions can vary significantly. Moreover, advancements in deep learning architectures, such as convolutional neural networks (CNNs), have further enhanced the ability of machine vision systems to extract relevant features from images, allowing for more accurate object detection and classification.

5.3.1 Algorithms tuning for specific environments

In order to attain dependable and consistent detection capabilities across a variety of challenging circumstances, machine vision algorithms are specifically engineered to adapt and respond to a range of influencing factors. These factors include but are not limited to, adverse weather conditions that may be classified as harsh, as well as performance considerations in environments with low levels of light. Additionally, these algorithms must account for variations in object appearance due to changes in perspective, occlusion, and the presence of dynamic elements within the scene. To enhance robustness, machine vision systems often employ techniques such as image preprocessing, feature extraction, and machine learning models that can learn from diverse datasets. By continuously improving their ability to recognize patterns and make decisions, these systems can achieve higher accuracy and reliability in various applications, including autonomous vehicles, medical imaging, and security surveillance. The outcome of their study indicates significant improvements in the ability to identify oil spills and other related phenomena from space-based observations [20].

The severe and challenging weather conditions necessitate the implementation of sophisticated algorithms that utilize various techniques specifically designed to counteract the negative impacts associated with inclement weather. These algorithms, for instance, may adjust the sensitivity of image processing parameters in a strategic manner to effectively reduce and mitigate the detrimental effects that elements such as rain or wind can have on visibility.

The performance of machine vision systems in low-light environments necessitates a specific capability that is significantly improved by incorporating advanced sensors designed for high-sensitivity image capture. This integration enables UAVs to operate efficiently and effectively during times such as dawn and dusk, as well as in various other low-light situations that are frequently experienced over bodies of water.

5.3.2 Remote sensing

The implementation of multispectral or hyperspectral sensors significantly enhances the capability of UAVs to effectively identify and monitor a diverse range of marine contamination. This advanced technology allows for precise detection of pollutants and contaminants in marine environments, even when faced with a variety of changing environmental conditions that may otherwise complicate such assessments. Moreover, the integration of machine learning algorithms enhances the capability of these systems to analyze large datasets, identifying patterns and trends that may not be immediately apparent through traditional methods. By employing real-time data collection and analysis, researchers can respond more swiftly to contamination events, enabling timely interventions to mitigate environmental damage.

Using multispectral or hyperspectral sensors that will lead to higher quality oil detection not only aids in the protection of marine ecosystems but also supports regulatory compliance and public health initiatives by ensuring that water quality standards are met and maintained [3].

Furthermore, previous experimental configurations that have been specifically designed to simulate scenarios involving oil spills offer a structured and controlled environment for evaluating the performance and effectiveness of these adaptive algorithms. These assessments focus on the algorithms' capabilities to detect oil spills that vary significantly in size and possess different characteristics, all while operating under conditions that closely resemble those found in real-world situations. The results of these evaluations indicate that the algorithms can successfully identify and classify oil spills with a high degree of accuracy, even in challenging environments such as turbulent waters or areas with heavy marine traffic. Furthermore, the adaptability of these algorithms allows them to learn from previous incidents, improving their performance over time. This continuous learning process is crucial, as it enables the algorithms to refine their detection methods based on new data and emerging patterns in marine behavior [2, 4].

Example: In the context of oil spill detection, the study utilized a comprehensive array of advanced image processing techniques to enhance the efficacy of identifying oil spills within captured images. Key techniques among these methodologies were Gaussian blur and Canny edge detection algorithms, both of which played pivotal roles in isolating and delineating the edges of the oil spill from the surrounding background. The Gaussian blur technique was employed initially to reduce noise and smooth the image, thereby facilitating more accurate subsequent edge detection.

As a result of implementing these sophisticated algorithms, the study achieved an impressive detection accuracy of 95%. This remarkable accuracy enabled the system to effectively distinguish the oil spill from its complex background, ensuring reliable recognition in varying conditions. Moreover, this precise detection capability allowed for the accurate measurement of the spill's circumference and area across multiple trials. The success of these machine vision techniques not only enhances the effectiveness of oil spill assessments but also highlights the critical role that image processing plays in environmental monitoring and response efforts. This foundation establishes a framework for future advancements in the automation and reliability of oil spill detection systems.

To conclude, the integration of machine vision technologies with UAVs presents a robust methodology for the detection and evaluation of oil spills in marine environments. The capability for real-time processing enables prompt intervention, while the adaptability of algorithms ensures precise detection across a range of complex environmental conditions. Anticipated advancements in remote sensing technology and processing methodologies are expected to enhance the effectiveness of these systems, thereby establishing them as indispensable tools in environmental monitoring and response strategies.

6. Wireless telecommunications

Robust telecommunication is crucial for the successful operation of UAVs in oil spill detection, allowing for seamless data transfer, coordination among multiple drones, and reliable interaction with ground control or monitoring systems.

6.1 Telecommunication framework

The telecommunication framework serves as a fundamental and essential component that underpins effective interaction. It provides a structured approach to understanding the dynamics of telecommunication, including the roles of the sender, receiver, and the medium through which messages are conveyed.

Reliable communication is crucial for multi-drone systems. To achieve this objective, the establishment of clear guidelines and protocols is essential. For instance, the implementation of standardized communication protocols can substantially improve coordination among drones. This includes defining specific channels for data transmission, establishing priority levels for different types of messages, and ensuring that all drones can interpret the information correctly. This will help to minimize misunderstandings and enhance the clarity of the information exchanged.

Additionally, incorporating redundancy measures, such as alternative communication pathways, can help maintain connectivity in case of signal loss. This approach ensures that critical data can still be transmitted through backup systems, thereby enhancing the overall reliability of the network.

In the process of designing or selecting an effective communication framework, two primary communication channels must be considered. The first is the link between drones and the ground station, while the second pertains to inter-drone communication. Both channels are examined in the following analysis.

6.1.1 UAV-to-ground communication

Several studies [21–24] highlight the use of various protocols for transmitting data between UAVs and ground stations. This includes both command/control signals and telemetry data related to the detection of oil spills. Effective communication is crucial for ensuring that UAVs can operate autonomously while relaying critical information back to operators in real time.

Various protocols, such as MQTT and CoAP, have been explored for their efficiency in facilitating communication between devices in the Internet of Things (IoT) ecosystem. These protocols are designed to minimize bandwidth usage and reduce latency, making them ideal for resource-constrained environments. MQTT, for instance, operates on a publish-subscribe model, which allows for efficient message distribution and reduces the need for constant polling. On the other hand, CoAP is specifically tailored for constrained devices and networks, making it suitable for applications in drone-to-ground communication.

Robust real-time data exchange is emphasized, ensuring that the ground control maintains up-to-date information on the UAV's location, mission status, and detected spill parameters. This capability is crucial for effective decision-making and rapid response to any anomalies that may arise during operations. Additionally, the integration of advanced sensors and communication technologies allows for seamless transmission of data between the UAV and ground control. This not only enhances situational awareness but also facilitates the implementation of automated adjustments to flight paths or mission parameters based on real-time environmental conditions.

Therefore, in the UAV-ground communication protocol, two factors should be considered. The first factor is the reliability of the communication link, which is crucial for ensuring that data is transmitted accurately and without interruption. This includes evaluating the potential for signal loss due to environmental obstacles, interference from other devices, and the distance between the UAV and the ground station. The second factor is the latency of the communication system, which can significantly impact the responsiveness of the UAV during critical operations. High latency can lead to delays in command execution, affecting the UAV's ability to react to dynamic situations in real time [2–4].

6.1.2 Inter-drone communication

The implementation of an ad-hoc network facilitates efficient data sharing among UAVs. This architecture enhances collaborative detection efforts, enabling one UAV to relay information to nearby units. Inter-drone communication in networked UAV systems is crucial for real-time data exchange, allowing for improved situational awareness and coordinated responses to dynamic environments. By leveraging protocols designed for low-latency communication, these systems can effectively share critical information such as location data, sensor readings, and mission updates.

The ability to establish secure communication among drones significantly enhances the operational efficiency of individual unmanned aerial vehicles (UAVs), allowing them to adapt to dynamic conditions and emerging threats. Moreover, the incorporation of advanced algorithms for data fusion and decision-making optimizes the collective performance of the UAV fleet, ensuring cohesive and effective operations across diverse environments.

In order to successfully achieve the aforementioned objectives in the realm of communication, it is absolutely essential to establish effective coordination among the various entities involved. To facilitate this process, sophisticated algorithms have been specifically developed for unmanned aerial vehicles (UAVs) that enable them to synchronize their flight trajectories. This synchronization is vital to ensure that the UAVs can collectively provide comprehensive coverage of the designated operational area while avoiding any unnecessary overlap in their paths. Such an approach is critical not only for optimizing the overall coverage of the area but also for significantly reducing the duration of the mission, thereby enhancing operational efficiency.

6.2 Communication technologies

Communication technologies have revolutionized interactions, facilitating real-time information exchange across vast distances, particularly in unmanned aerial vehicle (UAV) operations. By utilizing artificial intelligence and machine learning, drones equipped with advanced sensors can collect and transmit data instantaneously, improving monitoring and decision-making. Here are the key communication methods:

- *RF communication*: Primary means for long-range connectivity, utilizing RF links for reliable data transmission in surveillance, search and rescue, and environmental monitoring. Techniques like Frequency Hopping Spread Spectrum (FHSS) enhance signal integrity by spreading signals across multiple frequencies, minimizing interference, and optimizing capacity.

- *Cellular and satellite communication*: Cellular networks provide broad coverage for effective real-time monitoring, while advancements such as 5G enhance bandwidth and reduce latency. Satellite communication ensures connectivity in remote areas, utilizing low Earth orbit satellites to improve data transmission rates.

Robust communication systems prioritize reliability and redundancy, essential for critical UAV missions. Incorporating error detection and correction methods, such as parity checks and advanced error-correcting codes, mitigates data transmission errors. Adaptation techniques, like dynamic modulation schemes, adjust transmission rates based on signal quality, ensuring sustained connectivity.

Environmental factors lead to signal degradation, making mitigation strategies—such as error correction algorithms, adaptive antennas, and repeaters—necessary. Addressing communication latency, critical for real-time applications, ensures prompt decision-making in emergencies. Overall, enhancing communication technologies is vital for optimizing UAV operational effectiveness in dynamic environments [4]. Overall, addressing these communication challenges is vital for optimizing UAV operational effectiveness in dynamic environments.

6.3 Applications in oil spill detection

Oil spills pose significant environmental threats, necessitating effective detection and monitoring methods. Advanced technologies, such as remote sensing and satellite imagery, have been developed to identify and assess oil spills in real time. These methods utilize various spectral bands to differentiate between oil and water, allowing for rapid response efforts.

6.3.1 Real-time environmental monitoring

The robust communication capabilities enable real-time monitoring of oil spills, with UAVs transmitting data back to ground operators who can assess the situation promptly and coordinate appropriate response efforts. This rapid information exchange is crucial for minimizing missions' errors and therefore environmental damage and ensuring the safety of marine life.

6.3.2 Decision-making support

By ensuring reliable communication channels, UAV operators can receive immediate feedback from the UAVs, aiding in decision-making processes related to spill assessment and resource allocation during an emergency. This real-time data transmission allows for rapid analysis of the situation on the ground, enabling operators to adjust their strategies as new information becomes available. Furthermore, the integration of advanced sensors and imaging technologies on UAVs enhances their ability to detect environmental changes and assess the extent of spills more accurately. As a result, emergency response teams can deploy resources more effectively, minimizing the environmental impact and expediting recovery efforts.

6.4 Mathematical modeling

In the realm of wireless telecommunications, mathematical modeling plays a pivotal role in enhancing the performance and efficiency of communication systems. This section delves into several critical components that are fundamental for understanding and optimizing wireless communication networks. We begin with *communication models*, which provide the theoretical framework for analyzing signal propagation and transmission characteristics in various environments. Subsequently, we explore *error detection and correction*, essential for ensuring data integrity and reliability amidst the noise and interference inherent in wireless channels. The discussion extends to *dynamic modulation techniques*, which enable adaptive adjustments to modulation schemes based on real-time channel conditions, thereby maximizing throughput and maintaining connection quality. Additionally, we address *communication latency*, a crucial factor affecting user experience and system responsiveness, particularly in applications demanding real-time data processing. The section also emphasizes the importance of *reliability and redundancy modeling* to mitigate potential network failures through the implementation of backup systems and robust signaling strategies. Together, these subsections provide a comprehensive overview of the mathematical approaches that underpin current advancements in wireless telecommunications.

6.4.1 Communication models

Signal propagation refers to the movement of signals through a medium, which can include electrical signals in wires, electromagnetic waves through space, or sound waves through air or other materials. Understanding signal propagation is critical in various fields, including telecommunications, radio frequency engineering, and networking. In other words, signal propagation is a fundamental concept that affects the design and performance of communication systems, influencing how effectively information is transmitted from one point to another. The signal strength S at a distance d from a transmitter can be modeled using the Friis transmission equation:

$$S = Pt + Gt + Gr - L - 20\,log\,10(d) - 20\,log\,10(f) - 32.45 \tag{5}$$

Where S is received signal strength (dB), P_t is transmitting power (dBm), G_t is gain of the transmitting antenna (dB), G_r is gain of the receiving antenna (dB), L is losses (dB), and f is frequency (MHz).

This model helps assess how signal strength varies with distance and frequency, critical for maintaining robust communication.

6.4.2 Error detection and correction

Error detection with checksums is a technique used to verify the integrity of data during transmission or storage. A checksum is a value calculated from a data set and used to detect errors that may have occurred during its processing. The checksum allows the receiver to ascertain whether the received data is correct or if it has been altered. Checksums serve as a fundamental method for detecting errors in data transmission, playing a crucial role in ensuring data integrity across various applications.

A simple checksum technique can be calculated as follows for a message packet with bytes m_i:

$$C = \sum_{i=0}^{n} m_i \; mod256 \tag{6}$$

Where C is the checksum and n is the total number of bytes in the message. The checksum is sent along with the data; the receiver computes the checksum on the received data to verify integrity.

Cyclic Redundancy Check (CRC) is an error-detecting code used to identify changes to raw data in digital networks and storage devices. It provides a robust method for checking data integrity through polynomial division, allowing systems to detect accidental alterations or corruption. The Cyclic Redundancy Check (CRC) is a widely adopted and effective error detection scheme, known for its ability to detect a variety of error patterns in digital data transmission and storage.

For a binary data stream D and a generator polynomial G, the CRC can be computed as follows:

Append zeros to the data D based on the length of G:

$$D' = D \cdot 2^{|G|-1} \tag{7}$$

Divide D′ by G using binary division to obtain the remainder R:

$$R = D' \; modG \tag{8}$$

The CRC is then attached to the data D:

$$Transmitted \; Data = D \mid R \tag{9}$$

Where | denotes concatenation.

6.4.3 Dynamic modulation techniques

Adaptive modulation is a technique used in communication systems to optimize the modulation scheme based on the varying conditions of the communication channel. It allows a system to dynamically select the most suitable modulation format to ensure efficient data transmission while maximizing throughput and maintaining signal quality. In other words, adaptive modulation is a sophisticated technique that enhances communication efficiency by adjusting the modulation scheme to current channel conditions, leading to improved data throughput and reliability in various communication systems.

The modulation scheme can be adjusted based on the Signal-to-Noise Ratio (SNR). Given an SNR, the maximum data rate R can be determined using Shannon's theorem:

$$R = B \; log_2(1 + SNR) \tag{10}$$

Where R is the maximum achievable data rate (bps) and B is the bandwidth of the channel (Hz).

This formula allows for adaptive modulation schemes that alter the transmission characteristics based on real-time communication conditions.

6.4.4 Communication latency

Latency modeling is the process of analyzing, predicting, and characterizing the delays that occur in a system as data is transmitted from one point to another. It is a critical aspect of network design, performance analysis, and system engineering, particularly in applications where timeliness is paramount, such as real-time communications, video streaming, online gaming, and financial transactions. It is easier to say latency modeling is an essential practice in network and system design, focusing on analyzing and predicting the delays in data transmission to optimize performance and improve user experience across various applications.

The total communication latency D can be modeled as:

$$D = \frac{L}{R} + T_p + T_q \tag{11}$$

Where D is total delay (seconds), L is the size of the data packet (bits), R is data transmission rate (bps), and T_p is propagation delay (seconds), which can be modeled as:

$$T_p = \frac{d}{c} \tag{12}$$

where d is the distance between sender and receiver and c is the speed of light (approx. 3×10^8 m/s), T_q is queuing delay (seconds), which can vary based on network congestion.

6.4.5 Reliability and redundancy modeling

Redundancy assessment is a systematic evaluation process designed to evaluate the redundancy mechanisms in systems, processes, or networks to ensure reliability, availability, and robustness against failures. It involves analyzing various components to determine the extent of duplication or alternative pathways that have been implemented to maintain operations during component failures or adverse conditions. Redundancy assessment can also be described as a comprehensive evaluation process that identifies and enhances redundancy strategies within systems, ensuring operational continuity, reliability, and effective risk management in the face of potential failures.

The probability of successful communication can be modeled as follows, considering the probability of successful transmission P_s:

$$P_{total} = 1 - (1 - P_s)^n \tag{13}$$

Where P_{total} is the total probability of at least one successful transmission over n redundant channels.

This model helps in designing robust communication systems by evaluating the effectiveness of redundancy strategies.

7. Data acquisition

Data acquisition for oil spill detection using unmanned aerial vehicles (UAVs) involves systematic collection of environmental and imaging data necessary for identifying and quantifying spills. This process leverages advanced sensor technologies, including LiDAR, multispectral cameras, and thermal imaging, enabling UAVs to gather high-resolution information across diverse terrains. UAVs equipped with downward-facing high-resolution cameras provide continuous surveillance of ocean surfaces, enhancing the capability for effective spill detection. The integration of hyperspectral and multispectral sensors further allows for the identification of various marine contaminants.

Localization systems, utilizing Opti-Track infrared cameras, accurately determine the UAV's geographic position, facilitating precise mapping of identified spills. The accuracy of this data is ensured through measurement calibration, including the calculation of pixel-to-meter ratios from known reference objects. Data processing techniques play a critical role in analysis efficiency, incorporating image processing algorithms such as thresholding and edge detection to extract meaningful information from visual data. These algorithms assist in delineating oil spills and measuring their volume. Real-time data processing enables UAVs to quickly analyze and report incidents, enhancing decision-making and timely responses to environmental threats.

Overall, these advanced algorithms are instrumental in the effective detection and precise delineation of oil spills that may be present within the images that have been captured:

- Thresholding: Segments the oil in the foreground from the ocean background.

- Edge Detection: Identifies the edges of the oil spill, allowing for accurate measurement of volume and dimensions [1–3].

7.1 Real-time processing

Instantaneous data analysis provides unmanned aerial vehicles (UAVs) with the capability to analyze and process data in real time, which significantly enhances their ability to quickly detect and report incidents of oil spills. This capacity for immediate data processing is crucial for enabling timely and effective decision-making when it comes to addressing various environmental threats that arise from such spills. The swift identification and communication of these incidents are vital for implementing appropriate responses to mitigate potential damage to ecosystems [2, 3].

7.2 Data processing and reporting

The processes of data acquisition and reporting are fundamentally supported by various mathematical principles that enable their efficient and effective functioning. In the following sections, a detailed analysis will be conducted to explore these mathematical equations along with their specific functions and roles in the overall framework.

7.2.1 Sensor calibration and transformation

Sensor calibration is a critical process that ensures the accuracy and reliability of data collected from various sensors. This involves adjusting the sensor outputs to align with known standards or reference points, thereby minimizing measurement errors. Calibration can be performed using various methods, including static and dynamic calibration techniques, depending on the type of sensor and the application. Once calibrated, the sensor outputs can provide accurate and reliable data, which is crucial for effective monitoring and control in various systems. This accuracy is particularly important in fields such as environmental monitoring, industrial automation, and healthcare, where even slight deviations can lead to significant consequences. Furthermore, regular recalibration is necessary to maintain sensor performance over time.

The initial equation employed to examine the calibration and transformation of sensors is the pixel-to-meter conversion. Accurate data acquisition requires the conversion of pixel measurements obtained from images captured by UAV cameras into real-world metrics. This relationship is mathematically represented as:

$$PPMM = 2.35928h - 0.12456 \tag{14}$$

Where PPMM is pixels per millimeter, h is the altitude of the UAV in meters. This equation aids in determining the size of the detected oil spill in real-world measurements, essential for accurate reporting.

The second equation pertains to the examination of geometric transformations. To align the acquired imagery with real-world coordinates, geometric transformations are employed. These transformations may encompass translation and scaling, which can be represented as:

$$[x' \; y' \; 1] = \begin{bmatrix} s & 0 & t_x \\ 0 & s & t_y \\ 0 & 0 & 1 \end{bmatrix} \begin{bmatrix} x \\ y \\ 1 \end{bmatrix} \tag{15}$$

Where s is the scaling factor, tx and ty are translations in the x and y directions, x and y are original coordinates in pixels, and x' and y' are transformed coordinates in meters. This transformation ensures that data reporting is aligned with known geographic coordinates.

7.2.2 Image processing techniques

A crucial factor that must be taken into consideration when evaluating various image processing techniques is the precision and reliability of edge detection, as well as the calculation of the area affected by spills. In order to effectively assess these aspects, the Canny edge detection algorithm, which is widely recognized and utilized for the purpose of identifying the boundaries associated with oil spills, can be mathematically expressed through the application of convolution operations. For any given image denoted as I, the gradient magnitude G(x, y) can be determined using the following mathematical formulation:

$$G(x,y) = \sqrt{I_x^2 + I_y^2} \tag{16}$$

Where I_x is the partial derivative of the image in the x-direction and I_y is the partial derivative of the image in the y-direction [25].

Another aspect is to study the accuracy of estimating the spilled area. This involves analyzing various methodologies used to calculate the extent of the spill and comparing them against actual measurements taken in the field. Accurate estimation is crucial for effective response strategies, as it directly impacts the allocation of resources and the implementation of cleanup operations. Once edges are detected, the area of the oil spill can be estimated by integrating the detected region. If the spill boundary is defined by the curve C, the area A can be computed using Green's theorem:

$$A = \frac{1}{2}\oint_C (x\,dy - y\,dx) \tag{17}$$

This gives an accurate measurement of the oil spill area to facilitate reporting and planning interventions.

7.2.3 Data reporting models

The system often uses a delay model to ensure that data reporting meets the latency requirements of real-time operations:

$$D = \frac{C}{R} + L \tag{18}$$

Where D is total delay in seconds, C is the size of the data packet, R is the rate of data transmission, and L is processing latency in the UAV.

This model facilitates the equilibrium between data freshness and processing efficiency. By integrating diverse buffering techniques and prioritizing essential data streams, the system enhances performance while mitigating the risk of data loss. Furthermore, this model enables the optimization of transmission parameters to guarantee timely data reporting.

When reporting the detection events, statistical measures are employed to analyze spill frequency and characteristics:

$$\mu = \frac{1}{N}\sum_{i=1}^{N} A_i \tag{19}$$

Where A_i is the area of detected spill i, and N is the total number of detected spills.

$$\sigma = \sqrt{\frac{1}{N}\sum\nolimits_{i=1}^{N} (A_i - \mu)^2} \tag{20}$$

These metrics facilitate the assessment of spill trends within the monitored area. By analyzing the data collected over time, researchers can identify patterns that may indicate potential sources of contamination or areas at higher risk for spills. This information is crucial for developing targeted mitigation strategies and improving response protocols. Additionally, the metrics can help in evaluating the effectiveness of existing regulations and practices, allowing for adjustments that enhance environmental protection.

Example: Within the scope of this research, a robust data acquisition system was established to meticulously capture and analyze the coordinates of oil spills during the drone's trajectory. This study highlighted the importance of conducting multiple trials to attain a comprehensive dataset that accurately reflects the performance of the detection system. This systematic approach not only facilitated the detection of oil edges but also enabled precise location tracking of the identified spills throughout varying operational environments.

The significance of the recorded positions became evident as they were subsequently employed to calculate the areas of the detected spills. During the indoor trials, the results yielded spill area measurements of 2.348 m^2, 2.305 m^2, and 2.431 m^2, demonstrating notable consistency. The recorded values exhibited a tolerance of merely 0.126 m^2 from the actual known value of 2.332 m^2, underscoring the reliability and accuracy of the data acquisition method employed. This consistency across trials reinforces the credibility of the data collection process and illustrates its effectiveness in producing actionable insights for environmental response. Furthermore, the ability to generate such precise area calculations is critical for informing remediation efforts and enhancing overall spill response strategies.

8. Validation and trials

The validation and trials of UAV systems for oil spill detection are critical components to ensure their effectiveness, reliability, and accuracy in real-world applications. This overview captures the essential elements of validation methodologies, performance metrics, challenges, and outcomes derived from common themes in the literature.

8.1 Testing methodologies

Multi-drone systems for oil spill detection are evaluated through comprehensive testing methodologies focusing on collaborative operations and adaptive performance. Integrating multiple UAVs enhances coverage and efficiency, allowing real-time data sharing and task redistribution in dynamic environments.

Advanced machine vision algorithms, such as Canny edge detection, accurately delineate spill boundaries and are rigorously tested under various conditions to ensure reliability [3, 26]. Simulations of oil spills further assess detection capabilities, while the incorporation of multispectral and hyperspectral sensors boosts pollutant identification and facilitates swift responses to contamination events. Therefore, this methodology emphasizes the effectiveness of multi-drone systems in ensuring robust monitoring and timely interventions in marine environments [27, 28].

8.2 Reporting

Automated reporting is integral to the data reporting system for oil spill detection, enabling real-time generation of reports based on data analysis while minimizing manual effort and reducing human error. Advanced algorithms and machine learning techniques ensure adaptability to fluctuating data inputs, systematically compiling and communicating vital spill information, such as location, size, and extent, to relevant authorities [12].

Multi-drone systems enhance operational effectiveness through inter-drone communication, allowing simultaneous drones to share real-time data and improve situational awareness. This capability supports collaborative decision-making, particularly in emergency scenarios, enabling rapid dissemination of information about spills. For example, if one drone identifies a spill, it can quickly relay precise coordinates to nearby units, facilitating coordinated monitoring efforts.

Overall, these reporting mechanisms and advanced capabilities significantly enhance the effectiveness of UAV systems in managing oil spills, fostering transparency and trust among stakeholders while promoting prompt mobilization of resources for responsive actions [27–29].

Example: In the comprehensive validation phase of the study, a comparative analysis was conducted between the results obtained from indoor emulated experiments and those from outdoor tests carried out under real-world simulated conditions. This dual approach was instrumental in establishing the robustness and reliability of the developed detection system, as it sought to ensure that findings from controlled environments translated effectively to practical, dynamic settings.

The results from the outdoor trials revealed calculated spill areas of 33.89 m^2, 34.33 m^2, and 33.14 m^2. Notably, these measurements exhibited a tolerance of approximately 0.75 m^2 in relation to the actual spill area, which was determined to be 29.71 m^2. The minimal variations observed between the indoor and outdoor results underscore the consistency and accuracy of the detection algorithms applied throughout the trials. This strong correlation validates the effectiveness of the developed methodologies in real-world scenarios, thereby reinforcing the potential for wide-scale application in environmental monitoring and oil spill response initiatives. The successful integration of indoor and outdoor testing not only highlights the adaptability of the system but also establishes a reliable framework for future research and practical implementation.

9. Broader implications

The integration of AI and robotics in environmental monitoring through UAV systems holds significant implications for the oil and gas industry, specifically in terms of resource efficiency, safety, proactive measures, and sustainability. The following outlines each key area.

9.1 Resource efficiency

Heterogeneous AI-based systems have shown the potential to significantly reduce the human and financial costs associated with environmental monitoring. For example, automation in monitoring processes can lead to minimizing human intervention. Also, the use of advanced algorithms increases the ability of drones to collect and analyze data quickly and accurately. These significantly not only reduce labor costs and increase the accuracy and speed of detection, but also reduce the logistical burden associated with deploying human resources to remote or dangerous areas. Reference [3] discusses the economic implications of deploying UAVs in environmental applications.

9.2 Increased safety

As mentioned in Section 9.1, the use of autonomous systems reduces the use of human power. This leads to significant safety improvements in hazardous environments. UAVs can perform hazardous tasks such as monitoring oil spill sites, surveying damaged areas, forest fires, toxic operational areas. As a result, personnel exposure to potentially life-threatening situations is minimized. Reference [2] emphasizes the safety benefits of UAVs in hazardous environments.

9.3 Proactive measures

The use of real-time data and AI technology enables the implementation of preventive strategies. For example, stakeholders can quickly identify minor spills using advanced detection systems and real-time analysis, and take measures to mitigate them before they become larger environmental disasters.

These systems go a step further than real-time data analysis and detection, and by using big data, historical data analysis and real-time analysis, they can predict high-risk scenarios with the help of AI. Based on these analyses, legislators can recommend and implement timely and effective measures.

Reference [1] describes the role of AI in enhancing preventive response strategies in oil spill management.

9.4 Sustainability

Autonomous single-agent, swarm, or heterogeneous systems based on AI help to monitor and respond in more sustainable ways in the environmental monitoring sectors, especially in oil and gas industry. Improving environmental detection and response mechanisms and moving toward real-time monitoring can reduce environmental risks. For example, improving detection and rapid response mechanisms in the field of oceanic oil spills will minimize the ecological impact of oil spills and lead to less damage to marine and coastal ecosystems.

The use of these operational methods leads to more sustainable and efficient monitoring and can help oil extraction and transportation companies or regulatory bodies to adhere to regulatory standards. This helps them to improve the selection of the best and most sustainable detection and response strategies.

Reference [4] discusses AI-driven sustainability initiatives in the oil and gas sector.

Finally, the integration of AI and robotics in environmental monitoring represents a game-changing development for the oil and gas industry. Emphasizing the importance of sustainable and responsible practices, the adoption of these technologies will not only increase the sector's effectiveness in addressing environmental incidents, but also protect our oceans for future generations. By harnessing AI-powered drones and multi-drone systems, stakeholders can enhance their ability to respond to environmental challenges and create a more sustainable future.

It is worth noting that these systems are currently mostly in the research phase and their use in industrial sectors requires overcoming various and numerous challenges.

Acknowledgements

The author acknowledges the use of Isaaceditor to search for relative research works and language polishing of the manuscript.

Author details

Navid Nasiri[1*], Ahmed Al-Maashri[1], Hadj Bourdoucen[1], Said Al-Abri[1] and Nabil Aouf[2]

1 Department of Electrical and Computer Engineering, Sultan Qaboos University, Muscat, Oman

2 Department of Electrical and Electronic Engineering, City University of London, London, UK

*Address all correspondence to: nnerpr@gmail.com

References

[1] Saleem A, Al-Maashri A, Eldirdiry O, Ghommam J, Bourdoucen H, Al-Kamzari A, et al. Detection of oil spill pollution in seawater using drones: Simulation & lab-based experimental study. In: IOT, Electronics and Mechatronics Conference (IEMTRONICS). Toronto, ON, Canada: IEEE International; 2021

[2] Eldirdiry O, Nasiri N, Al-Maashri A, Bourdoucen H, Ghommam J, Saleem A, et al. Using AI-enhanced UAVs to detect and size marine contaminations. In: International Conference on Unmanned Vehicle Systems-Oman (UVS), Muscat, Oman. Muscat, Oman: Institute of Electrical and Electronics Engineers Inc.; 2024

[3] Al-Maashri A, Saleem A, Nasiri N, Eldirdiry O, Ghommam J, Bourdoucen H, et al. A multi-drone system for oil spill detection: A simulation and emulation platform. In: International Conference on Control, Automation and Systems (ICCAS), Muscat, Oman. Muscat, Oman: IEEE; 2022

[4] Eldirdiry O, Ghommam J, Al Rawas G, Al Maashari A, Bourdoucen H, Al-Kamzari A, et al. An emulated platform for detecting and size measuring of oil spills using an unmanned aerial vehicle system. In: International Conference on Mechanical, Automotive and Mechatronics Engineering. Dubai, UAE; 2023

[5] Huby AA, Sagban R, Alubady R. Oil spill detection based on machine learning and deep learning: A review. In: International Conference on Engineering Technology and their Applications (IICETA). Al-Najaf, Iraq; 2022

[6] Hammoud B, Wehn N. Recent advances in oil-spill monitoring using drone-based radar remote sensing. Marine Pollution - Recent Developments. 2022;**5**:1-30

[7] Juan V, Santos M, Andújar JM. Intelligent UAV map generation and discrete path planning for search and rescue operations. Complexity. 2018; **2018**(1):1-17

[8] Asadzadeh S, Oliveira WJD, Filho CRDS. UAV-based remote sensing for the petroleum industry and environmental monitoring: State-of-the-art and perspectives. Journal of Petroleum Science and Engineering. 2022;**208**(Part D):1-6

[9] Saeed AM, Gharaibeh A. Real-time obstacle avoidance for UAVs using LiDAR and RRT. Drones. 2021;**4**(5):81

[10] Yu Z, Si Z, Li X, Wang D, Song H. A novel hybrid particle swarm optimization algorithm for path planning of UAVs. IEEE Internet of Things Journal. 2022;**9**(22):22543-22552

[11] Muhammad K, Azar A, Koubaa A, Zaidi A. Disturbance-rejection-based optimized robust adaptive controllers for UAVs. IEEE Systems Journal. 2021;**15**(2): 2256-2265

[12] Wan Y, Zhong Y, Ma A, Zhang L. An accurate UAV 3-D path planning method for disaster emergency response based on an improved multiobjective swarm intelligence algorithm. IEEE Transactions on Cybernetics. 2023;**53**(4): 2658-2671

[13] Al-Ruzouq R, Gibril M, Shanableh A, Kais A, Hamed O, Al-Mansoori S, et al. Sensors, features, and machine learning for oil spill detection and monitoring: A review. Remote Sensing. 2020;**12** (20):1-42

[14] Liu P, Li Y, Liu B, Chen P, Xu J. Semi-automatic oil spill detection on X-band marine radar images using texture analysis. Machine Learning, and Adaptive Thresholding, Remote Sensing. 2019;**11**(7):1-19

[15] Jiao Z, Jia G, Cai Y. A new approach to oil spill detection that combines deep learning with unmanned aerial vehicles. Computers & Industrial Engineering. 2019;**135**:1300-1311

[16] Krestenitis M, Orfanidis G, Ioannidis K, Avgerinakis K, Vrochidis S. Oil spill identification from satellite images using deep neural networks. Remote Sensing. 2019;**11**(15):1-22

[17] Kerf TD, Gladines J, Sels S, Vanlanduit S. Oil spill detection using machine learning and infrared images. Remote Sensing. 2020;**12**(24):1-13

[18] Salem F, Kafatos M, El-Ghazawi T, Gomez R, Yang R. Hyperspectral Image Analysis for Oil Spill Detection. Washington, DC: NASA; 2001

[19] Jiang Q, Xiang X. Collaborative monitoring of oil spills using UAV swarms: An innovative approach for environmental management. Environmental Science and Pollution Research. 2023;**4**(30):1021-1035

[20] Xudong H, Biao Z, William P, Yingcheng L, Chen W. A novel deep learning method for marine oil spill detection from satellite synthetic aperture radar imagery. Marine Pollution Bulletin. 2022;**179**:1-13

[21] Li J, Zhou Y, Lamont L. Communication architectures and protocols for networking unmanned aerial vehicles. In: 2013 IEEE Globecom Workshops. Atlanta, GA, USA; 2013

[22] Alladi T, Naren G, Bansal VC, Guizani M. SecAuthUAV: A novel authentication scheme for UAV-Ground Station and UAV-UAV communication. IEEE Transactions on Vehicular Technology. 2020;**69**:15068-15077

[23] Khan NA, Jhanjhi NZ, Brohi SN, Nayyar A. Chapter three - emerging use of UAV's: Secure communication protocol issues and challenges. In: Drones in Smart-Cities. Amsterdam, Netherlands: Elsevier; 2020. pp. 37-55

[24] Atoev S, Kwon K-R, Lee S-H, Moon K-S. Data analysis of the MAVLink communication protocol. In: 2017 International Conference on Information Science and Communications Technologies (ICISCT). Tashkent, Uzbekistan: IEEE; 2017

[25] Dong S, Feng J. SGDBNet: A scene-class guided dual branch network for port UAV images oil spill detection. Marine Pollution Bulletin. 2024;**208**. Article number 117019

[26] Gharrad H, Jabeur N, Yasar A, Galland S, Mbarki M. A five-step drone collaborative planning approach for the management of distributed spatial events and vehicle notification using multi-agent systems and firefly algorithms. Computer Networks. 2021; **198**:1-11

[27] NOAA. Testing Oil Detection Technologies with a Collaborative Research Team. National Oceanic and Atmospheric Administration (NOAA) [Online]. Silver Spring, MD (NOAA HQ): NOAA; 2022. Available from: https://response.restoration.noaa.gov/testing-oil-detection-technologies-collaborative-research-team [Accessed: September 25, 2024]

[28] FDM. Field Determination of Multipollutant, Open Area Combustion

Source Emission Factors with a Hexacopter Unmanned Aerial Vehicle. U.S. Environmental Protection Agency (EPA) [Online]. Washington, DC (EPA HQ): EPA; 2017. Available from: https://cfpub.epa.gov/si/si_public_record_report.cfm?Lab=NRMRL&dirEntryId=339722 [Accessed: September 25, 2024]

[29] About WWF-GEF. World Wildlife Fund (WWF) [Online]. Available from: https://www.worldwildlife.org/pages/about-wwf-gef [Accessed: September 25, 2024]

Chapter 8

Agricultural UAVs in Recent Advances, Innovations and Applications

Rattana Boonprasert and Piyarat Vijuksungsith

Abstract

This chapter explores the future trends and advancements of Agricultural Unmanned Aerial Vehicles (Ag-UAVs), highlighting their revolutionary impact on modern agriculture. The discussion is organized into five key sections. Firstly, it examines fundamental principles and emerging trends, focusing on innovations in remote sensing mechanisms, including the use of electromagnetic spectrum analysis and vegetation indices (VIs). Secondly, it delves into the principles and applications of advanced technologies, such as high-resolution, multispectral imaging, Light Detection and Ranging (LiDAR), and thermal sensors, which enable precision tasks like targeted fertilizer and pesticide applications. The third section investigates essential components and recent advancements in Ag-UAVs, such as global positioning systems (GPS) modules, flight control systems, autonomous operating systems, and real-time mission tools, which optimize their performance for precision farming. The fourth section addresses the innovative applications of Ag-UAVs in crop monitoring, health assessment, and yield prediction, emphasizing their role in managing and optimizing agricultural practices. Finally, the integration of Artificial Intelligence (AI) enhances the capabilities of Ag-UAVs, enabling advanced data analysis for crop health assessment, pest detection, and growth monitoring. AI-driven precision operations and yield predictions further support farming by transforming traditional methods into efficient, data-driven ecosystems. In conclusion, the adoption of Ag-UAVs, coupled with advanced technologies such as AI and multispectral imaging.

Keywords: agricultural unmanned aerial vehicles (Ag-UAVs), vegetation index (Vis), temperature-vegetation dryness index (TVDI), crop health assessment, field crop monitoring

1. Introduction

Agricultural Unmanned Aerial Vehicles (Ag-UAVs) have become pivotal in transforming conventional agriculture into smart agriculture. These advancements integrate remote sensing technology, global positioning systems (GPS), artificial intelligence (AI), and the Internet of Things (IoT) to enhance the functionality and utility of Ag-UAVs. By leveraging these technologies, Ag-UAVs have emerged as essential tools for modern farmers engaged in smart farm management [1].

Key applications include sensor-based monitoring of vegetation indices, data analysis from high-resolution aerial imagery, and navigation systems equipped with imaging and sensory technologies, as shown in **Figure 1(a)**. Ag-UAVs provide farmers with in-depth, actionable insights, such as creating detailed 2D and 3D agricultural maps [2, 3]. These models support strategic planning for farm management, enabling the monitoring of crop health, growth patterns, and yield forecasting. Furthermore, Ag-UAVs play a critical role in assessing soil quality and improving overall productivity while simultaneously reducing waste. By enabling real-time communication and data-driven decision-making, Ag-UAVs empower farmers to enhance operational efficiency and achieve precise resource allocation. Specialized software further weed in the efficient collection and analysis of critical farm data, supporting rapid and accurate decision-making processes [4]. Modern Ag-UAVs also facilitate automation in various smart farming tasks, such as precision and autonomous spraying of pesticides, fertilizers, and growth stimulants [5], as shown in **Figure 1(b)**. The integration of AI enhances data processing capabilities, enabling predictive analytics for yield estimation and real-time farm management [6]. Despite these advances, challenges such as regulatory constraints, limited battery life, and payload capacity remain barriers to widespread adoption, as shown in **Figure 1**.

Nonetheless, the integration of remote sensing, GPS technology, AI, and IoT within Ag-UAV systems demonstrates significant potential for more efficient resource allocation and environmental management. These innovations pave the way toward a sustainable and efficient future for smart farming, addressing both current and emerging agricultural challenges [7]. These innovations also facilitate tasks like targeted application of fertilizers and pesticides, minimizing chemical usage, and ensuring uniform coverage as shown in **Figure 1(b)**. Despite their transformative potential, Ag-UAVs face challenges such as regulatory barriers, high initial costs, and the need for skilled

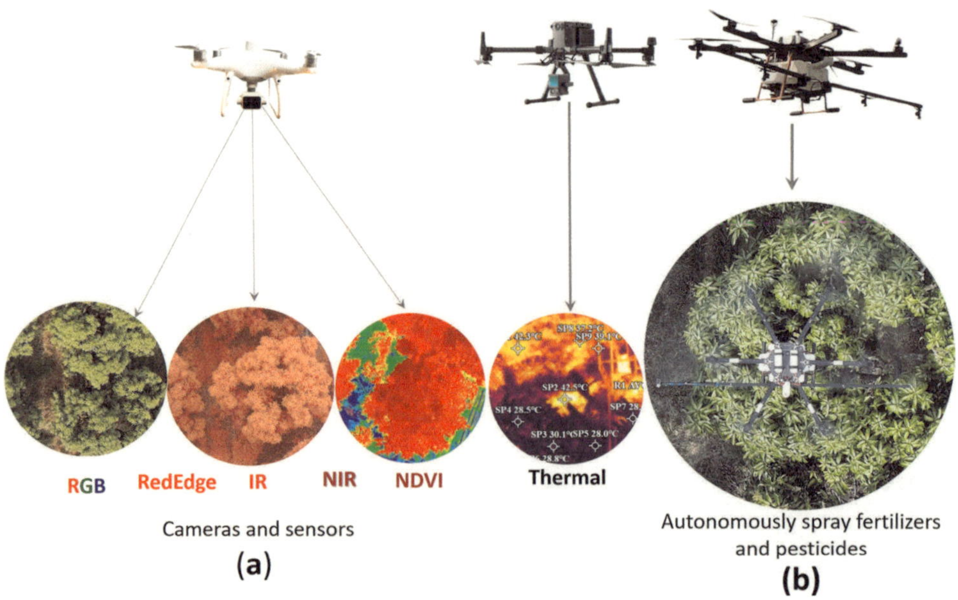

Figure 1.
Ag-UAVs are transforming farming operations: (a) High-resolution aerial imagery, multispectral and thermal imaging, (b) Innovations also facilitate tasks like targeted application of autonomous spray fertilizers and pesticides.

operators [5]. Limitations in battery capacity and payload also present constraints. However, continuous technological developments, including AI integration and IoT connectivity, are improving real-time data analysis and enhancing overall farm management [8]. These systems are not only driving efficiency but are also supporting sustainable practices by optimizing resources and reducing environmental impact. As costs decline and regulations adapt, Ag-UAVs are becoming increasingly accessible, benefiting farms of all sizes and shaping the future of agriculture as shown in **Figure 1**.

2. Basic principles and key future trends of Ag-UAVs in recent advances, innovations and applications

2.1 Basic principles of the electromagnetic spectrum of remote sensing mechanisms in agriculture

The electromagnetic spectrum includes a range of wavelengths that are essential for modern agricultural practices, especially when applied through Ag-UAVs. These Ag-UAVs are equipped with sophisticated sensors and imaging systems, allowing them to collect detailed data that helps identify issues such as crop diseases, irrigation inefficiencies, and nutrient deficiencies [9]. The use of specific spectral bands improves real-time monitoring of crop conditions and livestock activity, enhancing precision and efficiency in farm management. Ag-UAVs are particularly effective in the precision spraying of water and agrochemicals, utilizing environmental data to ensure targeted and efficient application [10]. This process reduces waste and supports sustainable practices. A critical aspect of their functionality involves leveraging specific parts of the electromagnetic spectrum, as shown in **Figure 2**. Key bands, such as Near-Infrared (NIR), Red Edge, and thermal wavelengths, are highly effective in evaluating vegetation health by analyzing indicators like chlorophyll levels [11], as shown in **Figure 3(a)**. Additionally commonly used wavelengths range from 300 nm to 2500 nm, capturing the effects of solar radiation [12] as shows in **Figure 3(b)** optical radiation in agriculture operates across a wide range from 100 to 1 mm, with each wavelength offering unique insights into various agricultural parameters. These advanced capabilities make Ag-UAVs indispensable tools in precision agriculture, supporting sustainable and data-driven farm operations as shown in **Figure 3**.

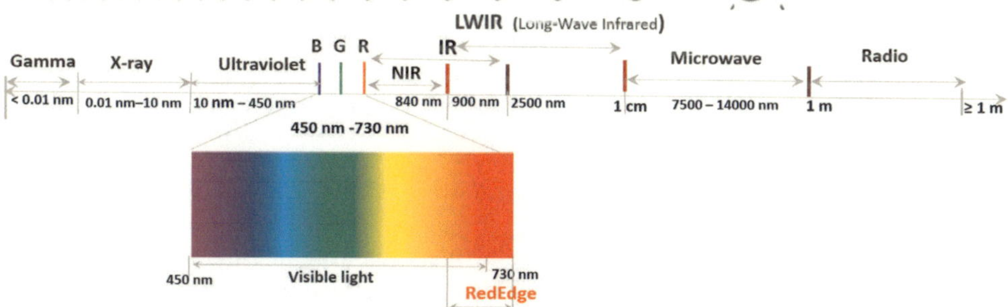

Figure 2.
A critical aspect of their functionality involves leveraging specific parts of the electromagnetic spectrum.

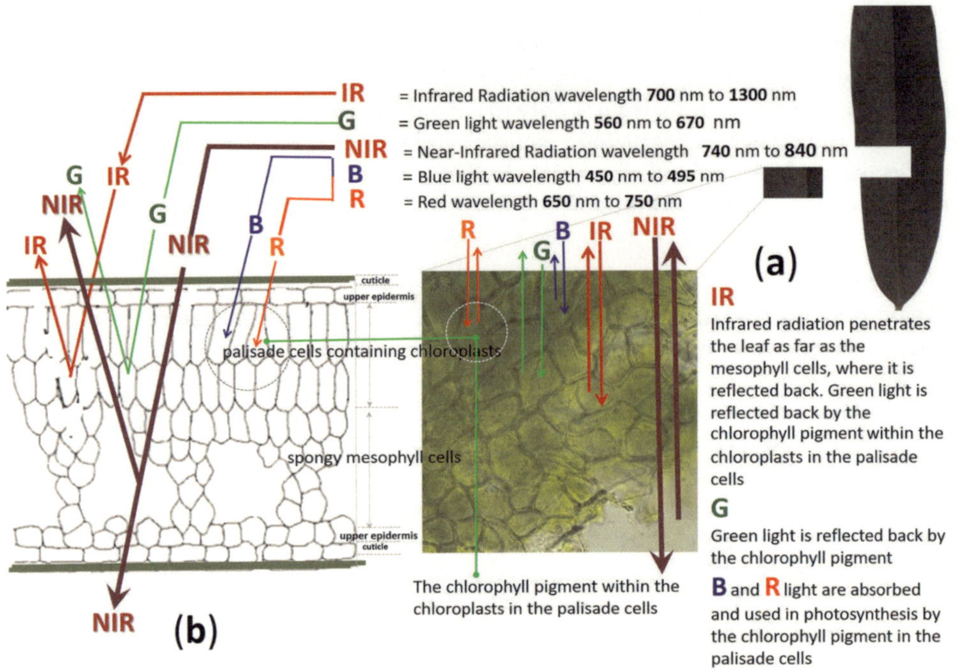

Figure 3.
Key bands, such as NIR, red edge, and thermal wavelengths, are highly effective in evaluating vegetation health: (a) the effects of solar radiation on cell structure and (b) analyzing indicators like chlorophyll levels.

2.2 Vegetation indices (VIs)

In the domain of Ag-UAVs and remote sensing, VIs play a crucial role in analyzing and interpreting various agricultural features [13]. They are instrumental in monitoring crop growth, distinguishing vegetation from non-vegetation areas, and providing detailed information on soil conditions and other related parameters [3]. VIs is particularly valuable for assessing plant health, vigor, and stress levels, enabling precise evaluations through Ag UAVs based remote sensing systems as shown in **Figure 3**. These indices assist in tracking vegetation coverage, biomass, and other agronomic metrics critical for effective farm management [14]. Among the commonly utilized vegetation indices are the Normalized Difference Vegetation Index (NDVI), the Soil-Adjusted Vegetation Index (SAVI), the Enhanced Vegetation Index (EVI), the Normalized Difference Red Edge Index (NDRE or RedNDVI), and the Tensor Structure Variation Index (TSVI), as shown in **Table 1**. Each index offers unique insights and applications in agriculture, helping optimize resource use and improve productivity when integrated with UAV technologies.

2.2.1 Role of VIs in Ag-UAVs-based agricultural monitoring

VIs derived from remote sensing data play a critical role in enhancing the capabilities of agricultural UAVs. These indices offer valuable insights into crop health, detect stress, and monitor variability across fields, enabling precise and large-scale vegetation analysis [3]. This is vital for improving productivity, identifying diseases, managing water stress, and optimizing overall farming practices [22].

Index	Bands	Eq.	Ref.
Normalized Difference Vegetation Index (NDVI)	NIR/Red Edge	NDVI = (NIR − R)/NIR + R)	[15–18]
Green Normalized Difference Vegetation (GNDVI)	G/NIR, Red Edge	GNDVI = (NIR − Green)/(NIR + Green)	[15]
Red Edge Index (NDRE or RedNDVI)/Effects of the spectral response functions of sensors on VIs	NIR, Red Edge	$RedNDVI = \frac{NIR - RED}{NIR + RED} = \frac{NIR - RE - 2RE}{NIR + RED} = \frac{2}{NIR + RE + 1}$	[13]
The enhanced vegetation index (EVI)	G/NIR, Red Edge	$EVI = G\frac{(N - R)}{N + C_1R - C_2B + X_{EVI}}$	[18]
Soil-adjusted vegetation index (SAVI)	NIR/Red Edge	$SAVI = \frac{(NIR - RED) \cdot (1 + X_{SAVI})}{NIR + RED + X_{SAVI}}$	[18, 19]
Tensor Structure Variation Index (TSVI)	NIR/Red Edge	$TSAVI = \frac{a(N - a.R - b)}{NIR + RED + X_{SAVI}}$	[16, 20]
		$TSAVI = \frac{a(N - a.R - b)}{a - N + a.b + X_{SAVI}(1 + a^2)}$	[18]
Optimized Soil-Adjusted Vegetation Index (OSAVI):	G/NIR, Red Edge	$OSAVI = \frac{NIR - G}{NIR + G}$	[21]

Table 1.
Key equations governing of remote sensing mechanisms in agricultural.

Among commonly used VIs, the NDVI is particularly effective for general assessments of crop health due to its simplicity and reliability. The SAVI is advantageous in areas with sparse vegetation or where soil interference is significant, while EVI is better suited for high-biomass environments, offering enhanced sensitivity to subtle variations in dense vegetation [23] in **Table 1**.

2.2.2 Use of VIs in Ag-UAVs applications

Ag-UAVs equipped with multispectral or hyperspectral sensors are capable of capturing reflectance data across a range of wavelengths, such as R, G, B, NIR, and SAVI [18]. These reflectance values are used to compute vegetation indices like NDVI, GNDVI, RedNDVI, EVI, SAVI, and TSAVI in **Table 1** by analyzing these indices [21]. Ag-UAVs provide valuable insights into crop health, detect stress, and assess variability across fields [6], as shown in **Figure 3**. This data supports effective decision-making for managing crops and optimizing yields. VIs is calculated using specific mathematical Eq. (1) tailored to these applications, enabling precision agriculture practices and the development of advanced technology is the key to rapid and non-destructive detection [24] as in Eq. (1):

$$VIs = f\ (NIR, R, G, B, sensor\ parameters) \tag{1}$$

Where:

f = monitoring crop growth index as in **Table 1**, and the sensor parameters reflect the specific Ag-UAVs sensors configuration and data captured as shown in **Figures 3** and **4**.

3. Principles of advantage technology in future and trends for Ag-UAVs

Developments in Ag-UAV applications are revolutionizing agriculture by using RGB cameras, multispectral imaging, LiDAR systems, thermal sensors, and other advanced technologies to enable precision tasks such as targeted fertilizer and pesticide applications, as shown in **Figure 4**.

3.1 RGB and high-resolution imaging

RGB cameras (visible light: RGB as shown in **Figure 3**) are high-resolution imaging tools widely used in agricultural UAVs for field mapping and crop monitoring. Operating within the visible light spectrum, these cameras provide detailed visual data on crop conditions, growth trends, and land utilization [1]. When paired with additional sensors, such as multispectral or thermal cameras, RGB cameras enhance the depth and accuracy of collected data, enabling a more comprehensive analysis of agricultural environments [5], as shown in **Figure 4(a)**. The advantages of RGB cameras are versatility and support for a wide range of applications, including crop health monitoring, field mapping, and tracking temporal changes in vegetation [25]. Their high-resolution imagery can identify key issues such as pest infestations, nutrient deficiencies, and signs of water stress [12]. Cost-effectiveness is another significant advantage, as RGB cameras are more affordable than specialized imaging sensors, making them accessible to farmers with varying budgets. Limitations: Despite their utility, RGB cameras have constraints, particularly in the range of spectral data they can capture. For analyses requiring more detailed spectral information, such as detecting subtle plant stress or specific nutrient imbalances, multispectral or hyperspectral sensors are necessary [26], as shown in **Figure 4(e)**. Applications in Agriculture: The integration

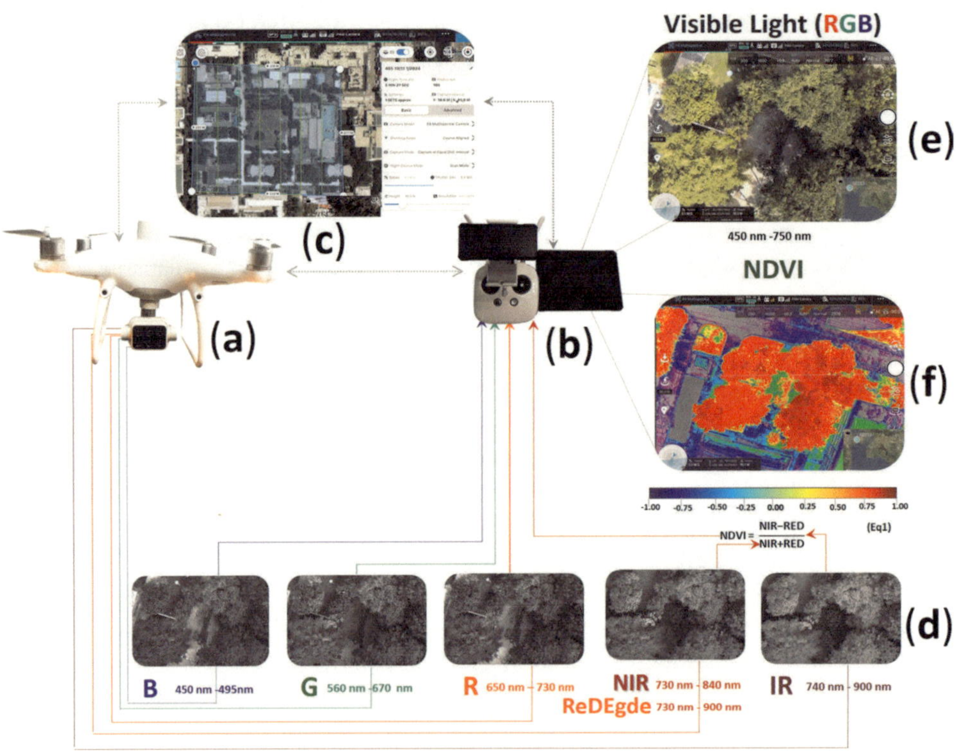

Figure 4.
Ag-UAVs are equipped with high-resolution cameras and advanced sensors: (a) Multispectral cameras, (b) Smart controllers, (c) Flight Control Systems (FCS) and autonomous systems in Ag-UAVs, (d) Multispectral imaging, (e) High-resolution imaging of RGB cameras, and (f) NDVI imaging.

of RGB cameras in Ag-UAVs has revolutionized farming practices. They are instrumental in various tasks, including crop monitoring, precision agriculture, soil and field mapping, irrigation management, weed detection, yield forecasting, and post-harvest evaluation [13]. These tools provide farmers with actionable insights, enhancing efficiency and productivity across the agricultural cycle [27].

3.2 Multispectral cameras

Applications in Ag-UAVs of multispectral cameras: Multispectral cameras support a wide range of agricultural applications, including crop monitoring, precision farming, and irrigation management [1]. They also aid in land use classification, disease detection, and yield prediction by leveraging VIs like NDVI and advanced tools such as machine learning algorithms [28]. By combining multiple indices, farmers can gain a more comprehensive understanding of vegetation health and variability [19], as shown in **Figure 4(f)**. It is an effective indicator of chlorophyll content and overall crop health during these critical phases. Benefits and Challenges: While multispectral cameras provide non-destructive, highly sensitive monitoring capabilities, challenges such as high initial costs, complex data requiring specialized expertise, and sensitivity to weather conditions persist [5]. However, the long-term benefits, including enhanced productivity, better resource management, and operational cost savings, make these cameras a worthwhile investment for improving agricultural efficiency, as shown in **Figure 4**.

A transformative tool in Ag-UAVs: Multispectral cameras integrated into agricultural UAVs have become indispensable in modern farming. These cameras operate across specific wavelengths in the electromagnetic spectrum, typically between 400 and 1000 nm, encompassing visible light (RGB) and NIR bands [11], as shown in **Figure 3**. Their high-resolution imaging capabilities allow for the precise detection of crop health, moisture levels, and nutrient deficiencies, as shown in **Figure 4(d)**. To ensure data accuracy, processes such as atmospheric correction, geometric correction, and radiometric calibration are applied during data analysis.

3.3 Thermal cameras in Ag-UAVs applications

Thermal cameras, equipped with infrared sensors, are invaluable in Ag-UAVs applications. These cameras detect infrared radiation emitted by objects, enabling non-contact temperature measurements within the 800–1400 nm wavelength range coverage as shown in **Figure 5(a)**. This capability supports critical tasks such as assessing plant health and optimizing irrigation by identifying subtle temperature variations. Thermal imaging has transformed agricultural practices, enabling precision monitoring and resource optimization while supporting sustainable farming practices [29]. By integrating these cameras into Ag-UAVs, farmers gain access to detailed, actionable insights that improve decision-making and productivity [30] in Eq. (2).

$$\mathrm{TVDI} = \frac{\mathrm{LST} - \mathrm{LST}_{\min}}{\mathrm{LST}_{\max} - \mathrm{LST}_{\min}} \tag{2}$$

Where:

TVDI = the Temperature-Vegetation Dryness Index. LST = Land surface temperature (LTS) at a given pixel (Thermal cameras equipped with thermal infrared sensors

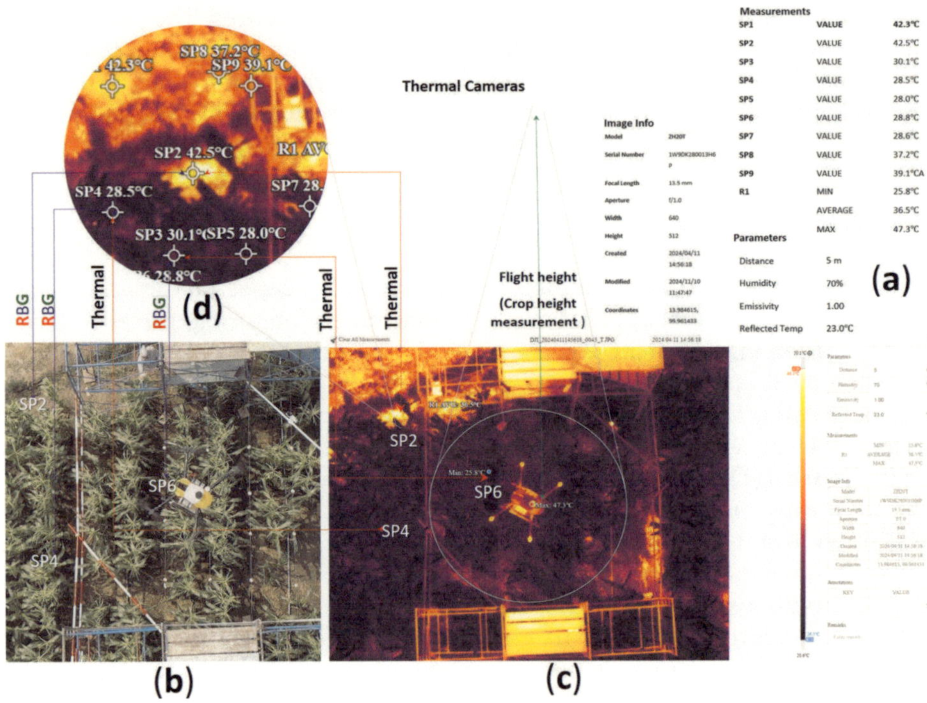

Figure 5.
Applications of thermal cameras in innovative solutions of Ag-UAVs for crop monitoring, managing, and optimizing agricultural practices include irrigation management: (a) Thermal cameras equipped with thermal infrared sensors the 800–1400 nm, (b) Crop monitoring, (c) Irrigation management, and (d) Distance: The spatial separation between the thermal camera and the target affects.

the 800–1400 nm) as shown in **Figure 5(c)**. LST_{min} = Minimum LST for a given NDVI value (wet edge). LST_{max} = Maximum LST for a given NDVI value (dry edge).

Key Steps:

- Plot the LST vs. NDVI for the study area.
- Identify the wet edge (low LST) and dry edge (high LST) by fitting linear relationships to the lower and upper boundaries of the scatterplot: wet edge: $LST_{min}\ (NDVI) = a_{wet}\ NDVI + b_{wet}$, and dry edge: $LST_{min}\ (NDVI) = a_{wet}\ NDVI + b_{wet}$.
- Substitute these linear equations into the TVDI Eq. to calculate it for each pixel [31]. A simplified version can be expressed as in Eq. (3):

$$\mathrm{TVDI} = \frac{\mathrm{LST} - \left(\mathrm{a_{WetEdge}.NDVI} + \mathrm{b_{WWetEdgeet}}\right)}{\left(\mathrm{a_{DryEdge}} \cdot \mathrm{NDVI} + \mathrm{b_{DryEdge}}\right) - \left(\mathrm{a_{WetEdget}} \cdot \mathrm{NDVI} + \mathrm{b_{WetEdge}}\right)} \tag{3}$$

Where:

This method allows for the computation, which serves as a spatial measure for assessing drought intensity and soil moisture levels. The linear coefficients such as (a_{wet}, b_{wet}, a_{dry}, b_{dry}) are determined through regression analysis of data points.

Key elements involved in this process include:

LST = represents the temperature value at specific pixels within the analyzed region as shown in **Figure 5(c)**. *Wet edge* = Corresponds to the lowest land surface temperature associated with a particular NDVI value, indicative of well-hydrated areas (*minimum LST*). Dry edge represents the highest land surface temperature observed for a given NDVI value in **Table 1**, which typically indicates arid or stressed conditions (*maximum LST*).

By leveraging these parameters, TVDI provides a comprehensive framework for identifying variations in soil moisture and drought conditions across landscapes. This tool supports precision agriculture by guiding irrigation strategies and assessing environmental stress on crops as shown in **Figure 5**.

3.3.1 Key measurements and parameters

Key measurements and parameters of thermal imaging relies on various parameters for accurate assessments as shown in **Figure 5(a)**.

- Distance: The spatial separation between the thermal camera and the target affects radiation intensity. Accurate readings are achieved when the camera operates within its calibration distance, defined during manufacturing. Significant deviations from this range can lead to measurement inaccuracies, as shown in **Figure 5(c)**.

- Relative humidity (RH): Reflecting environmental moisture content, RH impacts the accuracy of temperature readings. While a default of 70% is typical, adjustments can range from 20–100%, as shown in **Figure 5(a)**.

- Emissivity: This measures a surface's efficiency in emitting thermal radiation. Materials like plants and soil have specific emissivity values, which must be properly configured to avoid errors. Surface conditions, such as corrosion, can alter emissivity, necessitating calibration as shown in **Figure 5(a)**.

- Reflected temperature: This accounts for energy reflected by nearby objects. If no extreme temperature sources are nearby, the reflected temperature should align with the ambient environment as shown in **Figure 5(d)**.

- Ambient temperature: Representing the air temperature between the camera and the target, this parameter is adjusted based on environmental conditions. Advanced systems incorporate sensors to automatically detect and set this value as shown in **Figure 5(d)**.

- Thermal cameras can operate across a wide ambient temperature range, from −40–80°C (−40°F to 176°F), as shown in **Figure 5(d)**.

- Applications of the Temperature-Vegetation Dryness Index (TVDI) in agriculture as in Eqs. (3) and (4).

- Irrigation management: Thermal imaging helps monitor crop thermal signatures, allowing farmers to optimize water usage and ensure efficient irrigation. It can also estimate soil moisture levels, improving irrigation schedules and crop yield outcomes [30] as shown in **Figure 5(c)**.

- Plant health monitoring: By identifying temperature variations that indicate stress, thermal cameras enable early detection of issues like pest infestations or nutrient deficiencies [32] as shown in **Figure 5(d)**.

Drought assessment: TVDI is a drought indicator that correlates land surface temperature (LST) with vegetation health. Calculated using LST and NDVI, TVDI evaluates soil moisture status and drought severity. Higher values indicate severe drought, while lower values suggest milder conditions [31], as in Eqs. (3) and (4).

3.3.2 LiDAR systems

LiDAR (Light Detection and Ranging) is a remote sensing technology that uses pulsed laser beams to measure distances to various surfaces on Earth. In agricultural UAV applications, LiDAR is widely utilized for precise mapping of terrain, crop monitoring, and assessing biomass to model the functioning of a LiDAR system mounted on Ag-UAVs [23]. The key of considerations include both LiDAR and photogrammetric principles. Several critical parameters affect the effectiveness of LiDAR data collection: Transmitted Power (*P*): This is influenced by the specific LiDAR device being used and plays a significant role in determining the range and resolution of the measurements [33]. For example, the laser wavelength typically used in agricultural applications is around 905 nm.

Target reflectivity (*TR*): Different types of vegetation reflect LiDAR pulses differently, which directly impacts the quality of the signal received in Eq. (4).

Distance of LiDAR to target (D_{LiDAR}): This varies based on the UAV's altitude and is critical because signal strength decreases with the square of the distance from the target and Atmospheric Effects: Although atmospheric attenuation (signal degradation due to particles or moisture in the air) is generally minimal for UAV-based LiDAR systems, it can still be a factor when surveying larger areas or during specific weather conditions [33]. By considering these parameters, LiDAR systems on Ag-UAVs can provide highly accurate data for a range of agricultural applications, from topographical mapping to crop health assessment, improving the efficiency and sustainability of farming operations in Eq. (5).

$$TR = \frac{P_t \cdot G_t \cdot G_r \cdot \sigma}{(4\pi)^2 \cdot R^2} \cdot \eta \tag{4}$$

Where:

TR = the received power at the sensor (Target Reflectivity). P_t = the transmitted power of the LiDAR system (the power of the laser pulse. G_t = the gain of the transmitting optics related to the transmitter's ability to focus energy in a particular direction. G_r = the gain of the receiving optics. σ = the backscatter cross section of the target, which represents the reflectivity or scattering characteristics of the crop or soil.

LiDAR technology works by emitting laser pulses toward a target and measuring the time it takes for the reflected pulses to return to the sensor, allowing for precise distance measurements. Time-of-flight (TOF) LiDAR operates similarly to radar, but it uses light pulses instead of microwaves [33]. A TOF LiDAR system includes a laser transmitter that sends out rapid light pulses, a photoreceiver circuit that detects and times the pulses, and optics that focus the reflected light onto the receiver. The round-trip time (τ) between the emission and reflection of the light pulse is used to calculate the target distance (R) by accounting for the speed of light in a vacuum (c) and the refractive index of the optical path (n) in Eq. (5).

$$D_{\text{LiDAR}} = \frac{C \times \tau}{2} \tag{5}$$

Where:

D_{LiDAR} = light detection measurement systems distance measurement systems (distance of LiDAR). C = speed of light in a vacuum (C). τ = The round-trip time of flight (τ) between the emission of an outgoing laser pulse and the arrival of the pulse reflected by the target is used to calculate the target range (R) based on the average group refractive index of the optical path between the LiDAR system and the target (n).

The swath width of a LiDAR system is determined by factors such as the scan angle of the instrument and the altitude of the aircraft. When adjusting for boresight angles, it is crucial to utilize georeferenced points. To estimate the boresight angles, an optimization model is used, which incorporates the georeferencing process in relation to swath width, considering the scan angle of the instrument and the flying height of the UAV [25]. This model allows for the accurate calculation of the swath width based on these parameters. For each LiDAR return, georeferencing can be performed according to a specified equation that integrates these factors to ensure precision in the measurements [34] in **Table 2** as follows in Eq. (6):

$$\text{SL} = \text{AGL} \times \left(2 \times \tan\left(\frac{\text{FOV}}{2}\right)\right) \tag{6}$$

Where:

S_L = Swath width as a function of instrument scan angle and Ag-UAVs flying height shown in **Figure 6**. FOV Field of view. AGL = Above Ground Level of LiDAR scanner FOV (m).

The point density of the scan is the following in Eq. (7):

$$\text{Point Density} = (pts/s)/(S_L \times \mathit{Flight\ Speed}) \tag{7}$$

Where:

Point Density = Point density of the scan. *Pts/s* = LiDAR scan rate. S_L = Swath width as a function of instrument scan angle and Ag-UAVs flying height. *Flight Speed* = m/s.

LiDAR technology provides high-precision data by measuring variations in light travel time and reflection, allowing for the creation of detailed three-dimensional maps. This level of accuracy is especially valuable in agriculture, where spatial data is crucial for decision-making. In agricultural UAV applications, LiDAR plays a vital role in surveying and mapping, helping farmers assess terrain and crop conditions more effectively [23]. By capturing precise spatial information, it supports the analysis of land features, water distribution, and plant health, ultimately optimizing resource management and improving productivity in agricultural practices as shown in **Figure 6**.

Index	Sensor	Eq.	Ref.
the reflectance of the target feature	LiDAR/Radar/ RGB Imagery	$R_{Target} = \frac{DN_{Target}}{DN_{Reference\ plate}} R_{Reference\ plate}$	[14]
Offset target	LiDAR/Radar	$\text{Offset target} = \begin{bmatrix} \text{scale} & (x)\times x \\ \text{scale} & (y)\times y \end{bmatrix} (m)$	[34]
Automatic identification and mapping of /model performance assessment	Multispectral / Hyperspectral camera /RGB imagery / LiDAR/ Radar	$\text{Precision} = \frac{TP}{TP + FP} = \frac{\text{Correctly predicted individual trees}}{\text{All predicted individual trees}}$	[25]
		$\text{Recall} = \frac{TP}{TP + FP} = \frac{\text{Correctly predicted individual trees}}{\text{All ground} - \text{truthed individual tree}}$	[25]
		$F1 - \text{score} = \frac{\text{Precision} \times \text{Recall}}{\frac{\text{Precision+Recall}}{2}}$	[25]
		$\text{ToU} = \frac{bbx_{Pred} \cap bbx_{Ref}}{\frac{bbx_{Pred} \cup bbx_{Ref}}{2}}$	[25]
		$AP = \int_0^1 p(r)dr \approx \sum_{k=1}^{n} P_k(r_k - r_{k-1})$	[25]
Simple ratio between the size of the pattern in the real world and the image is used to convert the image's horizontal position error to the world frame	Multispectral/ Hyperspectral Camera/RGB Imagery/ LiDAR/Radar	$\text{WorldPosition}_{xy}(m) = ImagePosition_{xy}(px) \times \frac{WorldPattenSize(m)}{ImagePatternSIze(px)}$ $\text{WorldPosition}_{Z}(m) = FocalLength\ (px) \times \frac{WorldPattenSize(m)}{ImagePatternSIze(px)}$	[35]
The distance a single photon has traveled to and from an object is calculated			
The distance a single photon has traveled to and from an object	LiDAR/Radar	$d = c\ t/2,$	[33]
Phase shift measurement (PMS)	LiDAR/Radar	$d = c\Delta\theta/2\pi f$	[33]

Table 2.
Key equations governing sensors of lidar and radar provide to determine the effective monitoring range in plant data by measuring variations in light travel time and reflection in Ag-UAVs.

3.4 Radar technology

Synthetic Aperture Radar (SAR) technology is critical for accurate height measurement and agricultural monitoring when integrated into Ag-UAVs [36]. SAR uses the UAV's movement to simulate a larger antenna, producing high-resolution imagery of the ground and effectively measuring surface heights [36]. Different frequency bands such as L-band, C-band, and X-band are utilized, with the L-band being particularly useful in agriculture due to its superior ability to penetrate plant canopies. For precise data analysis, SAR data undergoes various processing techniques like signal filtering, noise reduction, and interferometric processing, which convert radar signals into accurate height measurements. Combining radar data with optical and multispectral sensor outputs enhances the overall accuracy, offering a more complete view of the agricultural landscape. In terms of data alignment [33], it is important to adjust coordinate systems to ensure consistency across measurements. The UAV's

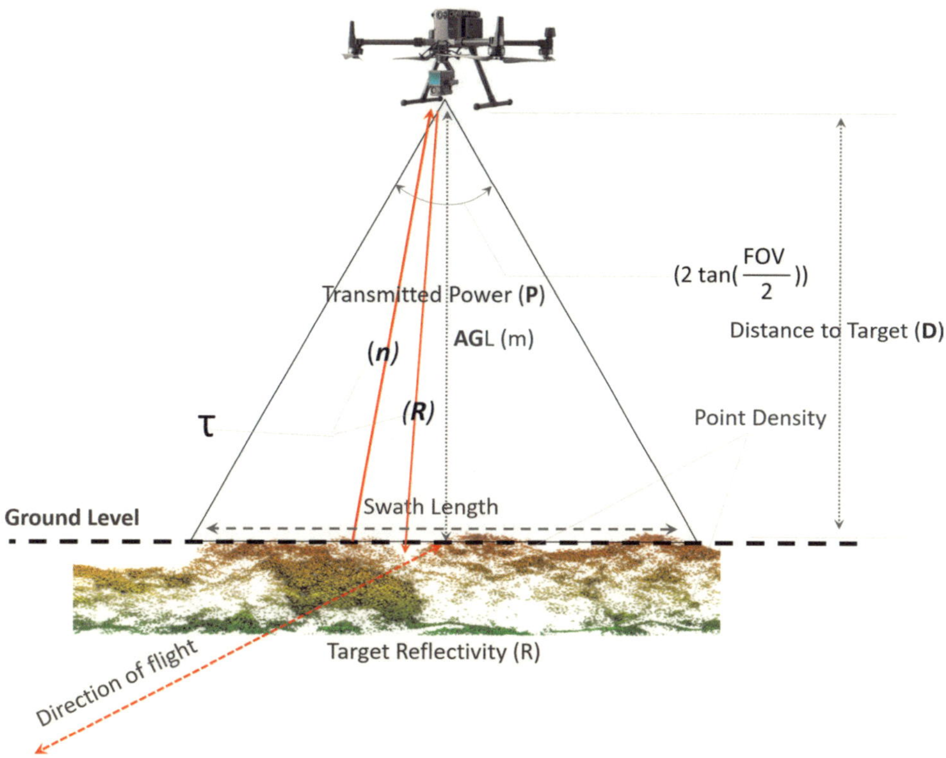

Figure 6.
The imaging equation aids in estimating parameters of swath width as a function of instrument scan angle and Ag-UAVs flying height in LiDAR system in Ag-UAVs.

coordinate system is used as the reference, with necessary rotations applied to the radar and Inertial Measurement Unit (IMU) data to achieve synchronization [8]. The radar outputs include critical metrics like the Radar Cross Section (RCS), which indicates the strength of reflection from an object, and range rate, representing the velocity of an object relative to the radar sensor [33]. This rich data set, which also includes range, azimuth, and elevation, contributes to the comprehensive monitoring and analysis of agricultural fields as shown in **Figure 6** as follows in Eqs. (8)–(10).

$$\mathrm{X} = (-X_{IMU} = Z_R) \tag{8}$$

$$\mathrm{Y} = (-Y_{IMU} = Y_R) \tag{9}$$

$$\mathrm{Z} = (-Z_{IMU} = X_R) \tag{10}$$

Where:

The following terms relate to the measurements and orientations used in UAV flight dynamics:

X = represents the area both in front of and behind the Ag-UAVs. *Y* = indicates the altitude of the UAV, or the distance it is from the ground. *Z* = refers to the flight height above the ground, essentially a measure of vertical distance from the surface. *ZR* = Refers to the elevation angles, specifying the UAV's up and down orientation relative to a horizontal plane. *YR* = represents the azimuth angle, which defines the UAV's left and right orientation relative to a reference direction. *XR* = Describes the distance measured directly ahead of the UAV, usually in terms of radar or other sensing equipment.

These parameters are essential for accurate positioning and navigation of Ag-UAVs in various applications. A bumper system in Ag-UAVs typically uses proximity sensors to detect nearby obstacles or the ground in **Table 2**. These systems often incorporate infrared (IR) sensors for measuring distances, providing a means to prevent collisions and ensure safe flight operations. The detection distance of such systems can be modeled using an equation similar to radar-based measurements, accounting for factors such as sensor calibration and environmental conditions as shown in **Figure 7**. The specific distance measurement can be calculated using the following in Eq. (11).

$$\mathrm{Bs}D = 2 \times SRF \times \Delta t \tag{11}$$

Where:

$B_S D$ = bumper system of distance in the detection distance of such systems. SRF = Speed of radar sensors of field. Δt = represents the time taken.

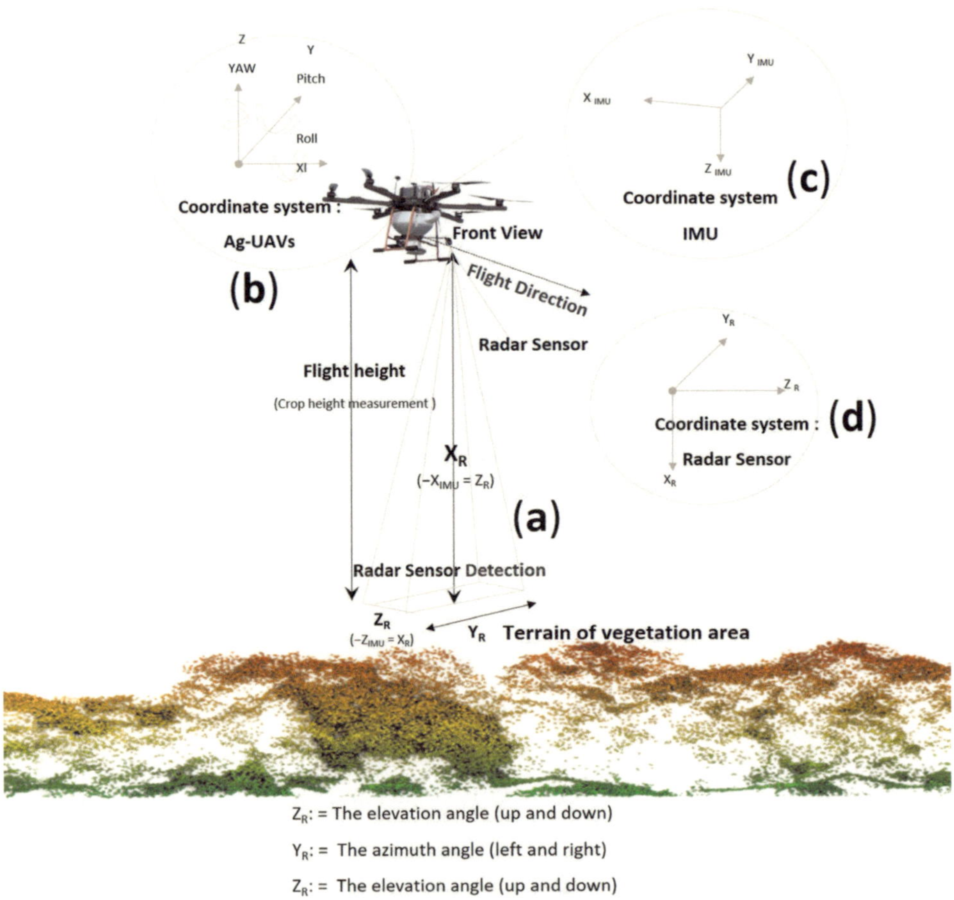

Figure 7.
The coordinate system of the UAV is designated as the target reference system. Both the Inertial Measurement Unit (IMU) and radar are adjusted accordingly to align with this system. (a) illustrates the radar sensor's field of view and the orientation axes of both the radar and the IMU on the Ag-UAV (SRF). *(b) shows the coordinate system for the UAV when it is positioned in front of the vehicle. (c) represents the coordinate system associated with the IMU, aligned with the UAV's movements and orientation.*

By adjusting the system to accurately measure this time delay, the bumper system can effectively monitor its proximity to obstacles, ensuring safety during Ag-UAVs operations.

4. Components and optimization in recent advances, new perspectives in technology of Ag-UAVs

Ag-UAVs are made up of several essential components that optimize their performance for precision farming. The airframe, often made of lightweight yet durable materials, forms the structural backbone of the UAV, ensuring strength while maintaining aerodynamics for efficient flight [8]. The propulsion system, consisting of motors and propellers, is crucial for providing the necessary lift and maneuverability, directly affecting both flight duration and operational capabilities [13]. The flight control system, which includes various sensors, gyroscopes, and accelerometers, is responsible for stabilizing the UAV during flight. Additionally, GPS technology is typically integrated into the system to provide precise positioning, ensuring accurate navigation during agricultural operations. These systems work together to enable Ag-UAVs to perform a wide range of tasks, from monitoring crop health to mapping fields efficiently [37], as shown in **Figure 8**.

4.1 GPS module technology in agricultural UAVs

The GPS module in agricultural UAVs integrates key components such as satellite systems, ground control stations, receivers, software, and mapping tools. Satellites transmit signals that enable the receiver to calculate precise locations by analyzing the signal travel time. GCS ensures satellite functionality and maintains accurate orbital paths [32]. UAV-installed GPS receivers process data from multiple satellites, often supported by Geographic Information Systems (GIS), which create detailed, actionable maps. This technology is highly valued for its precision, ability to cover vast areas efficiently, and real-time data access. However, challenges like signal interference, high costs, and complex data management can hinder widespread use. Despite these limitations, the long-term benefits, including enhanced productivity and cost savings, often outweigh initial investment challenges [38]. GPS modules in UAVs rely on microcontrollers or processors to interpret signals and integrate them with onboard systems like navigation and flight controls. Integration with Inertial Measurement Units (IMUs) improves accuracy by providing data on orientation, speed, and acceleration. Advanced algorithms and sensor fusion techniques enhance reliability, while robust communication protocols ensure seamless operation. A stable power source, typically from the UAV's primary battery, is essential for consistent GPS functionality [8], as shown in **Figure 8(b)**.

4.2 Flight control systems (FCS)

Flight Control Systems (FCS) and Autonomous Features in Agricultural UAVs: Flight control systems are fundamental for maintaining stability, precise navigation, and efficient operation of agricultural UAVs. These systems utilize a microcontroller to process sensor data and execute control algorithms. By integrating inputs from GPS and IMU sensors, they accurately determine the UAV's position and orientation, ensuring smooth flight. The IMU, comprising accelerometers and gyroscopes,

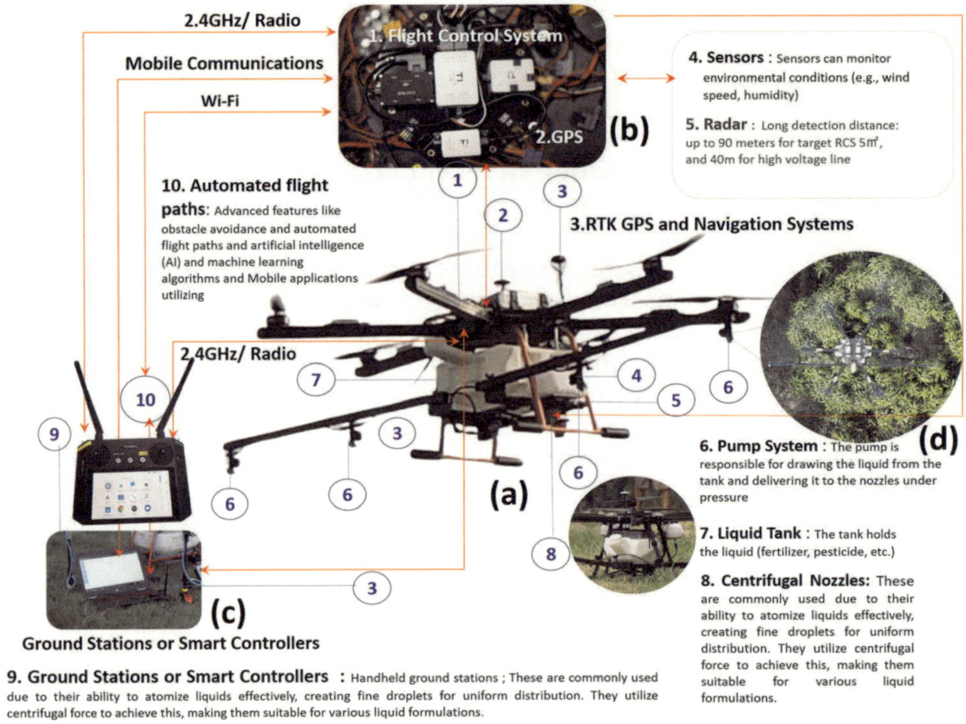

Figure 8.
Main Components of Ag-UAVs: (a) Airframe for autonomously spraying fertilizers and pesticides, (b) FCS and autonomous operating systems, (c) Ground Control Stations (GCS), and (d) Real-time operations.

provides real-time feedback on movement, aiding in stability during flight [8], as shown in **Figure 8(b)**. Key features of FCS include stabilization, autonomous navigation, and real-time sensor data processing. User-friendly interfaces make these systems accessible to operators with varying technical expertise, encouraging broader adoption. However, challenges persist, such as the high cost of advanced flight controllers, the need for technical training, and compliance with aviation regulations across regions. Addressing these concerns is crucial for maximizing UAV efficiency and unlocking their full potential in agriculture.

4.3 Autonomous systems

Autonomous systems within the flight control units (FCUs) of commercial agricultural UAVs are essential for efficient flight management, stability, and task execution. These systems play a key role in precision farming by facilitating tasks such as crop mapping and monitoring and optimizing inputs like water, fertilizers, and pesticides [39, 40]. The integration of autonomous flight control allows UAVs to cover large agricultural areas without the need for constant human oversight, making them ideal for scalable operations. Advanced flight controllers process data from various sensors in real time, enabling quick decision-making and providing farmers with timely insights on crop conditions. Additionally, modern controllers integrate seamlessly with technologies like GPS, LiDAR, and multispectral cameras, which enhance capabilities in crop health assessment and yield prediction [23].

User-friendly interfaces make these sophisticated systems accessible even to those with limited technical knowledge. Despite the benefits, the high cost of quality flight controllers may be a barrier for smaller-scale operations, and the complexity of the technology often requires training for proper usage as shown in **Figure 8(c)**.

4.4 Operating systems

Operating systems play a vital role in enhancing the precision and efficiency of agricultural UAVs [39]. These systems are powered by applications designed for flight and mission planning, allowing operators to plan and optimize UAV routes based on specific agricultural needs. These tools ensure that key tasks, such as crop monitoring, fertilization, and pesticide spraying, are carried out effectively [41]. By automating flight paths, these systems ensure optimal UAV performance in various agricultural environments, making them integral to precision farming practices as shown in **Figure 8(c)**.

4.5 Ground control stations (GCS)

GCS are crucial in managing UAV operations, providing a centralized platform for real-time flight monitoring and control [6]. The GCS enables operators to oversee UAV movements, monitor flight status, and maintain communication links with the UAVs during operations. Specialized software within the GCS also supports tasks like automated spraying and sowing, leveraging sensor data and algorithms to ensure precise application of resources [10]. This integration of technologies ensures that Ag-UAVs are used to their full potential, improving crop health and boosting yields while promoting sustainable farming practices as shown in **Figure 8(c)**.

4.6 Flight planning and mission tools

Flight planning applications and mission scheduling tools are critical for optimizing UAV operations in agricultural settings. These tools automatically generate flight paths based on mission objectives and terrain, allowing UAVs to efficiently cover large areas [38]. Real-time monitoring capabilities provide constant updates on flight status, helping operators make quick adjustments if needed. Additionally, mission planning tools help coordinate UAV operations to align with the needs of crops and environmental conditions, ensuring that agricultural tasks are completed on time and efficiently, as shown in **Figure 8(c)**. Data analysis tools, such as those processing NDVI for crop health assessments, offer valuable insights that enhance farm management decisions.

4.7 Real-time operations

Real-time operations are at the core of enhancing Ag-UAV efficiency and precision in farming practices. These operations utilize flight planning applications, ground control stations, data links, and specialized software for dynamic agricultural tasks, such as crop surveillance, spraying, and sowing [6]. By incorporating real-time data, including weather, field conditions, and crop health metrics, flight paths are optimized to maximize coverage and reduce flight time. The GCS serves as the command center, allowing operators to monitor flight status and manage UAV operations [42]. Data links ensure continuous communication between the UAVs and the GCS, enabling real-time adjustments based on telemetry data and enhancing the overall operational effectiveness.

4.8 Spraying system

Agricultural UAVs have revolutionized crop management, particularly in the application of fertilizers and pesticides, by integrating advanced spraying systems for precision agriculture [43]. These systems enable targeted delivery, reducing waste and enhancing efficiency. Essential components include specialized nozzles like centrifugal and electrostatic types. Centrifugal nozzles produce fine droplets for uniform coverage, while electrostatic nozzles improve adhesion to plant surfaces, reducing chemical drift [44] as shown in **Figure 8(d)**. For the application of UAVs in plant protection field, obtaining the distribution law of the unique downwash air flow is the key step to control and improve spraying quality [45] and other integral parts of the spraying system include:

- Pump System: Ensures consistent fluid flow during operation.
- Liquid Tank: Designed for easy refilling and maintenance.
- Control Mechanisms: Employ electronics and software to regulate spray patterns and rates.
- Sensors: Monitor environmental factors, such as wind speed and temperature, to optimize spraying conditions [46].
- Flight Control Integration: Maintains UAV stability and precise navigation during applications.

Index	Factors	Eq.	Ref.
Operation parameters and spraying liquid configuration Coefficient of variation	spraying operations	$S = \frac{CV = \frac{s}{x} \times 100\%}{\sqrt{\sum_{i=1}^{n}(x_i - x^-)^2/(n-1)}}$	[44]
Deposition level	Uniformity/ Nozzle design	$k = \frac{\beta_{dep}}{\beta_v} \times 10{,}000$	[44]
Drift rate and percentage	Uniformity/ Nozzle design	$\beta_{dep} = \int_2^{100} k(x)dx$	[44]
the reflectance of the target feature	flight altitude, and environmental condition	$R_{Target} = \frac{DN_{Target}}{DN_{Reference\ plate}} R_{Reference\ plate}$	[14]

Table 3.
The effectiveness of spraying operations is influenced by factors like droplet dynamics, spray uniformity, nozzle design, flight altitude, and environmental conditions.

The advantages of UAV spraying systems are notable, including precision application, reduced environmental impact, and the ability to cover extensive areas quickly, as shown in **Table 3**. However, barriers such as high setup costs, regulatory hurdles, and the need for skilled operation can affect widespread adoption [7]. Despite these challenges, the long-term benefits, such as reduced chemical usage, improved crop health, and labor efficiency, make these systems economically viable [42]. The effectiveness of spraying operations is influenced by factors like droplet dynamics, spray uniformity, nozzle design, flight altitude, and environmental conditions [44]. For example, the evaporation rate of sprayed liquids depends on temperature and relative humidity. An equation modeling chemical deposition on crop surfaces typically incorporates these variables to ensure optimal coverage and adherence. By combining precision technology and efficient design, UAV spraying systems contribute to sustainable and productive agricultural practices as follows in Eqs. (12) and (13).

$$D(x,y) = \frac{Q}{A} \cdot \eta(x,y) \cdot f_w(x,y) \cdot f_e(x,y) \tag{12}$$

A simplified version can be expressed as follows in Eq. (13):

$$D(x,y) = \frac{Q}{\pi(h\tan\theta)^2} \cdot e^{-\alpha u_w^2} \cdot (1 - k_e(1 - RH) \cdot T) \tag{13}$$

Where:

The distribution of chemicals from agricultural UAVs depends on various factors:

D(x,y) = deposition rate; this refers to the amount of chemical applied per unit area (e.g., kg/m^2) at specific locations, which is influenced by the Ag-UAVs altitude, speed, and nozzle configuration. *Q* = flow rate; the rate at which chemicals are dispersed, typically measured in liters per minute (L/min) or kilograms per second (kg/s). *c* = effective spray area; this is determined by factors such as the type of nozzle configuration used and the UAV's flying altitude, which together dictate the spread of the chemical. *η(x,y)η(x,y)* = droplet impingement efficiency; this describes how effectively droplets adhere to the target surface, influenced by leaf geometry and droplet size. *fw(x,y)fw(x,y)* = wind influence; Wind conditions play a significant role in the displacement of spray droplets, potentially affecting uniformity and coverage.

fe(x,y = evaporation effects; Environmental conditions, such as temperature and humidity, impact droplet size and mass due to evaporation, which can reduce the effectiveness of the spray.

4.9 Sowing systems

Sowing systems integrated into Ag-UAVs are designed to automate the seed planting process, delivering enhanced efficiency and precision in modern farming [47]. These systems combine advanced technology and engineering to optimize seeding operations across diverse terrains and crop requirements [10]. These systems bring significant advantages, including reduced labor costs, faster sowing times, and the ability to work in challenging terrains where traditional methods may be less effective [42]. However, factors such as initial investment, maintenance requirements, and the need for technical expertise should be carefully evaluated to ensure long-term

Key components	Details
Seed dispensers	Critical for the controlled distribution of seeds, these are available in pneumatic, mechanical, or gravity-fed configurations. Each type is suited for different seed sizes and planting environments, ensuring flexibility in agricultural operations.
GPS navigation system	High-precision navigation, often supported by RTK (Real-Time Kinematic) technology, enables accurate seed placement, minimizing wastage and ensuring uniformity in sowing patterns.
Control systems	These systems integrate flight management software with real-time sensors, allowing adjustments to flight paths and seeding parameters based on field conditions, maximizing operational effectiveness.
Data analytics tools	Tools such as soil moisture sensors and remote sensing technologies provide critical insights into soil conditions, weather patterns, and field topography [48]. This data supports informed decision-making and enhances the overall planting strategy.
Payload optimization	The UAV's payload capacity is a key factor, determining the volume of seeds that can be carried and distributed in a single flight, which directly impacts efficiency and coverage.

Table 4.
Key components are designed to automate the seed planting process, delivering enhanced efficiency in Ag-UAVs.

viability. By leveraging advanced navigation, data integration, and adaptive controls, UAV sowing systems are paving the way for more sustainable and precise agricultural practices in **Table 4**.

5. Applications and innovative solutions of Ag-UAVs for crop monitoring, managing, and optimizing agricultural practices

5.1 Crop monitoring and crop health assessment

The adoption of Ag-UAVs for crop monitoring has revolutionized the way farmers assess crop health [3]. These UAVs, equipped with advanced imaging systems like multispectral and hyperspectral cameras, enable precise analysis of agricultural fields over large areas. High-resolution aerial imagery captured by these drones facilitates the calculation of vegetation indices, such as the NDVI [17]. This index is instrumental in detecting crop stress, nutrient imbalances, and water deficiencies, allowing for timely adjustments to farming practices in **Table 5**. These models help optimize UAV utilization, ensuring maximum impact on crop management as follows in Eqs. (14) and (15).

$$E = f(\mathrm{VIs}, \mathrm{Y}, \mathrm{DID}, \mathrm{CE}, \mathrm{Psensor}, \mathrm{RT}, \mathrm{W}) \tag{14}$$

$$E = \alpha_1 \mathrm{VI} + \alpha_2 \mathrm{Y} - \alpha_3 + \mathrm{CE}\ \alpha_4 \mathrm{DID} + \alpha_5 \mathrm{Psensor} + \alpha_6 \mathrm{RT} + \alpha_7 \mathrm{W} \tag{15}$$

Where:

α1,α2, … ,α7α1,α2, … ,α7 are weighting factors that reflect the importance of each parameter in a specific agricultural setting.

VIs = effective vegetation monitoring is vital for understanding plant health and growth patterns. Indices such as NDVI, SAVI, EVI, NDRE, OSAVI, and TVDI in **Table 1**. *Y* = yield prediction and disease detection; Ag-UAVs significantly improve crop yield forecasting through techniques like biomass mapping and spectral analysis [50]. D_{ID} = Disease pattern identification: With tools like high-resolution imagery and

Key components	Details
Enhanced decision-making	Real-time data collection supports precise actions for irrigation, fertilization, and pest management, optimizing resource use and boosting yields [6].
Targeted crop management	Frequent surveys provide detailed insights into crop health variability across fields, enabling specific interventions that minimize waste and environmental impact [36].
Applications of VIs:	Indices like NDVI empower farmers to monitor plant health effectively and respond promptly to emerging issues. This capability not only improves productivity but also promotes long-term agricultural sustainability [16].
Representation of Ag-UAVs efficiency	The operational effectiveness of UAVs in agriculture can be quantified using mathematical models that integrate factors such as imaging resolution, flight coverage, and the frequency of data acquisition [39].
Sustainability	By reducing unnecessary inputs and focusing resources where they are most needed, UAVs contribute to more sustainable farming practices [1].

Table 5.
Benefits of based monitoring in applications and innovative solutions of Ag-UAVs.

thermal sensors, UAVs can identify disease patterns effectively. Indices such as OSAVI and TVDI are particularly useful for monitoring plant health and identifying problem areas early [50, 51]. C_E = Cost efficiency is critical for sustainable agricultural practices. Reducing operational costs without compromising quality or environmental impact enhances productivity and the economic feasibility of modern farming techniques [37]. P_{sensor} = High-precision sensors, including advanced cameras and hyperspectral systems, improve the data quality collected by UAVs. Enhanced sensor accuracy directly contributes to more reliable crop assessments and interventions [13]. RT = Real-time operations: The integration of real-time data collection and spraying capabilities increases operational efficiency. These technologies support dynamic adjustments, optimizing farming interventions [6]. W = Weed management; Accurate mapping and targeted spraying play a significant role in weed control. By reducing yield losses caused by weeds, UAVs contribute to effective weed management and improved crop health [49].

Looking ahead, future trends suggest a greater integration of artificial intelligence (AI) for predictive analytics, allowing farmers to anticipate and address potential issues like disease outbreaks or yield deficits [52]. The integration of advanced imaging technologies, such as hyperspectral sensors, into Ag-UAVs provides a practical and accessible tool for users, facilitating high-resolution data acquisition and comprehensive of agricultural crop analysis [53, 54]. Additionally, the Internet of Things (IoT) is emerging as a transformative force, connecting devices like sensors and drones for real-time monitoring and decision-making [52]. This interconnected approach supports precision agriculture by enabling continuous data flow and responsive farming practices, ultimately driving sustainability and productivity.

5.2 Field crop monitoring precision and yield prediction

The adoption of Ag-UAVs in field crop monitoring precision and yield prediction has revolutionized how data is collected and analyzed, enabling farmers to optimize their practices with unprecedented accuracy [5]. Equipped with cutting-edge imaging tools like multispectral and thermal cameras, UAVs capture detailed aerial data about fields. This data allows for in-depth analysis of crop health, soil quality, and environmental factors, aiding in smarter decision-making [55]. Ag-UAVs empower farmers to take a targeted approach to resource application. For instance, VIs like NDVI in **Table 1** help pinpoint areas needing specific inputs such as water or fertilizers [56]. This precise intervention minimizes waste, optimizes resource use, and reduces environmental impact while enhancing crop yields [21] as shown in **Figure 9(a)**. Regular UAV surveys throughout the growing season further support dynamic adjustments in management practices, promoting overall efficiency and sustainability. Developing a model to assess agricultural productivity using Ag-UAVs would involve variables that address crop health, field conditions, and yield metrics [40]. Such a framework could serve as a robust tool for optimizing agricultural outcomes while promoting eco-friendly practices, as follows in Eq. (16).

$$P = f(\mathrm{VIs}, C, M, S, \mathrm{Ef}) \tag{16}$$

Where:

The key factors that contribute to agricultural productivity can be expressed as follows:

P = represents agricultural productivity, which could be measured in terms of yield per hectare, crop health indices, or other related metrics. *VIs* = effective

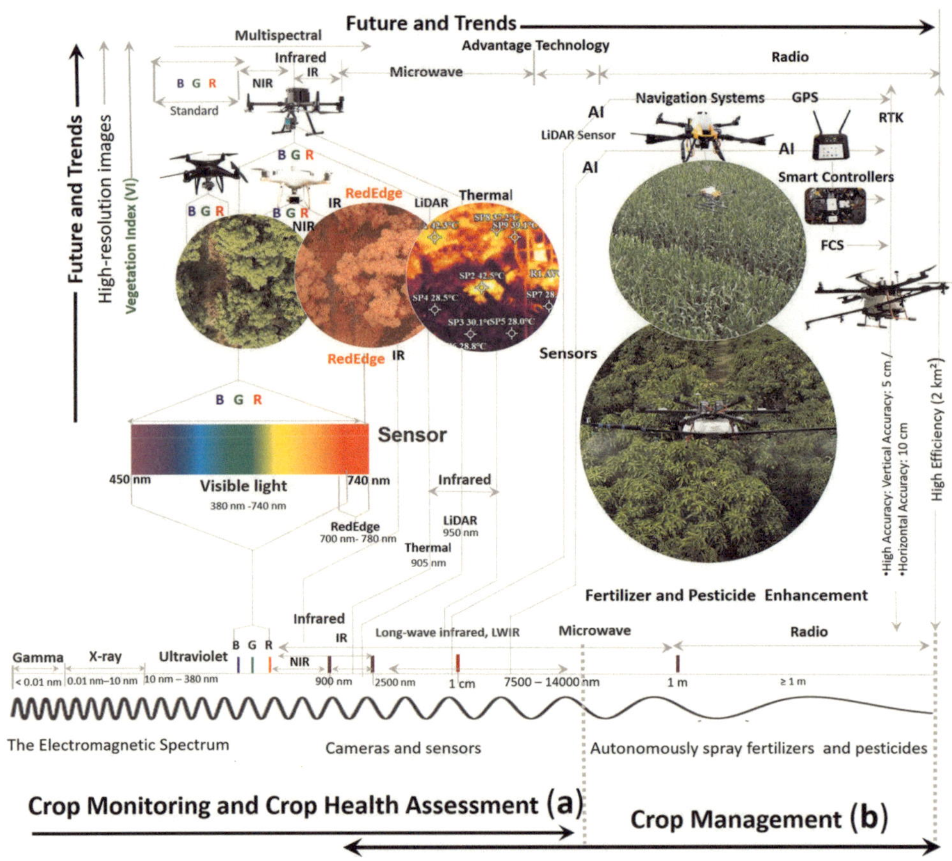

Figure 9.
Future and Trends of Ag-UAVs: (a) Crop monitoring and crop health assessment and (b) Crop management.

vegetation monitoring is vital for understanding plant health and growth patterns. Indices such as NDVI, SAVI, EVI, NDRE, OSAVI, and TVDI in **Table 1**. *C* = stands for crop characteristics, including factors like biomass, plant height, or chlorophyll content, all of which can be measured using UAV sensors or infrared (IR) technology in **Figure 3** [57]. *M* = represents management practices, such as fertilization and irrigation, which can be quantified and monitored through data captured by UAVs to optimize crop growth [58]. *S* = pertains to soil characteristics, including moisture levels and nutrient content, which can be assessed using UAV-mounted sensors or derived proxies (Factor of Soil-Adjusted Vegetation Index (SAVI) [18]). E_f = refers to environmental factors like temperature, rainfall, and humidity, some of which may be captured directly by UAVs or obtained from external datasets to influence crop performance.

5.3 Assessing agricultural productivity

Agricultural productivity can be effectively evaluated by employing models that incorporate key indicators such as NDVI, crop height in **Table 2**, and soil moisture levels in Eq. (4). A weighted approach allows for the assessment of each factor's contribution to overall productivity, enabling a more nuanced understanding of crop performance and resource needs in Eq. (17).

$$\mathrm{P} = \mathrm{a} \cdot \mathrm{NDVI} + \mathrm{b} \cdot \mathrm{H} + \mathrm{c} \cdot \mathrm{SMIndex} + \epsilon \tag{17}$$

Where:

The key factors that contribute to assessing agricultural productivity can be expressed as follows:

P = represents agricultural productivity, which could be measured in terms of yield per hectare, crop health indices, or other related metrics. *a,b,ca,b,c*: = Weighting coefficients determined via regression analysis or calibration. *SMIndex* = soil moisture levels in Eq. (4). ϵ: = Error term accounting for unmeasured variables.

5.4 Precision and assessing productivity

Precision agriculture is significantly enhanced by the utilization of Ag-UAVs. Equipped with advanced imaging technologies, such as multispectral and thermal cameras, UAVs enable farmers to collect high-resolution aerial data regarding their fields. This data facilitates a comprehensive analysis of crop health, soil conditions, and environmental factors, thereby supporting more informed decision-making processes [40]. In the context of precision agriculture, Ag-UAVs empower farmers to implement targeted interventions based on real-time data. By employing indices such as the NDVI, farmers can identify specific areas that require tailored inputs, such as fertilizers or irrigation, optimizing resource utilization and minimizing waste [15]. This targeted approach not only enhances crop yields but also reduces environmental impact by ensuring that inputs are applied only where needed. Additionally, Ag-UAVs play a crucial role in monitoring crop growth throughout the growing season, allowing farmers to dynamically adjust their management practices, which ultimately improves overall farm efficiency and sustainability [40].

Tools of precision in Ag-UAVs such as multispectral and hyperspectral imaging facilitate early detection of plant stress and disease Ag-UAVs have emerged as essential components of precision agriculture, offering high-resolution spatial data and the ability to cover extensive areas efficiently. Equipped with various sensors, UAVs capture images across different spectral bands, enabling comprehensive assessments of plant health and environmental conditions [32]. Additionally, ground-based sensors measure critical parameters such as soil properties and weather conditions, delivering real-time data that can be integrated with remote sensing information to enhance decision-making processes [15]. The integration of advanced data analytics and machine learning algorithms is crucial for interpreting the large datasets generated by UAVs and sensors. These technologies support the prediction of crop yields, identification of potential issues, and optimization of resource allocation.

6. Future and trends of Ag-UAVs

6.1 AI integration in Ag-UAVs

The integration of AI in Ag-UAVs is poised to revolutionize farming by enhancing operational efficiency and productivity. AI-driven advancements are shaping tools like flight and mission planning applications, enabling the automation of complex tasks and improving the accuracy of decision-making processes. These innovations empower farmers to optimize workflows and adapt to real-time field conditions [34] as shown in **Figure 9(a)**. AI enhances UAV capabilities in multiple applications. Equipped with sensors such as multispectral and hyperspectral cameras, UAVs collect detailed imagery and data that AI algorithms analyze to assess crop health, detect pest activity, and monitor growth stages. Machine learning models process this data to generate actionable insights, supporting farmers in tailoring their interventions to specific crop needs [59] as shown in **Figure 9**.

Precision operations powered by AI: AI-equipped UAVs play a pivotal role in precision agriculture. They can assess soil health by mapping properties and detecting nutrient deficiencies, providing critical information for determining fertilizer and irrigation needs. This targeted approach minimizes resource wastage while boosting yield potential [37]. Furthermore, precision spraying systems integrated with AI allow UAVs to identify and treat specific areas based on real-time conditions, reducing chemical use and mitigating environmental impacts as shown in **Figure 9(b)**.

Yield predictions and decision support: AI enhances yield prediction by analyzing historical data and current crop metrics, offering valuable insights for harvest planning and market strategies [15]. The ability to integrate UAV-collected data with external information, such as weather forecasts and market trends, enables comprehensive decision support systems [56]. These systems not only improve productivity but also promote sustainable agricultural practices by optimizing resource use and reducing environmental footprints.

Tools and advancements in precision agriculture: Ag-UAVs are pivotal in precision farming, leveraging advanced imaging technologies like multispectral and hyperspectral cameras to detect early signs of plant stress or disease [12] as shown in **Figure 9(a)**. These UAVs efficiently collect high-resolution spatial data, covering extensive areas and offering detailed insights into plant and environmental conditions. The data, combined with ground-based sensors that measure soil and weather parameters, creates a comprehensive framework for informed decision-making [16].

Integration of advanced technologies: the application of advanced analytics and machine learning enhances the value of the data gathered by UAVs and sensors [54]. These technologies process large datasets to predict crop yields, identify potential issues, and optimize input distribution, ultimately improving productivity and sustainability [39]. By integrating remote sensing with ground-based observations, farmers gain a holistic view of their fields, supporting proactive management strategies [1].

The future of Ag- UAVs lies in leveraging AI to foster smarter, data-driven farming, ultimately transforming traditional methods into sustainable and efficient agricultural ecosystems as shown in **Figure 9**.

6.2 Utilization of agricultural UAVs

The application of Agricultural UAVs (Ag-UAVs) is growing rapidly across various farming practices, including fertilizer application, monitoring vegetation growth, and assessing crop yields [17]. This expansion is driven by advances in technology, a focus on increasing agricultural efficiency, and global efforts to meet sustainability goals. Emerging trends suggest a shift toward automation and the integration of AI to optimize UAV operations. AI-driven systems enhance flight path planning and enable real-time analytics, improving adaptive spraying mechanisms that minimize chemical waste and environmental impact [7]. Ag-UAVs are becoming a cornerstone of precision agriculture, particularly with the use of hyperspectral and multispectral imaging. These technologies facilitate the early detection of pests and diseases, allowing for prompt interventions to safeguard crop health [51]. The large datasets generated by UAVs on crop conditions and field variability are processed using advanced analytical platforms, offering actionable insights to improve farm productivity and sustainability. Sustainability remains a key focus, with Ag-UAVs enabling targeted application techniques that reduce chemical usage. This includes using bio-compatible fertilizers and environmentally friendly crop protection measures [60]. Real-time pest detection, aided by AI and thermal imaging, allows for dynamic responses, such as applying treatment exclusively to affected areas, thereby reducing costs and improving crop outcomes [6]. Moreover, regulatory frameworks around the globe are adapting to better accommodate the integration of UAVs in agriculture. These frameworks address issues of safety, operational guidelines, and data privacy, creating a conducive environment for the widespread adoption of Ag-UAVs in modern farming practices.

7. Conclusion

In summary, the integration of UAVs into modern agricultural systems marks a pivotal shift toward more efficient and sustainable farming practices. With the use of various sensors, such as RGB, multispectral, thermal cameras, LiDAR, and radar technology, Ag-UAVs provide precise monitoring of crop health and optimize resource management. Advanced flight control systems and GPS enable accurate navigation, allowing for data-driven decision-making that improves efficiency while minimizing environmental impact. Ag-UAVs will play an increasingly vital role in boosting productivity and promoting sustainable food production. The integration of advanced technologies such as AI, multispectral imaging, and LiDAR into Ag-UAVs is driving a transformation in agriculture. These tools offer significant benefits, including improved productivity, enhanced resource management, and reduced environmental impact. Future advancements are expected to further optimize agricultural operations, paving the way for sustainable and efficient farming practices.

Acknowledgements

This research project has been funded by Mahidol University (Fundamental Fund: fiscal year 2021 by National Science Research and Innovation Fund (NSRF).

Author details

Rattana Boonprasert[1*] and Piyarat Vijuksungsith[2]

1 Faculty of Environment and Resource Studies, Mahidol University, Nakhon Pathom, Thailand

2 Faculty of Agriculture at Kamphaeng Saen, Central Laboratory and Greenhouse Complex, Research and Academic Service Center, Kasetsart University, Kamphaeng Saen Campus, Nakhon Pathom, Thailand

*Address all correspondence to: rattana.boo@mahidol.ac.th

References

[1] Ahmed S, Basu N, Nicholson CE, Rutter SR, Marshall JR, Perry JJ, et al. Use of machine learning for monitoring the growth stages of an agricultural crop†. Sustainable Food Technology. 2024;**2**:104-125. DOI: 10.1039/d3fb00101f

[2] Feng T, Lei J, Zeng Y, Qin X, Wang Y, Wang D, et al. Three-dimensional path-following control method for flying–walking power line inspection robot based on improved line of sight. Aerospace. 2023;**10**(945):1-21. DOI: 10.3390/aerospace10110945

[3] Kazemi F, Parmehr GE. Evaluation of RGB vegetation indices derived from uav images for rice crop growth monitoring. In: ISPRS Annals of the Photogrammetry, Remote Sensing and Spatial Information Sciences; 19–22 February 2023, Tehran, Iran (Virtual). GeoSpatial Conference 2022 (X-4/W1–2022). Tehran, Iran (virtual): ISPRS Journal Ph & RS; 2022. pp. 385-390. DOI: 10.5194/isprs-annals-X-4-W1-2022-385-2023

[4] Gallo I, Rehman AU, Dehkord RH, Landro N, La Grassa R, Boschetti M, et al. Deep object detection of CropWeeds: Performance of YOLOv7 on a real case dataset from UAV images. Remote Sensing. 2023;**15**(539):1-13. DOI: 10.3390/rs15020539

[5] Mukiibi A, Machakaire ATB, Franke AC, Steyn JM. A systematic review of vegetation indices for potato growth monitoring and tuber yield prediction from remote sensing. Potato Research. 2004;**133**:1-40. DOI: 10.1007/s11540-024-09748-7

[6] Alexandris S, Psomiadis E, Proutsos N, Philippopoulos P, Charalampopoulos I, Kakaletris G, et al. Integrating drone technology into an innovative agrometeorological methodology for the precise and real-time estimation of crop water requirements. Hydrology. 2021;**8**:131. DOI: 10.3390/hydrology8030131

[7] Chen P, Douzals JP, Lan Y, Cotteux E, Delpuech X, Pouxviel G, et al. Characteristics of unmanned aerial spraying systems and related spray drift: A review. Frontiers in Plant Science. 2022;**13**:870956. DOI: 10.3389/fpls.2022.870956

[8] Anderson K, Gaston KJ. Lightweight unmanned aerial vehicles will revolutionize spatial ecology. Frontiers in Ecology and the Environment. 2013;**11**(3):138-146. DOI: 10.1890/120150

[9] Daniels L, Eeckhout E, Wieme J, Dejaegher Y, Audenaert K, Maes WH. Identifying the optimal radiometric calibration method for UAV-based multispectral imaging. Remote Sensing. 2023;**15**(2909):1-22. DOI: 10.3390/rs15112909

[10] Lysych M, Bukhtoyarov L, Druchinin D. Design and research sowing devices for aerial sowing of Forest seeds with UAVs. Inventions. 2021;**6**:83. DOI: 10.3390/inventions6040083

[11] Gitelson A, Merzlyak MN. Signature analysis of leaf reflectance spectra: Algorithm development for remote sensing of chlorophyll. Journal of Plant Physiology. 1996;**148**(s3–4):494-500. DOI: 10.1016/S0176-1617(96)80284-7

[12] Bock CH, Nutter Jr. FW. Detection and measurement of plant disease symptoms using visible-wavelength photography and image analysis. Perspectives in Agriculture, Veterinary

Science, Nutrition and Natural Resources. 2021;**6**(27):1-15. DOI: 10.1079/PAVSNNR20116027

[13] Deng L, Mao Z, Li X, Hu Z, Duan F, Yan Y. UAV-based multispectral remote sensing for precision agriculture: A comparison between different cameras. ISPRS Journal of Photogrammetry and Remote. 2018;**14**:124-136. DOI: 10.1016/j.isprsjprs.2018.09.008

[14] Xu S, Xu X, Blacker C, Gaulton R, Zhu Q, Yang M, et al. Estimation of leaf nitrogen Contentin Rice using vegetation indices and feature variable optimization with information fusion of multiple-sensor images from UAV. Remote Sensing. 2023;**15**:854. DOI: 10.3390/rs15030854

[15] Guebsi R, Mami S, Chokmani K. Drones in precision agriculture: A comprehensive review of applications, technologies, and challenges. Drones. 2024;**8**(686):1-30. DOI: 10.3390/drones8110686

[16] Qi J, Chehbouni A, Huete AR, Kerr YH, Sorooshian S. A modified soil adjusted vegetation index. Remote Sensing of Environment. 1994;**48**:119-126. DOI: 10.1016/0034-4257(94)90134-1

[17] Wahab I, Hall O, Jirström M. Remote sensing of yields: Application of UAV imagery-derived NDVI for estimating maize vigor and yields in complex farming Systems in sub-Saharan Africa. Drones. 2018;**2**:28. DOI: 10.3390/drones2030028

[18] Zhen Z, Chen S, Yin T, Chavanon E, Lauret N, Guilleux J, et al. Using the negative soil adjustment factor of soil adjusted vegetation index (SAVI) to resist saturation effects and estimate leaf area index (LAI) in dense vegetation areas. Sensors. 2021;**21**(2115):1-14. DOI: 10.3390/s21062115

[19] Jianga Z, Huetea AR, Li J, Qi J. Interpretation of the modified soil-adjusted vegetation index isolines in red-NIR reflectance space. Journal of Applied Remote Sensing. 2007;**1**(013503):1-12. DOI: 10.1117/1.2709702

[20] Lawrence RL, Ripple WJ. Comparisons among vegetation indices and Bandwise regression in a highly disturbed heterogeneous landscape. Remote Sensing of Environment. 1998;**64**:91-102. DOI: 10.1016/S0034-4257(97)00171-5

[21] Steven MD. The sensitivity of the OSAVI vegetation index to observational parameters. Remote Sensing of Environment. 1998;**63**(1):49-60. DOI: 10.1016/S0034-4257(97)00114-4

[22] Karmakar P, Teng SW, Murshed M, Pang S. Crop monitoring by multimodal remote sensing: A review. Remote Sensing Applications: Society and Environment. 2024;**33**:101093. DOI: 10.1016/j.rsase.2023.101093

[23] Zhao K, García M, Liu S, Guo QC, Gang Zhang X, Zhou Y, et al. Terrestrial lidar remote sensing of forests: Maximum likelihood estimates of canopy profile, leaf area index, and leaf angle distribution. Agricultural and Forest Meteorology. 2015;**209–210**:100-113. DOI: 10.1016/j.agrformet.2015.03.008

[24] Huang Y, Ren Z, Li D, Liu X. Phenotypic techniques and applications in fruit trees: A review. Plant Methods. 2020;**16**(107):1-22. DOI: 10.1186/s13007-020-00649-7

[25] Beloiu M, Heinzmann L, Rehush N, Gessler A, Griess VC. Individual tree-crown detection and species

identification in heterogeneous forests using aerial RGB imagery and deep learning. Remote Sensing. 2023;**15**:1463. DOI: 10.3390/rs15051463

[26] Su W, Zhang M, Bian D, Liu Z, Huang J, Wang W, et al. Phenotyping of corn plants using unmanned aerial vehicle (UAV) images. Remote Sensing. 2019;**11**(17):1-19. DOI: 10.3390/rs11172021

[27] Freeman PK, Freeland RS. Agricultural UAVs in the U.S.: Potential, policy, and hype. Remote Sensing Applications: Society and Environment. 2015;**2**:35-42. DOI: 10.1016/j.rsase.2015.10.002

[28] Impollonia G, Croci M, Ferrarini A, Brook J, Martani E, Blandinières H, et al. UAV remote sensing for high-throughput phenotyping and for yield prediction of Miscanthus by machine learning techniques. Remote Sensing. 2022;**14**(2927):1-24. DOI: 10.3390/rs14122927

[29] Bhandari M, Xue Q, Liu S, Stewart BA, Rudd JC, Pokhrel P, et al. Thermal imaging to evaluate wheat genotypes under dryland conditions. Agrosystems, Geosciences & Environment. 2021;**4**:e20152. DOI: 10.1002/agg2.20152

[30] Chen A, Jiang J, Luo Y, Zhang G, Hu B, Wan X, et al. Temperature vegetation dryness index (TVDI) for drought monitoring in the Guangdong Province from 2000 to 2019. PeerJ. 2023;**11**(e16337):1-30. DOI: 10.7717/peerj.16337

[31] Li H, Li C, Lin Y, Lei Y. Surface temperature correction in TVDI to evaluate soil moisture over a large area. Journal of Food, Agriculture & Environment. 2010;**8**(3&4):1141-1145

[32] Awais M, Li W, Hussain S, Cheema MJM, Li W, Song R, et al. Comparative evaluation of land surface temperature images from unmanned aerial vehicle and satellite observation for agricultural areas using In situ data. Agriculture. 2022;**12**:184. DOI: 10.3390/agriculture12020184

[33] Farhan SM, Yin J, Chen Z, Memon MS. A comprehensive review of LiDAR applications in crop management for precision agriculture. Sensors. 2024;**24**:5409. DOI: 10.3390/s24165409

[34] Almalki FA, Soufiene BO. Modifying Hata-Davidson propagation model for remote sensing in complex environments using a multifactional drone. Sensors. 2022;**22**:1786. DOI: 10.3390/s22051786

[35] Moreira M, Azevedo F, Ferreira A, Pedro D, Matos-Carvalho J, Ramos A, et al. Precision landing for low-maintenance remote operations with UAVs. Drones. 2021;**5**(103):1-33. DOI: 10.3390/drones5040103

[36] Omia E, Bae H, Park E, Kim MS, Baek I, Kabenge I, et al. Remote sensing in field crop monitoring: A comprehensive review of sensor systems, data analyses and recent advances. Remote Sensing. 2023;**15**:354. DOI: 10.3390/rs15020354

[37] FHL F, Heldens WB, Kong Z, Lange ES. Drones: Innovative Technology for use in precision Pest management. Journal of Economic Entomology. 2020;**113**:1-24. DOI: 10.1093/jee/toz268

[38] Shamshiri RR, Hameed IA, Balasundram SK, Ahmad D, Weltzien C, Yamin M. In: Luque A, Hegedus S, editors. Books of Agricultural Robots. London, UK: IntechOpen; 2018. pp. 91-114. DOI: 10.5772/intechopen.80936

[39] Kim J, Kim S, Ju C, Son H. Unmanned aerial vehicles in agriculture:

A review of perspective of platform, control, and applications. IEEE Access. 2019;7:105100-105115. DOI: 10.1109/ACCESS.2019.2932119

[40] Tsouros DC, Bibi S, Sarigiannidis PG. A review on UAV-based applications for agriculture †. Information. 2019;**10**: 349. DOI: 10.3390/info10110349

[41] Qi P, Zhang L, Wang Z, Han H, Müller J, Li T, et al. Effect of operational parameters of unmanned aerial vehicle (UAV) on droplet deposition in trellised pear orchard. Drones. 2023;7:57. DOI: 10.3390/drones7010057

[42] FVAD S. Analysis of preliminary design requirements of a heavy LiftMultirotor drone for agricultural use. Chemical. Engineering Transactions. 2017;**58**:625-630. DOI: 10.3303/CET1758105

[43] KRG A. An autonomous UAV for pesticide. Journal of Trend in Scientific Research and Development (IJTSRD). 2019;**3**(3):986-990. DOI: 10.31142/ijtsrd23161

[44] Wang J, Ma C, Chen P, Yao W, Yan Y, Zeng T, et al. Evaluation of aerial spraying application of multi-rotor unmanned aerial vehicle for Areca catechu protection. Frontiers in Plant Science. 2023;**14**:1093912. DOI: 10.3389/fpls.2023.1093912

[45] Zhang Z, Zhu L. A review on unmanned aerial vehicle remote sensing: Platforms, sensors, data processing methods, and applications. Drones. 2023; 7(398):1-42. DOI: 10.3390/drones7060398

[46] Yang FB, Xue XY, Zhang L, Sun Z. Numerical simulation and experimental verification on downwash air flow of six-rotor agricultural unmanned aerial vehicle in hover. International Journal of Agricultural and Biological Engineering. 2017;**10**(4):41-53. DOI: 10.25165/j.ijabe.20171004.3077

[47] Pan Y, Zhu N, Ding L, Li X, Goh H-H, Han C, et al. Identification and counting of sugarcane seedlings in the field using improved faster R-CNN. Remote Sensing. 2022;**14**:5846. DOI: 10.3390/rs14225846

[48] Pruthviraj U, Kashyap Y, Baxevanaki E, Kosmopoulos P. Solar photovoltaic hotspot inspection using unmanned aerial vehicle thermal images at a solar field in South India. Remote Sensing. 2023;**15**:1914. DOI: 10.3390/rs15071914

[49] Eide A, Koparan C, Zhang Y, Ostlie M, Howatt K, Sun X, et al. UAV-assisted thermal infrared and multispectral imaging of weed canopies for glyphosate resistance detection. Remote Sensing. 2021;**13**(4606):1-18. DOI: 10.3390/rs13224606

[50] Kouadio L, El JM, Belabess Z, Laasli SE, Roni MZK, Amine IDI, et al. A review on UAV-based applications for plant disease detection and monitoring. Remote Sensing. 2023;**15**:4273. DOI: 10.3390/rs15174273

[51] Neupane K, Baysal-Gurel F. Automatic identification and monitoring of plant diseases using unmanned aerial vehicles: A review. Remote Sensing. 2021;**13**(3841):1-23. DOI: 10.3390/rs13193841

[52] Chukwu N, Ogwugwa EC. Applications of artificial intelligence in agriculture: A review. Engineering, technology and applied science. Research. 2019;**9**(4):4377-4383. DOI: 10.48084/etasr.2756

[53] Lukas V, Huˇnady I, Kintl A, Mezera J, Hammerschmiedt T, Sobotková J, et al.

Using UAV to identify the optimal vegetation index for yield prediction of oil seed rape (*Brassica napus* L.) at the flowering stage. Remote Sensing. 2022; **14**:4953. DOI: 10.3390/rs14194953

[54] Yu J, Wang J, Leblon B. Evaluation of soil properties, topographic metrics plant height and unmanned aerial vehicle multispectral imagery using machine learning methods to estimate canopy nitrogen weight in corn. Remote Sensing. 2021;**13**:3105. DOI: 10.3390/rs13163105

[55] Mogili UR, Deepak BBVL. Review on application of drone Systems in Precision Agriculture. Procedia Computer Science. 2018;**133**:502-509. DOI: 10.1016/j.procs.2018.07.063

[56] Rejeb A, Abdollahi A, Rejeb K, Treiblmaier H. Drones in agriculture: A review and bibliometric analysis. Computers and Electronics in Agriculture. 2022;**198**:107017. DOI: 10.1016/j.compag.2022.107017

[57] Maguire MS, Neale CMU, Woldt WE. Improving: Accuracy of unmanned aerial system thermal infrared remote sensing for use in energy balance models in agriculture applications. Remote Sensing. 2021;**13**(1635):1-17. DOI: 10.3390/rs13091635

[58] Yan W, Jiang J, Lanwu H, Zhao W, Nair R, Wang X. Correcting land surface temperature from thermal imager by considering heterogeneous emissivity. International Journal of Applied Earth Observation and Geoinformation. 2024; **129**:103824. DOI: 10.1016/j.jag.2024.103824

[59] Ezzy H, Charter M, Bonfante A, Brook A. How the small object detection via machine learning and UAS-based remote-sensing imagery can support the achievement of SDG2: A case study of vole burrows. Remote Sensing. 2021;**13** (3191):1-18. DOI: 10.3390/rs13163191

[60] Huu BV, Hieu NQ, Hieu LT. Monitoring growth and predicting crop yield through UAV-mounted spectral camera analysis of the interplay between soil compaction and vegetation index. Emirates Journal of Food and Agriculture. 2024;**36**:1-10. DOI: 10.3897/ejfa.2024.118256

Section 3

General Applications

Chapter 9

Application of Unmanned Aerial Vehicles in Industrial Intelligence Inspection

Fan Gao

Abstract

Regular safety inspection and maintenance of key equipment and devices is the top priority of industrial enterprises. The traditional manual inspection method is restricted by natural and geographical conditions and is difficult to meet the actual needs. With the advent of the era of artificial intelligence, industrial intelligent inspection has become a research hotspot. With the rapid development of technologies such as Unmanned Aerial Vehicle and data processing, currently, the technology of using UAV for industrial inspection has become relatively mature in some developed countries. Moreover, a customized intelligent inspection model featuring 'UAV inspection + condition perception + data processing and analysis + data application and visualization display' has been formed. This chapter introduces the application scenarios of this customized intelligent inspection model, including wind turbine blade damage inspection, transmission line inspection, pole tower inspection, metallurgical industry blast furnace temperature inspection, and reinforced concrete bridge damage inspection, through the above cases which briefly introduced typical application scenarios of Unmanned Aerial Vehicles in industrial intelligence inspection.

Keywords: UAV inspection, remote condition monitoring, high precision data acquisition, airborne camera, image recognition

1. Introduction

1.1 Preliminary exploration of applying UAV to industrial inspection

Unmanned Aerial Vehicle (UAV) can easily fly to places that are inaccessible or dangerous for humans to reach. Based on this characteristic, after being equipped with cameras and sensors, UAV could be utilized for industrial inspection [1]. **Table 1** presents the exploration scenarios of applying UAV to industrial inspection. In the future, UAV is expected to become an important tool for inspection in various industries and make greater contributions to improving production efficiency and safety.

Time	Country	Application scenario	Practical application value
2000	United Kingdom	The UAV was used to inspect the high voltage transmission line by University of Wales and EA Technology	Improves inspection efficiency and reduces the burden of manual line inspection
2004	Canada	The photoelectric pod mounted on UAV was used to carry out high-voltage transmission line inspection by Canada Avcan and United Kingdom EA Technology	Greatly reduces the cost of line inspection
2004	United States	The UAV was used for regular inspection of operating power lines by United States NASCENT Technology and Massachusetts Institute of Technology	Improves inspection efficiency, and ensures the normal operation of the line
2011	United Kingdom	The UAV was used for close aerial inspection of living torch tower by United Kingdom Cyberhawk	The world's first close aerial inspection of a living air torch tower
2012	China	The UAV was used for very close autonomous flight and tracking inspection by China Shandong Electric Power Research Institute	Timely finds line defect and ensures the normal operation of the line

Table 1.
Application scenario of UAV in inspection.

1.2 Introduction to the sensor configuration on the UAV

A wide variety of sensors are installed on UAV in industrial inspection scenarios to meet detection requirements in different scenarios and improve inspection efficiency and accuracy. An introduction to the sensor configuration on the UAV is shown in **Table 2**:

No.	Sensor	Concrete type	Deployment location	Type of data collected	Application scenarios
1	Camera	Visible light camera; infrared camera; multispectral camera	Bottom or top of the UAV fuselage	Image; Video	Target identification; environmental monitoring, etc.
2	Thermal imaging camera	Uncooled thermal imaging camera; refrigerated thermal imaging camera	The bottom or side of the UAV fuselage	Thermal images, temperature data	Heat source detection
3	Laser radar	Single-wire laser radar; multiline laser radar	The bottom or side of the UAV fuselage	Point cloud data (3D coordinate points)	Terrain mapping, obstacle detection, and 3D modeling
4	barometer	Absolute barometer; relative barometer; digital barometer	Inside of the UAV	Barometric value	Height measurement
5	Temperature and humidity sensor	Capacitive; semiconductor; digital; MEMS sensors	Outside of the UAV	Temperature and humidity	Monitors air quality and meteorological changes

Table 2.
Introduction to the sensor configuration on the UAV.

By carrying a variety of sensors, the UAV could achieve all-round and multi-dimensional data acquisition in industrial inspection and improve the efficiency and accuracy of inspection.

2. Application of UAV in industrial intelligence inspection

2.1 Application of UAV in wind turbine blade damage inspection

According to Global Wind Report from the Global Wind Energy Council, the global wind industry installed a record 117GW of new capacity in 2023, represents a 50% year-on-year increase from 2022, the annual installed capacity of onshore wind power exceeded 100GW in 2023, reaching 106GW, represents a 54% year-on-year increase from 2022. The total installed capacity of offshore wind power reached 10.8GW (**Figure 1**) [2].

Today, with the rapid development of wind power generation technology, the quality inspection of wind power units has increasingly become a bottleneck restricting the high-quality development of the wind energy industry [3], and the operating costs of the units in the life cycle account for about 20% of the total cost of the units. In recent years, due to the vigorous development of UAV, it is possible to apply computer vision technology to the field of blade defects and damage, which has broad application prospect and scientific research value. Its main work includes using the image acquisition equipment to shoot the blade surface graphics and using the computer to proceed image preprocessing, feature extraction, and damage recognition (**Figure 2**).

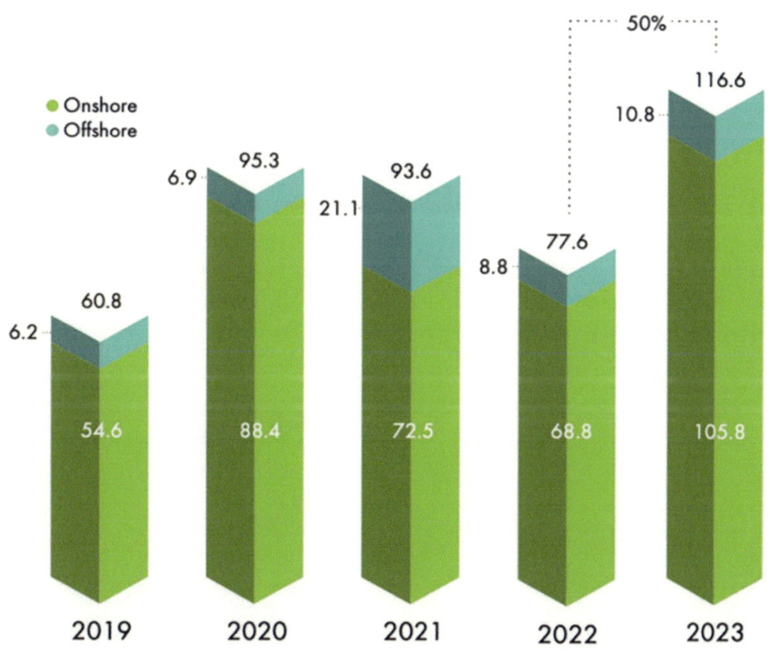

Figure 1.
New installation of global wind (GW) industry.

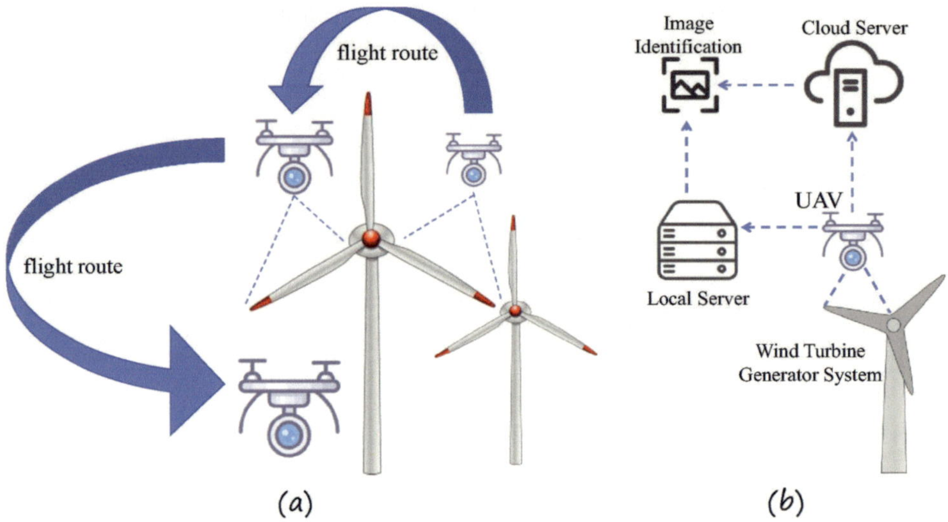

Figure 2.
Operation diagram of wind turbine blade damage inspection, (a) Flight route of UAV, and (b) Inspection system architecture.

The UAV could carry out close inspection on the blade of wind turbine, and through the flexible flight of the high-definition camera and the UAV, as shown in **Figure 3**, it could clearly photograph the surface of the blade, such as cracks, damage, corrosion, and other problems [4], and could also use the obstacle avoidance function of the UAV to carefully inspect the complex parts of the leading edge and the rear edge of the blade.

In addition, the UAV could carry out inspection of the tower barrel. The UAV takes off from the ground, gradually rises along the tower barrel, conducts a comprehensive inspection of the appearance, welds, bolts, etc., timely finds the corrosion, deformation, bolt loosening and other problems of the tower barrel, and ensures the structural safety of the tower barrel [5, 6].

2.2 Application of UAV in transmission line inspection

UAV inspection of transmission line means that visible light cameras, infrared sensors, and other task equipment were fitted and mounted with the UAV to carry out flight inspection, providing a basis for managers to make judgments and decisions.

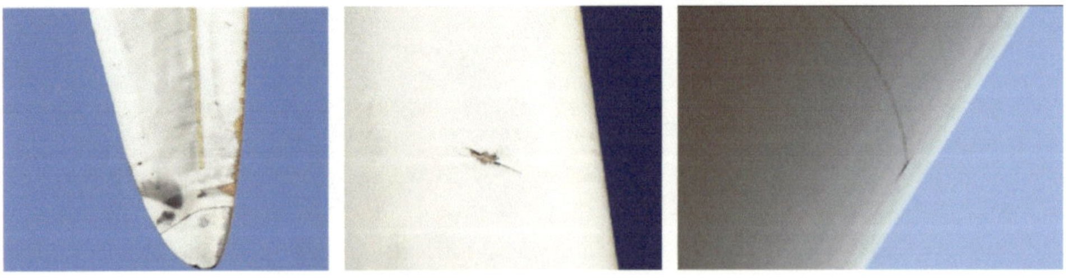

Figure 3.
UAV inspection result of wind turbine blade damage.

Small electric UAV operation could achieve fine diagnostic inspection of transmission lines [7, 8]. As shown in **Figure 4**, through high-precision control system, the transmission line could be inspected with high frequency, and the low speed or hovering flight could also be carried out in the short distance from the pole and the wire, so as to realize the detailed inspection of the transmission line guide ground, iron towers, fittings, insulators and ancillary facilities [9, 10].

Compared with the conventional manual inspection method, the UAV equipped with high-definition camera could be used to observe the missing pins, missing nuts, and various equipment defects of the transmission line from multiple angles by hovering in different spatial positions (**Figure 5**). By equipped with infrared equipment, it can also collect heat defects in wire joints, wire clips, tensioning pipes, insulators, and other parts (as shown in **Figure 6**), completely eliminating the "dead angle" of manual inspection, and providing a new technical means for power grid operation inspection [11, 12].

Based on the safe, flexible and convenient characteristics of UAV inspection, it improves the efficiency of on-site operation, and technical level of routine operation, and improves emergency handling of lines in high-risk and high-demand operations such as emergency repair, hidden trouble investigation and scene investigation of ultra-high voltage transmission lines [13].

2.3 Application of UAV in pole tower inspection

With the increasingly mature UAV technology, the continuous development of artificial intelligence technology, as well as the significant progress in computer vision technology, automation control technology, and sensor technology, UAV has been

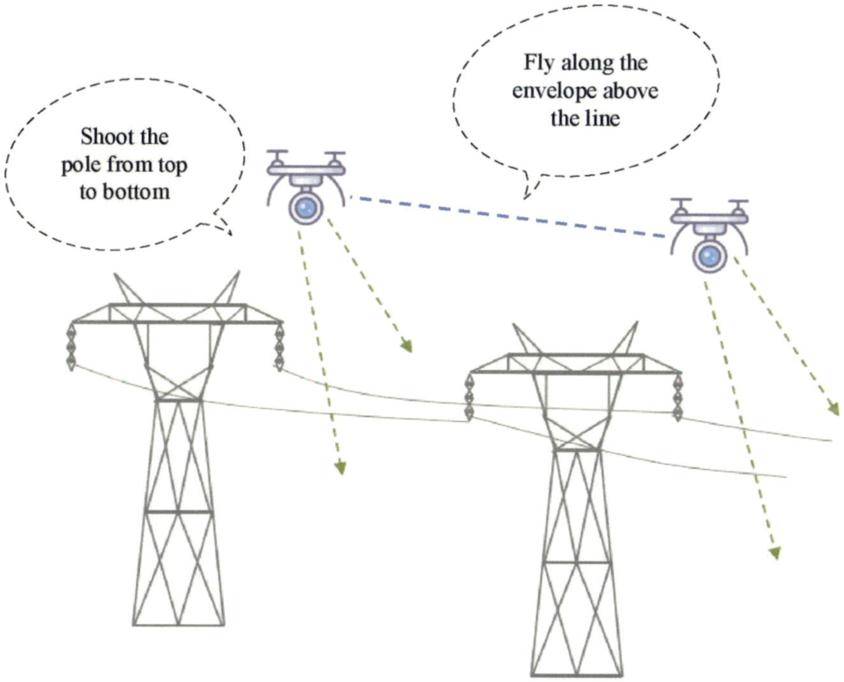

Figure 4.
Inspection operation diagram of fixed wing UAV.

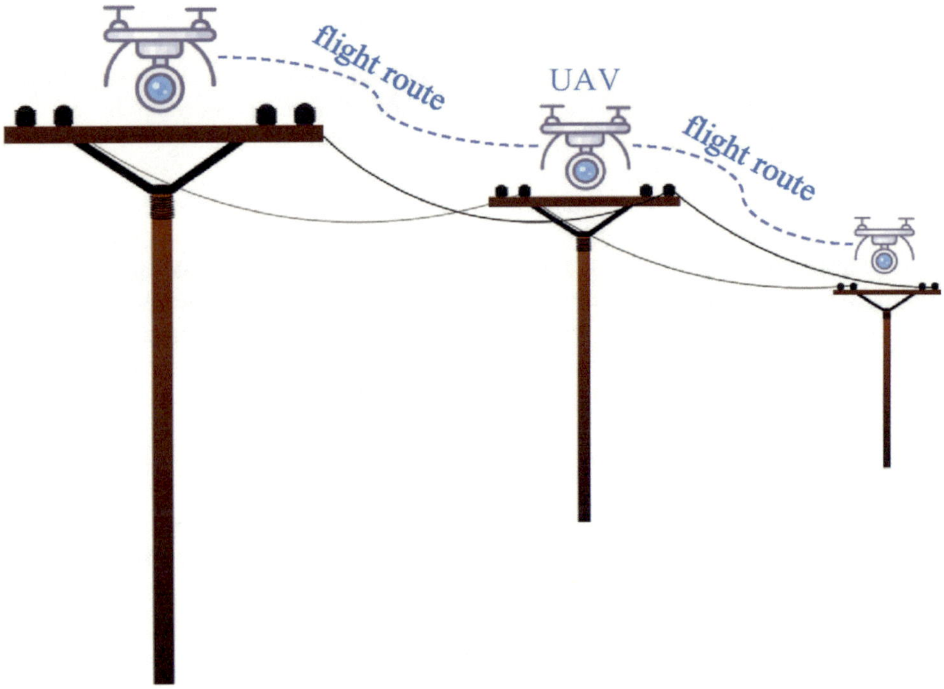

Figure 5.
Inspection operation diagram of multi-rotor UAV.

Figure 6.
UAV inspection results of transmission line (bolt missing pin).

widely applied in power line inspection. UAV can reach places that inspectors cannot or are not convenient to reach, gradually liberating inspectors from the high-intensity physical labor. Based on their advantages of "accurate inspection, stable monitoring and fast transmission," using unmanned aircraft for detailed inspections of power towers and power lines has become the best tool for inspectors to complete inspection tasks efficiently and safely.

Based on the UAV inspection operation, the "fully automatic UAV power precise inspection solution" introduced in this chapter has greatly improved the problems caused by traditional manual UAV inspection [14–16], such as "high labor costs for UAV pilots, large commuting expenses, poor timeliness, low accuracy and consistency, and short flight range and duration". As shown in **Figure 7**, it has realized functions such as on-site task deployment, automatic take-off and landing of UAVs, automatic inspection flight, and remote control to execute tasks.

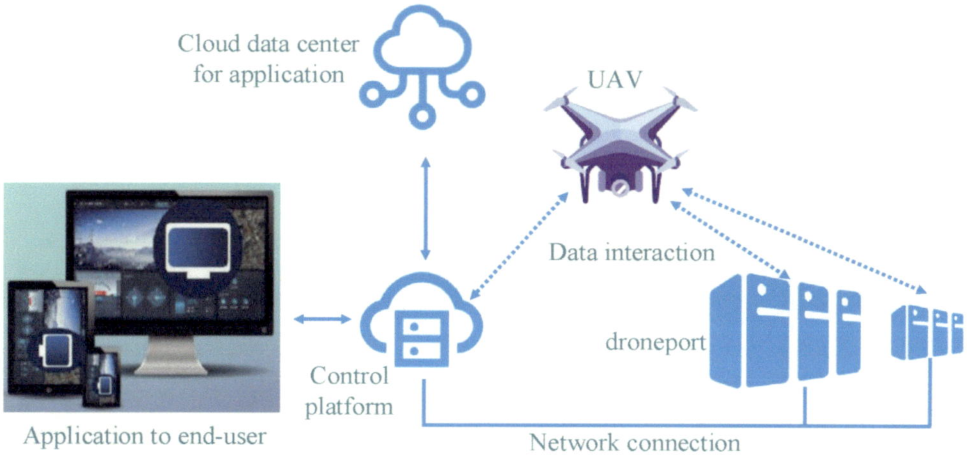

Figure 7.
Network architecture of automatic inspection system.

The shooting plan for a single tower adopts the method of manually marking points to plan the flight path of the unmanned aerial vehicle from the automatic airport to the target tower. As shown in **Figure 8**, for the 10 target components of the target tower, the shooting paths are planned as 1 → 10, and the unmanned aerial vehicle will execute the tasks in sequence.

The inspection team for the factory area's transmission towers, following the existing arrangement of the towers, as shown in **Figure 9**, three towers were divided the into one

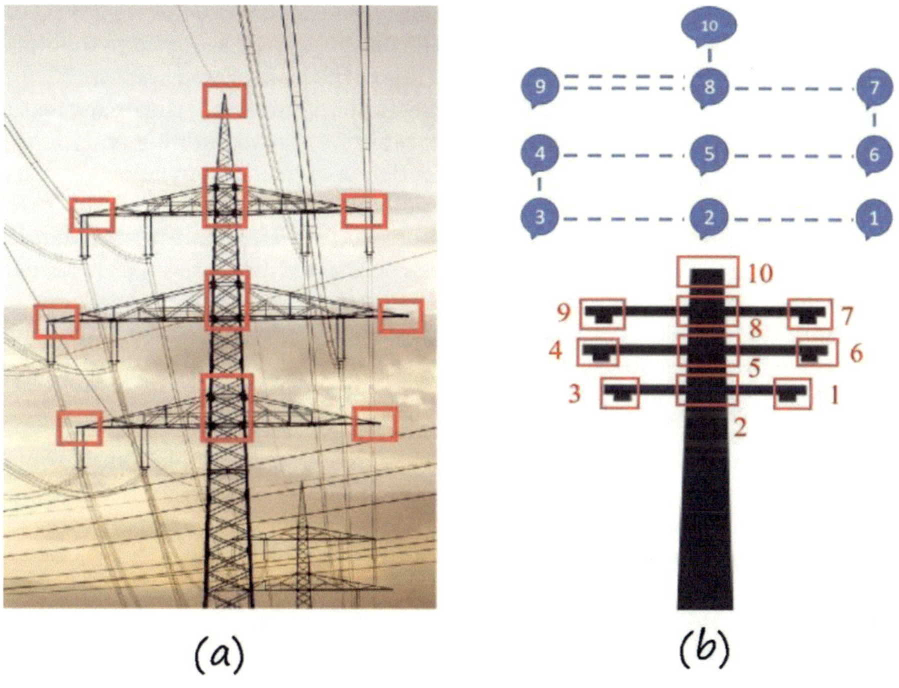

Figure 8.
Flight route of single pole power inspection, (a) actual photograph, and (b) elevation.

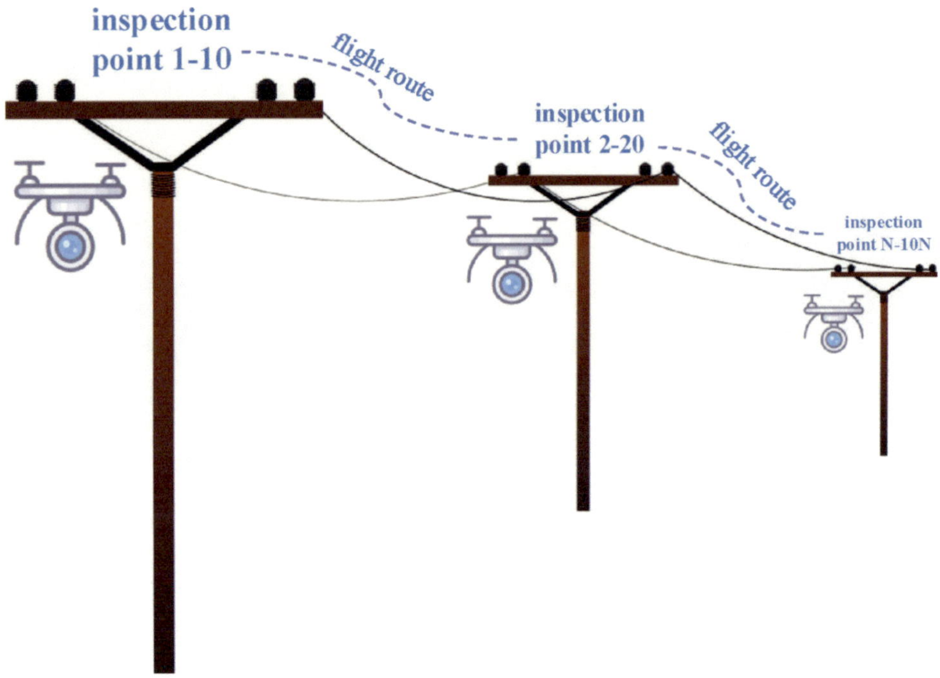

Figure 9.
Path planning of multiple pole power inspection.

group and the operation route were planned by marking points manually. During each operation, any one of the routes was executed, and the unmanned aerial vehicle (UAV) followed the sequence. After taking photos of the three towers, it returned to the automatic airport to transmit the photos taken this time to the background system.

As shown in **Figure 10**, after the UAV inspection is completed, the image features captured are integrated and analyzed to achieve automatic positioning and identification of insulator components. Based on the set defect identification rules, corresponding defect analyses are conducted for the insulator components to realize the analysis and identify common defects of tower insulators [17, 18]. The analysis and identification results are summarized and processed. According to the component type, defect type, and defect grade, they are classified for easy classification query based on requirements, and local magnification display of specific components is carried out to complete the refined inspection operation.

After obtaining the detailed inspection images of insulators, the background processing system platform conducts data processing and intelligent analysis including automatic association of inspection images with tower account books, automatic defect annotation, and information entry. It automatically records the key data and defect analysis results during the inspection flight in a document and generates the inspection operation analysis results of power poles [19, 20].

2.4 Application of UAV in metallurgical industry blast furnace temperature inspection

The metallurgical industry is the basic industry of the national economy and one of the important roles of modernization. The intelligent unmanned aerial

Figure 10.
UAV inspection results of pole power (Tower corrosion).

vehicle (UAV) inspection system for blast furnaces can realize functions such as temperature measurement of blast furnace pipelines, temperature measurement of blast furnaces and hot blast stoves furnace walls, environmental monitoring, inspection of factory roof, inspection of chimney top, and inspection of overhead power lines. For high-risk areas such as blast furnaces, high-altitude pipelines, and hot blast stoves, precise temperature detection can be achieved, allowing for timely identification of overheated areas and prompting the inspection personnel to conduct focused re-inspections in these areas. At the same time, due to the ease of operation of the UAV automatic flight system, areas that are difficult to reach for inspections can be transformed into regular inspection areas. This makes the intelligent UAV inspection system the best tool for inspection personnel to complete inspection tasks efficiently and safely, as shown in **Figure 11**, enabling the UAV to detect equipment hazards that inspection personnel cannot reach or are inconvenient to reach, thereby ensuring the long-term stable operation of the equipment. At the same time, in the event of emergencies, inspection reconnaissance UAVs can be quickly launched for inspection and reconnaissance, quickly locating the source of the accident, and real-time transmitting the on-site situation back to the command center [21].

After the flight route planning is completed, the UAV takes off automatically from the on-site automatic airport and flies along the planned route. When the UAV reaches the infrared temperature measurement point, it will adjust the shooting angle, focal length, etc., according to the preset point position instructions. The platform can monitor the temperature values of the infrared thermal imaging in the shooting picture of the UAV in real time. If the temperature value in the shooting area of the current waypoint exceeds the temperature threshold of that waypoint, the alarm mechanism will be automatically triggered. The system will automatically send the alarm information to the platform, mobile phone text message, or email. Users can locate the specific position of the blast furnace alarm through the alarm information. The thermal imaging pictures taken by the UAV show different colors due to the temperature differences in the monitoring area. Manual judgment of the images can also assist in identifying high-temperature points and abnormal points, helping to eliminate safety hazards.

The intelligent UAV inspection scheme for blast furnaces introduced in this chapter has advantages such as ultra-long-distance image acquisition, real-time image transmission, and real-time temperature monitoring (**Figure 12**) [21]. It has realized remote, intelligent, and automatic temperature measurement and inspection work for blast furnaces, effectively improving the efficiency, quality, and safety of blast furnace inspection and liberating labor force.

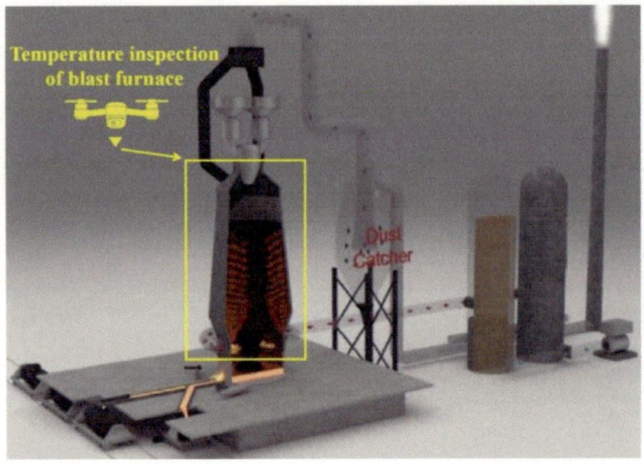

Figure 11.
Temperature inspection operation of blast furnace.

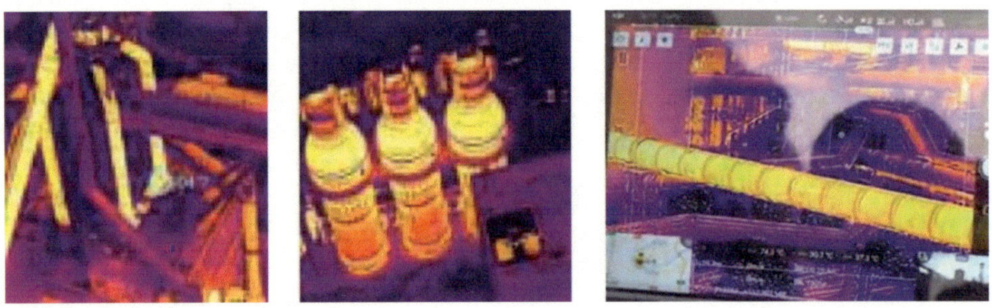

Figure 12.
Inspection operation of multi-rotor UAV.

2.5 Application of UAV in reinforced concrete bridge damage inspection

Application of UAV in bridge engineering inspection is mainly the appearance check [22], and the routing of UAV inspection is shown in **Figure 13**. The first stage, according to the key information of the bridge structure and the key inspection area to formulate the inspection plan. In the second stage, risk assessment was conducted on the bridge and surrounding area to determine the potential risk area of UAV flight. The third stage is to formulate the flight route of UAV, as shown in **Figure 13**. There were three routings of bridge inspection. In the fourth stage, the UAV carries out inspection according to flight routes and inspection plans and transmits live video of inspection and inspection pictures of critical areas in real time.

The high-precision sensor carried by the UAV could obtain high-resolution images and data, and through computer vision technology, it could identify cracks on the surface of the bridge structure (**Figure 14**) [23].

3. Conclusion

Through the introduction of application cases in this chapter, it shows the outstanding advantages of UAV in industrial inspection, including the efficiency of overall inspection, ensuring the safety of inspection, and high-precision data acquisition with high practical application value. High-resolution optical cameras could

DOI: http://dx.doi.org/10.5772/intechopen.1010545

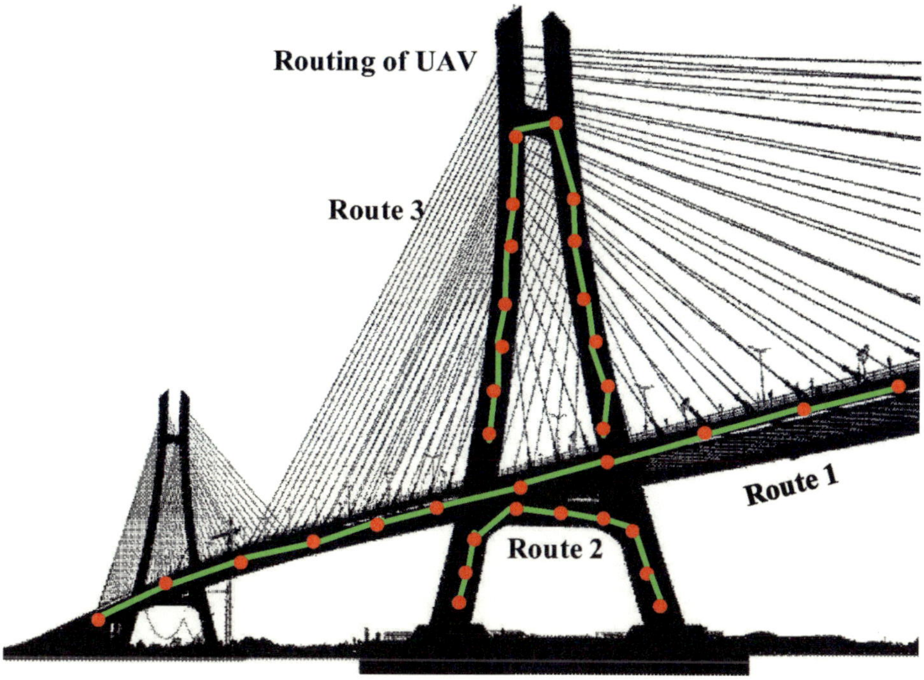

Figure 13.
Application of UAV in bridge damage inspection.

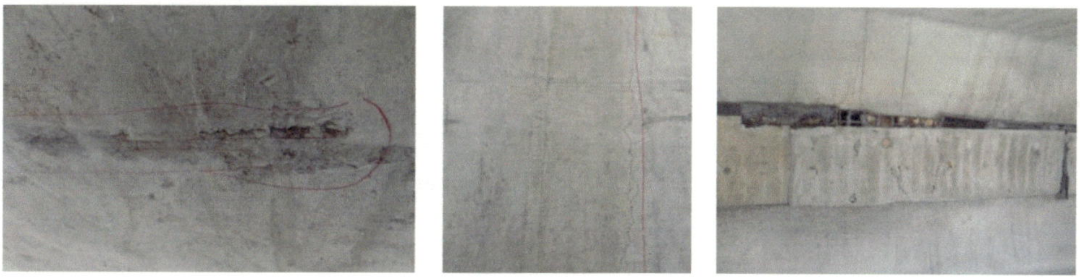

Figure 14.
UAV inspection results of bridge damage.

photograph tiny cracks and corrosion on the surface of industrial equipment; The infrared thermal imager can detect the temperature distribution of the equipment and find the overheating part of the equipment in time, and the Lidar sensor could accurately measure the distance and shape of the object, which is very helpful for checking the structural deformation of industrial facilities. Through these sensors, UAV can collect rich and accurate data, which provides strong support for the status assessment and fault diagnosis of industrial equipment.

Look to the future, UAV will be more and more intelligent in industrial inspection, automatically judge the severity of faults, and flight path planning will be more intelligent and automatically optimizes inspection paths and improves inspection efficiency. In addition, multi-UAV collaborative inspection will become a development trend, multiple UAVs can work together to inspect different areas or different types of equipment at the same time, improving the efficiency and comprehensiveness of the overall inspection.

Author details

Fan Gao
Chongqing Chuanyi Automation Co., Ltd., Chongqing, China

*Address all correspondence to: gaofan_sic@sina.com

References

[1] Fang Z, Andrey S. Strategies for optimized UAV surveillance in various tasks and scenarios: A review. UAV. 2024;**8**(5):193. DOI: 10.3390/UAV8050193

[2] Global Wind Energy Council (GWEC). Global Wind Report 2023 [Internet]. Brussels: GWEC; 2023 [cited 2024 Dec 21]. Available from: https://www.gwec.net/reports/globalwindreport/2023

[3] Zhang K, Pakrashi V, Murphy J, Hao G. Mint: Inspection of floating offshore wind turbines using multi-rotor unmanned aerial vehicles: Literature review and trends. Sensors. 2024;**24**(3):911. DOI: 10.3390/s24030911

[4] Electric Power Research Institute. A White Paper On Wind Turbine Blade Defect and Damage Categorization [Internet]; 2024. Available from: https://restservice.epri.com/publicdownload/000000003002019669/0/Product

[5] SkySpecs. Blade Inspections [Internet]; 2024. Available from: https://skyspecs.com/product/inspections/

[6] Cyberhawk Innovations Limited. Comprehensive Close Visual Inspection [Internet]; 2024. Available from: https://thecyberhawk.com/renewable-energy

[7] Zheng X, Jia R, Aisikaer LG. Component identification and defect detection in transmission lines based on deep learning. Journal of Intelligent Fuzzy Systems. 2021;**40**(2):3147-3158. DOI: 10.3233/jifs-189353

[8] Kim S, Kim D, Jeong S, Ham J-W, Lee J-K, Ki-Yong O. Mint: Fault diagnosis of power transmission lines using a UAV-mounted smart inspection system. IEEE Access. 2020;**8**:149999-150009. DOI: 10.1109/ACCESS.2020.3016213

[9] Niu WN, Ning B, Zhou H. Mint: Design of data transmission system of human-autonomous devices for UAV inspection of transmission line status. Journal of Ambient Intelligence and Humanized Computing. 2019. DOI: 10.1007/s12652-019-01504-x

[10] Meng Y, Tang Y, Huang X. Mint: A lightweight insulator detection methodology for UAVs in power line inspection. Journal of Circuits, Systems and Computers. 2023. DOI: 10.1142/s0218126624500695

[11] Luo Y, Xue Y, Yang D, Zhou B. Mint: A survey of intelligent transmission line inspection based on unmanned aerial vehicle. Artificial Intelligence Review. 2022:56173-56201. DOI: 10.1007/s10462-022-10189-2

[12] Tian D, Chen J, Wang X. Application research of UAV infrared diagnosis technology in intelligent inspection of substations. Energy Informatics. 2024. DOI: 10.1186/s42162-024-00364-w

[13] Weizhi L, Li Q, Zhang W, Mei L, Cai D, Li Z. Mint: Management of power equipment inspection informationization through intelligent unmanned aerial vehicles. Artificial Life and Robotics. 2024;**29**:579-584. DOI: 10.1007/s10015-024-00963-6

[14] Gao F, Long Z. Research and application of intelligent automatic UAV port and image recognition in precise inspection of pole tower. In: Liu Z, Li R, He X, Zhu Z, editors. Advances and Challenges in Advanced Unmanned

Aerial Systems. 2024. pp. 99-110. DOI: 10.1007/978-981-99-8045-1_8

[15] Li H. Application of 5G in electric power inspection UAV. In: Journal of Physics: Conference Series, 2021 2nd International Conference on Electrical, Electronic Information and Communication Engineering (EEICE 2021), 16-18 April. Tianjin, China; 2021. DOI: 10.1088/1742-6596/1920/1/012048

[16] Li H. Application research of transmission line ubiquitous inspection technology via 5G UAV. Computer Science and Application. 2020. DOI: 10.12677/csa.2020.108159

[17] Yang M, Zhou Z, You X. Mint: Research on trajectory tracking control of inspection UAV based on real-time sensor data. Sensors. 2022;**22**(10):3648. DOI: 10.3390/s22103648

[18] Zhang Z, Cai D, Zhang Z. Mint: Review on online operation insulator identification and fault diagnosis based on UAV patrol images and deep learning algorithms. Frontiers in Energy Research. 2022. DOI: 10.3389/fenrg.2022.912453

[19] Yang L, Li D, Li D. Mint: A lightweight insulator defect detection model based on UAV images. UAV. 2024;**8**(9):431. DOI: 10.3390/UAV8090431

[20] Yin L, Jing H, Wang W. Mint: Parameters optimization of UAV for insulator inspection on power transmission line. IEEE Access. 2022;**10**:97022-97029. DOI: 10.1109/access.2022.3192643

[21] Zhu M, Gao F, Guo L, He W. Research and application of 5G and condition monitoring in predictive maintenance of ironmaking blast furnace. In: Dong J, Zhang L, Cheng D, editors. Lecture Notes in Electrical Engineering. 2024. pp. 392-406. DOI: 10.1007/978-981-97-2757-5_42

[22] Li Z, Zhang B. Application study of UAV and IOT Technology in Intelligent Detection of bridge engineering. In: Proceedings - International Conference on Machine Learning, Cloud Computing and Intelligent Mining, MLCCIM 2022; August 5-7 2022. Xiamen. China: IEEE; 2022. pp. 13-18

[23] Liu Q. Mint: An overview of route planning for bridge inspection UAV. Computer Science and Application. 2022. DOI: 10.12677/csa.2022.1212270

Chapter 10

Multirotor Microgravity Platforms

Siddhardha Kedarisetty and Joel George Manathara

Abstract

This chapter introduces a novel application of using multirotor unmanned aerial vehicles (UAVs) as microgravity platforms. Conventional microgravity platforms that create microgravity (near-zero gravity), such as space stations and drop towers, are expensive and have limited access. In this chapter, we show that multirotors can be turned into affordable microgravity platforms. Toward this, a vertical microgravity enabling maneuver suitable for multirotors and an acceleration control strategy are developed. The proposed maneuver design and control methodology are validated through successful flight tests demonstrating sustained microgravity conditions. Finally, experiments are conducted onboard one of the multirotors executing a microgravity enabling maneuver to observe the effect of microgravity on liquid level in a capillary and liquid meniscus shape in a glass cuvette. These experiments and the microgravity enabling flight tests establish multirotors as viable microgravity platforms.

Keywords: multirotor UAVs, microgravity platforms, zero-gravity maneuvers, parabolic flight, acceleration control, microgravity experiments

1. Introduction

The current capabilities for space exploration require astronauts to live for months in conditions of negligible gravity, even when traveling to our nearby planet. In near-zero gravity, called *microgravity*, the behavior of the natural phenomena we experience daily on Earth, such as convection, capillary action, flame propagation, and combustion, is different [1, 2]. Moreover, most biological processes, including human muscle strength and bone density, are also affected by microgravity [3, 4]. Since various physical, chemical, and biological processes affect how astronauts conduct themselves in space, understanding these processes in microgravity became essential, leading to a new branch of research known as '*microgravity science*'. However, to conduct experiments in microgravity, we first require some stable and reliable means of enabling microgravity.

Experiencing microgravity on or near Earth is possible through free-fall motion. On Earth, we experience gravity only when we try to defy it. A stationary body experiences gravity of $1g$.[1] When an accelerometer measures the vertical acceleration of an object at rest, it shows $1g$, since accelerometers output the experienced gravity.

[1] $1g \approx 9.81\,\mathrm{ms}^{-2}$

The gravity experienced by an object is computed by adding 1g to its translational vertical acceleration.[2] An object accelerating toward Earth at 1g (a negative translational acceleration by our convention) is said to be in a state of free-fall and consequently experiences microgravity. The necessary and sufficient condition for an object to be in free-fall is that the net force acting on the object must be equal to Earth's gravity on the object. Utilizing the principle of free-fall, researchers have developed various test platforms to create a microgravity environment within Earth's gravitational field [2].

1.1 Microgravity platforms

The microgravity research community has been using a few types of microgravity platforms for so long that their performance values are well documented. These platforms are known to be standard microgravity platforms. The metrics used to measure the performance of a microgravity platform include g-time[3], g-level[4], payload capability, altitude of operation, and waiting time to get access to these platforms.

The standard microgravity platforms listed in **Table 1** provide us with near-zero g-levels and long g-times. However, accessing these platforms involves a long waiting time. Also, the cost of accessing any standard microgravity platform is not affordable for many educational and research organizations. Nevertheless, advancements in technology are giving rise to new microgravity platforms focused on reducing costs and shortening waiting times. Emerging microgravity platforms include: (a) single-engine piloted aircraft [11], (b) gliders [12], (c) laboratory free-fall equipment [13], and (d) UAVs [14, 15]. Although these platforms offer limited g-time and payload capacity, they can support several microgravity research areas. For example, research experiments such as capillary effects [16], surface tension variation [17], and flame propagation in thin fuels [18]—typically conducted on traditional microgravity platforms—can be performed on emerging platforms, as they require only 1 to 6 seconds

Platform	g-time	g-level	Operating altitude	Payload mass	Wait time
Space stations [5]	months	10^{-5}-$10^{-6}g$	400 km	≈500 kg	years
Satellites [6]	months	10^{-5}-$10^{-6}g$	> 500 km	≈200 kg	years
Space shuttle [7]	days	10^{-3}-$10^{-5}g$	> 300 km	≈500 kg	years
Sounding rocket [8]	5-6 min	10^{-3}-$10^{-4}g$	400 km	≈500 kg	years
Balloon drop [2]	60s	10^{-2}-$10^{-3}g$	32-41 km	≈500 kg	NA
Manned flights [9]	10-25s	10^{-2}-$10^{-3}g$	> 3 km	≈5 kg	months
Drop towers [10]	1.5-9s	10^{-2}-$10^{-5}g$	0-146 m	≈300 kg	months

Table 1.
List of standard microgravity platforms.

[2] Here the upward direction is considered positive.

[3] g-time of a platform is the maximum duration it can experience or offer microgravity.

[4] g-level is the average gravity experienced by the platform during this time, and it is expressed in terms of Earth's gravitational acceleration (g).

of g-time and payloads of a few kilograms. In particular, UAVs piqued the interest of researchers due to their affordability and widespread availability. Their ease of assembly, operation, and maintenance further enhances their potential as popular microgravity platforms.

1.2 UAVs as microgravity platforms

A few studies have explored the use of UAVs as microgravity platforms. The gravity levels achieved by these platforms are shown in **Figure 1**. Higashino and Kozai [19] conducted one of the earliest in-flight demonstrations of microgravity using a small-scale fixed-wing UAV. However, a gravity level of less than $0.2g$ was sustained for only 2 seconds, as illustrated in ` **1a**. Hofmeister and Blum [14] were able to achieve microgravity of $0.1g$ g-level for 3 seconds using a small-scale fixed-wing UAV, as depicted in **Figure 1b**. Their attempt with a medium-scale fixed-wing UAV extended the microgravity duration to 12 seconds; however, the fluctuations in the experienced acceleration were of the order of $0.4g$, as shown in **Figure 1c**. The reason for these fluctuations is the altitude at which they operated. To perform parabolic flights, fixed-wing UAVs must fly at high altitudes for an unobstructed flight path, but the prevalent wind speeds at such altitudes are comparable to the UAV's operating speed, which significantly affects the acceleration experienced by the UAV.

After the parabolic flight attempts using fixed-wing UAVs, there was little interest in using UAVs as microgravity platforms until the use of variable pitch quadrotors as microgravity platforms [20]. In that work, a proportional-integral-quadratic-ramp control structure was used for the quadrotor to maintain near-Martian gravity for 1.5 seconds, as shown in **Figure 1d**. Though the variable pitch quadrotor in Ref. [20] did not achieve microgravity, the work opened up the possibility of using multirotors as microgravity platforms.

Multirotors, unlike fixed-wing UAVs, can operate at low altitudes and in small open spaces. Further, they can take off without the need for a runway. Nevertheless, multirotors cannot be directly used to enable microgravity.

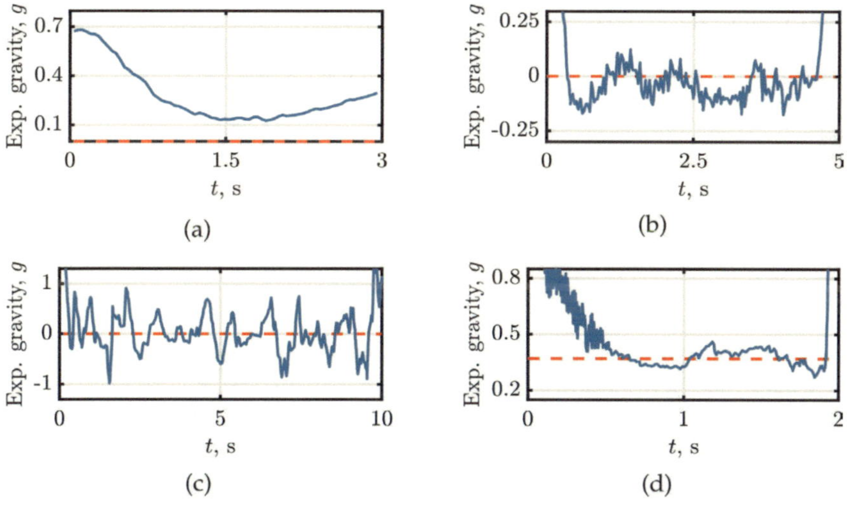

Figure 1.
Gravity experienced by the existing MUAV microgravity platforms. (a) Higashino and Kozai [19]; (b) Hofmeister and Blum (UAV-1) [14]; (c) Hofmeister and Blum (UAV-2) [14]; (d) Afman et al. [20].

1.3 Challenges of using multirotors as microgravity platforms

The two major challenges in using multirotors to enter free-fall and enable microgravity are (a) aerodynamic drag and (b) propeller performance variation in axial flight.

The major hindrance for an object to free-fall within Earth's atmosphere is the aerodynamic drag. In vacuum, a falling object accelerates toward Earth at 1*g* and experiences microgravity—as gravity is the only force acting on it. On the other hand, an object falling under atmospheric conditions cannot achieve microgravity due to drag. Thus, merely stopping the multirotor's propellers and letting it fall does not help to achieve microgravity. To maintain microgravity acceleration levels, we need to provide continuous thrust commands to the multirotor to compensate for the drag (D) acting on it.

$$D = \frac{1}{2} C_D \rho V|V|S \tag{1}$$

where C_D is the drag coefficient, ρ is the air density, V is the multirotor velocity, and S is the multirotor surface area. However, the drag coefficient of the multirotor C_D, essential for calculating drag, is not readily available.

For multirotors to be microgravity platforms, they must perform vertical maneuvers with varying velocities and accelerations. To perform these maneuvers while countering the drag, it is essential for the multirotor's propellers to generate the desired thrust by commanding the corresponding motors' angular speed. However, the propeller thrust coefficient varies with changes in the airflow they encounter. The thrust coefficient (C_T) of a propeller is a non-dimensional quantity that determines the thrust (T) generated by a propeller as

$$T = \frac{1}{2} C_T \rho \omega^2 \pi R^4 \tag{2}$$

where ω is the angular speed of the propeller and R is the radius of the propeller. To generate the desired thrust, knowing C_T allows determining the correct angular speed commands for the motors. However, like the drag constant, the propeller thrust coefficient is not readily available.

1.4 Contributions

The main objective of the work described in this chapter is to establish multirotors as a viable microgravity platform. To accomplish this objective, it is required to develop a vertical microgravity enabling maneuver suited for multirotors, accurate mathematical models, and acceleration control strategies. The major contributions of this work are listed below.

- A hexrotor test platform is developed to perform microgravity enabling maneuvers. A corresponding mathematical model is developed to predict its behavior during highly maneuvering axial flight. The model incorporates the propeller's thrust coefficients for climb and descent, derived from CFD simulations and wind tunnel tests. The motor-propeller dynamics, influenced by propeller inflow and motor dynamics, is modeled using a thrust measurement test stand. An axial flight model integrating these parameters is formulated and used to design a model-based acceleration control law.

- A feedback linearization-based acceleration control law is designed to achieve the desired acceleration despite variations in the drag force and propeller thrust coefficients. Additionally, a strategy to estimate the thrust coefficient is developed. When the control law is augmented with this estimator, the acceleration's convergence to the desired value is ensured despite estimation errors in other parameters, such as the drag coefficient.

- Multiple microgravity enabling maneuvers were performed using the hexrotor, achieving microgravity levels of approximately $10^{-2}g$ for over 1.5 seconds of g-time. The hexrotor is equipped with a payload comprising capillary tubes and a glass cuvette. During a 1-D parabolic maneuver, the experiments revealed a rise in water levels within the capillary and changes in the meniscus shape due to the absence of gravity. These observations, along with acceleration data from flight tests, demonstrate the feasibility of using multirotors as microgravity platforms.

2. Microgravity enabling vertical maneuvers for multirotors

An object in a gravitational field must be in a state of free-fall for it to experience microgravity. All existing microgravity platforms rely on this concept to achieve microgravity. Microgravity platforms that execute these maneuvers can have orbital, parabolic, or vertical trajectories. Microgravity platforms, such as balloon drops and drop towers, employ a vertical trajectory—dropping the payload from a certain altitude [2]. If the net force on the payload is equal to Earth's gravity, its trajectory, although vertical in space, is parabolic in time (a 1-D parabola). This section introduces and discusses a 1-D parabolic microgravity enabling maneuver suitable for multirotors.

The proposed microgravity enabling maneuver is a combination of multiple maneuvers, which are referred to as phases, and the multirotors and the onboard payload experience microgravity only during one of these maneuvers. The specific maneuver during which the payload experiences microgravity is referred to as the microgravity phase. The proposed 1-D microgravity enabling maneuver is shown in **Figure 2**. The phase-wise description of the 1-D maneuver is provided below.

- Take-off phase: In this phase, the multirotor performs a take-off from the ground and hovers at a steady height (h_{1_r}) for a small duration of time (t_{1_t}). The purpose of this phase is to a) check the multirotor flight readiness and b) maintain a flat attitude above the ground to avoid unnecessary lateral movements during the rest of the phases. The altitude of the multirotor at the end of this phase is denoted as h_1.

- Accelerated climb phase: In this phase, the multirotor climbs with a constant acceleration greater than $1g$ until it reaches a specified velocity (w_{2_t}). Thus, the multirotor experiences hypergravity during this phase. The time interval for this phase is denoted as t_2.

- Microgravity phase: Upon achieving the terminal velocity of the accelerated climb phase (w_{2_t}), the microgravity phase commences. During this phase, the

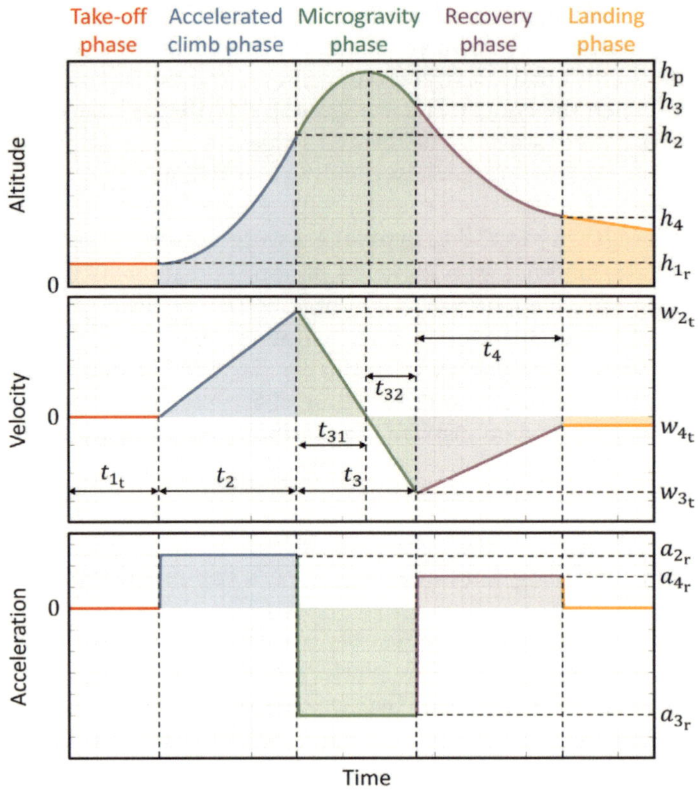

Figure 2.
Proposed 1-D Microgravity Enabling Maneuver.

multirotor maintains $-g$ acceleration (a_{3_d}) and experiences microgravity. The duration of microgravity experienced by the multirotor is t_3. Note that microgravity phase consists of both climb and descent flight.

- Recovery phase: The microgravity phase ends when the multirotor attains a specified velocity (w_{3_t}) upon which the recovery phase is initiated, and in this phase, the multirotor breaks the free-fall by maintaining acceleration (a_{4_r}), which is greater than zero.

- Landing phase: Upon achieving a low descent velocity (w_{4_t}), the multirotor maintains this velocity to ensure a safe and soft landing.

The variation of altitude, velocity, and acceleration with time during these phases is shown in **Figure 2**. The variables denoting the reference quantities to be tracked are marked with the subscript 'r'. A change in the background color in **Figure 2** indicates the transition between two maneuvers, and the quantities at the termination of a maneuver are indicated using subscript 't'. Some of the maneuver variables such as $h_{1_r}, t_{1_t}, w_{3_t}, w_{4_t}$ are left for the user to choose.

Phase-wise kinematic relations of the entire maneuver are given below.

$$
\begin{aligned}
&\text{Phase-1}: \left\{ t_{1_t}, h_{1_r} : \text{User choice} \right.\\
&\text{Phase-2}: \begin{cases} w_{2_t} = w_{3_t} - a_{3_r} t_3, \quad a_{2_r} = \dfrac{\left(w_{3_t} - a_{3_r} t_3\right)^2}{2\left(h_p + \dfrac{1}{2}\dfrac{\left(w_{3_t} - a_{3_r} t_3\right)^2}{a_{3_r}}\right)} \\[2ex] t_2 = \dfrac{w_{2_t} - w_{1_d}}{a_{2_r}}, \quad h_2 = h_{1_r} + \dfrac{1}{2} a_{2r} t_2^2 \end{cases}\\
&\text{Phase-3}: \left\{ w_{3_t} : \text{User choice}, \quad h_3 = h_p + \dfrac{w_{3_t}^2}{2a_{3_r}} \right.\\
&\text{Phase-4}: \left\{ w_{4_d} : \text{User choice} \right.
\end{aligned}
\tag{3}
$$

3. Multirotor test platform

For microgravity enabling multirotors, the key performance criterion is the duration of experienced microgravity. Bidirectional thrust capability is crucial to maintaining free-fall during both the climb and descent parts of the microgravity phase, (refer to **Figure 2**). The downward thrust generation compensates for the upward drag force during descent, allowing the multirotor to experience a longer duration of microgravity. To enable this, a hexrotor test platform with two inverted rotors is developed, as shown in **Figure 3**. The four upward rotors and the two inverted rotors provide bidirectional thrust, facilitating microgravity during both climb and descent.

The propellers that generate downward thrust are intentionally chosen to be small as they need to produce thrust only to nullify the drag during the descent part of the microgravity phase. In contrast, larger upward propellers are chosen as they must generate thrust to support the weight of the hexrotor, accelerate when needed, and overcome the drag acting on it during the climb in accelerated climb and microgravity phases. The inverted propellers are kept at a distance from the upward propellers using lengthier arms to avoid any wake recirculation that can cause instabilities during

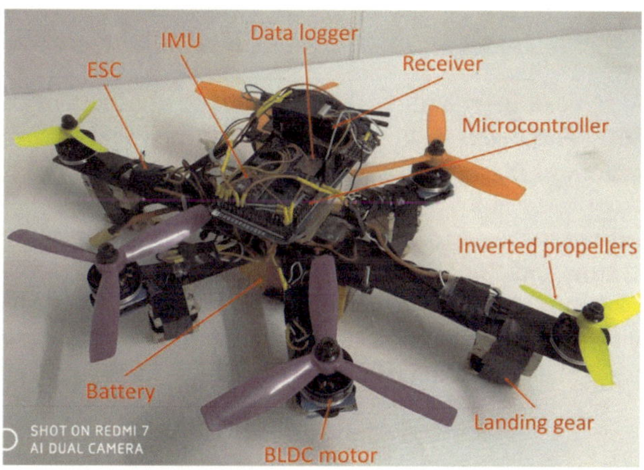

Figure 3.
Proposed hexrotor with two inverted propellers.

Parameter	Value
m	1.16 kg
I_{xx}	0.00179 kgm^2
I_{yy}	0.00281 kgm^2
I_{zz}	0.00373 kgm^2
l_u	0.114 m
l_r	0.152 m

Table 2.
Hexrotor's physical parameters.

Component (Specifications)	Function
Lithium Polymer battery (4 S, 1500 mAh, 100 C)	Powers all the multirotor components
Battery eliminator circuit (5 V, 3 A output)	Powers electronic components
Inertial measurement unit (MPU6050 and BMP180)	Measures angular rate, acceleration, and altitude
Guidance controller (Arduino Mega 2560)	Maintains the desired acceleration/velocity
Autopilot (Omnibus F4)	Maintains desired attitude
Data logger	Records the flight data
Receiver (2.4 GHz FS-i6)	Receives the commands from transmitter
Electronic speed controller ESC (30 A Spedix)	Supplies the motor with power proportional to the thrust commands
Brushless DC motor (2300 kv)	Rotates at angular speeds based on the power supplied by the ESCs
Upward propellers (3x5045)	Generate upward thrust
Inverted propellers (3x3045)	Generate downward thrust

Table 3.
List of multirotor components.

the flight. The moment of inertia and other physical parameters of the hexrotor are provided in **Table 2**. The x-axis is along an arm with the inverted propeller, and therefore, the moment of inertia about its x-axis is lesser compared to that about its y-axis.

The list of components used in the assembly of the hexrotor, along with their specifications and functions, is provided in **Table 3**. The hexrotor presented in this section is used to execute microgravity enabling maneuvers. However, for it to maintain microgravity for the specified g-time, an acceleration control law is required. Toward this, a mathematical model of the proposed hexrotor is necessary.

4. Hexrotor axial motion modeling

This section develops a mathematical model that governs the motion of a well-stabilized hexrotor with its flight restricted to the vertical axis.

4.1 Rotor thrust modeling

The thrust modeling is divided into a) steady-state thrust model and b) motor-propeller dynamics. The standard multirotor propeller thrust model is of the form $k\omega^2$, where ω is the angular speed of the rotor and k is a constant that is independent of the axial speed of the vehicle [21]. This model accurately predicts the thrust produced by the multirotor for applications involving hover and low-speed maneuvers, but not for flights involving high-speed maneuvers, wherein the assumption of a constant k in the thrust model does not suffice.

Toward characterizing the thrust generated by a propeller over a range of axial velocities, we performed computational fluid dynamics (CFD) analysis[5] to compute the thrust produced by the rotor at various axial speeds, including climb and descent. Further, we validated the CFD results with wind tunnel experiments by subjecting the propeller to various axial flight conditions. The recorded variation of the thrust coefficient with non-dimensional axial velocity ($\lambda_a = w/(\omega R)$) is plotted in **Figure 4**. Here, T is the thrust produced by the rotor of radius R with angular speed ω in a steady axial flow of velocity w.

From **Figure 4**, it can be seen that, if the rotor thrust is modeled as $k\omega^2$, then k should depend on the non-dimensional axial velocity.[6] Therefore, to obtain the correct propeller thrust in axial flight, the hover thrust model needs to be corrected by multiplying it with k_T—what we call the steady-state thrust gain.

$$k_T = \frac{C_T(\lambda_a)}{C_T(\lambda_a = 0)} \tag{4}$$

The propeller thrust model that includes the thrust coefficient variation and the motor and propeller inflow dynamics is

$$\dot{T} = -\frac{1}{\tau}T + \frac{k_T}{\tau}T_{\text{des}} \tag{5}$$

where τ is a time constant that incorporates the dynamics of the motor and the propeller inflow, and T_{des} is the desired thrust.

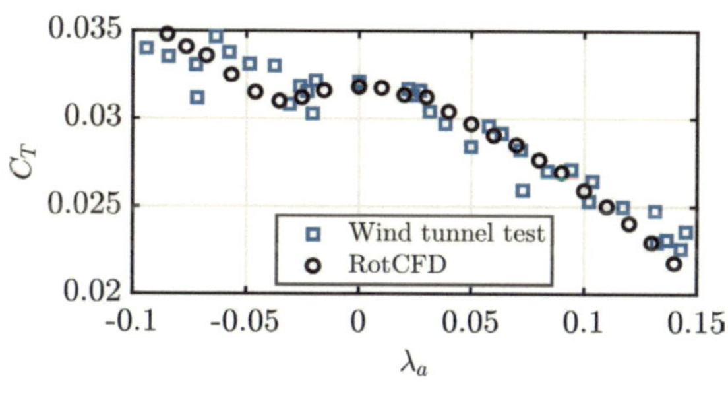

Figure 4.
Coefficient of thrust dependence on axial velocity: results from CFD analysis and wind tunnel experiments.

---

[5] We used the commercial software RotCFD to perform the CFD analysis.

[6] Since if $T = k\omega^2$, then $k = 4\rho R^4 C_T$ and C_T is a function of λ_a.

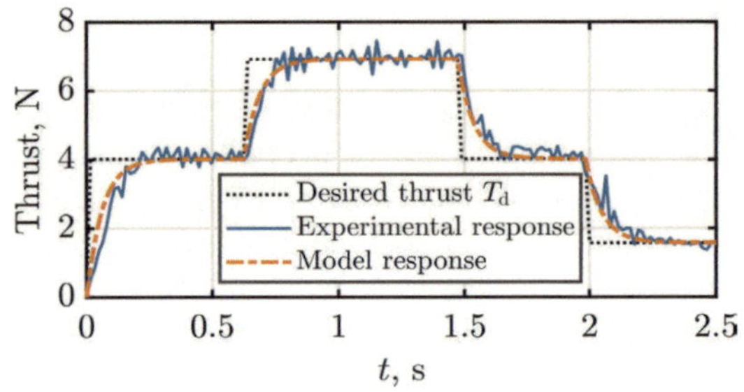

Figure 5.
Thrust dynamics.

A thrust measurement test stand that contains a load cell is used to compute τ for the chosen motor-propeller combination. For a desired thrust profile T_d shown in **Figure 5**, the measured thrust response as well as the thrust response generated from the model (Eq. (5)) with $\tau = 0.053$ seconds are plotted. The response predicted by the thrust model matches well with the mean experimental response, justifying the use of a first-order thrust model.

4.2 Axial acceleration model

In order to derive the vertical axis acceleration model, we assume that the hexrotor attitude is well stabilized with a flat attitude and the translation is only axial. Further, the effect of external disturbances such as gusts and atmospheric turbulence are either negligible or compensated for by the controller. The resultant axial acceleration of the hexrotor due to the forces acting on it—upward and reverse thrusts, drag, and weight—is

$$\frac{\mathrm{d}w}{\mathrm{d}t} = \frac{1}{m}(T_\mathrm{u} - T_\mathrm{r}) - \frac{k_D}{m} w|w| - g \tag{6}$$

where k_D is the drag constant (Drag $= k_D w^2$), and T_u and T_r are thrust generated by the upward and reverse rotors of our hexrotor, respectively.

Further, we neglect thrust time constant τ in Eq. (5) as the hexrotor motors have negligible transients. Accordingly, we can express T_u and T_r as

$$T_\mathrm{u} = k_\mathrm{u} T_{\mathrm{u}_\mathrm{des}} \quad \text{and} \quad T_\mathrm{r} = k_\mathrm{r} T_{\mathrm{r}_\mathrm{des}} \tag{7}$$

where k_u and k_r are the steady-state thrust gains, and $T_{\mathrm{u}_\mathrm{des}}$ and $T_{\mathrm{r}_\mathrm{des}}$ are the desired thrusts of the upward and the reverse rotors, respectively.

From Eqs. (6) and (7), the axial flight model of hexrotor is

$$\frac{\mathrm{d}w}{\mathrm{d}t} = \frac{1}{m}\left(k_\mathrm{u} T_{\mathrm{u}_\mathrm{des}} - k_\mathrm{r} T_{\mathrm{r}_\mathrm{des}}\right) - \frac{k_D}{m} w|w| - g \tag{8}$$

5. Acceleration controller design

In this section, we design a control law for the hexrotor to maintain the desired acceleration despite the opposing drag force and varying propeller performance in axial flight conditions. Before discussing the acceleration control law design, the hexrotor is made to perform the microgravity maneuver with a well-tuned PID controller at hover. The acceleration responses of the hexrotor in the climb and microgravity phases are plotted in **Figure 6**. The vehicle's acceleration does not converge to the desired value because of the drag force and propeller thrust coefficient variation. Since the PID controller does not explicitly consider these varying flight conditions and disturbances of 1-D microgravity maneuver, the desired acceleration cannot be tracked throughout the flight.

Consider the simplified hexrotor axial flight model in Eqation (8),

$$\frac{dw}{dt} = \frac{1}{m}\left(k_u T_{u_{des}} - k_r T_{r_{des}}\right) - \frac{k_D}{m} w|w| - g \tag{9}$$

Toward linearizing the axial translational dynamics of the hexrotor, the following control law is proposed

$$T_{u_{des}} = \frac{1}{k_u}\left(ma_d + k_D w|w| + mg + k_r T_{r_{des}}\right) \tag{10}$$

where a_d is the commanded desired acceleration. The control law in Eq. (10) will linearize the system in Eq. (8) to $\frac{dw}{dt} = a_d$.

Note that the control law in Eq. (10) assumes that the system parameters (k_D, k_u, and k_r) are precisely known. In reality, these parameters can only be estimated. Hence, the control law is re-written as

$$T_{u_{des}} = \frac{1}{\hat{k}_u}\left(ma_d + \hat{k}_D w|w| + mg + \hat{k}_r T_{r_{des}}\right) \tag{11}$$

where $\hat{k}_D$, $\hat{k}_u$, and $\hat{k}_r$ are the estimates of k_D, k_u, and k_r, respectively. Accurate estimation of these parameters is computationally expensive and requires additional sensors. Therefore, a method to estimate k_u from the axial velocity and acceleration estimates is provided, and it is shown that the convergence of the vehicle acceleration to the desired value under the control law in Eq. (11) then becomes invariant to the estimation errors in k_D and k_r to a large extent.

k_u is estimated as

$$\hat{k}_u = \frac{\hat{T}_u}{T_{u_{des}}} = \frac{m(a_z + g) + \hat{k}_D w|w| + \hat{k}_r T_{r_{des}}}{T_{u_{des}}} \tag{12}$$

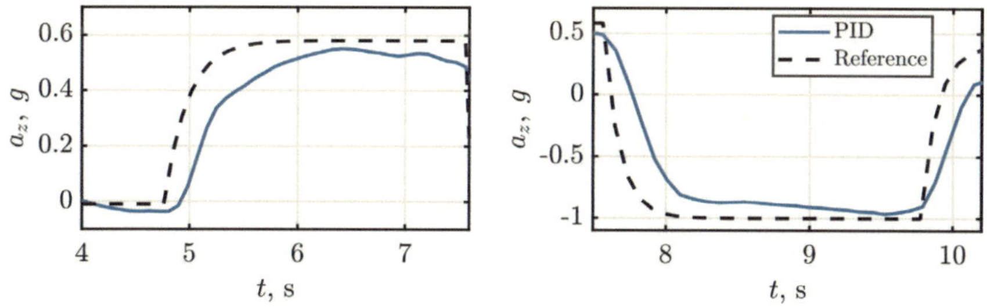

Figure 6.
Acceleration response with PID control law.

where $\hat{T}_u$ is an estimate of the upward thrust, and a_z is multirotor acceleration along z-axis of the Earth reference frame. We use the control law in Eq. (11) along with the estimate of k_u in Eq. (12) to achieve acceleration convergence to the desired value. Substituting Eq. (12) into Eq. (11) yields $a_z = a_d$. In the continuous-time domain, the hexrotor's acceleration converges to the desired value unconditionally—for any value of $\hat{k}_D$ and $\hat{k}_r$. However, it is not possible to implement a continuous-time control law. For implementation, discrete forms of the proposed control and estimation schemes used are

$$\begin{aligned} T_{u_{des}}[n] &= \frac{1}{\hat{k}_u[n-1]}\left(ma_d[n] + \hat{k}_D w[n]|w,[n]| + mg + \hat{k}_r T_{r_{des}}[n]\right) \\ \hat{k}_u[n] &= \frac{ma_z[n] + mg + \hat{k}_D w[n]|w,[n]| + \hat{k}_r T_{r_{des}}[n]}{T_{u_{des}}[n]} \end{aligned} \tag{13}$$

The discrete version of the acceleration control law and parameter estimator does not converge the hexrotor's acceleration to the desired value for any choice of $\hat{k}_D$ and $\hat{k}_r$. Nevertheless, the following theorems guarantee the acceleration convergence to the desired value for a wide range of $\hat{k}_D$ and $\hat{k}_r$.

If $T_{r_{des}}$, $\hat{k}_D$, and $\hat{k}_r$ satisfy

$$\begin{aligned} T_{r_{des}} &> \frac{m}{k_r}(a_d + g) - \frac{k_D}{k_r}w^2; \quad \hat{k}_D > -\frac{m}{2w^2}(a_d + g) + \frac{k_D}{2} + \left(\frac{k_r}{2} - \hat{k}_r\right)\frac{T_{r_{des}}}{w^2}, \quad \text{if } w > 0, \\ T_{r_{des}} &> \frac{m}{k_r}(a_d + g) + \frac{k_D}{k_r}w^2; \quad \hat{k}_D < \frac{m}{2w^2}(a_d + g) + \frac{k_D}{2} - \left(\frac{k_r}{2} - \hat{k}_r\right)\frac{T_{r_{des}}}{w^2}, \quad \text{if } w < 0 \end{aligned} \tag{14}$$

then the estimate of ku converges to $\hat{k}_u = k_u \frac{m(a_d+g)+\hat{k}_D w|w|+\hat{k}_r T_{r_{des}}}{m(a_d+g)+k_D w|w|+k_r T_{r_{des}}}$ for a constant desired acceleration and under the quasi-steady assumption of constant velocity.

Proof: Refer [22] □

Theorem 1.2 If $\hat{k}_u$ converges, then the vehicle acceleration converges to a_d.

Proof: Refer [22] □

Adhering to the conditions in Theorem 1.1, we choose $\hat{k}_D = 0.046$ and $T_{r_{des}}$ as

$$T_{r_{des}} = \begin{cases} T_{min} + \hat{k}_D w^2, & \text{if } w < 1\ \text{ms}^{-1} \text{ in the microgravity phase} \\ 0, & \text{otherwise} \end{cases} \tag{15}$$

where T_{min} is the minimum thrust required by the upward rotors to maintain a stable and flat attitude, and the reverse rotors are allowed to operate mainly during the descent part of the microgravity phase. The chosen drag constant corresponds to the drag coefficient of a flat plate. Note that the conditions in Theorem 1.1 allow one to choose $\hat{k}_D$ within a wide interval (anywhere between 0.023 and 0.072 in our case), which corresponds to a broad range of shapes, for acceleration convergence to the desired value.

To reduce the impact of uncertainties and disturbances such as accelerometer measurement noise, gusts, and prevalent winds on acceleration, we augment the proposed control law, which uses feedback linearization (FL), with a PID controller. The equations of the FL-PID control law and the estimation scheme in discrete form, as implemented for flight tests, are

$$
\begin{aligned}
T_{\mathrm{u_{des}}}[n] &= \frac{1}{\hat{k}_{\mathrm{u}}[n-1]}\left(k_{\mathrm{p}}e_a[n] + k_{\mathrm{d}}\frac{e_a[n]-e_a[n-1]}{\Delta t}\right.\\
&\left. +k_{\mathrm{i}}\sum_{i=0}^{n} e_a[i]\Delta t + \hat{k}_D w[n]|w,[n]| + mg + \hat{k}_{\mathrm{r}}T_{\mathrm{r_{des}}}[n]\right) \qquad (16)\\
\hat{k}_{\mathrm{u}}[n] &= \frac{ma_z[n] + mg + \hat{k}_D w[n]|w,[n]| + \hat{k}_{\mathrm{r}}T_{\mathrm{r_{des}}}[n]}{T_{\mathrm{u_{des}}}[n]}
\end{aligned}
$$

where Δt is the sampling interval, e_a is the acceleration error $(a_{\mathrm{d}} - a_z)$, and k_{p}, k_{i}, and k_{d} are the proportional, integral, and derivative gains, respectively.

6. Flight tests and onboard experiments

This section presents the results of multiple 1-D parabolic flights (described in Section 2) performed by the developed hexrotor employing the acceleration control law developed in the previous section.

6.1 Flight tests

The chosen maneuver parameters for the flight tests are provided in **Table 4**. The desired acceleration and terminating velocity of the accelerated climb phase computed using the kinematic equations in Eq. (3) are also given in **Table 4**. The peak altitude in these flights was restricted to 20 m so that the pilot can judge the attitude of the multirotor. Using the parameters specified in **Table 4**, 1-D parabolic maneuver flights are carried out in an open space, as shown in **Figure 7**.

The altitude, vertical velocity, vertical acceleration, and attitude of the hexrotor from the flight tests are plotted in **Figure 8**. From the translation plots, we can observe that the hexrotor successfully executed each phase of the 1-D maneuver. At the end of the fifth second, the hexrotor began its accelerated climb and maintained the desired acceleration of $0.6g$ until it reached a velocity of $12\,\mathrm{ms}^{-1}$, which is the terminating velocity of the accelerated climb phase. Subsequently, the hexrotor progressed into the microgravity phase by reducing its thrust, thereby maintaining the body acceleration near $-g$. During this phase, it experienced microgravity for approximately 1.6 seconds. A much lower magnitude of $4\,\mathrm{ms}^{-1}$ is chosen for the latter to allow a smooth transition of the vehicle from the microgravity to the recovery phase. From **Figure 8**, we can observe that the pilot maintained a flat attitude throughout the maneuver.

The acceleration experienced by the hexrotor in the microgravity phase is within the range of $\pm 0.05g$ for a g-time greater than 1.6 seconds in every flight test. These results indicate that with the help of the developed acceleration control strategy, the hexrotor maintains steady microgravity levels.

Chosen maneuver parameters						Computed variables	
h_{p}	t_3	$w_{1_{\mathrm{d}}}$	t_1	$w_{3_{\mathrm{t}}}$	$w_{4_{\mathrm{d}}}$	$w_{2_{\mathrm{t}}}$	$a_{2_{\mathrm{d}}}$
20 m	1.6 s	$0.4\,\mathrm{ms}^{-1}$	5 s	$-4\,\mathrm{ms}^{-1}$	$-1\,\mathrm{ms}^{-1}$	$12\,\mathrm{ms}^{-1}$	$0.6g$

Table 4.
Microgravity enabling maneuver parameters for flight tests.

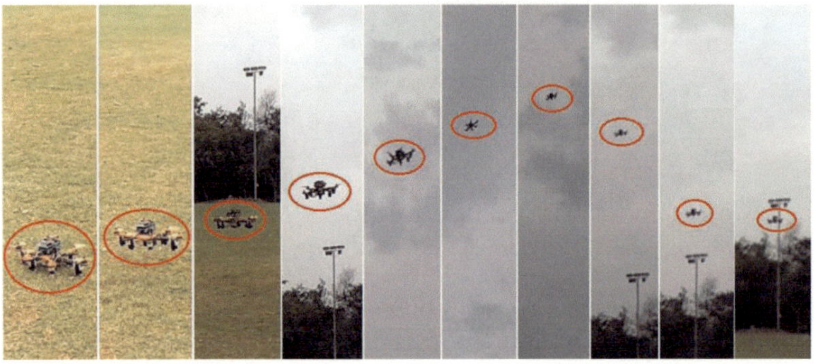

Figure 7.
A collage of snapshots of a microgravity flight test.

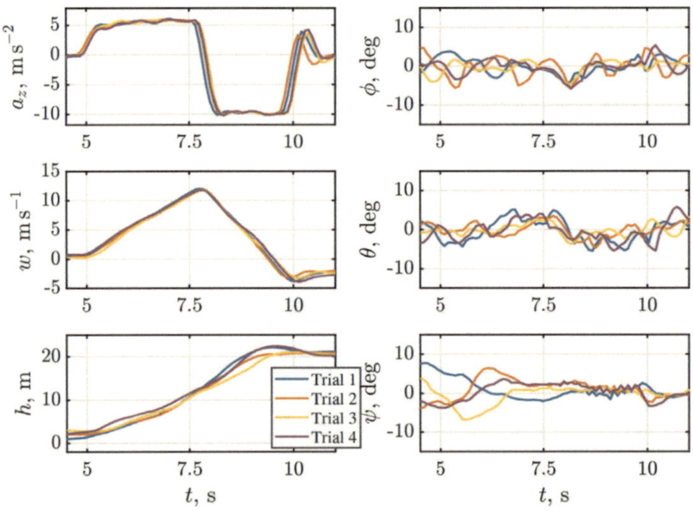

Figure 8.
Translation acceleration and attitude responses of hexrotor during the 1-D parabolic maneuver.

7. Onboard experiments

This section describes the microgravity experiments conducted onboard the hexrotor by equipping it with a payload containing a glass cuvette and two capillary tubes with 1mm and 2 mm diameters, as shown in **Figure 9**. An onboard camera is used to capture the effect of microgravity on capillary action and fluid meniscus shape. The acceleration experienced by the hexrotor and payload during the flight test is plotted in **Figure 10**. From this plot, we can observe that the experienced acceleration is within the range of $\pm 0.05g$ about all three body axes directions.

The meniscus shape of the fluid in a glass cuvette and fluid level variation in a capillary tube are physical phenomena that are highly influenced by the gravitational force, and therefore, we can observe the effect of microgravity on them. The rise of liquid in a capillary tube occurs when the molecular forces between the liquid and the tube (called interfacial tension) are stronger than the corresponding forces within the liquid (called surface tension). We refer to this rise in the liquid level as capillary action. The liquid inside the capillary tube settles at a level where the Earth's

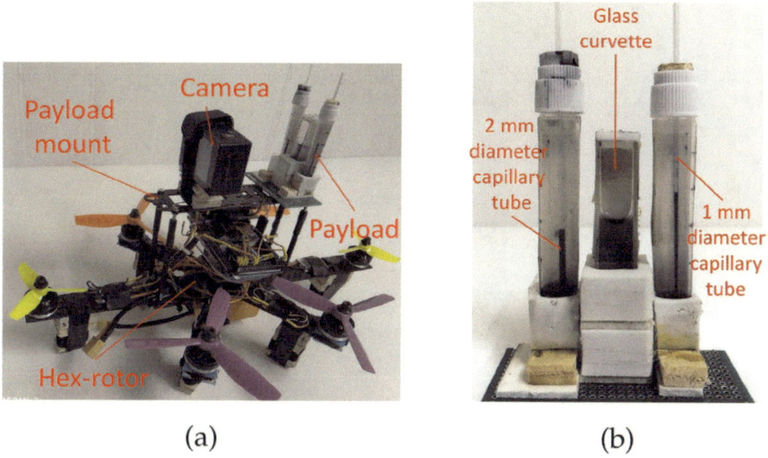

Figure 9.
Hexrotor used as a microgravity platform and microgravity experimental setup. (a) Hexrotor with payload; (b) Payload.

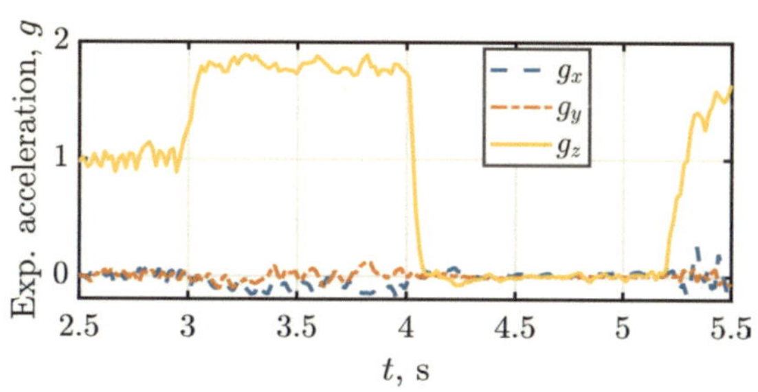

Figure 10.
Acceleration experienced by the hexrotor with payload during 1-D parabolic maneuver.

gravitational force and the capillary tube's adhesive force strike an equilibrium. The capillary rise in the 1 mm capillary tube is higher than in the 2 mm capillary tube, as shown in **Figure 11a**, because the capillary action increases as the diameter decreases.

In **Figure 11**, snapshots of the payload are shown in the hover, accelerated climb, and microgravity phases. The liquid levels in both capillary tubes dropped in the accelerated climb phase compared to the hover phase, as the experienced acceleration is about 1.8 times the acceleration due to Earth's gravity. As seen in **Figure 11c**, the liquid in the capillary tube during the microgravity phase rose to the top because the payload in that phase did not experience a gravitational force that would counteract the capillary rise. Similarly, we can observe that the shape of the meniscus in the glass cuvette is more pronounced (like the 'U' shape) in the microgravity phase compared to the hover and climb phases. There is no force apart from the liquid's cohesive force to balance the adhesive force due to the cuvette's wall in the absence of gravity. As a result, the top layer of the liquid climbs around the walls, creating a more pronounced meniscus shape.

From the flight test and onboard experimental results presented in this chapter, we establish that our control strategies enable the use of multirotors as microgravity platforms. Although a small multirotor with limited payload capacity and short-duration microgravity capability was used for demonstration, the developed acceleration control strategy can be applied to larger multirotors with higher payload capacities [23].

(a) (b) (c)

Figure 11.
Payload in a 1-D parabolic maneuver. (a) Hover; (b) Accelerated climb; (c) Microgravity.

8. Conclusions

We demonstrated the feasibility of using multirotors as microgravity platforms by making a hexrotor execute the designed microgravity enabling maneuver with the help of the developed acceleration control law. Along with the proposed maneuver and acceleration controller, factors like low cost, component availability, and quick assembly make multirotors affordable microgravity platforms. The methods and algorithms developed in this chapter are generic, allowing for the development of multirotor microgravity platforms with higher payload capacities. Additionally, multirotors can be programmed to maintain specific accelerations, enabling reduced gravity environments, like on the Moon and Mars, making them versatile microgravity platforms.

Author details

Siddhardha Kedarisetty[1]* and Joel George Manathara[2]

1 Indian Institute of Technology Bhilai, Bhilai, India

2 Indian Institute of Technology Madras, Chennai, India

*Address all correspondence to: siddhardhak2010@gmail.com

References

[1] Takahashi F, Katta VR, Hicks MC. Cool-flame burning and oscillations of envelope diffusion flames in microgravity. Microgravity Science and Technology. 2018;**30**(4):339-351. DOI: 10.1007/s12217-018-9630-9

[2] Thomas VA, Prasad NS, Reddy CAM. Microgravity research platforms - a study. Current Science. 2000;**79**(3): 336-340. DOI: www.jstor.org/stable/ 24103367

[3] Schneider S, Peipsi A, Stokes M, Knicker A, Abeln V. Feasibility of monitoring muscle health in microgravity environments using Myoton technology. Medical & Biological Engineering & Computing. 2015;**53**(1):57-66. DOI: 10.1007/ s11517-014-1211-5

[4] Nagatomo F, Kouzaki M, Ishihara A. Effects of microgravity on blood flow in the upper and lower limbs. Aerospace Science and Technology. 2014;**34**(4): 20-23. DOI: 10.1016/j.ast.2014.01.009

[5] Lee MC, Israelsson UE. New microgravity fundamental physics research areas in the ISS era. Acta Astronautica. 2001;**48**(5–12):597-602. DOI: 10.1016/S0094-5765(01)00029-7

[6] Li C, Zhao H, Ni R. China's recoverable satellites and their onboard experiments. Microgravity Science and Technology. 2008;**20**(2):61-65. DOI: 10.1007/s12217-008-9009-4

[7] Hale W, Lane H, Chapline G, Lulla K. Wings in Orbit: Scientific and Engineering Legacies of the Space Shuttle, 1971–2010. NASA; 2011

[8] Jonsson R. SSC microgravity sounding rocket program MASER. Acta Astronautica. 1988;**17**(1):39-43. DOI: 10.1016/0094-5765(88)90126-9

[9] Martin PK. Review of NASA's Microgravity Flight Services. Technical Report, NASA, IG-10-015. NASA; 2010

[10] Belser V, Breuninger J, Reilly M, Laufer R, Dropmann M, Herdrich G, et al. Aerodynamic and engineering design of a 1.5 s high quality microgravity drop tower facility. Acta Astronautica. 2016;**129**:335-344. DOI: 10.1016/j.actaastro.2016.09.031

[11] Perez-Poch A, González DV, López D. Hypogravity research and educational parabolic flight activities conducted in Barcelona: A new hub of innovation in Europe. Microgravity Science and Technology. 2016;**28**(6): 603-609. DOI: 10.1007/s12217-016- 9516-7

[12] Pletser V, Frischauf N, Cohen D, Foster M, Spannagel R, Szeszko A, et al. First Middle East aircraft parabolic flights for ISU participant experiments. Microgravity Science and Technology. 2017;**29**(3):209-219. DOI: 10.1007/ s12217-017-9539-8

[13] Beitz E, Güttler C, Blum J, Meisner T, Teiser J, Wurm G. Low-velocity collisions of centimeter-sized dust aggregates. The Astrophysical Journal. 2011;**736**(1):34. DOI: 10.1088/ 0004-637X/736/1/34

[14] Hofmeister PG, Blum J. Parabolic flights home. Microgravity Science and Technology. 2011;**23**(2):191-197. DOI: 10.1007/s12217-010-9249-y

[15] Siddhardha K. Microgravity enabling multirotors: Compact like drop towers and programmable like parabolic flights. Microgravity Science and Technology. 2021;**33**(3):36. DOI: 10.1007/s12217-021- 09889-1

[16] Wollman A, Weislogel M. New investigations in capillary fluidics using a drop tower. Experiments in Fluids. 2013; **54**:1-13. DOI: 10.1007/s00348-013-1499-1

[17] Meseguer J, Sanz-Andrés A, Pérez-Grande I, Pindado S, Franchini S, Alonso G. Surface tension and microgravity. European Journal of Physics. 2014;**35**(5):055010. DOI: 10.1088/0143-0807/35/5/055010

[18] Carney A, Li Y, Liao Y-T, Olson S, Ferkul P. Concurrent-flow flame spread over thin discrete fuels in microgravity. Combustion and Flame. 2021;**226**: 211-221. DOI: 10.1016/j.combustflame.2020.12.005

[19] Higashino SI, Kozai S. Automatic microgravity flight system and flight testing using a small unmanned aerial vehicle. Japan Society of Microgravity Applications. 2010;**27**(1):3-10. DOI: 10.15011/jasma.27.1.3

[20] Afman J, P, Feron E, Hauser J. Triple-integral control for reduced-G atmospheric flight. In: Proceedings of American Control Conference, Milwaukee, USA: IEEE; 2018. pp. 392-397

[21] Tian B, Liu L, Hanchen L, Zuo Z, Zong Q, Zhang Y. Multivariable finite time attitude control for quadrotor UAV: Theory and experimentation. IEEE Transactions on Industrial Electronics. 2018;**65**(3):2567-2577. DOI: 10.1109/TIE.2017.2739700

[22] Kedarisetty S, Manathara JG. Acceleration control of a multi-rotor UAV towards achieving microgravity. Aerospace Systems. 2019;**2**(2):175-188. DOI: 10.1007/s42401-019-00031-z

[23] Kedarisetty S, Manathara JG. Performance assessment framework for multirotor unmanned aerial vehicle microgravity platforms. Microgravity Science and Technology. 2023;**35**(5):52. DOI: 10.1007/s12217-023-10074-9

Chapter 11

Using Reinforcement Learning for Unmanned Aerial Vehicle Conflict Resolution in a CTR Environment

Joaquin Vico Navarro and Juan A. Vila Carbó

Abstract

Growing demand for Unmanned Aircraft System (UAS) operations in urban areas within Controlled Traffic Regions (CTRs) around airports poses a significant challenge to UAS traffic management. Current U-space regulations allow temporarily segregating sections of the CTR airspace to carry out these operations, and UAS must react to changes in the airspace structure of the CTR, which restrict flights into segregated areas by terminating the flight. This work faces the problem of UAS performing less restrictive operations of UAS inside a CTR. These operations are assumed to be defined by a flight plan that does not necessarily enclose them into a segregated area. This is the case, for example, of UAS flying between two heliports inside a CTR. Achieving such operational level in a CTR is based on the concept of Dynamic Airspace Reconfiguration (DAR), which allows the definition of temporary no-fly zones (NFZs) to preserve safety of manned aviation and lets ATC dynamically restructure them upon a safety event. The proposed solution enables UAS to react to airspace restructuring without necessarily terminating the flight and to self-manage Conflict Resolution (CR) to keep traffic separations without the intervention of ATC. This is achieved using a Multi-Agent Reinforcement Learning (MARL) system with decentralized decision-making that provides UAS guidance after a CTR restructuring and keeps separation with all types of traffic in the CTR while accomplishing the predefined mission. This offers several benefits, including dynamic rerouting for UAS, increased efficiency, and greater scalability with reduced reliance on a centralized traffic control unit.

Keywords: conflict resolution, deep reinforcement learning, unmanned traffic management, dynamic airspace reconfiguration, air traffic control

1. Introduction

Operations within a Controlled Traffic Region (CTR) or controlled zone mean flying in an airspace around an airport where Air Traffic Control (ATC) service is provided to, at least, Instrumental Flight Rules (IFR) flights [1]. Flights under Visual Flight Rules (VFR) can also fly inside it, usually through a set of well-defined corridors. Most urban areas of big cities fall under these airspaces, and so does the increasing traffic generated by Unmanned Aircraft (UA) and Urban Air Movility (UAM). The integration of Unmanned Aerial System (UAS) traffics with IFR and VFR traffics into a CTR is one of the big challenges for the development of unmanned aviation, and it requires taking action at three different levels: legislative, technological, and organizational [2, 3]. All these aspects have been addressed by the U-space concept [4] in Europe and UTM (Unmanned Aircraft System Traffic Management) [5] in the USA. Both of them provide a set of ConOps and a set of specific services and procedures designed to ensure safe and efficient access to airspace for unmanned aviation based on high levels of digitalization and automation. This chapter focuses on the technological support of the proposed problem. To ensure harmonization across EU member states at the legislative level, a Commission Implementing Regulation [6] known as SERA (Standardized European Rules of the Air) was created. Currently, most state members' legislation only allows UA traffic in segregated areas. According to EUROCONTROL and EASA [7], the integration of UAS in CTRs relies on the technology and equipment of the aircraft. Proposed solutions include geo-fencing (U-space service) or innovative onboard DAA (Detect and Avoid) systems. Some of these systems are based on the concept of "electronic conspicuity," which refers to some technology that can help users and air traffic services be aware of what is operating in surrounding airspace.

The initial proposal of U-space for integrated operation is based on the Dynamic Airspace Reconfiguration (DAR) [8]. This concept will enable ATC units to reconfigure the airspace to ensure that manned aircraft and UAS traffic remain segregated. Pilots/operators and onboard systems will have to deal with configuration before and during the flight, most likely through U-space services. Implementing this service will require appropriate transmission networks and technological interfaces or platforms that allow exchange between Air Traffic Management (ATM) and Unmanned Traffic Management (UTM). Previous studies have analyzed the impacts of the usage of DARs in controlled airspace, demonstrating a high impact on UAS operations [9]. This work deals with the problem of keeping manned and unmanned air segregated upon a DAR and, additionally, keeping the maximum operational level and providing conflict resolution between UAS after a DAR.

The contents of this chapter are organized as follows. Section 2 introduces the background of Conflict Resolution (CR) in manned and unmanned aviation as well as recent Machine Learning (ML) approaches to solving it. Section 3 discusses the methods applied in our proposal. Section 4 describes the characteristics of the environment developed for the simulations. Section 5 details the components of the Reinforcement Learning (RL) agent, and Section 6 shows the training process and results. Section 7 displays the validation results when the method is applied to a CTR. Lastly, Section 8 contains the conclusions.

2. Background

Several CR strategies to keep air-traffic separation have been proposed in the bibliography [10–12]: from completely centralized to completely decentralized, several solutions are possible. A centralized resolution strategy assumes the existence of a service provider that coordinates the trajectories of all aircraft involved in the conflict and commands them to simultaneously execute a single set of coordinated maneuvers that provide safe separation between all relevant aircraft pairs. On the other hand, a decentralized resolution strategy solves conflicts locally: each aircraft solves its own conflicts without the need for a coordinator. This is also known as self-separation.

The previous classification has been made attending to the decision making agent, usually referred as the separator. But different levels of centralization can be also devised attending to the traffic data source: a centralized traffic data source assumes that some central agent provides all separators with a snapshot or system-wide traffic information of a given airspace (coming a radar for example), whereas a decentralized traffic data source assumes that each separator has its own perception of nearby traffic.

Figure 1 shows three strategies with different levels of centralization:

Figure 1(a) shows a centralized CR structure with a central controller that, based on system-wide traffic information, computes a coordinated and joint action that is then broadcast to all the agents. System-wide information can be obtained from its own information source, like a radar, or by aggregating local information from the participants in the airspace. This approach requires constant communication between the separator and the agents. In both **1(b)** and **(c)**, there is no central controller and are thus considered decentralized structures where every agent performs self-separation based on its own decision making. In **1(b)**, there is communication between agents during the decision-making process and they perform coordinated actions. This structure is common in cooperative Multi Agent Reinforcement Learning (MARL) settings, and it may include several information exchange steps before reaching a solution, so it requires a constant and stable connection to exchange information. In **1(c)**, the agents are fully decentralized, with no explicit information exchange with each other. They only use their local information to make their decisions.

Some studies have been performed to study the performance of centralized and decentralized strategies [13]. Results show that, although centralized strategies are more efficient, they are less reliable under communication failures and are difficult to scale. Using a decentralized approach shares the decision-making load among all participants, enabling the CR process to be run at a higher frequency, leading to faster responses to the changes and, thus, better adaptability.

Current technology for collision avoidance systems, like the ACAS X (Air-borne Collision Avoidance System X) family of algorithms, are based on Markov Decision Process (MDP) [14]. These techniques have evolved to the use Artificial Intelligence (AI) techniques with promising results for CR in manned aviation [15–18]. However, manned aviation studies assume lower traffic densities than the expected density of Unmanned Aerial Vehicle (UAV) in U-space environments.

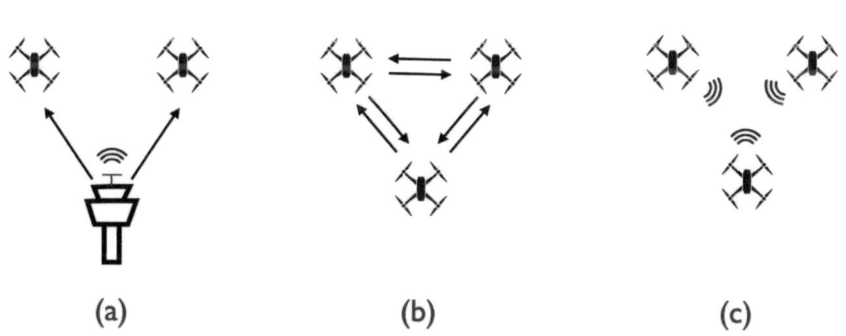

Figure 1.
Separator centralization levels.

These CR strategies are based RL and, more specifically, on a subfield of RL named MARL. RL is an area of machine learning concerned with how an intelligent agent should take actions in a dynamic environment in order to maximize a reward signal, improving its performance by interacting with the environment and learning from the experiences. In MARL, multiple agents interact in the same environment. MARL structures differ in the agent hierarchy and information exchanged between the agents. This way, the structures of MARL also respond to the different levels of centralization shown in **Figure 1**.

CR strategies proposed in AI can be broadly classified into pair-wise CR and Multi-Aircraft Conflict Resolution (MACR). Several methods have introduced heuristics to transform pair-wise CR into MACR. Some of these methods are based on hierarchically processing the conflicts and restricting the solution envelope for subsequent conflicts [15]. Some others employ neural network architectures that include agent communication in the decision-making process [16], as in **Figure 1(b)**. Although effective, this method requires either to be executed centrally and resolutions delivered to the participants, affecting scalability as the number of participants increases, or a high bandwidth communication link between UAVs, which is unrealistic in a real-world scenario.

Other studies have developed decentralized CR algorithms based on heuristics to determine the most relevant intruders to include in the observation space [17]. These approaches provide good results in the manned aviation space; however, as stated before, the increased traffic density and flight dynamics of UAVs make selecting which information is more relevant to the agent increasingly difficult.

The strategy proposed in this work is based on a centralized information source provided by U-space services, with decentralized decision-making, with each UAS being able to process the information and choose the optimal path. The objective of each aircraft is to avoid the loss of separation from other aircraft, avoid entering segregated airspace and perform its mission, minimizing the distance traveled.

Finally, many learning-based CR techniques come from the field of robotics where they were extensively studied for static obstacle avoidance [19, 20]. This way, the Optimal Reciprocal Collision Avoidance (ORCA) framework [21] is one of the most widely used in crowd simulation and multi-agent systems. ORCA is a system for collision avoidance in a short time horizon and can easily be scaled to handle large systems with many robots. It assumes robots to have perfect sensing about the surrounding agents. This requirement can be relaxed using communication protocols [22, 23] to share the state information. A collision avoidance policy for multiple robots in decentralized scenarios where each robot generates its own paths without observing other robots' states and intents has been also shown to be feasible in [24].

3. Strategy for UAS separation in a CTR

The problem of separating UAS in the CTR is twofold: on one hand, UAS must be separated from IFR and VFR traffic and, on the other, from other UAS.

In this proposal, the separation of UAS from IFR and VFR traffic in the CTR is accomplished through the enforcement of No-Fly Zones (NFZs), which set the limits of areas where UAS cannot penetrate. They protect the areas for the departure and approach procedures of IFR traffic and the corridors for VFR traffic inside the CTR. Departure and approach areas are areas located on both sides of the runway axis between the runway threshold and a distance where IFR fly at an altitude where UAS

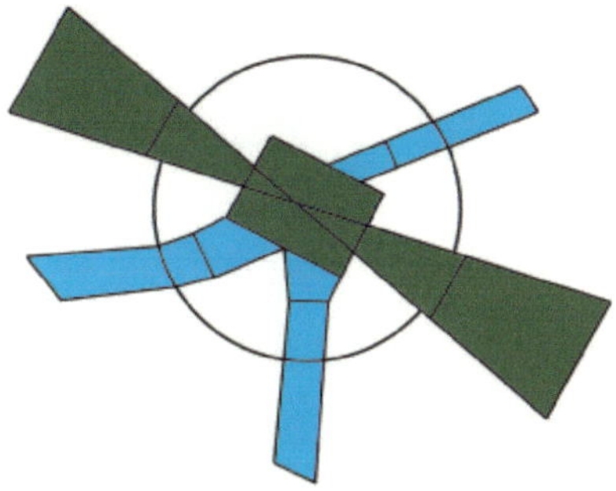

Figure 2.
LEVC CTR with IFR protected areas in green and VFR in cyan.

cannot fly. VFR corridors define the routes for VFR traffic to enter or leave the CTR to takeoff or land. **Figure 2** displays an example of a CTR area.

We assume that ATM can temporarily activate and deactivate the NFZs or dynamically reconfigure them as needed in order to protect VFR and IFR traffic using the DAR concept. We also assume that the information about the state of the currently active NFZs will be made available to UAS through some U-space (or UTM) service.

The separation of UAS from other UAS is done in two stages: strategic and tactical. In the strategic phase, they are separated by properly deconflicting (in time or space) the flight plans of the UAS, but due to uncertainty during this phase, some conflict may arise in the tactical phase. As discussed in Ref. [9], after a DAR, previously strategically deconflicted flight plans may not remain conflict-free and modifications to the routes are needed to maintain separation.

This work proposes a system where decision-making is entirely decentralized, so self-separation is performed by each UAS independently, but we assume the existence of some U-space service that provides all separator agents with the relevant traffic information for each participant.

In order to implement the proposed scheme, each aircraft is equipped with an RL agent. The agents need information from the current state of the environment to choose their actions. The proposed method uses an observation space that provides information of all nearby UAS and the segregated areas defined by the DAR. This information is encoded as an image and allows the representation of segregated areas with arbitrary shapes and the current position of the intruders, their separation minima, and their intent. The current kinematic state of the current UAS is also provided as a vector. This approach can cope with mobile intruders (i.e., other drones in the area) and static barriers (i.e., dynamically segregated sections of the airspace). This technique is explained in more detail in Section 5.1.

The UAS are assumed to fly in a U-space environment, with a Network Identification Service (NIS) available for the agents to gather information about their surrounding aircraft and a Flight Authorisation Service (FAS) that registers and can provide flight plan information to the CR system to deduce future intent of other drones. Although the information source is centralized on the U-space services, it is not realistic to assume that all drones would receive a complete picture of the airspace. Instead, only the information relevant to each drone would be provided. This information may be supplemented by onboard sensors such as embedded RADAR, but it is not required for the proposed system.

These constraints are programmed in a simulation environment for the MARL algorithm to learn the optimal policy to solve the separation problem. MARL is often

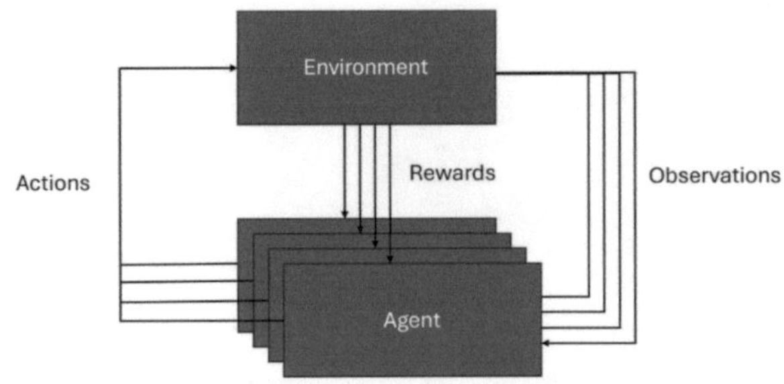

Figure 3.
Environment and agent interaction.

defined as a Decentralized Partially Observable Markov Decision Process (Dec-POMDP) or *Markov games* [25]. MDPs is a framework for modeling decision-making problems with discrete time steps and stochastic models. This model assumes the state transitions are *Markovian*, the state at time t only depends on the state, and actions taken at $t - 1$. MDP assumes perfect observability of the current state and a single actor or agent interacting with the environment. Extensions of the MDP model that accounts for partially observable states and multiple actors led to the Dec-POMDP.

A Dec-POMDP for $\mathbb{N}$ agents is defined by the set of possible states $\mathcal{S}$, the set of agent actions $\mathbb{A} = \times_{i \in \mathbb{N}} \mathbb{A}_i$, a state transition function $T : \mathcal{S} \times \mathbb{A} \times \mathcal{S}[0, 1]$ that defines the probability of transitioning from the state $s \in \mathcal{S}$ to $s' \in \mathcal{S}$, a set of observations $\mathbb{O}$. The agents receive feedback from the environment with the reward function $R : \mathbb{S} \times \mathbb{A} \rightarrow \mathbb{R}$.

To choose the actions, each agent i uses its current observations and a stochastic policy $\pi_{\theta_i} : \mathbb{O}_i \times \mathbb{A} \rightarrow [0, 1]$. The objective of the agents is to tune the policy to maximize its total expected return $G_i = \sum_{t=0}^{T} \gamma^t r_i^t$ where γ is a discount factor and h is the time horizon.

The core concepts of a RL algorithm are shown in **Figure 3**. The environment simulates the state transitions and provides the agents with their local observations. The agents choose a set of actions according to their policy, and after the actions are simulated, the environment outputs a set of rewards used to evaluate such actions.

To tackle this optimization problem, several RL algorithms have been developed. In this work, the Proximal Policy Optimization (PPO) algorithm is used to train the agents as it provides a good balance between sample complexity and algorithm simplicity. PPO was developed for single-agent reinforcement learning but has demonstrated adequate performance in MARL problems, especially in cooperative environments with homogeneous agents such as the environment described in this work [26].

4. Airspace environment modeling

A model of the airspace needs to be created so that reinforcement agents can learn an optimal policy to solve the problem. This mathematical model is composed of four components: (1) the CTR, (2) the drone model, (3) the separation management model, and (4) flight plan generation.

4.1 CTR modeling

The CTR used for this environment is a set of sections of the airspace defined by the coordinates of each of their vertex. Each section or NFZ can be dynamically segregated, denying an airspace area for drone traffic. The agents' objective is to complete their missions while avoiding entering an activated section and maintaining safe separation from the rest of the agents. If a drone is within a NFZ when activated, it should depart the area as soon as possible.

For the development of the airspace model, two different section models were made, one for training and another for evaluation.

The training CTR model comprises a randomly generated set of restrictions. This is done so the agents do not learn to solve a specific CTR environment and can generalize to any location. To generate the random CTR, $n_{obstacle}$ polygons of n sides, with $n \in \mathbb{N} : 3 \leq n \leq obs_{max}$, and a circumradius of $r \in \mathbb{R} : 0.5 obs\_size_{max} \leq n \leq obs\_size_{max}$ The positions of these obstacles are randomly distributed among the environment, and overlap between two or more sections is allowed. A new CTR is generated for each training episode.

For evaluation, a real CTR was modeled as an example of what the agents may encounter when deployed. The evaluation CTR is based on the CTR for LEVC in Valencia (Spain) as of Airac 2310 [9]. This CTR was chosen as it offers several complex shapes to challenge the routing of the agents as the different sections are activated. **Figure 2** shows the outline of the CTR, centered on the airport area.

Each section in the CTR may be independently segregated and desegregated during the execution of the episode. Upon the start of an episode, each section starts deactivated, and it is assigned a random period $T_{act} \in \mathbb{R} : 250 \leq T_{act} \leq 750$ seconds. The section is toggled after T_{act} seconds.

4.2 Drone modeling

The drones in the environments are represented by several agents, with the state S for the agent i being composed of the coordinates of the agent in the environment (x_i, y_i), the current speed (v_i), and heading (χ_i).

$$s_i^t = \begin{bmatrix} x_i \\ y_i \\ v_i \\ \chi_i \end{bmatrix}^t \tag{1}$$

The transition between states after applying the action for a given speed and heading change $(\Delta v_i, \Delta \chi_i)$ is defined in Eqs. (2) and (3):

$$\begin{bmatrix} v_i \\ \chi_i \end{bmatrix}^{t+1} = \begin{bmatrix} v_i \\ \chi_i \end{bmatrix}^t + \begin{bmatrix} \Delta v_i \\ \Delta \chi_i \end{bmatrix}^t \tag{2}$$

$$\begin{bmatrix} x_i \\ y_i \end{bmatrix}^{t+1} = \begin{bmatrix} x_i \\ y_i \end{bmatrix}^t + \begin{bmatrix} cos\,(\chi_i) v_i \\ sen(\chi_i) v_i \end{bmatrix}^{t+1} \tag{3}$$

The performance parameters for the agent, such as the limits for Δv_i and $\Delta \chi_i$, optimal velocity (v_{nom}), minimum (v_{min}), and maximum (v_{max}), are defined as

Parameter	Description	Value
Δv_{max}	Acceleration	$1m/s^2$
$\Delta \chi_{max}$	Track change rate	$17^{\circ}/s$
v_{min}	Minimum speed	$0\ m/s$
v_{nom}	Nominal speed	$10\ m/s$
v_{max}	Maximum speed	$15\ m/s$

Table 1.
Drone performance parameters.

parameters for all agents. Their starting position, flight plan, and separation minima are assigned at the start of the episode, as described in Sections 4.4 and 4.3, respectively.

Table 1 contains the main parameters used to model the drone's performance. The performance parameters where obtained from the average drone performance model used in Ref. [27].

In our implementation, the drones are able to hover in place. Aircraft that cannot hover in place, such as fixed-wing drones, may be included in future research, enabling the use of several performance profiles and drone types, such as multi-copter and fixed-wing.

4.3 Separation modeling

The separation minima between drones is simulated as a "bubble" around the drone. This separation model was based on previous research for the integration of drones in U-space environments. In Ref. [28], authors determined a separation loss as an intrusion of the Separation Threshold volumes. These volumes are determined by a series of factors, like drone category, the environment's density environment, and the performance of the Communications, Navigation and Surveillance (CNS) infrastructure available. For this text, the values selected for the Separation Threshold were obtained from the BUBBLES Validation exercises, Scenario 2, Exercise [29] and can be found in **Table 2**.

At the start of each episode, each drone is randomly assigned a category and Separation Threshold from **Table 2**.

Category	Separation threshold (m)
A1	102.00
A2	102.00
A3	198.36
SAIL I-II	234.20
SAIL III-IV	263.64
SAIL V-VI	281.90
Certified (no passenger)	471.01
Certified (Passenger)	640.19

Table 2.
Horizontal separation distances.

4.4 Flight plan creation

The intent of the current agent and the rest of the traffic is important for the optimization of the trajectories. Flight plans are created to simulate a realistic trajectory for the agents.

Agents in the environment aim to complete their flight plan. The flight plans are created at the initialization of the episode and are composed of a number (n_{wp}) of waypoints defined by their coordinates $\left(x_{wp}(i), y_{wp}(i)\right)$. The first waypoint is used as a takeoff location, and the last as a landing site. Once the agent reaches a waypoint, it is marked as completed and the agent moves on to the next. When the drone reaches the last waypoint, the agent is considered "landed" and removed from the simulation.

For the experiments in this chapter, random flight plans were used, with points randomly selected within a certain distance of the previous $(WP_{maxDist})$, and the agents followed them in order. The waypoints are resampled if it is within a no-fly zone to ensure that the agents can complete their flight plans even if ATC segregates that section of the airspace.

5. Multi-agent reinforcement learning setup

This section discusses the development of the different aspects of the RL setup used to solve the environment defined in 4. The environment created for this chapter contains N independent agents. These agents will learn a shared policy during training then the policy will be independently deployed for validation.

5.1 Observation space

For this work, we developed a hybrid observation approach composed of a matrix with information about the airspace and an array of information related to the agent and its target. For each agent, the observation is defined as $o^t = \left[o_a^t, o_s^t\right]$, with o_a^t being an image extracted from the state of the airspace and o_s^t containing information derived from the state of the drone $\left(s_i^t\right)$. Similar approaches have been used to process input from lidar sensors in obstacle avoidance problems [30].

In o_a^t, the section of the airspace around the current agent is represented as an image that conveys the following information:

1. Intent and separation minima of the current agent.

2. Any active NFZ surrounding the agent.

3. Any other agent near the agent and its current speed, intent, and separation minima.

This image is centered on the agent's position and oriented in the direction of the current heading (χ_i).

The size of the area represented by the image is a square with a 5 km side with a resolution of 256 by 256 pixels with three layers, resulting in 19.5 m/pxl. The 5 km

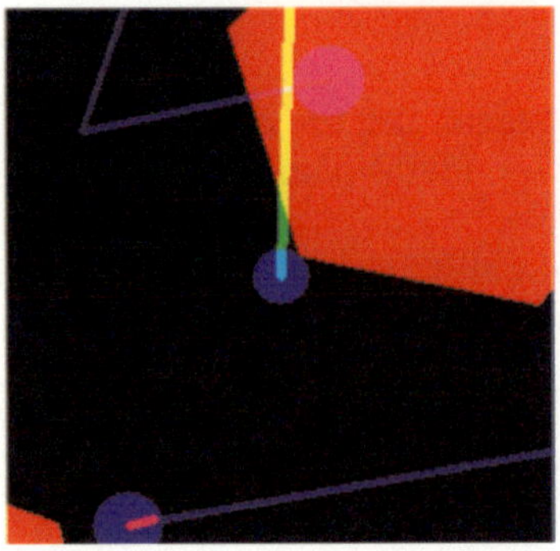

Figure 4.
Representation of the observation o_a^t for an agent.

figure was chosen to balance the size of the matrix used for the observations and the resolution in meters per pixel. This takes into account the performance of the drones used in the experiment; UASs with higher performance characteristics may require observations covering more area.

The main advantage of representing the airspace this way is that the model does not have a limit to the number of intruders used to calculate the optimal trajectory and resolve conflicts, as all intruders in the 5 km area are represented. Previous approaches [17] needed heuristics to decide which agents to consider and which to ignore. This representation also allows the inclusion of NFZs of arbitrary shape. That, combined with the position and intent of the rest of the agents, provides the information needed to avoid conflicts.

This enables the model to leverage the future intent of the rest of the agents in the decision-making process, allowing the agent to optimize its path to reduce future conflicts and distance traveled. **Figure 4** shows an example of the observation received by an agent. The NFZs appear as red areas. The other agents are shown as blue circles defining their separation minima, with a blue line showing their next waypoints and red lines their speed vectors. In the center, the current agent appears with its separation minima and path to the next waypoint.

The agent also receives information about its state in the form of a vector composed of the normalized distance to the target, the sine, and the cosine of the relative hearing to the target, and its normalized velocity. The vector observation is defined in Eq. (4).

$$o_s^t = \begin{bmatrix} dist_{target}/env_{size} \\ cos\,(\chi_i - \psi_i) \\ sin\,(\chi_i - \psi_i) \\ v/v_{nom} \end{bmatrix} \tag{4}$$

5.2 Action space

In this work, the environment is limited to a 2D space and the agent has two controls: acceleration and turn rate. The action is modeled as $a_i(t) = [a_T, a_\chi]$: $a_T, a_\chi \in [-1, 1] \subset \mathbb{R}$, with a_T being the action controlling the acceleration or thrust and a_χ the action controlling the turn rate. In order to obtain the values used to update the state, the actions are multiplied by scaling factors to obtain the Δv and $\Delta \chi$ used in Eq. (5).

$$\begin{bmatrix} \Delta v_i \\ \Delta \chi_i \end{bmatrix}^t = a_i^t \begin{bmatrix} \Delta v_{max} \\ \Delta \chi_{max} \end{bmatrix} \tag{5}$$

5.3 Reward function

The reward function used in this work has been designed to consider several factors. Eq. (6) describes the reward function for the agent i after executing the action a_i^t. It is composed of the following components: reward for approaching the next waypoint in the flight plan $\left(r_i^{target}\right)$, conflict avoidance reward $\left(r_i^{conflict}\right)$, nominal speed reward $\left(r_i^{vel}\right)$, and efficiency reward $\left(r_i^{eff}\right)$.

$$r_i = r_i^{target} + r_i^{conflict} + r_i^{vel} + r_i^{eff} \tag{6}$$

The reward calculation uses the constants W_{target}, W_{conf}, W_{vel}, W_{thust}, and W_χ that are defined at training time. The values used in this training are in **Table 3**.

First, the reward for approaching a target $\left(r_i^{target}\right)$ is the change in distance to the next waypoint during the step. It is divided by the nominal speed to normalize the value.

$$r_i^{target} = W_{target} \frac{\left(dist_{i-target}^t - dist_{i-target}^{t+1}\right)}{v_{nom}} \tag{7}$$

If the target is reached in the current step, $r_i^{target} = 1$.

Parameter	**Description**	**Value**
n_{agents}	Number of agents	10
max_{steps}	Maximum number of steps per episode	2500
env_{size}	Environment size	30,000
$n_{obstacle}$	Number of NFZ	15
obs_sides_max	Maximum number of sides of a section	6
obs_size_{max}	Maximum of random NFZs	4000
$W_{maxDist}$	Maximum distance between waypoints	15,000
W_{target}	Weight for target reward	1
W_{conf}	Conflict avoidance reward	−0.75
W_{vel}	Nominal speed reward	−0.15
W_{thust}	Efficiency reward for speed changes	−0.05
W_χ	Efficiency reward for track changes	−0.05

Table 3.
Environment parameters.

Then, the reward for avoiding conflicts should punish the agent when it gets closer to another agent or a geofence and reward slightly when the agent increases the separation. However, more importance should be given to agents closer to the current drone. A discounting function $(f_d(dist))$ was developed to do so.

The resulting r^{conf} is defined as follows:

$$r_c = W_{conf} \times \sum_{j \in \mathcal{N} \setminus \{i\}} f_d\left(dist_{i-j}^{t+1}\right) \frac{\left(dist_{i-j}^{t} - dist_{i-j}^{t+1}\right)}{v_{max}} \quad (8)$$

$$r_i^{conf} = \begin{cases} r_c & \text{if } dist_{i-j}^{t} - dist_{i-j}^{t+1} > 0 \\ r_c/2 & \text{otherwise} \end{cases} \quad (9)$$

The calculation of the distance between the agent and an obstacle $(dist_{i-j})$ is different depending on whether the obstacle j is a drone or an active NFZ. The distance between the exterior of their Separation Thresholds is used for the drones. For the distance between the drone and an active NFZ, the distance between the drone's position and the point closest to the drone on the polygon defining that NFZ is used. **Figure 5a** and **b** show the distances are measured for other UAS and NFZ respectively.

Eq. (9) reduces the reward received by the agent if it is separating from an obstacle. This is done to ensure that the cumulative reward received if an agent gets closer to an obstacle and then separates is lower than if it maintains the separation.

And the discount function $f_d(dist)$ is as follows:

$$f_d(dist) = \left(1 - \frac{1}{1 + e^{\alpha(-dist+\beta)}}\right) \quad (10)$$

This discount function is commonly used as a [0,1] continuous approximation of the step function [31]. The parameters α and β may be adjusted to suit the application; in this case, the values are 0.01 and 500, respectively. **Figure 6** shows the resulting function.

It is important to remark that this reward function is compatible with agents that are within a currently active NFZ, as the path of maximum reward is to exit through the closest side.

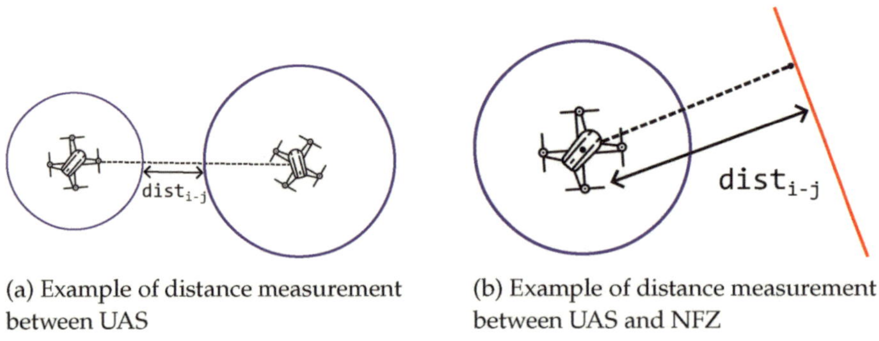

(a) Example of distance measurement between UAS

(b) Example of distance measurement between UAS and NFZ

Figure 5.
Distance calculation for reward. (a) Example of distance measurement between UAS (b) Example of distance measurement between UAS and NFZ.

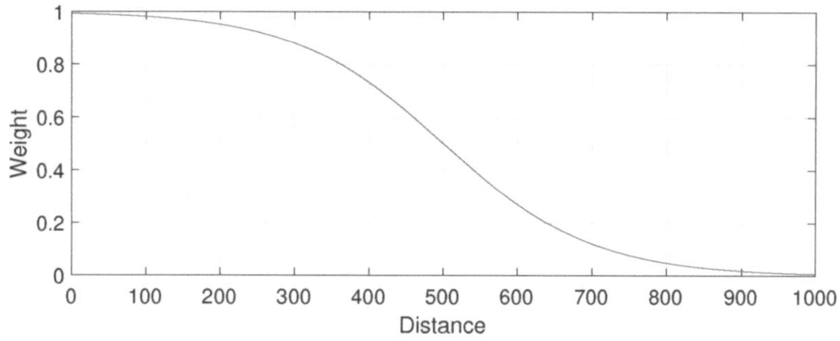

Figure 6.
Discount function.

If a drone invades an active NFZ or a loss of separation between agents occurs, W_{conf} is added to the reward per instance.

The reward also takes into account if the agent is flying at the nominal velocity, slightly punishing any deviation from that value.

$$r_i^{vel} = W_{vel} \frac{\left|v_i^t - v_{nom}\right|}{v_{nom}} \tag{11}$$

Lastly, an efficiency reward was added. This reward slightly punishes any speed or heading change to encourage the agents to maintain course and speed when not influenced by other factors.

$$r_i^{eff} = W_{thust}\left|a_T^t\right| + W_\chi \left|a_\chi^t\right| \tag{12}$$

6. RL algorithm training

The agent was trained using the environment detailed in Section 4 using an implementation of the PPO algorithm [32, 33]. The model is composed of a Convolutional Neural Networks (CNN) based feature extractor for the image observation (o_a^t) that is later concatenated with the vector observation (o_s^t) and passed through Fully Connected (FC) layers.

The agents are trained under the *Centralized Training Decentralized Execution* paradigm, each agent receives its local observation and chooses the action sampled from the shared policy π, which is trained with experiences from all agents.

The training was performed using 10 agents in a randomized environment as explained in Section 4.1. For each episode, the environment was regenerated with random NFZs, flight plans and separation values for the drones. The randomness of the environment helps the agents learn generalizable rules for routing instead of learning a specific pattern. The parameters defining the constraints environment are in **Table 3**. During training, the NFZs were constantly activated, while in evaluation, the NFZs may be activated or deactivated. The architecture used for the neural network does not have a memory mechanism, that is, the only input for a decision is the current state, so no issues were found in the transition from training to evaluation. It was trained for 2 million steps, with the hyperparameters defined in **Table 4**. The step size used was $\Delta t = 1s$, with the maximum duration of an episode limited to 2500 steps. The episode may terminate early if all drones have finished their missions.

Parameter	Value
Learning Rate	$1e-3$
Number of steps	2,000,000
Batch size	512
Rollout buffer	1024
Discount factor	0.99
Generalized Advantage Estimator (GAE) parameter	0.95

Table 4.
Training Hyperparameters.

6.1 Training results

Figure 7 contains the results of the training. The experiences were generated by 10 agents during 2 million steps. During training, the following variables were monitored: mean reward per episode, mean episode length, sum of unique losses of separation, and total distance traveled.

The training results behave as expected, with the mean reward per episode across agents increasing as the training progresses, showing that the agents are learning a better policy as they gather information from the environment. Similarly, the mean episode length also decreases over time, showing that the agents are able to complete their mission before the step limit, reaching a plateau defined by the average mission length.

Unique losses of separation is a metric that measures the number of times that a drone has intruded the separation threshold of another object. A unique loss of separation is counted as one, independently of the duration. **Figure** 7 shows the progression of the

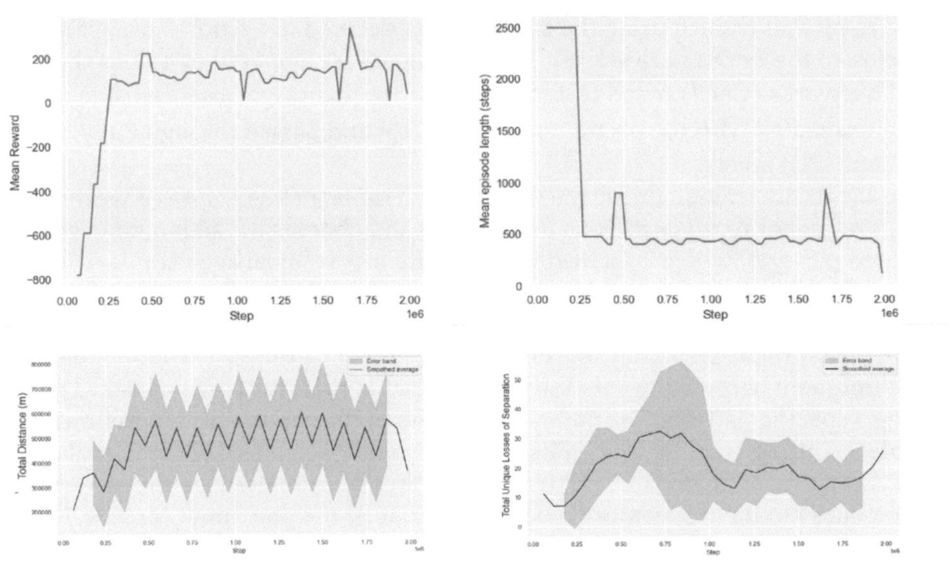

Figure 7.
Training results showing Mean reward, Mean episode length, Unique losses of separation per drone, Total distance traveled.

number of unique losses of separation per episode as the agents learn to solve the environment. An important caveat is that the number of losses of separation is expected to lower as training progresses, but it may not reach zero as the configuration of the environment does not prevent the agents from being initialized inside an active NFZ or in close proximity to another drone. No such provisions were made as in the real environment a NFZ may be activated while there are still drones flying over. The agents must learn to vacate an activated NFZ as soon as possible. This is consistent with the results obtained as the total steps in separation loss per episode reduces as training progresses.

The total distance traveled is a good indicator that the agents are learning, as at the start of the training, the agents tend to remain still or get stuck in situations they cannot solve. As training progresses, the total distance traveled increases and plateaus once the agents learn to traverse the environment.

7. Validation with a CTR environment

After training with the generic environment, the agents are evaluated with the CTR environment. This environment shares the same parameters as the training environment, with the difference that more agents are used (15) and instead of randomly generated polygons, the NFZs are defined by the LEVC CTR as described in Section 4.1. This evaluation is performed for 25 episodes.

For each episode, the NFZs of the CTR begin deactivated, allowing drone traffic. Then, the sections are periodically toggled according to their randomly assigned period as described in Section 4.1.

The agents are able to solve the environment without any loss of separation in 9 out of the 25 episodes, with their average length being 113 seconds. The results in **Figure 8** show that the number of unique losses of separation per episode is relatively low, especially taking into account the high density of the airspace. The number of steps in separation loss determines the length of time that the agents were intruding on their separation thresholds during an episode, showing that the agents tend to resolve the conflicts that arise relatively quickly. Lastly, the deviation from the flight plan shows that the agents perform their missions effectively. As with the previous metrics, zero deviation from the original flight plan is not possible as parts of the CTR and other drones affect the trajectory of the agent.

As an example of the situations that arise in this environment, **Figure 9a** shows the initial configuration of a simulation on the east section of the environment. In this illustration, the drones are shown as triangles, each with a different color. The trajectories are also shown the same color as the drone. The circle around the agents represents their separation minima bubble. It is blue if there is no loss of separation and red if there is. The waypoints on the flight plan are represented by squares colored with the same color as the drone. They are connected by a line in the order the drone needs to reach them. The CTR is outlined, but it is not yet active; drones start their flights without restrictions. Active NFZs will be represented by golden areas as the simulation proceeds. We will focus on the marked area in the following analysis. **Figure 9b** contains the last steps of the simulation, with the trajectories followed by the drones.

Figure 10 shows the progression of the simulation as the agents fly their missions. Arrows have been added to remark the intention of each drone when it deviates from its original flight plan.

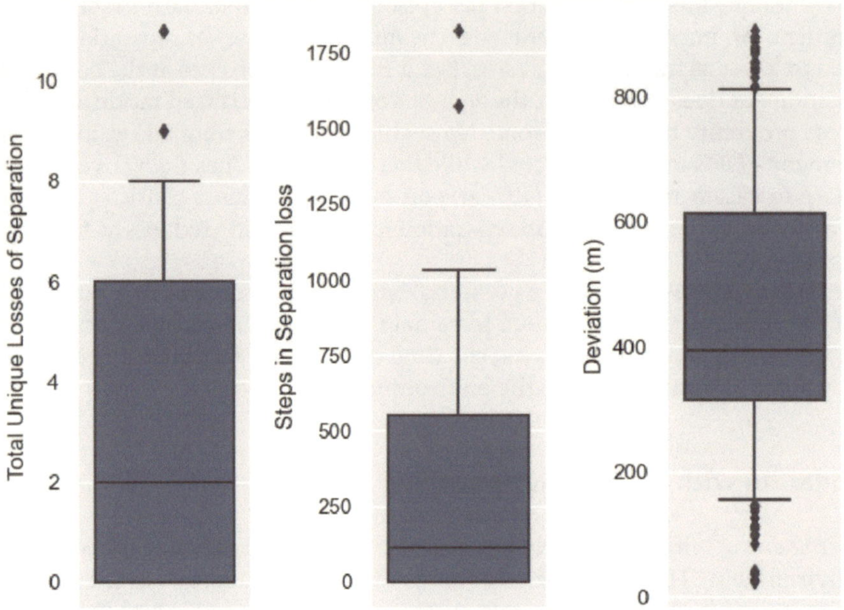

Figure 8.
Results of 25 episodes on the CTR environment.

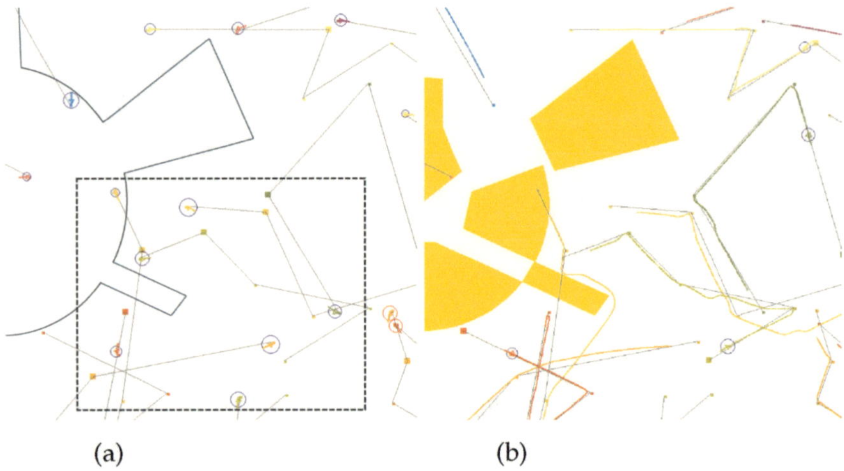

Figure 9.
CTR Simulation. (a) Simulation step 0 (b) Simulation step 1640.

We would like to remark on three situations marked with circles in the figures. In situation (1), an NFZ has been recently activated, and the agent has to avoid the zone while progressing to its next waypoint. In situation (2), the orange and green drones avoid losing separation by modifying their trajectories. The orange drone continues with its flight plan and, in situation (3), has to maintain separation from the lime drone with crossing plans. The separation is momentarily lost in 10c and promptly recovered. In **Figure 10e**, the drones proceed to their next waypoint once the conflict is resolved.

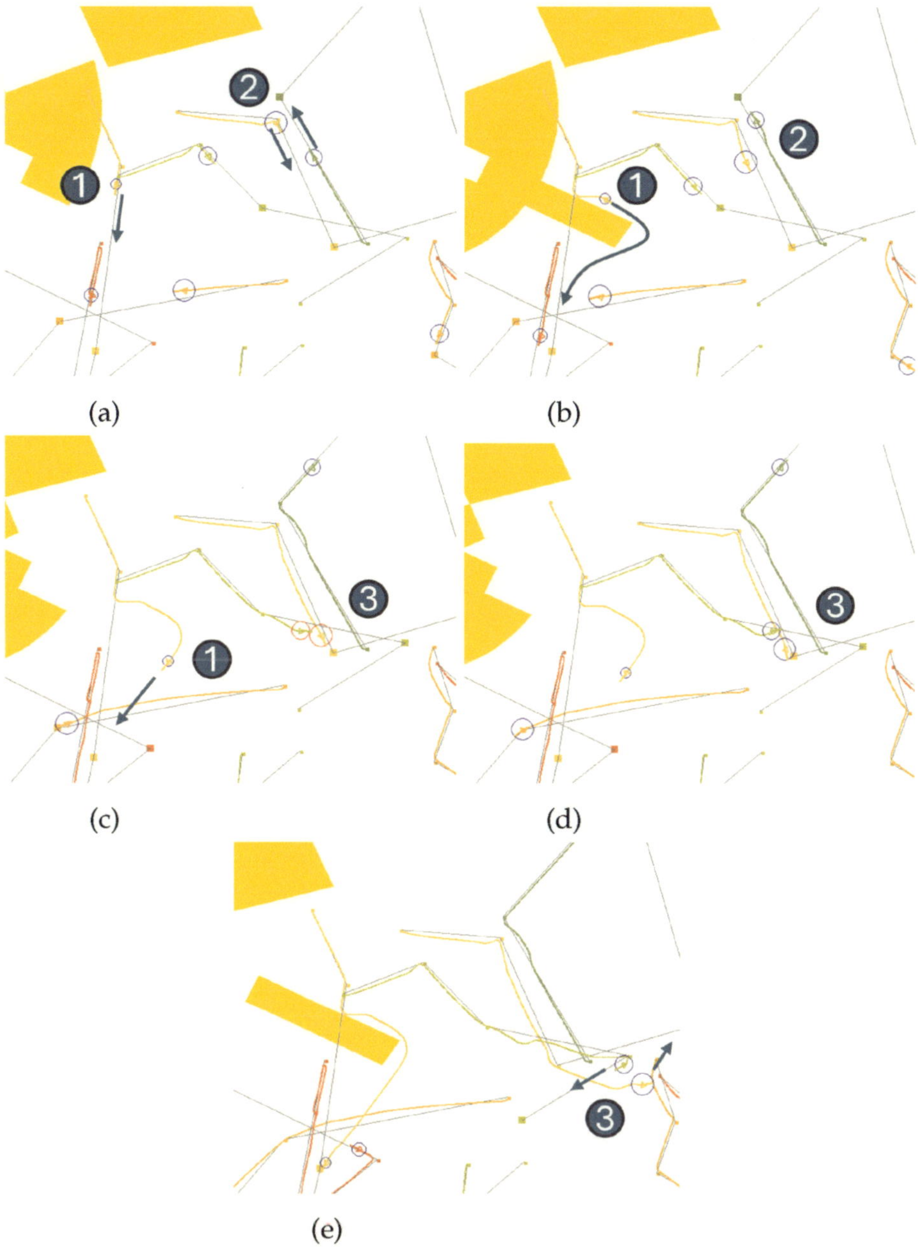

Figure 10.
Example of CTR environment execution. (a) Simulation step 400 (b) Simulation step 560 (c) Simulation step 880 (d) Simulation step 900 (e) Simulation step 1300.

8. Conclusions

This text puts forward a Deep Reinforcement Learning (DRL) model for MACR in close proximity to a CTR with special emphasis on the DAR and its effects on the operations of the drones. The results indicate that the observation space developed allows the agents to correctly process the information of their surroundings, extract insights and act accordingly. The model was trained using generic environments and then validated using a known CTR, proving its generalization capabilities and demonstrating that it could be deployed in any airspace, independent of its shape and structure.

In future work, the inclusion of different performance profiles for each of the agents and the inclusion in the simulation of position noise and communication failures would validate the performance of the model under real-world situations. It is expected to include a comparison with other RL and traditional ATC methods to validate the results obtained. Another aspect that fell outside of the scope of this chapter is the implementation of different priorities. This would allow situations like emergency services to receive priority in congested airspace. Lastly, the inclusion of the vertical dimension in the actions and states is expected.

Acknowledgements

This research was conducted with funding from Generalitat Valenciana under an ACIF grant (CIACIF/2021/489).

Author details

Joaquin Vico Navarro* and Juan A. Vila Carbó
Instituto Universitario de Automática e Informática Industrial, Universitat Politècnica de València, Valencia, Spain

*Address all correspondence to: joavina1@itaca.upv.es

References

[1] ICAO. Annex 2 - Rules of the air. Technical report. 2025

[2] Kleczatský A, Hulínská Š, Kraus J. Enabling UAS BVLOS flights in CTR. Journal of Physics: Conference Series. 2023;**2526**(1):012094. DOI: 10.1088/1742-6596/2526/1/012094

[3] Politi E, Purucker P, Larsen M, Reis RJD, Rajan RT, Penna SD, et al. Enabling technologies for the navigation and communication of UAS operating in the context of BVLOS. Electronics. 2024;**13**(2):340. DOI: 10.3390/electronics13020340

[4] EUROCONTROL. U-space concept of operations (CONOPS). Technical report, SESAR Joint Undertaking. 2023

[5] FAA (Federal Aviation Administration). UTM concept of operations version 2.0 (UTM ConOps v2.0). Technical report, NextGEN. 2020

[6] ECAC. European Commission. Commission implementing regulation (EU) No 2012/923 of 26 September 2012 laying down the common rules of the air and operational provisions regarding services and procedures in air navigation and amending Implementing Regulation (EU) No 1035/2011 and Regulations (EC) No 2007/1265, (EC) No 2006/1794, (EC) No 2006/730, (EC) No 2006/1033 and (EU) No 2010/255 (Text with EEA relevance). Technical report. 2012. Available from: https://www.ecac-ceac.org/images/news/uas-bulletin/UAS_Bulletin_2021_02.pdf

[7] EASA. Easy access rules for standardised European rules of the air (SERA). Technical report. 2024. Available from: https://www.easa.europa.eu/en/document-library/easy-access-rules/easy-access-rules-standardised-european-rules-air-sera

[8] ECAC. European Commission. Commission Implementing Regulation (EU) 2021/664 of 22 April 2021 on a regulatory framework for the U-space (Text with EEA relevance). Technical report. 2021. Available from: http://data.europa.eu/eli/reg_impl/2021/664/oj/eng

[9] Janisch D, Sánchez-Escalonilla P, Cervero JM, Vidaller A, Borst C. Exploring tower control strategies for concurrent manned and unmanned aircraft management. In: 2023 IEEE/AIAA 42nd Digital Avionics Systems Conference (DASC). Barcelona, Spain: IEEE; 2023. pp. 1-10. DOI: 10.1109/DASC58513.2023.10311233

[10] Ribeiro M, Ellerbroek J, Hoekstra J. Review of conflict resolution methods for manned and unmanned aviation. Aerospace. 2020;7(6):79. DOI: 10.3390/AEROSPACE7060079. ISSN 2226-4310

[11] Bilimoria K, D, Lee HQ, Mao ZH, Feron E. Comparison of centralized and decentralized conflict resolution strategies for multiple-aircraft problems. In: 18th Applied Aerodynamics Conference. Reston, VA, USA: American Institute of Aeronautics and Astronautics (AIAA) Inc.; 2000. DOI: 10.2514/6.2000-4268. Available from: custserv@aiaa.org

[12] Xiangmin GUAN, Renli LYU, Hongxia SHI, Chen J. A survey of safety separation management and collision avoidance approaches of civil UAS operating in integration national airspace system. Chinese Journal of Aeronautics. 2020;**33**(11):2851-2863. DOI: 10.1016/j.cja.2020.05.009. Available from: https://www.sciencedirect.com/science/article/pii/S100093612030220X. ISSN 1000-9361

[13] Xue M. Urban air mobility conflict resolution: Centralized or decentralized? In: AIAA 2020 Aviation Forum. Session: Modeling and Simulation for Urban Air Mobility (Invited). Reston, VA, USA: American Institute of Aeronautics and Astronautics (AIAA) Inc.; 2020. DOI: 10.2514/6.2020-3192. Available from: custserv@aiaa.org

[14] Mueller ER, Kochenderfer M. Multi-rotor aircraft collision avoidance using partially observable Markov decision processes. In: AIAA Modeling and Simulation Technologies Conference. Session: UAV Path Planning and Collision Avoidance. Reston, VA, USA: American Institute of Aeronautics and Astronautics (AIAA) Inc.; 2016. DOI: 10.2514/6.2016-3673. Available from: custserv@aiaa.org

[15] Honghai Z, Jinlun Z, Zongbei SHI, Yike LI, Jinpeng Z. DDQNC-P: A framework for civil aircraft tactical synergetic trajectory planning under adverse weather conditions. Chinese Journal of Aeronautics. 2024;**37**(12):434-457. DOI: 10.1016/j.cja.2024.07.014. Available from: https://www.sciencedirect.com/science/article/pii/S1000936124002693. ISSN 1000-9361

[16] Dalmau R, Allard E. Air traffic control using message passing neural networks and multi-agent reinforcement learning. In: 10th SESAR Innovation Days (SID). Virtual Event. Brussels, Belgium: SESAR 3 JU; 2020

[17] Chen Y, Hu M, Yang L, Xu Y, Xie H. General multi-agent reinforcement learning integrating adaptive Manoeuvre strategy for real-time multi-aircraft conflict resolution. Transportation Research Part C: Emerging Technologies. 2023;**151**:104125. DOI: 10.1016/j.trc.2023.104125. ISSN 0968-090X. Available from: https://www.sciencedirect.com/science/article/pii/S0968090X23001146

[18] Ribeiro M, Ellerbroek J, Hoekstra J. Determining Optimal Conflict Avoidance Manoeuvres at High Densities with Reinforcement Learning. Brussels, Belgium: SESAR 3 JU; 2020

[19] Feng S, Sebastian B, Ben-Tzvi P. A collision avoidance method based on deep reinforcement learning. Robotics. 2021;**10**(2):73. DOI: 10.3390/robotics10020073. ISSN 2218-6581

[20] Song S, Saunders K, Yue Y, Liu J. Smooth trajectory collision avoidance through deep reinforcement learning. In: 2022 21st IEEE International Conference on Machine Learning and Applications (ICMLA). Nassau, Bahamas: IEEE; 2022. pp. 914-919. DOI: 10.1109/icmla55696.2022.00152

[21] van den Berg J, Guy SJ, Lin M, Manocha D. Reciprocal n-body collision avoidance. In: Pradalier C, Siegwart R, Hirzinger G, editors. Robotics Research. Berlin, Heidelberg: Springer; 2011. pp. 3-19. ISBN 978-3-642-19457-3

[22] Hennes D, Claes D, Meeussen W, Tuyls K. Multi-robot collision avoidance with localization uncertainty. In: Proceedings of the 11th International Conference on Autonomous Agents and Multiagent Systems. Vol. 1. 2012. pp. 147-154

[23] Godoy J, Karamouzas I, Guy S, Gini M. Implicit coordination in crowded multi-agent navigation. In: Proceedings of the AAAI Conference on Artificial Intelligence. Vol. 30(1). San Mateo, CA, USA: Association for the Advancement of Artificial Intelligence (AAAI); 2016. DOI: 10.1609/aaai.v30i1.10131. Available from: https://ojs.aaai.org/index.php/AAAI/article/view/10131

[24] Long P, Fan T, Liao X, Liu W, Zhang H, Pan J. Towards optimally decentralized multi-robot collision avoidance via deep reinforcement learning. In: 2018 IEEE International Conference on Robotics and Automation (ICRA), Brisbane, QLD, Australia. 2018. pp. 6252-6259. DOI: 10.1109/ICRA.2018.8461113

[25] Littman ML. Markov games as a framework for multi-agent reinforcement learning. In: Cohen WW, Hirsh H, editors. Machine Learning Proceedings 1994. San Francisco (CA): Morgan Kaufmann; 1994. pp. 157-163. DOI: 10.1016/B978-1-55860-335-6.50027-1. Available from: https://www.sciencedirect.com/science/article/pii/B9781558603356500271. ISBN 978-1-55860-335-6

[26] Yu C, Velu A, Vinitsky E, Gao J, Wang Y, Bayen A, et al. The surprising effectiveness of PPO in cooperative multi-agent games. In: Proceedings of the 36th International Conference on Neural Information Processing Systems, NIPS'22. Red Hook, NY, USA: Curran Associates Inc; 2024. ISBN 9781713871088

[27] BUBBLES Consortium. Algorithm for Analysing the Collision Risk. Technical Report. Valencia, Spain: Universitat Politècnica de València (UPV); 2021

[28] Vila Carbó JA, Balbastre Tejedor JV, Pallarés PM, Pérez PY. Risk-based method for determining separation minima in unmanned aircraft systems. Journal of Air Transportation. 2023; **31**(2):57-67. DOI: 10.2514/1.D0326. ISSN 2380-9450

[29] BUBBLES Consortium. Concept validation test plan (CVALP). Technical report. Universitat Politècnica de València (UPV); 2022

[30] Choi J, Lee G, Lee C. Reinforcement learning-based dynamic obstacle avoidance and integration of path planning. Intelligent Service Robotics. 2021;**14**(5):663-677. DOI: 10.1007/s11370-021-00387-2. ISSN 1861-2784

[31] Gao S, Wu W, Lee C-H, Chua T-S. A maximal figure-of-merit learning approach to text categorization. In: Proceedings of the 26th Annual International ACM SIGIR Conference on Research and Development in Information Retrieval, SIGIR'03. New York, NY, USA: Association for Computing Machinery; 2003. pp. 174-181. DOI: 10.1145/860435.860469. ISBN 1581136463

[32] Raffin A, Hill A, Gleave A, Kanervisto A, Ernestus M, Dormann N. Stable-baselines3: Reliable reinforcement learning implementations. Journal of Machine Learning Research. 2021; **22**(268):1-8. Available from: http://jmlr.org/papers/v22/20-1364.html

[33] Schulman J, Wolski F, Dhariwal P, Radford A, Klimov O. Proximal Policy Optimization Algorithms. arXiv; 2017. Available from: https://arxiv.org/abs/1707.06347